PUNISHING PUTIN

INSIDE THE GLOBAL
ECONOMIC WAR
TO BRING DOWN RUSSIA

STEPHANIE BAKER

SCRIBNER

NEW YORK LONDON TORONTO SYDNEY NEW DELHI

Scribner
An Imprint of Simon & Schuster, LLC
1230 Avenue of the Americas
New York, NY 10020

First Scribner hardcover edition September 2024

SCRIBNER and design are trademarks of Simon & Schuster, LLC

Simon & Schuster: Celebrating 100 Years of Publishing in 2024

For information about special discounts for bulk purchases,
please contact Simon & Schuster Special Sales at 1-866-506-1949 or
business@simonandschuster.com.

The Simon & Schuster Speakers Bureau can bring authors to
your live event. For more information or to book an event,
contact the Simon & Schuster Speakers Bureau at 1-866-248-3049
or visit our website at www.simonspeakers.com.

Manufactured in the United States of America

1   3   5   7   9   10   8   6   4   2

Library of Congress Cataloging-in-Publication Data

Names: Baker, Stephanie, 1967– author.
Title: Punishing Putin : inside the global economic war to bring down
Russia / Stephanie Baker.
Description: First Scribner hardcover edition. | New York : Scribner, 2024. |
Includes bibliographical references and index.
Identifiers: LCCN 2024022279 (print) | LCCN 2024022280 (ebook) |
ISBN 9781668050583 (hardcover) | ISBN 9781668050606 (ebook)
Subjects: LCSH: Economic sanctions—Russia (Federation) | Russia
(Federation)—Foreign economic relations.
Classification: LCC HF1558.2 .B33 2024 (print) | LCC HF1558.2 (ebook) |
DDC 337.47—dc23/eng/20240605
LC record available at https://lccn.loc.gov/2024022279
LC ebook record available at https://lccn.loc.gov/2024022280

ISBN 978-1-6680-5058-3
ISBN 978-1-6680-5060-6 (ebook)

CONTENTS

KEY PLAYERS

U.S. GOVERNMENT

WHITE HOUSE

Jake Sullivan—National Security Adviser from 2021.

Daleep Singh—Deputy National Security Adviser for International Economics (February 2021–April 2022 and again from February 2024). Helped devise U.S. economic penalties at the U.S. Treasury in 2014 and served as Biden's sanctions architect in 2022.

John Bolton—National Security Adviser in the Trump administration, April 2018–September 2019.

Rory MacFarquhar—Special Assistant to the President and Senior Director for Global Economics on the National Security Council (2013–16). Helped craft U.S. sanctions against Russia in 2014.

TREASURY

Janet Yellen—Secretary from 2021, chair of the Federal Reserve (2014–18).

Wally Adeyemo—Deputy Secretary from 2021. Helped lead the sanctions response to Putin's invasion in 2022.

Brian Nelson—Under Secretary for Terrorism and Financial Intelligence from December 2021. Led diplomatic efforts to enforce U.S. sanctions against Russia worldwide.

Elizabeth Rosenberg—Assistant Secretary for Terrorist Financing and Financial Crimes from December 2021 to February 2024. Worked on the price cap and global sanctions enforcement.

Ben Harris—Assistant Secretary for Economic Policy and Counselor to the Secretary (2021–23). Helped design and sell the price cap on Russian oil.

Catherine Wolfram—Deputy Assistant Secretary for Climate and Energy Economics (2021–22). Helped design the price cap on Russian oil.

Steve Mnuchin—Secretary in the Trump administration, 2017–21.

JUSTICE DEPARTMENT

Lisa Monaco—Deputy Attorney General from 2021. Oversaw the campaign to go after sanctions evasion.

Andrew Adams—head of the KleptoCapture task force (March 2022–July 2023) and former Assistant U.S. Attorney in the Southern District of New York. Oversaw multiple Russian organized crime and sanctions evasion cases.

STATE DEPARTMENT

Victoria Nuland—Under Secretary for Political Affairs (2021–24), Assistant Secretary for European and Eurasian Affairs (2013–17). Played a key role in the U.S. response to Russia's annexation of Crimea in 2014 and its full-scale invasion of Ukraine in 2022.

Daniel Fried—Coordinator for Sanctions Policy (2013–17), who led U.S. efforts to work with Europe on sanctions against Russia.

COMMERCE DEPARTMENT

Matthew Axelrod—Assistant Secretary for Export Enforcement at the Bureau of Industry and Security from December 2021. Spearheaded efforts to stop Russia from getting hold of U.S. technology for its defense industry.

EUROPEAN UNION

Ursula von der Leyen—President of the European Commission and Germany's former Defense Minister. Led the EU's response to Putin's invasion.

Björn Seibert—Head of Cabinet for von der Leyen, who helped forge a consensus on sanctions among the twenty-seven EU member states.

U.K.

Boris Johnson—U.K. Prime Minister, 2019–22.

Kwasi Kwarteng—former Secretary of State for Business, Energy, and Industrial Strategy (2021–22), and Chancellor (September 6–October 14, 2022).

Jonathan Black—Johnson's G7 sherpa, who coordinated U.K. economic penalties with Western allies.

ITALY

Mario Draghi—Italian Prime Minister (February 2021–October 2022) and President of the European Central Bank (2011–19). Played an important role in the decision to immobilize Russia's $300 billion in central bank assets.

HUNGARY

Viktor Orbán—Prime Minister from 2010, who frequently opposed EU efforts to impose sanctions on Russia.

THE SANCTIONED TYCOONS

Roman Abramovich—former owner of Chelsea Football Club, who met regularly with Putin. Largest shareholder in Evraz, Russia's second-biggest steel producer. Used his connection to the late tycoon Boris Berezovsky to get a controlling stake in oil company Sibneft, which he sold to Gazprom in 2005, pocketing about $10 billion.

Oleg Deripaska—owns 45 percent of En+ Group, which in turn holds a controlling stake in Rusal, Russia's largest aluminum producer. Cemented his fortune in the aluminum wars of the 1990s, when people were killed in the fight to control the industry. The U.S. Justice Department seized his homes in New York and Washington.

Suleyman Kerimov—owns the superyacht *Amadea*, according to allegations made by the U.S. Justice Department. A senator in Russia's upper house of parliament since 2008. Made his early money trading oil and investing in Gazprom using loans from Russian state-controlled banks. Most of his current fortune comes from Polyus, Russia's largest gold producer, which his family controlled until early 2022, when it sold part of its stake and transferred control of the remainder to a foundation.

Eduard Khudainatov—claimed to be the owner of the superyacht *Amadea*, seized by the United States. Former CEO of Rosneft and founder of the Independent Oil and Gas Company.

Mikhail Fridman—fled London in September 2023 after the U.K dropped a lengthy sanctions evasion probe. The largest shareholder in Alfa Group, an investment company that holds stakes in banking, telecoms, and retail. Pocketed $14 billion with his partners in 2013 when they sold their stake in the oil joint venture TNK-BP to state-controlled Rosneft. Set up LetterOne private equity firm in London.

Vladimir Potanin—Russia's richest man, with the biggest single stake in Norilsk Nickel, the world's largest producer of high-grade nickel. Bought stakes in Tinkoff Bank and Rosbank after Russia's invasion of Ukraine. Used to play ice hockey with Putin.

Viktor Vekselberg—cofounded Renova Group with fellow billionaire Len Blavatnik. Made his early fortune in aluminum and then investing in the oil joint venture TNK-BP. The Justice Department seized his homes in the United States and his superyacht *Tango* in the Spanish port of Mallorca on charges of sanctions evasion.

Igor Sechin—Chairman and CEO of state-controlled oil giant Rosneft, who helped Putin regain control of Russia's oil industry. Former KGB officer who worked with Putin in the St. Petersburg's mayor office. Has been called Putin's grey cardinal and a leading representative of the *siloviki*, or security forces.

Arkady Rotenberg—billionaire who made his fortune from state construction contracts as the owner of Stroygazmontazh, which built the bridge linking Crimea to Russia and sections of Nord Stream 2, the gas pipeline to Germany. Childhood friend of Putin's from St. Petersburg, where they practiced judo together. Sold Stroygazmontazh in November 2019 for $1.3 billion.

Konstantin Malofeyev—close confidant of Putin's known as Russia's Orthodox Oligarch. Founder of Tsargrad TV, a key node in Putin's propaganda machine, and a financial supporter of Russians promoting separatists in Crimea and eastern Ukraine.

Gennady Timchenko—friends with Putin since the early 1990s. Made his early money trading oil products. Helped found a St. Petersburg judo club, of which Putin was the honorary president. Set up a commodities trading firm, Gunvor, which he sold on the eve of being sanctioned in 2014. Owns a 23.5 percent stake in the gas company Novatek, the largest non-state-owned gas producer in Russia.

Yuri Kovalchuk—took over Bank Rossiya with other Putin-connected businessmen in 1991. The United States called him Putin's "personal banker" when it added him to the sanctions list in 2014. Referred to as the Rupert

Murdoch of Russia because of his control of National Media Group, which owns television and newspapers that toe the Kremlin's line.

THE RUSSIAN GOVERNMENT

Sergei Lavrov—Foreign Minister since 2004 and the Kremlin's mouthpiece to the world.

Alexander Novak—Deputy Prime Minister from 2020 and former Minister of Energy between 2012 and 2020. Helped the Kremlin navigate the G7 oil price cap.

Anton Siluanov—Minister of Finance since 2011. Vowed to freeze foreign assets in response to Western sanctions.

Elvira Nabiullina—Governor of the Bank of Russia since 2013. Led Putin's campaign to build Fortress Russia.

FRIENDS AND FIXERS

Evgeniy Kochman—founder of Imperial Yachts.

Graham Bonham-Carter—London-based property manager for Deripaska.

Olga Shriki—New York–based fixer for Deripaska.

Vladimir Voronchenko—friend of Vekselberg's.

Ekaterina Voronina—Deripaska's girlfriend and mother of two of his children.

Jack Hanick—former Fox TV producer who worked for Malofeyev.

PART I

THE ECONOMIC
WAR BEGINS

WE ARE COMING FOR YOUR SUPERYACHT

On February 24, 2022, a superyacht called *Amadea* lay anchored off Sint Maarten in the Caribbean, a portrait in assured opulence. The luxurious 348-foot white-hulled vessel had all the trappings of a Russian billionaire's floating mansion. On the foredeck was a large helipad with a glide-path indicator. A thirty-three-foot infinity pool lined with blue mosaic tiles sparkled on the stern side. Quirky features were spread across five decks: a lobster tank, a firepit, and a spa pool that converted into a stage for DJs. Inside, walls covered in fake leather book spines surrounded a hand-painted Pleyel piano. Michelangelo clouds adorned the ceiling above the dining room table. A cinema on the bridge deck was replete with a retractable projector, a popcorn machine, and motion-controlled sofas that vibrated with the action on the large screen.

Estimated as one of the seventy largest superyachts in the world, *Amadea* stood out when it dropped anchor in the turquoise waters off the port of Philipsburg, the island's Dutch capital, where tourists frolicked on the white sand beaches. After Russian president Vladimir Putin ordered his troops to cross the border into Ukraine earlier that morning, *Amadea*, which was known to be Russian owned and managed, found itself in trouble. As the shock of the full-scale invasion reverberated around the world, outrage quickly translated into cutting off these expensive playthings of Putin's elite, sending Russian-linked superyachts on the run. *Amadea*'s crew had watched the political climate change almost overnight. Suppliers were refusing to sell fuel to *Amadea*. The crew were the only passengers on board, but the port agent told them it was best not to stay.

On the same day, U.S. president Joe Biden announced a sweeping set of sanctions against Russian banks and elites as he vowed to roll out more punishing restrictions to respond to Putin's brutal invasion. The European Union and the U.K. had imposed asset freezes and travel bans on a handful of wealthy Russians, some of whom were known to own superyachts. The noose was tightening.

By early March, many Russian-owned superyachts were racing from all corners of the world in search of safe waters, often turning off their transponders so no one could track their movements. Many in the Caribbean booked it east across the Atlantic to the Seychelles or Dubai, where Western sanctions were unlikely to be applied. But the Russian-owned company that managed *Amadea*, Imperial Yachts, plotted to sail the superyacht in the other direction, to the Pacific and out of the Western Hemisphere. In search of fuel, it set off for nearby Antigua, where some of the crew demanded answers from the management company given internet gossip that the owner was on the U.S. sanctions list. "If we find ourselves supporting internationally wanted criminals, we are not in for that," one of the crew told a manager at Imperial Yachts. Normally, any superyacht captain has documents that list what company owns the boat. The captain can show that document at ports for routine checks, but the paperwork doesn't always spell out *who* is the ultimate beneficial owner. A manager at Imperial Yachts told the crew that they were good to go.

From Antigua, *Amadea* prepared to cruise seven thousand nautical miles through the Panama Canal to Fiji, where it planned a short stop to restock and allow a relief crew to take over. But by the time it was approaching the Panama Canal, *Amadea* was at the center of intense scrutiny. Unbeknownst to the crew, federal agents in Washington and New York were tracking its every move as part of a task force chasing Russian assets. Investigators thought it might be heading toward Vladivostok in Russia's east, but the crew were mostly South Africans or Brits who had no Russian visas and would be forbidden from entering the country, preventing them from flying home.

After *Amadea* made its way through the Panama Canal, the United States asked Mexican authorities to search the vessel for evidence of who owned or controlled it. First, around ten members of the Mexican military, dressed in camouflage and sporting pistols, pulled up beside *Amadea*, demanding to inspect the vessel. With its paperwork in order and no sanctioned individuals on board, it was allowed to cruise on before being waved down again in the middle of the ocean by an imposing Mexican navy frigate, which launched a speedboat carrying a search team. They boarded *Amadea* with a ladder in choppy waters and thoroughly searched the vessel, taking pictures of insurance and registration documents. It was again let go and motored northwest to refuel in the port of Manzanillo on Mexico's west coast, where the military searched it again for several hours, this time with sniffer dogs. The crew didn't know what they were looking for. During these searches, the captain handed over documents showing the owner was a company registered in the British Virgin Islands, Millemarin Investments Ltd., controlled by an unsanctioned Russian. But the paperwork didn't show which Russian billionaire actually owned the vessel. With nothing indicating a sanctions violation, Mexican authorities let the boat restock and refuel before departing.

After eighteen days at sea, *Amadea* sailed past the swaying palm trees and sugarcane plantations of Fiji, destined for the port of Lautoka in mid-April. The superyacht was three hours ahead of schedule. To kill time, the captain shut off the engine and drifted off the coast to let some of the more than thirty crew members go for a swim in the hot afternoon sun.

They finally glided into the port just before sunset. To their surprise, agents from the U.S. Federal Bureau of Investigation (FBI) were waiting for them, ready with a warrant to search the boat and its computers. They hauled the captain and several others into an air-conditioned shipping container at the port for interrogation, which dragged on until the early hours of the morning.

The FBI agents grilled the crew members with questions about the superyacht and its owner. "Why do you need all these people?" A boat this big requires a lot of people, the crew answered. "Why are you using code names—G-1, G-2—for guests on board? You're trying to conceal the yacht's true owner." The crew denied hiding anyone's identity and said using code names over open radios was standard practice.

Around the same time, more than five thousand miles away at Los Angeles airport, FBI agents had intercepted *Amadea*'s British-born relief captain and two other crew members en route to Fiji, aggressively questioning them for hours about who owned the superyacht. The agents canceled their U.S. visas, cloned their cell phones for evidence, and promptly deported them. Back in Fiji, *Amadea*'s fate hung in the balance.

*   *   *

By the time *Amadea* got to Fiji in mid-April, Russian forces had recently withdrawn from the town of Bucha, leaving behind hundreds of dead Ukrainians, some shot in the head with their hands tied in horrific images of apparent war crimes. As the number of killed or wounded in Ukraine continued rising, the hunt for Russian assets such as *Amadea* became a symbol of U.S. efforts to impose costs on the elite who were propping up Putin's regime. U.S. officials hoped the moves would isolate Russia from the global economy and expose the corruption of Kremlin cronies in an attempt to show Russians they were getting "ripped off," as one White House official put it. Busting tycoons for sanctions evasion and seizing their assets wasn't just an empty gesture. It had one potential real-world impact: the U.S. Justice Department planned to sell the yachts, artwork, and real estate of Russian oligarchs who violated sanctions and channel the proceeds to Ukraine—making these toys of Russia's billionaires the possible beginning of war reparations.

Amadea, worth an estimated $300 million, represents only a small fraction of the assets linked to Russia's so-called sanctioned oligarchs and targeted by Western governments since the start of the invasion. Most of the country's top twenty richest men—and they all are men—are under sanctions in the United States, EU, or U.K., with almost $60 billion in private Russian assets already frozen worldwide. Attempts to seize this much wealth have sparked some of the biggest legal battles in history.

But the economic war on Russia goes far beyond taking away the lavish possessions of Russia's billionaires. Desperate to avoid a direct military confrontation with a country that has more nuclear warheads than any other, Western allies have deployed unprecedented sanctions against Russia in response to the largest land war in Europe since World War II. In Washington, London, Brussels, and beyond, Western governments have launched a full-scale assault on the Russian economy in a bid to degrade Putin's military might. It's a war that spans the globe, with battles playing out from Dubai to Cyprus to Moscow. Never before has this arsenal of economic weapons been turned against a major market economy. Western allies blocked roughly $300 billion in Russian state funds, banned technology exports, expelled banks from the international financial system, and capped the price of Russian oil. In doing so, they have reordered global political alliances and trade and turned what was once the world's eleventh-largest economy into a global pariah. The steps they took will reverberate for decades.

After the full-scale invasion, Russia became the most sanctioned country in the world, with more than eighteen thousand designations of individuals and entities now in place across the United States, EU, U.K., Japan, Canada, Switzerland, and Australia. Never before has such a large coalition—more than thirty countries representing more than half of the global economy—tried to isolate a major economy through coordinated economic penalties. Before February 2022, Iran was the only country that came close, with roughly thirty-six hundred designations. But the Russian economy is much bigger and far more integrated into the global financial system.

Russia's vast natural resources mean it's impossible to completely wall off its economy. In some ways, Russia is too big to sanction, turning this form of targeted economic warfare into a giant experiment. Because it is such a big producer of oil, gas, and metals, the West couldn't impose a full embargo without tipping the global economy into a recession. So officials in Washington, Brussels, and London came up with new tools to try to bleed Putin of resources to fund his military-industrial complex.

The economic war on Russia is in some ways a clear sign of things to come. Over the past three decades, sanctions have become a central tool of Western foreign policy, merging economics with national security. With the majority of global trade in dollars, the United States can deliver an enormous financial shock to anyone it deems undesirable. But the war in Ukraine has turbocharged the use of such economic leverage.

"Putin put us into a Cold War for ten to fifteen years, unfortunately, for everyone," Mikhail Khodorkovsky, the exiled Russian opposition leader who spent more than a decade in prison on trumped-up political charges, told me. "Many of the sanctions that have been introduced are designed to last many years." This new conflict between East and West has revived the transatlantic alliance in ways that few could have predicted and brought Russia and China (along with Iran and North Korea) closer together as repressive bedfellows. In Cold War II, as the historian Niall Ferguson has argued, China and Russia are cooperating in a powerful economic axis to challenge Western values and American dominance of the world. But unlike in the first Cold War, Russia is now the junior partner to China, forging a parallel economy designed to avoid sanctions. While Washington urges the rest of the world to match Western restrictions, some countries, such as Brazil and India, are hedging their bets and trying to maintain a nonaligned path by continuing trade ties with the Kremlin. In fact, more than two-thirds of the world's population are in countries that have not backed the sanctions against Russia. That means greater opportunities for Russian evasion and an increasingly divided world.

The current battle will influence Western leaders long after the last shot has been fired in Ukraine. Putin's invasion of Ukraine has been a crash course in how to impose economic penalties on a major economy without causing catastrophic consequences for the rest of the world. Should China invade Taiwan, the West would face much greater costs if it tried to pursue a similar economic war in response. China's economy, worth about $18 trillion, is about ten times the size of Russia. Still, the Group of Seven (G7), the club of the world's wealthiest democracies, has learned how difficult it is to implement economic penalties and deny technological know-how in ways that don't cause harm at home. In the process, there have been hastened efforts to diversify supply chains. These tactics, along with many others developed in the aftermath of the war on Ukraine, form the beginnings of a playbook for the new art of economic war.

*   *   *

The story I'm telling here is the product of a lifetime of work. After the fall of the Soviet Union, I covered Russia's economic transition to a market economy as a bright-eyed young reporter in Moscow in the mid-1990s, chronicling the U.S. and European companies flocking to Russia to invest. I watched firsthand as Western governments and international financial institutions haphazardly lent billions to Russia to help it transition to a free market underpinned by an elected government. What they got instead was a kleptocracy, a corrupt state where politicians at every level were on the take.

Since the 1990s, I have personally interviewed many of Russia's business tycoons as they maneuvered to consolidate and protect their fortunes. I also bring deep experience reporting from Ukraine in the run-up to Putin's invasion when I investigated the role of Trump's former campaign chairman Paul Manafort as an adviser to Ukraine's former pro-Russian president and Rudy Giuliani's work with pro-Russian officials. Since 2022, I've chronicled the sanctions against Russia, charting what amounts to the end of an era.

Three decades after the fall of the Soviet Union, when Putin tried to bolster his popularity by whipping up Russian nationalism and invading Ukraine, the Western money that had once flooded into Russia started pouring back out again. More than fifteen hundred Western companies—some of the same ones I'd seen flock to the country in the 1990s—quit or curtailed their operations in Russia, walking away from billions of dollars of assets they'd spent years building up during an unprecedented period of globalization. Some of the world's biggest companies—McDonald's, Ford, Exxon—sold their assets to local tycoons for token sums or had their businesses expropriated by the Kremlin, closing out thirty years of Western investment into Russia. But more than two thousand Western companies stayed and continued doing business in Russia, paying taxes to Putin's regime and weakening efforts to deprive the Kremlin of resources to wage war.

This book reveals the behind-the-scenes drama on both sides of the economic war, from the halls of power in Washington, London, and Brussels to the desperate maneuvers of sanctioned oligarchs to keep their mansions and superyachts. To understand how the most expansive sanctions regime ever came together, I've spoken to more than a hundred officials and business leaders in the United States, Europe, and Russia. I've also drawn from thousands of pages of court filings and public documents. This book will tell the human stories behind the largest business exodus from a single country in history and the lengths to which Russia's billionaires have gone to hold on to their money and influence.

Will the economic war succeed? Or will it harm others more than Russia? The principal failure of the economic war has been the slow rollout of penalties and the lack of enforcement of the restrictions, which has allowed

Putin to continue earning billions of dollars through the illicit trade in oil and gold. Moscow has managed to reshuffle the global oil trade to find new buyers such as India, which has served as a backdoor route for Russia to sell hydrocarbons around the world. The Kremlin has been able to circumvent bans on the import of Western technology by creating front companies to buy components that are crucial for its production of precision-guided weapons. The biggest hole in the Western strategy: China. By buying oil and exporting semiconductors, Beijing has helped prop up the Russian economy and blunted the effect of sanctions. Without better enforcement, the West's restrictions will fail to degrade Putin's ability to sustain his military.

To be sure, as in any war, there has been collateral damage where ordinary Russians who oppose Putin have been unnecessarily penalized, their bank accounts closed for no reason. The often blanket bans on everything and everyone tied to Russian has helped Putin use sanctions to demonize the West and create a victim narrative at home. Khodorkovsky, the exiled opposition leader, told me the West should have done more to help Russians trying to flee the country to avoid serving in the army. "Sanctions against banks hit ordinary Russian citizens because they couldn't use their cards or open accounts in the West," he told me. "Antiwar Russians returned to Russia with the conviction that the West is not fighting the Putin regime, but Russians."

Putin is waging a war of attrition, waiting until the United States and Europe tire of supporting Ukraine and hoping that Biden will be replaced by Donald Trump, who has vowed to end the war in a day. Increasingly the sanctions have turned into an economic war of attrition. Like a protracted land battle, the economic war has seen both advances and retreats. While reporting this book, I encountered many people who told me that sanctions are pointless because they haven't stopped the war, but in fact that argument is a key plank in Russian propaganda aimed at undermining support for the restrictions in the West. Though the sanctions haven't been as crippling to the Russian economy as some thought they would be at the outset, Putin is bankrupting Russia, sacrificing the country's long-term prosperity for short-term gains. The Kremlin more than doubled defense spending to a level not seen since the collapse of the Soviet Union—it's now almost a third of all government spending. That's boosted growth, but it all depends on Russia being able to sell its oil at lofty prices while the West tries to squeeze the

Kremlin's revenues. Russia already lost an estimated $168 billion in oil and gas export earnings in the first two years of the war because of Western restrictions and Europe finding other sources of energy.

Pressure from sanctions caused the Russian ruble to tumble almost 45 percent by the second anniversary of the invasion from a wartime high in June 2022. Perhaps more important, hundreds of thousands of Russia's best and brightest have left the country, a brain drain that will hobble the country for years to come. U.S. deputy secretary of the treasury Wally Adeyemo has argued the goal is to put "sand in the gears" of the economy. Sanctions were never meant to be a magic bullet. Rather, the economic war was designed to work alongside the military one, to undermine Putin's ability to fund his military-industrial complex while arming Ukraine to give it the best chance of heading off a Russian victory. Yet on both fronts, the West has moved too slowly, adhering to a path of gradual escalation that has failed to diminish Putin's will to keep fighting.

At the time this book went to press, Putin's invasion had claimed the lives of tens of thousands of Ukrainians. A third of Ukraine's population had been displaced, while its economy had shrunk by more than 25 percent. Russian forces have destroyed schools, hospitals, bridges, power plants, and apartment buildings, indiscriminately targeting civilian infrastructure and hobbling Ukraine's ability to fight back. No amount of money can compensate for such carnage.

But one of the key questions is whether the billions of dollars of frozen Russian assets can be used to help war-torn Ukraine finance its reconstruction, which the World Bank estimates will cost at least $486 billion. The ability of Ukraine to survive as Russia pummels it with relentless attacks depends in part on it getting the funds to rebuild critical national infrastructure even as the war continues. Even relatively small amounts of money can make a difference. For all the obstacles standing in the way, selling a Russian superyacht could help pay to rebuild thousands of destroyed homes. It remains the central question of the economic war, one that will be asked again and again: Who will pay for Putin's catastrophic invasion?

CHAPTER 1

ATTACKING FORTRESS RUSSIA

At 3:00 a.m. eastern time on February 24, 2022, just hours after Putin announced the start of his "special military operation" and Russian missiles began raining down on Ukraine, Daleep Singh woke up at his home in northwest Washington, DC. He'd only slept a few hours and, bleary-eyed, immediately reached for his phone to check the news. Russian tanks were rolling across the Ukrainian border from the north, east, and south. Explosions were being reported across many major Ukrainian cities, including the capital, Kyiv.

Singh, a forty-five-year-old North Carolinian with a crop of thick dark hair, was Biden's deputy national security adviser for international economics and a key architect of sanctions against Russia. His wife had gotten used to his texting and emailing from bed in the middle of the night as the crisis had deepened. With Russia amassing troops at the border, he'd been rising early and working late into the evening for months, helping devise a response to the looming threat of an invasion. The images from Ukraine on his phone were as bad as he thought it could get. As Russian troops invaded from three sides, residents clogged the main road out of Kyiv, trying to flee. Russian forces were attacking a major international cargo airport outside the city and moving into the exclusion zone around the Chernobyl nuclear power plant, the site of the world's worst nuclear disaster.

Earlier in the week, Singh had already announced an initial round of U.S. sanctions in response to Russia recognizing the independence of Ukraine's separatist regions in its east, and the Biden administration had prepared another package to be announced as soon as the inevitable invasion started. But it wasn't clear exactly how far Russian troops would go. As the brutality of the invasion unfolded in those early hours, he realized that the measures they'd prepared weren't enough. Western allies needed to ramp up the economic pressure immediately, or Russian troops might overrun Ukraine in days. They wanted to stun Putin with major sanctions to buy time to send Ukraine more military aid so it could defend itself.

Trying not to wake his wife or teenage kids, Singh tiptoed downstairs to his home office to call Björn Seibert, head of cabinet to European Commission president Ursula von der Leyen in Brussels. Seibert, a bespectacled former German defense ministry official, is the most powerful guy you've never heard of, with an almost sphinxlike ability to broker deals behind the scenes in Brussels. Seibert and Singh had been talking daily for weeks about what it would take to drive consensus for tougher sanctions. The stakes for Europe were higher. It was heavily dependent on Russian energy, which made the prospect of unprecedented economic penalties more costly.

Seibert told Singh that the visuals of a Putin invasion would be critical in their efforts to implement ambitious sanctions. For European leaders, images of war on the Continent would trigger a visceral emotional reaction and unblock resistance to wider economic penalties. It quickly became clear they were watching the start of the biggest war in Europe since World War II, one that justified deploying the most extensive sanctions ever against a major economy.

"Okay, I see the visuals," Seibert said.

"It's go time," Singh replied.

*   *   *

For nearly a year, Biden had been trying to head off Russia's invasion of Ukraine using a mix of traditional diplomacy and unconventional tactics. The tension first started to build in April 2021, just months after Biden entered the White House. Putin began testing Washington by amassing troops on the border with Ukraine in what was Russia's largest deployment since his annexation of Crimea in 2014. The troop buildup represented the first significant threat of a full-scale invasion of Ukraine, which led U.S. officials to warn of consequences if Russia provoked a wider war. In a call that month with Putin, Biden urged him to deescalate and said he wanted to develop what the U.S. president called a "stable and predictable relationship," proposing a U.S.-Russia summit. Putin listed his grievances over Ukraine but eventually accepted the invitation.

Determined to correct the Trump administration's soft-pedaling on Russia, Biden pushed ahead, just days after the call, with a package of sanctions to respond to Russian provocations, which included Moscow's meddling in the U.S. elections, the poisoning of the late Russian opposition activist Alexei Navalny, and the Russian-backed cyber hack on the U.S. tech company SolarWinds Corp., which exposed multiple U.S. government agencies to data breaches.

The Biden administration viewed the sanctions as an act of housekeeping, making up for Trump's unwillingness to respond to Russia's malign actions. The penalties were limited to barring U.S. institutions from the primary market for ruble-denominated bonds and blacklisting thirty-two entities and individuals for trying to influence the 2020 election—more of a signaling exercise without major impact. The same day, the Pentagon canceled plans to send two navy destroyers into the Black Sea because of rising tensions between Ukraine and Russia in what some viewed as a sign of U.S. weakness. A week later, Putin reacted angrily to the sanctions in his state-of-the-nation speech, saying that "picking on Russia without any reason" had become a "new sport." He didn't mention the military buildup, but Russia announced the next day it would be withdrawing some of its troops from the Ukraine border by May 1.

Biden's tougher stance on Russia was delicately balanced with his efforts to revive the transatlantic alliance after Trump's tempestuous presidency. At the end of May, the Biden administration waived sanctions on Nord Stream 2 AG, the company set up to build and operate the controversial new $11 billion, 767-mile gas pipeline from Russia to Germany under the Baltic Sea that bypassed Ukraine, adding capacity to an existing route. Biden's desire to rebuild relations with Germany, badly damaged by Trump, drove the waiver—"It was all about alliance management," one administration official told me—but the president remained opposed to the project, convinced the pipeline would give Putin more influence over Europe.

For all his wariness of Putin's intentions, Biden believed communication between the world's two leading nuclear powers was essential for global stability. When he finally sat down with Putin at the eighteenth-century Villa La Grange on Lake Geneva in June 2021, it looked like a superpower showdown from the Cold War. "This is not a kumbaya moment," Biden told Putin during the three-hour summit. "It's clearly not in anybody's interest, your country's or mine, for us to be in a situation where we're in a new Cold War." But he later admitted that Putin still felt "encircled" and believed that the United States was looking to "take him down." Besides some talk of working groups on arms control and cybersecurity, Biden came out of the summit with no important commitments from Putin.

For the moment, the summit appeared to stifle Putin's hunger for territory. As the threat of a new Russian invasion of Ukraine receded so did any further talk of sanctions. For Singh and other Biden advisers, there were bigger economic problems to grapple with, such as postpandemic inflation.

That soon changed. A month later, Putin published a rambling five-thousand-word essay "On the Historical Unity of Russians and Ukrainians," laying out his historical claims on Ukrainian territory, which resurrected Russian imperial myths that the two countries are really "one people." In the essay, he questioned Ukraine's borders, arguing the nation occupied lands that were historically Russian. The essay was read with alarm inside the White House, but the administration was soon engulfed by the crisis sparked by the withdrawal of U.S. troops from Afghanistan, a disastrous episode that some believed encouraged Putin to think the United States wouldn't respond if Russia invaded Ukraine. Just weeks after the evacuation from Kabul, the United States started getting credible intelligence that Russia was again building up its forces on the border under the cover of a routine military exercise, but the intelligence indicated Moscow was sending different types of units than in previous years.

As representatives from the Group of 20, an organization of the world's major economies, descended on Rome at the end of October 2021 for their annual summit, Biden pulled aside the leaders of France and Germany to start sharing intelligence for the first time on Russia's troop buildup. It was a wake-up call. "We made a strategic decision that we were not going to give Putin the element of surprise," Singh recalls of the National Security

Council's idea to start sharing sensitive intelligence. "We didn't want him to use false flags."

U.S. officials began warning Russia of severe economic consequences if Putin went ahead with the invasion. Biden dispatched CIA director Bill Burns to Moscow to talk to Putin and make it clear that the response would be much more severe than it had been in 2014. Putin was isolating during a severe COVID outbreak, but Burns told him by phone that Russia would pay a "heavy price" if he launched an invasion. His message fell on deaf ears. A few weeks later, Putin accused the West of ignoring Russia's "red lines" on Ukraine and NATO expansion.

After returning from Rome, Jake Sullivan, Biden's national security adviser, started convening daily meetings with Singh and other officials who worked on military, intelligence, and diplomacy to come up with a comprehensive response. Diplomacy wasn't working, so sanctions were one of the few tools they had at their disposal. "Economics was really a central part of the discussion," Singh told me. "We knew that the asymmetric advantages we collectively possessed were in capital and cutting-edge technology." That reflected an enduring tenet of sanctions: they needed to harm the target harder than the country imposing the penalties. Denying Russia access to Western financial markets and know-how could hurt Russia without imposing huge costs on the United States and Europe.

For European officials, the turning point came in November 2021 when von der Leyen, with Seibert, visited the White House for the first time to meet Biden, who sounded the alarm on Russia's troop buildup. "It struck me how much time the U.S. president, with his full agenda, was devoting to what's happening on Europe's borders," Seibert told me. Detailed discussions on coordinated sanctions among the G7, the informal bloc of the world's industrialized democracies, got underway. In December, Biden held a two-hour video call with Putin warning him that the United States and its allies would impose "economic consequences like none he's ever seen" if he sent troops into Ukraine. Deterrence was primarily focused on the economic threat rather than the military one.

While Biden was sharing U.S. intelligence about the amassing of troops on the border of Ukraine, not everyone agreed on what it all meant. "Some allies thought it was a bluff," Eric Green, then senior director for Russia and Central

Asia at the National Security Council (NSC), told me. "We said, 'Even if we're wrong, let's at least plan for the worst in case we're right.'" Russian officials repeatedly denied they were planning to invade. But by January 2022, U.S. intelligence indicated Russia was moving blood supplies and other medical equipment near the border with Ukraine. In Brussels, Seibert, von der Leyen's head of cabinet, watched the buildup with apprehension, having monitored previous Russian military exercises as a defense analyst. He began convening weekly meetings with small groups of ambassadors on the thirteenth floor of the European Commission's headquarters to try to forge a consensus across the twenty-seven member states on possible sanctions. The ambassadors started calling the meetings, held usually on Sundays, confessionals, where they aired their concerns.

Many officials harbored doubts about the U.S. intelligence, even in Kyiv. At the beginning of February, with one hundred thousand Russian troops at Ukraine's border, Ukrainian president Volodymyr Zelensky was talking down the threat of an invasion. Social media memes were comparing his response to the Russian troop buildup to the Netflix film *Don't Look Up*, in which two astronomers try to warn an apathetic world of an incoming comet that will destroy the planet. "We are looking up," Zelensky told reporters. "But we've been in this situation for eight years," alluding to Russia's 2014 annexation of Crimea and the ongoing war in the east.

The threats of severe economic consequences designed to deter Putin kept coming. Europe's dependence on Russian energy supplies became a major point of contention. In early February, Biden met with Germany's chancellor, Olaf Scholz, in Washington, where the U.S. president publicly vowed to "bring an end" to Nord Stream 2 if Russia invaded. But Scholz, then just two months on the job, still wasn't taking a clear stance on the pipeline.

U.K. prime minister Boris Johnson, who had developed a close relationship with Zelensky, thought the Germans were being very cautious. "One key issue on sanctions was whether the package should be announced in anticipation of Putin's action, in the hope of deterring him," Johnson told me. "Olaf spoke of the need for 'strategic ambiguity'—not tipping our hand until the invasion had actually happened, which is what we did. I'm not sure how effective that was."

Two days before the invasion, Germany halted approvals for the new pipeline after Russia formally recognized the self-proclaimed republics of

Luhansk and Donetsk in eastern Ukraine. At the same time, the United States tried to up the pressure by imposing full blocking sanctions on two of Russia's biggest banks—Vnesheconombank (VEB) and Promsvyazbank—instantly freezing their U.S. assets, and blacklisting five Kremlin-connected elites, including the director of the FSB, the successor to the KGB—a move that froze their U.S. dollar holdings. The next day, Washington went ahead with sanctions on the company behind Nord Stream 2, and its German CEO Matthias Warnig, a former East German Stasi officer with links to Putin.

In the end, none of it stopped Russia from invading. Whether tougher sanctions ahead of the invasion might have deterred Putin is impossible to say with hindsight. Some thought he was intent on trying to take Ukraine regardless of the economic costs. The West was not about to risk a direct military confrontation with a nuclear-armed Russia by sending NATO troops into Ukraine. That meant the theater of war would need to be economic and technological combat pushed to its limits.

*   *   *

Giving his dog a bone to keep her quiet, Singh left home on the day Putin launched his invasion around 4:00 a.m. after his call with Seibert. It was cold and dark as he drove along the Potomac River to the White House, steeling himself for one of the most consequential days of Biden's presidency. Up until then, he'd felt as if he'd been pushing a boulder up a hill for months trying to build a global consensus for economic penalties to respond to Putin's belligerent massing of troops on the border. Biden had spoken with Zelensky late at night from the White House soon after the invasion began and told him he'd rally support the next day for severe sanctions.

U.S. and U.K. intelligence indicated that Russia would try to quickly take all of Ukraine in a shock-and-awe operation. Inside the White House, officials were operating under the assumption the war could be over in days. Singh thought Western economic penalties against Russia needed to strike a devastating blow as quickly as possible. Others agreed. "Once the scale of the invasion became apparent, we could imagine half of Ukraine would be under occupation, including Kyiv, so there was a desire to go big on the economic side and throw everything at them," one former senior administration official told me. But because Russia was one of the world's top producers of oil, gas, and critical metals, it was impossible to do a full embargo without sparking a major economic slump.

One idea they'd been working on was cutting off Russia's biggest banks from SWIFT, the financial-messaging platform that connects banks around the world to facilitate international financial flows. SWIFT is like the Gmail of the global banking system—a secure messaging system for worldwide payments. Kicking Russian banks out of SWIFT would make it difficult for money to move in and out of the country. The move would deny them access to Western correspondent banking accounts, hampering cross-border payments for trade of all kinds. There was a precedent: SWIFT blocked Iranian banks in 2012, but they weren't as wired into the global financial system as Russian banks were. Cutting Russia off wasn't as simple and straightforward as it looked to some, economically or politically. For one, there were concerns that Europe would suddenly be unable to pay for its natural gas supplies from Russia if SWIFT blocked all of the country's major banks.

While Russia might be able to find workarounds to a SWIFT ban, Singh thought the moment was right for a move that would deal a more devastating blow: blocking Russia's central bank. He wanted to hit Putin's Fortress Russia—a war chest of around $630 billion in reserves it had built up since 2014. Those reserves were made up of assets in dollars, euros, sterling, yen, renminbi, and gold mostly held at financial institutions outside Russia that it could sell to support the value of the ruble against other currencies. Without access to that full stockpile, the central bank would struggle to prevent the ruble from dropping in value, potentially precipitously. Despite trying to cultivate a reputation as a master tactician, Putin had made a strategic error by leaving around half of those reserves parked at financial institutions in the West, where he laid himself open to a financial attack.

The United States had used this financial weapon before, but the sheer size of Russia's reserves made it a radical step. In August 2021, Biden froze Afghanistan's $7 billion in reserves held on American soil after the U.S. withdrawal allowed the Taliban to sweep to power. The United States had taken similar steps to block the reserves of other sanctioned countries, such as Iran and Venezuela, but the amounts were relatively small. Immobilizing some $300 billion of Russia's reserves represented a whole new category of economic combat. Never before had the world's biggest economies teamed up to freeze so much money in response to a global security threat.

Singh realized that putting a block on the Russian central bank's foreign exchange reserves was, financially at least, the nuclear option, but it was the only way to make Fortress Russia buckle. He wasn't alone in thinking Russia's reserves were fair game; Italian prime minister Mario Draghi, who'd served as president of the European Central Bank for eight years, had already thought of targeting Russia's central bank and was discussing the idea with counterparts in Europe soon after the invasion started. Russia's full-scale invasion of Ukraine, replete with troops and tanks heading for Kyiv, marked such a blatant violation of the post–World War II world order that it justified a move that might have been seen as reckless just days earlier. Putin had upped the ante the morning he launched the invasion by delivering a chilling speech that contained a veiled threat of using nuclear weapons. He warned that countries that tried to stand in Russia's way would suffer "consequences you have never seen in your entire history." Targeting the reserves was one of the most drastic economic steps to take, but sitting idly by was even more dangerous.

The freeze would no doubt undermine Putin's control of the economy. Singh believed the move would cause the Russian currency to crash as everyone rushed to the door, trying to exchange rubles for dollars. The block would disarm Russia's capacity to intervene to stabilize the currency. The Russian economy depended on the U.S. dollar for half of its international trade and 80 percent of its daily foreign exchange transactions. Russia's central bank was the lender of last resort to its commercial banks. But the domino effect of such a move in international financial markets was impossible to predict. No major central bank had ever been blocked in this way. Politicians were in uncharted territory, working under extreme time pressure with the highest possible stakes. It was hard to know if Russia was exposed to what Singh called "dry tinder," or complex derivatives, which could set off fires at financial institutions outside Russia's borders. Freezing $300 billion could affect the global financial system in ways that were difficult to anticipate.

The proposal also raised the specter of an accelerated de-dollarization of the global economy. Other central banks might respond by paring back their dollar holdings to reduce their vulnerability to sanctions. The ability of countries to freely borrow from one another remains the cornerstone of the international financial system. By freezing Russia's central bank reserves, there were concerns that other countries would view the dollar or euro as unsafe because they could be unilaterally targeted by Washington and Brussels.

Some economists and policymakers argued that the block on Russia's reserves threatened to undermine the trust built up over decades of countries honoring debts across borders. If the United States and the EU could freeze dollar and euro reserves held at other financial institutions in an act of economic warfare, then the rules of the game had fundamentally changed.

Singh believed the move was justified because Russia had egregiously violated the rules-based order by trying to change borders by force. And Draghi wasn't worried about such a move undermining financial stability, people familiar with his thinking told me. But the freeze would require unprecedented international consensus and coordination, and the unknowable risks involved made the decision all the more fraught.

In those first hours after Putin launched his invasion, leaders on the other side of the Atlantic were already holding tense talks. At 10 Downing Street, U.K. prime minister Boris Johnson was messaging with his key advisers in a WhatsApp group: "We want the toughest possible next tranche of sanctions. We have to make them bite. Putin cannot succeed. He must fail." Johnson held an anxious call with Zelensky that morning. "We were thinking, 'Is this guy going to get killed?'" one aide who listened to the conversation told me. Zelensky's life was at risk, but one of the things he asked for was a Russian ban from SWIFT, a sign of how important he saw it to degrading Putin's war machine. Zelensky's vow to stay in Kyiv to lead Ukraine's defense despite Russian threats to assassinate him injected a sense of gravity into talks on the need for tougher economic penalties and urgent military aid.

As a result of Zelensky's plea, Johnson became a vocal advocate for a SWIFT ban. Johnson then spoke with German chancellor Olaf Scholz, who was about to host an emergency call with the leaders of the G7. Johnson told him the G7 should shut down Russia's access to SWIFT as quickly as possible. "SWIFT would really hurt us," Scholz retorted. Germany relied on Russia for about half its gas imports. How would Germany pay for Russian gas if all Russian banks were kicked out of the global financial system for sending payments? Johnson pushed the German leader hard on the need for Europe to wean itself off Russian hydrocarbons. "So will you put all the oligarchs in jail?" Scholz shot back, clearly annoyed.

The exchange highlighted each country's vulnerability. The U.K. had been a magnet for illicit Russian wealth for over two decades as tycoons bought luxury mansions in London and sent their kids to British private schools. But having left the EU, the U.K. had a bare-bones sanctions regime that couldn't quickly respond to Russia's invasion. Meanwhile, Germany had agreed to phase out nuclear power plants thinking it would have an endless supply of cheap Russian gas. Downing Street sources told me Johnson privately viewed Scholz as weak and soft on Putin, but Johnson publicly talked up European unity. His motivations for sounding tough on Putin were both entirely genuine and politically expedient. As a biographer of Winston Churchill, Johnson saw the invasion as his moment to cast himself as a wartime leader and restore his popularity just as domestic scandals about parties at Downing Street during the pandemic lockdown were threatening to end his political career. Supporting Ukraine wasn't a hard call politically.

Hard-line voices came from an unusual corner: Canada. Though one of the smallest economies in the G7, Canada has the second-largest Ukrainian diaspora in the world, which made Russia's invasion a visceral issue. Chrystia Freeland, Canada's deputy prime minister and finance minister, was pitching the idea of freezing Russia's central bank reserves to prime minister Justin Trudeau after talking to Ukrainian officials. Her late mother was a Ukrainian lawyer who had helped draft Ukraine's constitution. Fluent in Ukrainian and Russian, Freeland understood Putin and the Russian economy, having been Moscow bureau chief of the *Financial Times* in the 1990s and seeing the logic of attacking the reserves.

European leaders were in shock when they gathered for the G7 video call later on the day the invasion began. Zelensky had declared martial law, saying the government would give weapons to all Ukrainians willing to defend their country. Russia claimed it had neutralized Ukraine's air defenses. Casualties were mounting. "They couldn't quite believe that this was happening on our continent again," one diplomat who listened to the call told me, "particularly for some of the Europeans who were less certain it was going to happen." Scholz was the leader most shocked by the invasion. He'd been in office for less than three months after protracted coalition talks that saw him replace

Angela Merkel, one of Germany's longest-serving leaders. Over an hour, the G7 leaders discussed the intelligence assessment suggesting the war would be over quickly—an assessment that turned out to be wrong. "In the German case, they also gave the impression that they believed that of all the options, a speedy outcome—ghastly though it was—might perhaps be the most sparing of human life and suffering," Johnson told me.

As the G7 leaders debated how to respond, Johnson, von der Leyen, and Trudeau sounded the most hawkish. Fresh from speaking with Zelensky, Johnson joined the G7 call pushing for a Russian ban from SWIFT, while Trudeau floated the idea of blocking Russia's enormous foreign central bank reserves, after Freeland urged him to do so. Singh had thought about the possibility of freezing the reserves ever since his time working at the U.S. Treasury in 2014 when Putin annexed Crimea, but the idea hadn't been raised at the level of the leaders until then. For such a radical step to be taken, Singh felt timing was everything. It looked as if the moment had finally come.

The sanctions that had been prepared in advance to roll out if Putin invaded looked weak juxtaposed with images of Russian missile strikes across Ukraine. The measures included a series of U.S. blocks and restrictions on some Russian banks and sanctions against some elites, but these were far from a knockout blow. Biden announced the package with a broad brush, facing down questions about why the penalties didn't stop Putin and why a Russian ban from SWIFT wasn't included. "It's always an option, but right now, that's not the position the rest of Europe wishes to take," Biden said. Singh was scheduled to follow later that day with a more detailed dissection of the package for the media, which he knew needed to go further. Unlike Seibert, who worked behind the scenes in Brussels on the EU's second sanctions package, Singh had taken on an increasingly public role articulating Biden's sanctions policy through a series of press briefings and appearances on CNN and MSNBC to explain the economic pressure campaign against Putin.

In fact, Singh had been so central to devising U.S. sanctions against Russia that some were calling the economic response the "Daleep doctrine." He came armed with an Ivy League pedigree and a gold-plated résumé. After studying economics at Duke University, he had earned a joint MBA and master's in public administration from the Massachusetts Institute of Technology and Harvard University focusing on international economics.

He'd worked at Goldman Sachs, and then the U.S. Treasury and the New York Federal Reserve. Singh explains the world with a disarming clarity and convincing faith in the ability of the United States to uphold the rules-based liberal world order. Coming from his mouth, the measures sounded smart, strategic, sensible. No one wanted to go to war with a nuclear-armed Russia, but an economic battle sounded like an astute way to make Putin pay a steep price. "Back by popular demand," Biden's spokesperson Jen Psaki introduced him to the Washington press corps at 5:30 p.m. on the day Russia's invasion began, "Daleep is back."

"This is a briefing I never wanted to give," Singh began. "President Biden has said from the start of this crisis, if Putin chooses to invade, the cost to Russia will be immediate and profound—to its financial system, to its economy, to its technology base, and to its strategic position in the world." He ticked off a series of economic penalties: cutting off Russia's largest bank, Sberbank, from the U.S. financial system; full blocking sanctions on Russia's second-largest bank, VTB, and three others; restricting thirteen of Russia's biggest companies from U.S. financing; blacklisting ten Russian elites; and a bar on Russia's ability to import cutting-edge technology.

The sanctions on day one went further than the United States had gone ever before, with commercial bank penalties that were hard fought, but the immediate reaction from the media could be summed up as "That's all you got?" Biden had warned of punishing sanctions if Putin invaded, but now the penalties looked feeble. Putin had ordered the biggest attack by one state against another in Europe in more than seventy years, but the Kremlin leader himself was not sanctioned. The administration hadn't even fully blocked Russia's biggest bank, Sberbank.

Pressure for more drastic measures built after Zelensky urged EU leaders to impose more punishing sanctions, warning them during an emotional video call from his bunker in Kyiv later that day, "This might be the last time you see me alive."

* * *

The next day, as Russian attacks on Ukrainian cities continued, Biden's national security team were working frantically inside the White House, surviving on pizza, chicken fingers, and espressos from a machine that was growing green fuzz from neglect in Singh's office. Images of the war on social media and televisions were shocking people around the world, while calls to deploy obscure economic weapons were seeping into the public consciousness. Outside the White House, protesters in Lafayette Square were holding placards saying BAN RUSSIA FROM SWIFT. "I'm not even sure if people who were holding these signs knew what SWIFT was. But it had just become this rallying cry," Singh told me. While SWIFT had caught the public's attention, freezing Russia's reserves had not.

The idea to block Russia's central bank suddenly took on an urgency because of French intelligence that the Kremlin was already starting to withdraw assets from Europe, which meant an agreement to freeze was needed by Monday or tens of billions could disappear. As the U.S. Treasury finally slapped sanctions on Putin himself along with other top officials, Singh was writing up a succinct one-page memo outlining a plan to block Russia's mammoth $300 billion in central bank reserves held in Western financial institutions, to de-SWIFT its largest banks, and to launch a task force to go after sanctioned assets. In conversations with Biden and his national security adviser, Jake Sullivan, Singh argued it was time to strike big. They were expecting Russia to try to topple the Ukrainian government, so waiting made no sense. The severity of the invasion was at the upper bounds of what they had expected. "If not now, when are we going to deliver the full scale of our sanctions arsenal?" he told them.

Singh was Biden's G7 "sherpa," named after the Himalayan mountain guides. Singh hopped on a call with Seibert and Jonathan Black, sherpas to von der Leyen and Johnson, respectively, to strategize how to build consensus to strike against Russia's biggest economic target—Russia's central bank—by harnessing the emotional valence of the moment. "We were trying to figure out how to get the whole G7 to move at once," Singh told me. The wider group of G7 sherpas were supposed to talk later that day, and the trio wanted to devise the most convincing pitch. When the sherpas all convened, they talked about de-SWIFTing some of Russia's biggest banks and going after sanctioned oligarch assets. Singh went last with his pitch for blocking $300 billion in reserves in the West—a ban on anyone transacting with Russia's central bank, arguing it would generate an economic shock and awe.

"This is an extreme measure to take, but if we do it together, it will be seen as a collective defense of core principles that we all share to underpin peace and security," Singh told them.

"The issuers of the world's major reserve currencies were all represented on that call—euros, dollars, pound, and yen. That's all you needed," he told me. The sherpas agreed to push the proposal up their chains of command. Yet they were venturing into the unknown. "Nobody knew the exact size of the assets," Seibert told me. "But we knew most of the money was in Europe."

In London, Johnson spoke with Zelensky again as Russian troops marched toward Kyiv. As usual, they started out with a translator, first talking about weapons supplies and Johnson telling him the whole world was praying. But then Zelensky began speaking English. "You like Shakespeare, Boris, right?" Zelensky said, knowing that Johnson had a deal to write a biography of the Bard. "To SWIFT or not to SWIFT? That is the question," Zelensky said. As a former TV comedian, Zelensky knew how to deliver a rehearsed line for maximum effect even in his halting English. Johnson assured him they were making progress on SWIFT.

Fresh from the call with Zelensky, Johnson went to his 9:00 a.m. meeting with his key political advisers and SWIFT at the forefront of his mind. "We really need to get SWIFT done," he told them. "The Europeans have got to come through on this."

Europe was split on whether to exclude Russia from SWIFT, with Germany, Italy, and Austria initially expressing doubts about the move. Johnson was trying to rally support for the ban. Johnson texted his advisers that Dutch prime minister Mark Rutte was on board: "Rutte is sound on SWIFT and the bank-asset freeze," referring to Russia's central bank reserves. "We need a way of moving all this on," Johnson said. "A country is being destroyed before our eyes. And the West is still bickering about how tough to be." His hard-hitting stance was all the easier because kicking Russian banks out of SWIFT and freezing the reserves cost the U.K. little. Going after Russian money in the U.K. would be much harder.

Back in Washington, Singh knew the clock was ticking; the proposal to block Russia's reserves had to be kept under wraps, or Putin would continue to move the money out of Western financial institutions. Singh isn't just a policy wonk; he's a markets guy. He'd most recently worked as head of the markets team at the New York Federal Reserve. He knew a proposal had to be agreed upon before trading began on Monday. That actually meant Sunday, when New Zealand's currency markets opened. "Is this going to work?" his boss, Jake Sullivan, asked him. Singh thought it would cause the ruble to go into freefall. They couldn't wait with the situation on the ground in Ukraine worsening by the hour.

When Singh and others huddled in Sullivan's office for a National Security Council meeting on Saturday morning, Biden, connected remotely from Wilmington, Delaware, asked Sullivan about freezing Russia's reserves. When Singh presented the plan, the president asked him to explain why blocking the reserves would matter to Putin. "Because he's not expecting it," Singh said. Everyone was on board, but U.S. treasury secretary Janet Yellen hesitated about rushing it through. She was unsure about the ramifications of freezing Russia's reserves and how it might affect global markets. Yellen was also doubtful that enough other countries would back the move to make it a global initiative and was reluctant to support the freeze if it was just the United States going ahead. "I want more time to consider it," she told the group.

The meeting ended without a decision. Without Yellen's support, the proposal was going nowhere. It had been discussed conceptually by senior Treasury officials before, but the speed of the decision-making and the possible ripple effects made them nervous. Yellen was the last obstacle to the plan moving forward at a time when Ukraine's very existence as an independent state was in doubt. Russian forces were engaged in urban warfare in northwestern Kyiv and were attacking the key port city of Mariupol.

Singh called Seibert and said, "We have a problem."

Yellen needed convincing, and the only person who could possibly persuade her was Draghi, then the Italian prime minister. Yellen is known to be cautious in the face of uncertainty, but she's widely respected on Wall Street for helping bring the global financial system back from the brink as the former vice chair and then chair of the Federal Reserve. Draghi had worked with Yellen as equals on the world stage for years. He commanded enormous respect after navigating the European sovereign-debt crisis in the early 2010s, giving his now-famous speech saying he'd do "whatever it takes" to prevent the euro from crashing.

"They spoke the same language, and I'm not talking about English," one former senior European diplomat told me. "They understand each other at a glance." For Draghi, the horrors unfolding in Ukraine pushed any worries about financial stability to the back of his mind. He viewed immobilizing the reserves as an obvious step to take. Seibert asked von der Leyen to call Draghi to see if he could convince Yellen. When he called her to discuss the proposal, Yellen was in a meeting at the U.S. Treasury's office on Pennsylvania Avenue with senior officials discussing their doubts that enough countries would agree to the plan to make it work. She stepped out to speak to Draghi and returned sounding more convinced. "Italy wants to do this," she said. "They think they can get consensus."

With Yellen on board, Singh rushed to finalize the statement announcing the historic steps the G7 was planning to take. He wanted it to go out by 5:00 p.m. Eastern time.

Then, in the middle of the afternoon, Singh got a call from his daughter, who was home alone, telling him a man had been lurking on their front lawn and broken into their house in northwest Washington. Singh dropped everything, called the Secret Service, and rushed home. The man fled the scene in a BMW sedan. He was relieved to find that she was fine. Nothing had been stolen. There was no evidence the episode was linked to Singh's high-profile sanctions work, but it could certainly have been a Russian attempt to rattle him. Russian spies have a history of orchestrating "home intrusions" designed to harass and intimidate diplomats.

Shaken, Singh returned to the White House, and several hours later Western allies announced an economic blitzkrieg. The United States, the U.K., Germany, France, Canada, and the European Commission committed to removing selected Russian banks from SWIFT and restricting Russia's central bank from using its foreign reserves. (Japanese leaders, who were asleep when the statement went out, joined later.) In a concession to European countries, not all Russian banks would be kicked out of SWIFT, in part to allow payments for Russian energy to keep flowing.

Agreeing to freeze $300 billion of Russian assets in one swoop was an uphill battle. Now, as Russia launched missile strikes across Ukraine, they had to wait and see what would happen.

*   *   *

The next day, Singh woke up to reports that freezing the reserves and de-SWIFTing Russia's largest banks might have a bigger impact than expected. He began to worry that this unprecedented action could spark global market chaos. "Taking out the central bank means we're running the risk of catastrophic success," he told Sullivan. "We'll need eyes wide open to the risk of an uncontrolled financial crisis that spreads beyond Russia's borders."

The effect on Russia was immediate and profound. On Monday, the ruble plunged almost 30 percent—and even more in international markets—as companies and individuals rushed to try to exchange the Russian currency for dollars. Singh was in real-time contact with the Fed and other regulators to monitor the fallout. A tumbling ruble meant higher import costs, which would fuel Russian inflation, causing an economic downturn. The Russian central bank announced the Russian stock market, first closed when the war began, would not open, in a bid to limit the financial repercussions. It would remain closed for a month. Shares trading in London of Russia's largest bank, Sberbank, plunged more than 70 percent.

The assault initially played out exactly as Singh had predicted, and, fortunately, his concerns about possible financial "dry tinder" igniting outside Russia didn't materialize. Putin hadn't seen it coming. Western leaders began to gloat that the Russian economy would soon collapse. France's finance minister, Bruno Le Maire, declared that the West was "waging an all-out economic and financial war on Russia." Critics piled in. "To do this to a fellow central bank involves breaking the assumption of sovereign equality and the common interest in upholding the rights to property," the economic historian and Columbia University professor Adam Tooze wrote on his influential blog.

With Russia thrust into its most precarious economic position in decades, Putin was lucky to have one of the world's smartest central bankers in his corner: Elvira Nabiullina. Then a fifty-eight-year-old economist, Nabiullina, with her black-rimmed glasses and bobbed auburn hair, exudes a no-nonsense "don't mess with me" air. She had worked with Putin ever since he entered the Kremlin, including the previous nine years as central bank governor. Western investors had lauded her as one of the world's best monetary policymakers and praised her for trying to clean up the country's notoriously corrupt and bloated banking sector, shutting down more than three hundred institutions. She was renowned for sending signals to the market by the type of brooch pinned to her collarless jackets before rate decisions. When she showed up with a dove or a swan brooch, the rate went down. When she wore a hawk or a leopard, it signaled a rate rise.

When the war started, Nabiullina wanted to step down, but Putin ordered her to stay for another five-year term, according to people close to her. Quitting would have been seen as a betrayal of Putin, with unknown consequences for her and her family. Resigning would effectively mean fleeing the country. It was yet another sign of how fear had become the cornerstone of Putin's Russia. While other lower-ranking employees quit, some more prominent officials also felt trapped.

The freeze took Russian central bank officials by surprise. Before the invasion, they had modeled scenarios for Russia's banks getting cut off from SWIFT, but they didn't think the reserves would be blocked. With the ruble in free fall, the normal strategy would be to sell some of the central bank's stash of dollars and euros to bolster the currency. With half the reserves out of reach, though, Nabiullina had limited firepower. So she used other tools: On the Monday after the G7 announced the freezing of reserves, she more than doubled interest rates, increasing demand for rubles, and imposed capital controls to stop cash from fleeing the country. (Curiously, she donned all black and wore no brooch on the day of her announcement; her brooch signals have all but disappeared since the invasion.) The government also required Russian businesses earning foreign currency abroad to swap 80 percent of their proceeds into rubles. That same day, Putin chaired an emergency meeting with the central bank after the Kremlin admitted the sanctions "significantly changed Russia's economic reality." In a video to her staff just days after the invasion, Nabiullina said, "All of us would have wanted for this not to happen," adding to speculation she privately opposed the war. Whatever her leanings, her efforts helped stabilize the ruble by the end of March and staved off the immediate ruin of the Russian economy. In the end, she did more to help Putin sustain the war than almost anyone.

*   *   *

The freeze, coupled with expelling some of the country's largest banks from SWIFT, sparked a financial crisis that was contained within Russia's borders, but the Kremlin was able to recover because the West had left one major hole in the sanctions: energy. Russia was still earning petrodollars from the sale of oil and gas, which hadn't been touched by the economic war because Europe remained heavily dependent on Russian supplies. But the resolve to ratchet up the economic pressure on Putin only increased as more Russian atrocities in Ukraine came to light. If the threat of economic penalties couldn't prevent Putin from launching his war, the goal shifted from behavior change to a containment strategy. "Sanctions can degrade and impair a country's ability to project power and exert influence," Singh told me. "But are the effects decisive enough to stop an autocrat from conducting a physical land grab? Almost never. It was always unlikely that sanctions by themselves would deliver a knockout blow to Putin's plans before or in the early days of the invasion. Their impact accumulates over time."

That buildup could only happen with a sustained collective effort. The G7, working as part of a coalition of more than thirty countries, would go on to roll out new sanctions daily, weekly, and then monthly, mostly coordinated but sometimes in a helter-skelter fashion. It froze the assets of some of Russia's richest men, blacklisted more banks and companies, and imposed trade restrictions, but the measures had less of an impact than the nuclear option of freezing the reserves. "We made policy in a very open way," Black, Johnson's sherpa, told me. "We shared things that normally we'd be quite careful about, everything from legislative overload to financial stability. There was a lot of trust in that group of people."

The West had united in its efforts to isolate Russia like never before, unlocking tactics that turbocharged the use of economic war. Europe was considering how it might wean itself off Russian energy in what would be a major shift in the post–Cold War economic model.

But the U.K. faced one of the most difficult challenges: the oligarchs. So much illicit Russian money had flooded into the capital that it had developed the nickname Londongrad. Soon after the invasion, Johnson was preparing for Prime Minister's Questions, the weekly face-off in parliament, with the opposition Labour leader, Keir Starmer, and Johnson was expecting to be attacked for not doing enough to respond to Putin's aggression. Helping him prep was Michael Gove, a cabinet minister whose role would involve him in the handling of sanctioned Russian mansions. Johnson turned to him and said with his bombastic flourish, "You need to be the Henry VIII of modern Britain, seizing the assets of the oligarchs like Henry VIII seized the monasteries." Gove countered, "No, that's you. I'm Cromwell," referring to the king's chief minister, who helped him disband the monasteries in the 1500s, expropriating their income. There were no Cromwell-like confiscations, but it was a sign of the dilemma they faced. They had no legal basis to actually seize anything unless an oligarch had committed a crime or was involved in unlawful conduct; many Russian tycoons had earned their fortunes from historical corruption but most were by then invested in legitimate businesses.

Many saw Johnson as soft on Russia because of his relationship with Alexander Lebedev, a former KGB agent turned businessman with a hotel in Crimea, and his son, Evgeny, the owner of London's *Evening Standard* newspaper. In 2018, Johnson had met Alexander at a weekend-long party held at Evgeny's palazzo in Italy, while Johnson was U.K. foreign secretary, without civil servants or his security detail present, an episode that raised questions about the nature of their relationship. Johnson billed the weekend as purely social.

Whatever his relationship with the Lebedevs, Johnson was now pushing for more sanctions on Russia's elite. The move was popular among a British public outraged by pictures of carnage from Ukraine. "It's embarrassing that we're still mucking around with our list of oligos," he texted his advisers in a WhatsApp group. "We need to sanction them all much faster." Less than a week after the invasion, the U.K. targeted Russian billionaire Alisher Usmanov, freezing his £48 million Beechwood House in north London and his sixteenth-century Sutton Place estate in Surrey, outside the capital. That meant he couldn't sell the properties or pay for their upkeep without approval from U.K. authorities. But it turned out Usmanov was one step ahead. He'd already transferred those properties into trusts of which he was no longer a beneficiary, complicating efforts to block the assets.

In March, Russian foreign minister Sergei Lavrov compared the Western sanctions to thievery. "They didn't give a damn about all their principles that they planted on the international stage, including when they began to seize the assets of both the Russian central bank and our private companies. It's just theft," he told Al Jazeera. "They have now simply crossed out these rules and returned to the gangster, wild capitalism of the times of the gold rush."

Trumpeting the power of the penalties, Biden for the first time articulated the policy of economic war. "Taken together, these economic sanctions are a new kind of economic statecraft with the power to inflict damage that rivals military might," he said in a speech to an assembled crowd at the Royal Castle in Warsaw at the end of March. "These international sanctions are sapping Russian strength, its ability to replenish its military, and its ability to project power." Framing it as a battle between autocracy and democracy, Biden went out of his way to make clear that the Russian people were not "our enemy."

The West hadn't imposed a full blockade on Russia, instead relying on a complex web of restrictions. Global banks trying to keep up were often so risk averse that they just stopped doing business with anyone connected to Russia, fearful of running afoul of the U.S. Treasury. Low-income countries also suffered from higher food prices because the difficulty of processing payments to Russia made Western importers shy away from buying Russian grain, even though it was not subject to sanctions. The unintended casualties in the economic war undermined efforts to build a wider global coalition for sanctions.

Imposing asset freezes on this company or that oligarch in an attempt to squeeze Putin's resources, or, as one U.S. official put it, add "sludge" to the system, continued unabated. More Russian banks were banned from SWIFT. But it was the freezing of Russia's central bank reserves—done over a weekend—that arguably had the biggest impact on Putin's ability to sustain the war over the long term, even if Russia recovered on the back of soaring energy prices. For the first time, hundreds of billions of dollars had been immobilized in the West as a direct response to a global security threat. It inextricably linked economic power with a set of values and norms and forced a rethinking of the risks of economic interdependence. And it set off a protracted global fight over whether the G7 was legally justified to actually confiscate Russia's $300 billion in reserves to rebuild war-torn Ukraine.

CHAPTER 2

HUNTING RUSSIAN KLEPTOCRATS

O n Monday, February 28, 2022, just four days after Putin's invasion began, Andrew Adams got an unexpected call from Washington. At the time, he was overseeing several secret investigations targeting high-profile Russian oligarchs as an assistant U.S. Attorney in the Southern District of New York (SDNY)—the most powerful federal prosecutor's office in the country, based in lower Manhattan. Adams had risen up the ranks to become the cochief of SDNY's money-laundering and transnational-criminal-enterprises unit, a position that gave him unique insight into the workings of Russian corruption not just in New York but around the world. When he woke up that morning, Putin's war against Ukraine was intensifying, with reports of civilians trying to block the column of Russian tanks rumbling toward Kyiv and artillery attacks on Ukraine's second-biggest city, Kharkiv.

The night before, Adams had told his wife he would leave SDNY to accept a job as a partner at a prestigious Manhattan law firm. He'd spent almost a decade in public service, where prosecutors typically earn a tenth of what they could pull in private practice. As much as he loved his job at SDNY, it was time to move on. But, unbeknownst to him, in Washington, the White House had just asked the Justice Department to form what it called the KleptoCapture task force to aggressively enforce sanctions on Russian officials and elites with ties to Putin. Hunting down the yachts, jets, and mansions involved in sanctions evasion, the goal was to step up the attack on money laundering and flush Russian illicit finance out of the West. It was envisioned as an all-hands-on-deck initiative, pulling in multiple agencies, from the FBI to the Internal Revenue Service, the U.S. Marshals, and Secret Service. Deputy Attorney General Lisa Monaco was told to stand up the group as quickly as possible.

When Adams answered his phone that morning, a top Justice Department official who worked with Monaco told Adams they wanted him to lead the new high-profile push. "He told me, 'We would really love it if you would do this, and by the way, we would really love it if you could give us an answer in the next forty-five minutes,'" Adams recalled. Though he'd been investigating Russian oligarchs for years, Adams knew that leading the task force was a huge opportunity but not one without risks. "These cases are not easy, but they have possibilities for really aggressive action," he said. For one, he quickly realized Putin's invasion had finally galvanized Western allies to act in a way that would unlock international cooperation and create opportunities to build cases like never before. The partnership at the white-shoe law firm could wait. "So, I called my wife and then the law firm and said, 'Sorry guys, this is too momentous of a situation, so I'm going to stick with it.'"

The following evening, Biden delivered his State of the Union address, during which he announced the new task force. The war in Ukraine dominated his speech as he vowed to choke off Russia from the international financial system. "Tonight, I say to the Russian oligarchs and the corrupt leaders who've bilked billions of dollars off this violent regime, 'No more,'" Biden said. "We're coming for your ill-begotten gains."

Adams, then just thirty-nine, doesn't look like a hard-nosed criminal prosecutor. Tall and thin, with his dark blond hair neatly combed back, he has an earnest demeanor that belies his tenacity in going after mobsters and drug kingpins. "Over the years, you see different prosecutors—some of them are like cowboys who want to bust heads," Adams's old boss at SDNY, Sharon Cohen Levin, told me. Adams didn't fit that mold. He'd earned a reputation as someone who successfully cooperated with teams of FBI agents on complex cases, making tricky judgment calls under pressure.

Within days, Adams was leading the biggest-ever coordinated drive to lock down Russian assets around the world, from superyachts to private jets, while helping to fast-track stalled cases with a surge in resources. The

KleptoCapture task force had around twelve prosecutors working under Adams, including trial attorneys from the units focused on money laundering, organized crime, counterintelligence, and export controls. He enlisted a handful more from U.S. Attorneys' offices from around the country. "You're here to do the extremely tight turnaround cases," Adams told them.

The task force would be housed within Monaco's office and would sit above all of the DOJ's key divisions: national security, criminal, tax, and civil. Crucially, it would not be just a coordinating task force but would be allowed to cut its own subpoenas, giving it power to run with an investigation. "All the signals were, 'We want to treat this like we're on a wartime footing,'" he recalled. "'Move quickly and you'll have money, you'll have support.'"

The United States leads the world in prosecuting money laundering and corruption, with teams of FBI agents able to follow the money like no other law enforcement body in the world. America has long been criticized for overreach, acting as the world's policeman, judge, and jury—a position it enjoys because of the widespread use of the U.S. dollar. But the task force marked a sea change in approach. After years of paying lip service to cracking down on Putin's cronies and confronting his "malign" influence operations, the Biden administration decided to put some real teeth into sanctions enforcement by targeting Russian assets involved in evasion. Congress helped, allocating about $60 million in funding soon after the task force was established.

In May 2022, Monaco sent a chill through C-suites by declaring, "Sanctions are the new FCPA," or Foreign Corrupt Practices Act, which had been used by the Justice Department to aggressively prosecute executives and fine U.S. companies for bribing foreign officials. The anti-corruption law had been on the books since the 1970s, but the Justice Department only started seriously enforcing it in the 2000s, when it began handing out eye-watering fines to multinational corporations around the world. Monaco was signaling that just as the United States aggressively enforced anti-corruption laws, it would start pouring resources into prosecuting sanctions violations.

At the outset, the task force sent out an email to all ninety-three U.S. Attorneys' offices to find out if they were already working on any Russian-sanctions or export-control cases in an effort to pool efforts and avoid duplication. Adams was able to fast-track resources to offices that had already started Russia-related investigations. And he could help smooth the way with international partners now that governments around the world were a bit more willing to cooperate, opening up possibilities for unprecedented action.

The task force began by targeting Russian oligarchs who had already been sanctioned as a way of demonstrating the penalties would finally have real teeth. Working with the FBI and the Department of Homeland Security, they drew up a list of roughly twenty Russian oligarchs who could give them a shot at bringing charges of sanctions violations or money laundering. It wasn't necessarily driven by their importance to the Russian economy but by whether the oligarch had U.S. assets or other ties that would give the U.S. jurisdiction to make a case.

At the same time, a robust debate took place behind the scenes about whether targeting Russia's top tycoons would make a difference. There was an acknowledgment that dialing up the pressure on Russia's wealthiest businessmen wouldn't necessarily force Putin to roll back from Ukraine. The Kremlin had a history of seizing assets from oligarchs who went against Putin, and there were plenty of examples of Russian businessmen dying under mysterious circumstances. Refraining from sanctions to entice them to provide intelligence hadn't worked before, but the hammer of an indictment became a central tool. "It was the carrot-versus-stick conversation," said one former top counterintelligence source involved in the discussions at the time. "We spend a lot of time trying to recruit oligarchs and get info. There was not a lot of track record of them responding to the carrot. But we weren't sure if leaning on the oligarchs really was the soft underbelly of Putin. They liked coming to the U.S. with their houses. But they weren't going to do anything that would put their health or family at risk. They're making a mental calculation. If I cooperate with the U.S. government, I can keep my yacht and my bank account, but I could fall out of a window."

Once the KleptoCapture task force was formed, the emphasis was clearly on the stick. Even if putting the oligarchs under stress did little to change Putin's decision-making, they needed to enforce the existing sanctions and make sure Russia's elite were prosecuted for illegal activity. The sanctions were meaningless without enforcement. The task force was partly about increasing costs on the Russian oligarchs through prosecution and partly about purging Russian money and influence from Western economies. It created opportunities to seize Russian assets and channel the proceeds to Ukraine using forfeiture, a complex legal process that involves proving in a court that the assets were involved in unlawful activity and therefore can be confiscated. But Russian tycoons were masters at using offshore shell companies to hide their wealth, which raised the risk that KleptoCapture would end up in a costly multiyear game of cat-and-mouse chases.

*   *   *

Adams, with his track record of working on Russian money laundering and organized crime cases, was a natural pick to lead KleptoCapture. He'd been inspired by the legendary Spanish prosecutor José Grinda Gonzalez, who spent years hunting the Russian Mafia in Spain. "He talked about Russian organized crime as a form of civilizational assault," Adams recalled during a talk at the Hudson Institute in Washington, DC. "That remains a sort of foundational text for me and this task force."

The son of a nurse and a pediatrician, Adams grew up in Baton Rouge, Louisiana, and then Dallas, Texas, before getting his law degree at the University of Michigan. Following in the footsteps of many ambitious law graduates, he kicked off his career with two clerkships, including at the influential U.S. Court of Appeals for the Second Circuit, where Supreme Court justices Thurgood Marshall and Sonia Sotomayor once served. Both the judges he'd clerked for had been assistant U.S. Attorneys, so he saw it as an attractive career path.

In 2013, he landed a coveted position as a prosecutor at SDNY, where he was one of more than 220 assistant U.S. Attorneys. The office is known for its political independence from the mainline Justice Department in Washington, so much so that its nickname is the Sovereign District of New York. It has jurisdiction over Manhattan and, therefore, the finance industry, giving it another moniker: the Sheriff of Wall Street. It has a history of aggressively prosecuting high-profile insider-trading and financial-fraud cases, including those of Michael Milken and Bernie Madoff. Adams chose an unusual path at the storied office. After a year at SDNY, most prosecutors often join the narcotics unit to get experience in bread-and-butter criminal cases. But Adams could see that those who were promoted to supervisors had once worked in the forfeiture unit, so it looked like a fast track. It was traditionally considered a backwater that no one wanted to join. "It wasn't sexy," as one former SDNY prosecutor explained it to me.

With roots in English law, forfeiture goes back centuries. It's what allowed English customs officials in the colonial period to use "writs of assistance" to seize suspected contraband, ensuring that goods landing in American ports were taxed or, if not, confiscated. Outrage over these seizures helped spark the American Revolution. After independence, the first U.S. Congress adopted forfeiture laws modeled on the British statutes to help collect customs duties. Forfeiture was rarely used for almost two centuries, apart from during Prohibition, when it was used to seize cars used for illegally selling alcohol. Present-day forfeiture grew out of the war on drugs in the 1980s, as prosecutors around the country went after drug kingpins, turning forfeiture into a potent weapon to fight crime. Instead of just putting drug dealers in prison, prosecutors used new forfeiture laws to seize property that was the proceeds of their crimes—the fast cars, the private jets, and the mansions—and, where possible, transfer funds to the victims. Under new civil forfeiture laws, prosecutors were able to seize property if there was evidence it was connected to unlawful activity, even if the owners weren't charged with a crime. In the United States, civil forfeiture has been controversial, sometimes used by local authorities for minor offenses in a zeal to seize assets.

At SDNY, the forfeiture unit was doing the painstaking work of tracing financial assets involved in crime, often carrying the water for other prosecutors in the office. But Adams realized it was a way to work as a junior prosecutor on bigger cases, such as complex frauds. And he'd be learning the ropes from Levin, whom *Forbes* once called the "Babe Ruth of Forfeiture" due to her success in seizing assets. "Most people, when they come to the U.S. Attorneys' office, they're pretty young, and their vision is 'I'm going to put the bad guys in jail,'" Levin told me. "That's not what we did in the forfeiture unit. But I was able to convince people to join me by telling them it was an opportunity to work on cutting-edge cases." Levin's sales pitch worked on Adams. "You could parlay the position into getting into cases as a relatively junior prosecutor that you would otherwise never be able to touch. You could go to the securities unit and say, 'I'll do your forfeiture, but I also want to be on the trial for this big insider-trading investigation,'" Adams told me.

After learning how to grab millions from fraudsters and insider traders, Adams joined the Violent and Organized Crime unit of SDNY, a step up where he could prosecute serious offenses and use his forfeiture skills. Adams essentially acted as in-house legal counsel to the FBI's Eurasian Organized Crime unit, whose flagship squad is in New York. The Russian Mafia was on its doorstep. "We worked hand in glove with them a lot," Adams told me. He spent three years chasing down Russian mob figures in Brooklyn's Brighton Beach, which had been a magnet for émigrés since the 1980s and a base for Mafia murders, drug dealing, and fraud schemes that often stretched across the country.

Around 2015, Adams began working with the FBI as it zeroed in on a Mafia leader named Razhden Shulaya, aka Roma, or Brother, a Soviet Georgian raised in St. Petersburg. He was a *vor v zakone* or "thief-in-law," the top rank in Russian organized crime, akin to an Italian godfather. Unlike the Italian Mafia, which is dominated by family ties, the Russian mob is less organized and hierarchical. A *vor*, a term that grew out of the Soviet prison system, is more likely to broker opportunistic partnerships. Shulaya was a product of Putin's Russia, having reportedly emerged from the Georgian Mafia group Kutaisi, which battled with a rival Georgian mob over contracts for the 2014 Sochi Olympics. He was arrested in Lithuania in 2013 during a Europe-wide crackdown on Soviet Georgian gangsters, but he somehow made his way to Edgewater, New Jersey, later that year. Shulaya's gang was a sign of how Russian organized crime was expanding across the United States, growing in strength as an offshoot of Putin's kleptocracy.

The Shulaya case had all the elements of a classic mobster movie. Adams, working with the FBI's Eurasian Organized Crime unit, was soon onto Shulaya thanks to informants working undercover. Investigators watched how a flow of counterfeit jewelry, cases of contraband cigarettes, and ten thousand pounds of stolen chocolate flowed his way. There were even plans for a "romance scam" to use an attractive woman to lure a man to Atlantic City, drug him with chloroform, and steal his money. Shulaya operated out of a poker house running rigged games above a restaurant in Brighton Beach, where he once threatened the owners and demanded $100,000 in payment. As a *vor*, Shulaya was entitled to receive tributes, or *obshchak*, common funds or goods from other criminals under his protection. The parking lot of the Whole Foods in

Edgewater was the setting for his verbal lashings of underlings. When Shulaya was unhappy with his level of *obshchak*, he brought in his enforcer, a Georgian professional middleweight boxer named Avtandil Khurtsidze, aka Mini Mike Tyson, who'd enjoyed considerable success during his fifteen-year career.

Shulaya's case was a classic racketeering prosecution from a bygone era. Adams and his FBI team made headway by getting a warrant to spend six months wiretapping phones, with Russian and Georgian translators working the case. "It was thousands and thousands of hours of investigation," Adams told me. "We were hopping from phone to phone. Now nobody uses standard phone lines."

In January 2017, investigators realized Shulaya had bigger ambitions. He was plotting an elaborate scheme to defraud casinos by using devices and software that could predict the behavior of particular models of electronic slot machines. The devices would let Shulaya's gang figure out when a machine was likely to pay out a large prize. It represented a more sophisticated form of Russian organized crime that could be used in casinos nationwide.

He never got that far. In early June 2017, Shulaya collapsed on his bed in his hotel room at Caesars Palace in Las Vegas. He'd been up for days, losing at blackjack, snorting cocaine, and having sex with a woman he met at the casino. A few days later, the FBI arrested him at a Walgreens in Vegas in coordinated arrests across the country that also charged thirty-two others, the culmination of an investigation that had lasted years. It was hailed as the most important arrest in the expanding world of Russian organized crime.

Adams co-led the trial a year later, when Shulaya was convicted of racketeering for schemes involving extortion, fraud, theft, and trafficking in stolen goods. Shulaya was sentenced to forty-five years in prison and ordered to forfeit more than $2 million in assets. "It was the first racketeering conviction of a *vor*," Adams told me. The case was a win for U.S. law enforcement trying to combat the constantly evolving activity of the Russian Mafia in the United States. For Adams, the racketeering case was a crash course in the structure and inner workings of Russian organized crime.

Learning about the Russian criminal underworld helped Adams when he started investigating oligarchs close to Putin, who used the *obshchak* model— payments from a common cash pot—on a grand scale to run Russia as a Mafia state. As the historian Mark Galeotti has observed, the term *obshchak* had started to take on new meanings as the ways of the *vory* started to be used by the Kremlin to enrich those around Putin. And under Putin's rule, Russian criminal gangs had gone global, using sophisticated financial networks.

SDNY was retooling in response to the changing nature of the threat they saw. Major bank investigations routinely saw organized criminal networks pumping money through the U.S. financial system. Likewise, every organized crime probe involved some attempt to exploit U.S. banks. After successfully convicting Shulaya, Adams rose to co-lead SDNY's forfeiture unit with another prosecutor, Alex Wilson. They suggested to their boss, then U.S. Attorney Geoffrey Berman, that they stop siloing forfeiture and require every prosecutor to learn how to trace and seize assets stemming from crime or unlawful activity. It reflected how forfeiture had become a central tool of U.S. law enforcement. "The vision was, if you're a prosecutor and you don't know how to use this tool, then you're not doing all of your job," Adams said. Berman agreed and renamed the unit the Money Laundering and Transnational Criminal Enterprises unit.

In March 2018, it became clear the threat from Russia was much bigger than anyone had realized. Sergei Skripal, a former military intelligence officer who'd worked as a double agent for MI6, and his daughter, Yulia, were found frothing at the mouth and slumped on a bench in Salisbury, a small town southwest of London. He had been living quietly in the U.K. since 2010. The Skripals survived, but authorities determined they'd been exposed to a nerve agent called Novichok, smuggled into the country in a perfume bottle by agents from Russia's military intelligence service, the GRU, in a botched hit job. A British woman later died after being accidentally exposed. The Kremlin denied responsibility, but the nerve agent had only been produced at one site in Russia. The poisoning amounted to a Russian state-sponsored chemical weapons attack on British soil.

Outrage over the Skripal poisoning was a turning point that led to the creation of Operation Accordable, a joint U.S.-U.K. project to go after sanctioned Russian oligarchs operating in the West. Ostensibly, the FBI and the Justice Department joined forces with the U.K.'s National Crime Agency (NCA) to pursue targets together, but they weren't always on the same page.

A month after the Skripal poisoning, the Trump administration slapped sanctions on seven Russian tycoons after coming under pressure from

Congress over the Kremlin's meddling in the 2016 presidential election. The new sanctions widened the pool of oligarchs for Operation Accordable to track. In theory, anyone under U.S. sanctions becomes radioactive and has their dollar assets blocked, usually by banks, which need to monitor government lists of designated individuals. Businesses, in turn, are required to inform the Treasury if they have blocked assets belonging to sanctioned individuals. But the U.K. and the EU didn't always follow with their own matching sanctions, enabling some of the tycoons to operate freely in Europe. Investigators on both sides of the Atlantic told me that unmatched political will to go after Russian tycoons frustrated U.S. efforts to bring criminal charges against sanctions evaders.

Operation Accordable drew up a list of oligarch targets who were operating in the West. One of the first cases Adams began overseeing was against Konstantin Malofeyev, known as Russia's Orthodox Oligarch because of his support of the Russian Orthodox Church. A Russian billionaire with a bushy brown beard, Malofeyev was first sanctioned by the United States in 2014 for being one of the main sources of financing for Russians promoting separatists in Crimea and eastern Ukraine. He is one of Putin's top propagandists and an ardent monarchist, who made his fortune after founding a private equity firm called Marshall Capital Partners and investing in Russia's state-controlled telecom company, Rostelecom. He reportedly hired a former FSB colonel, Igor Girkin, to provide security during his visits to Crimea in 2014 in the weeks before Putin annexed the peninsula. (Girkin, whose nom de guerre is Strelkov, or "shooter" in Russian, would go on to become the self-proclaimed minister of defense in Donetsk, in eastern Ukraine. In 2023, he was arrested and later sentenced to four years in prison in Russia for inciting extremism after accusing Putin of not being aggressive enough in Ukraine.)

Malofeyev was pouring money into a pro-Putin media empire, setting up a TV channel called Tsargrad, the Slavic name for Constantinople. The Orthodox Oligarch wasn't just a Putin crony; he was using the Western financial system to spread Russian propaganda in Europe using an American media executive. Malofeyev was firmly ensconced in Russia out of Operation Accordable's reach, but Adams's team focused on the tycoon's weak link: Jack Hanick, the former news director at Fox News. Malofeyev hired him in 2013 to help build the channel in Moscow, re-creating a Russian version of Fox News catering to the religious right. Hanick, a Harvard grad and former documentary filmmaker, helped the late disgraced Fox News chief Roger Ailes build the conservative network. In 2013, two years after leaving Fox, he was invited to Moscow to speak about internet censorship, where he met Malofeyev. Hanick came to view Russia as standing up for traditional Christian values, unlike the decay he claimed to see in the United States. In 2013, he moved with his family to Moscow and continued working for Malofeyev even after the U.S. Treasury imposed sanctions on him in 2014—a crime under U.S. law.

When Tsargrad TV launched in 2015, Malofeyev likened it to the Fox News of Russia, broadcasting a conservative take on global news. Ignoring the sanctions on his boss, Hanick helped Malofeyev launch and operate a pro-Russian television network in Greece. Secretly, Hanick was also helping him try to set up media businesses in Bulgaria, using a Greek businessman as a front. In 2015 Hanick attempted to help Malofeyev transfer a $10 million investment in a Texas-based bank holding company, held by an offshore company in the Seychelles, to a Greek associate. But banks blocked the money because Malofeyev was sanctioned.

Catching Hanick would send a powerful message that doing business with a sanctioned Russian oligarch would not be tolerated. But the investigation took years. FBI agents interviewed Hanick in February 2021 near Miami, asking about his work for the Russian oligarch, and he allegedly lied to them, saying he didn't know Malofeyev was involved in the Bulgarian TV network until he read about it in the news. But to indict him, they had to find evidence he willfully intended to violate the sanctions.

SDNY's breakthrough on the case came after it got a warrant that summer to search Hanick's email, where it found his draft memoir, saved to his Google drive, about his time working for Malofeyev. In the memoir, Hanick recalls how a trip to Moscow to attend a conference was really to meet investors in Malofeyev's proposed television station. The memoir was enough to give the investigators proof that Hanick knowingly violated sanctions by doing business with Malofeyev. They indicted him under seal in November 2021.

But he was already out of their reach. Soon after agents interviewed him in Florida, Hanick got on a plane to London. The Justice Department asked the U.K.'s NCA to arrest him and extradite him back to the United States to stand trial. Under their mutual legal assistance treaty, the U.K. should have picked him up as soon as it got the sealed indictment and the extradition request. Despite being part of Operation Accordable, the U.K. authorities dragged their feet. The NCA is effectively a British version of the FBI but without the same resources or expertise. The agency's comparatively tiny budget means it's fearful of taking action that could land it in costly litigation in British courts.

But by early February 2022, with Russian troops massing on Ukraine's border, there was a palpable shift in political will as intelligence reports indicated an invasion was imminent. London's Metropolitan Police finally arrested Hanick with a view to extradite him to the United States. Then the case went quiet; he's not been convicted. (Hanick's lawyer declined to comment.) The Justice Department moved to forfeit $5.4 million in an account Malofeyev held in the United States, the first transfer of funds from sanctioned oligarchs to Ukraine. ("It will not be the last," Attorney General Merrick Garland said.) Adams called the amount minuscule compared to the cost of Russia's damage to Ukraine, but he saw it as the beginning of KleptoCapture making assets available to victims of the war. "Giving money to Ukraine is really the crux of the whole mission," Adams told me.

The forfeiture of Malofeyev's funds seemed an inconsequential punishment for a man who had described Russia's 2022 invasion of Ukraine as a "holy war" against "satanists" and "pagans." Malofeyev responded to the order by saying "Biden's criminal group" had "defrauded" him, while Putin's spokesman, Dmitry Peskov, said the decision would "boomerang," warning that Russia would reciprocate. But there were even bigger assets allegedly involved in sanctions evasion that would test KleptoCapture's ability to peel back the layers of secrecy hiding the wealth of Russian billionaires.

*   *   *

In its first days, the KleptoCapture task force, led by Adams, began tracking a list of superyachts they believed to be owned by sanctioned Russian tycoons. If there was ever a symbol of opaque, outrageous Russian wealth, it's the superyacht. Russian billionaires owned some of the biggest boats in the world, usually registered in tax havens such as Bermuda or the Cayman Islands. To some critics, the hunt for superyachts was a populist push to satisfy public anger over Russia's invasion, one that would do little to affect Putin's desire to grab territory in Ukraine. It certainly created discontent among the elite in Moscow, but the superyacht chase offered one tantalizing concrete benefit: if they were involved in sanctions violations, it opened up possibilities for the United States to seize and sell them under U.S. forfeiture laws, eventually channeling the proceeds to war-torn Ukraine.

As soon as the war began, many of the yachts cruised in search of waters beyond the reach of the West—Turkey, Dubai, Sochi. But Adams's team eventually homed in on one yacht in particular, motoring south to the Panama Canal: *Amadea*. It was traveling through waters friendlier to the United States, giving KleptoCapture a crack at catching it. At the same time, task force investigators were working overtime to track down brokers in the tight-knit superyacht industry to dig up evidence of who owned the vessel. Brokers told them that Suleyman Kerimov, the secretive Russian gold tycoon, had bought *Amadea* in 2021 after touring it in 2020.

Kerimov isn't just any Russian billionaire: he's a senator in Russia's upper house of parliament and closely aligned with the Kremlin. Born in Dagestan, a mountainous region in Russia's North Caucasus, Kerimov trained as an economist before going on to build up stakes in a bank, an airline, and an oil trading company during the chaos of the 1990s. But he hit the big time in the early 2000s under Putin when he borrowed billions from state-owned banks to invest in Russia's biggest and most politically sensitive companies, including gas giant Gazprom and the country's biggest bank, Sberbank. He had an appetite for risk-taking. He almost died in 2006 when he crashed his Ferrari Enzo into a tree while speeding along the Promenade des Anglais in the French city of Nice. The car burst into flames, and Kerimov was badly burned.

With his rimless glasses and close-cropped gray hair, Kerimov had developed a reputation as a kind of Jay Gatsby of Putin's Russia because of his penchant for throwing extravagant parties at his villa in the Riviera. At a 2008 bash, Beyoncé sang to Western bankers as markets began cratering. He lost billions in the financial crash but survived to rebuild his fortune. The United States imposed sanctions on him in 2018. Kerimov went on to own, through his son, a controlling stake in Russia's biggest gold mining company, PJSC Polyus, before reducing the family's shares to less than 50 percent in April 2022 as sanctions enforcement ramped up and investigators closed in on *Amadea*.

When *Amadea* reached Fiji in mid-April, FBI agents boarded the vessel along with local law enforcement to conduct a search. Among their finds: what they thought might be a Fabergé egg—a symbol of Russian opulence. (It turned out to be a glass egg from Murano, an island in Venice.) More important, the KleptoCapture task force discovered that the computer system on *Amadea* was loaded with evidence. There was a detailed paper trail showing the sanctioned tycoon's family used the superyacht, along with invoices for payments in U.S. dollars. For instance, when *Amadea* passed through the Panama Canal toward the Pacific Ocean, it had to pay a $56,000 transit fee. It is illegal for anyone under U.S. sanctions to conduct transactions in U.S. dollars, or for others to make such payments on their behalf. In total, prosecutors allege that *Amadea*'s management paid more than $1.2 million in maintenance and fuel costs that were processed by U.S. banks on behalf of Kerimov.

Emails showed the crew preparing for the visit of Kerimov, then code-named GO by the crew. "GO apparently has two things that have to be immaculate. Stainless and teak," according to handover notes found on board. "GO has requested the quickest [Jet Skis] available so we will be getting new ski's [*sic*] at some point." Kerimov's daughter, code-named G2, was ordering more permanent changes to be made. "Please add new/more accessible plug socketing in the bathrooms with your designs for presentation to the G2," the captain said in an email to a designer. The FBI agents said they found evidence of Kerimov's family ordering a new pizza oven and spa bed. Crew members reportedly told investigators that Kerimov was the true owner and that the superyacht had been transferred to the tycoon in a "backdoor Russian deal," an allegation that was later contested.

Initially, U.S. prosecutors unearthed evidence showing that a below-the-radar Russian oil magnate named Eduard Khudainatov was the ultimate owner of *Amadea* through elaborate layers of offshore shell companies. Khudainatov is what some might call a minigarch—he's not one of the country's top oligarchs, but he's connected to some of the most powerful people in Russia. He was once the CEO of state-controlled Rosneft when it was chaired by Igor Sechin, one of Putin's closest confidants. When Khudainatov left Rosneft in 2013 to set up his own energy business, Independent Oil and Gas Company, he quietly acquired lucrative oil and gas assets and did several deals with Rosneft. In 2020, the state-owned oil giant paid him around $11 billion to purchase oil fields in Russia's far north. A Russian state-owned company paying that much to a businessman for a deal would inevitably require the

Kremlin's approval. And anyone building a fortune in Russia's oil industry—a strategic sector—would de facto need Putin's blessing.

But prosecutors alleged Khudainatov was merely a "straw owner" of *Amadea*—a front for his fellow blacklisted tycoon, Kerimov. Khudainatov denied the allegation, saying he was the true owner, and he decided to fight the United States to get *Amadea* back, throwing a wrench in KleptoCapture's efforts to seize it.

On paper at least, prosecutors discovered that Khudainatov also purportedly owned another superyacht, the $700 million, 460-foot *Scheherazade*—almost the length of a naval destroyer but with two helipads and a pool that can be transformed into a dance floor—through a company in the offshore tax haven of the Marshall Islands. Italian authorities blocked *Scheherazade* in a marina in Tuscany soon after the war began after reports indicated it was Putin's yacht. Anti-corruption activists working for the late opposition leader Alexei Navalny dug up *Scheherazade*'s crew list. It showed several of them had worked for Russia's Federal Guard Service (FSO), which provides Putin and other high-ranking officials with security. Navalny's team had learned from previous investigations into Putin's properties never to take anything at face value; evidence of who controlled an asset mattered more than who technically owned it. They concluded it was unlikely so many federal officers would be on the crew list unless Putin had used the superyacht.

"The fact that Khudainatov is being held out as the owner of *two* of the largest superyachts on record, both linked to sanctioned individuals, suggests that Khudainatov is being used as a clean, unsanctioned straw owner to conceal the true beneficial owners of these vessels," the FBI special agent working the case wrote in an April 2022 affidavit. Lawyers for Khudainatov deny Putin ever used *Scheherazade*, arguing the Russian president would never have used a boat with Western-made radar systems for fear of being tracked. Khudainatov later emerged as the owner on paper of a third superyacht, the $600 million, 443-foot *Crescent*, which Spanish authorities froze for reported links to Rosneft's Sechin in Port Tarraco, about an hour from Barcelona. Sechin, however, denied owning it. Whoever technically owned it, I was told Sechin was intimately involved in the design of *Crescent* before it was delivered in 2018. Indeed, U.S. prosecutors allege that Sechin and his then wife met with the interior designer of *Crescent* in Moscow in December 2014.

Why would one tycoon, whom few people had even heard of, own three superyachts worth more than $1.5 billion? Khudainatov, for his part, maintained through his lawyers he bought all three of them from the German shipyard Lürssen as an investment. The Kremlin denied Putin had links to *Scheherazade*. While Ukrainian forces tried to push back Russian troops in the east of Ukraine, on the other side of the world, KleptoCapture was trying to get the bottom of the corporate equivalent of a matryoshka doll, or nesting structure of secretive offshore companies and transactions that hid the ownership of *Amadea*.

After a protracted legal battle in Fiji, the island's Supreme Court rejected Khudainatov's bid to stop *Amadea*'s seizure, concluding ownership of the boat needed to be decided in a U.S. court. In June 2022, the U.S. marshals replaced *Amadea*'s Cayman Islands flag with a U.S. one and sailed it to San Diego, where it sat beside a dock, fenced off with barbed wire and signs warning against trespassing. However, it wasn't possible to just lock up the superyacht and leave it there indefinitely. The U.S. government had to maintain its value for an eventual sale, or if it lost its claim to forfeit it. Fees to maintain the boat quickly mounted. Normally operated by a crew of thirty-three, *Amadea* still needed at least half that many—from engineers to deckhands—rotating on board, available in case of fuel spills or fires. The exterior needed regular washing, or the boat might need a multimillion-dollar repaint job. Then there was insurance and port fees. The monthly costs: $750,000. To maintain its insurance, it had to go into a dry dock for repairs at a cost of $5.6 million.

These colossal expenses surprised the White House. Soon after *Amadea*'s seizure, U.S. national security adviser Jake Sullivan complained about how ridiculous the situation was. "You know what the craziest thing is? When we seize one, we have to pay for upkeep," he said on a hot mic before an event at the Center for a New American Security. "Some people are basically being paid to maintain Russian superyachts on behalf of the United States government."

After it sailed to San Diego, Khudainatov again appealed the seizure in Fiji's Supreme Court and argued the task force had failed to prove Kerimov owned the vessel. Khudainatov commissioned the superyacht from Lürssen with a plan to flip it, but he struggled for years to find a buyer. When Kerimov viewed *Amadea* in Abu Dhabi in 2020, the tycoon thought it was old-fashioned with a loud engine, according to Khudainatov's lawyer. Apparently a lot of people thought it was ugly—a gaudy over-the-top Russian design with gold hardware and wood paneling—which made it hard to sell. While U.S.

prosecutors maintain Kerimov bought it using a front, Khudainatov's lawyers argued Kerimov's daughter Gulnara merely decided to arrange a long-term charter of the superyacht.

Why Kerimov's family would charter it if he thought it was so unappealing isn't entirely clear. But allegedly his daughter's charter of the 426-foot *Flying Fox*, kitted out with the first cold therapy cryosauna ever installed on a superyacht, was coming to an end, and she wanted to do a winter cruise through the Caribbean. Kerimov used *Amadea* in October 2021 in the south of France when he stayed on the owner's deck. The crew had strict instructions to follow his preferences. "Ensure the carpet is vacuumed and free of foot prints." When unpacking his bags, "items should be hung in the wardrobe in groups from light to dark." "All water must be served at room temperature, except during his morning workout." Kerimov was certainly planning a trip on *Amadea*, according to the emails the FBI found on the boat. But Khudainatov's lawyers denied he'd sold it to his fellow sanctioned billionaire. Requesting changes to the yacht was normal for a long-term charter, they added. Fiji's Supreme Court rejected the appeal.

As the legal fight dragged on, *Amadea* remained docked in San Diego while Khudainatov's lawyers tried negotiating a deal with U.S. prosecutors to get it back without going to court. Some eighteen months after the United States seized it, the talks broke down and the Justice Department formally filed a claim to forfeit the vessel.

That's when U.S. prosecutors introduced a sudden plot twist. Khudainatov was no longer being held out as the straw owner. Prosecutors alleged that Khudainatov sold *Amadea* to another company in the Cayman Islands, which was owned on paper by Evgeniy Kochman, the founder of Imperial Yachts, the Monaco-based company that worked for numerous Russian tycoons and managed *Amadea*. They said Kochman paid 225 million euros ($240 million) to Khudainatov's company for the superyacht in two installments in September and October of 2021, around Kerimov's stay on *Amadea* in the South of France. "The boat has been sold," a crew member wrote in a memorandum. "Boss trip expected in the middle of October." They were now presenting new evidence to argue that Kochman, not Khudainatov, was the straw owner holding *Amadea* for Kerimov. Khudainatov denied he'd sold it, saying they drew up paperwork as part of a plan to have Kochman take over *Amadea*, but the deal wasn't completed. While the title for the superyacht remained in the name of Khudainatov's company, he had relinquished all rights to it after receiving 225 million euros, prosecutors alleged.

It wasn't the first time Washington had targeted Kochman, a dark-haired forty-one-year-old entrepreneur known for courting Russia's wealthy elite. In June 2022, Washington imposed sanctions on him and Imperial, saying the company provided "services to Russia's elites, including those in President Putin's inner circle." The U.S. Treasury said he was helping tycoons who were sanctioned. Operating out of offices overlooking the port of Monaco, Kochman's company acted as a high-end concierge service to Russian billionaires, doing everything from overseeing the construction of new superyachts to selling vessels, hiring crew, and chartering boats. Together with his sister Julia, Kochman worked closely with German shipbuilders and yacht designers in Monaco and Italy on behalf of wealthy clients.

Imperial sat at the center of an elaborate nexus that facilitated the flow of billions of dollars from Russian tycoons through a web of shell companies to the luxury superyacht industry. Kochman was renowned in the opaque world of superyachts for his attention to detail and for operating under strict secrecy, often putting onerous demands on crew to sign stringent nondisclosure agreements. In one of its biggest projects, Imperial oversaw German shipyard Lürssen's construction of *Amadea*, codenamed Project Mistral, with the renowned Norwegian superyacht architect Espen Oino and interior designer François Zuretti, after which it managed *Amadea* for years.

As further evidence that *Amadea* really belonged to Kerimov, prosecutors disclosed emails from Dinar Khalikov, who said he represented the tycoon and was listed on documents as the "owner's representative," requesting changes to the superyacht. The Kerimov family were planning extensive renovations of the interior, including a new gym. Imperial hired Zuretti to "refit" *Amadea* over a twenty-month period at a cost of $1 million in design fees alone. Emails from the captain to Zuretti and Imperial detailed changes requested during a "walk around with Dinar," including removing bright red carpet and draped curtains that "collect dust." Kochman and Khalikov had asked the crew to keep Kerimov's Nike sneakers on board for his next visit.

The fight over *Amadea* is ongoing, and it's proving costly: the U.S. government had spent an estimated $17 million maintaining *Amadea* by the end of April 2024, when it was transferred to a dry dock in Washington state for two months of repairs that were estimated to cost another $5.6 million. In March 2024, prosecutors filed a motion to sell it, citing the "excessive" cost of maintaining it, a move that Khudainatov's lawyer labeled "premature." After almost two years in U.S. custody, appraisers valued *Amadea* at only $230 million.

As a test case for the KleptoCapture task force, *Amadea* may not be an easy win. When it comes to Russian billionaires, what's on paper doesn't always reflect reality. Russian tycoons are known to operate by unwritten agreements and sometimes arrange to have others hold assets on their behalf. Prosecutors maintain the emails and paper trail show that Kerimov was using fronts to control *Amadea*, but Khudainatov hasn't given up and continues to insist he owns it. Almost two years after the seizure, the case has dragged on longer than some anticipated at the outset. It even outlasted Adams, who finally left for private practice in July 2023 and was replaced by Michael Khoo and David Lim, two Justice Department veterans. "Mr. Khudainatov, to the extent he maintains he's the actual owner, has always said it was his intent to sell *Amadea*," Khoo told me. "Let's reduce it to a pile of cash and the litigation will proceed with respect to the money in a bank instead of a ship sitting unused and draining resources in the meantime." In May 2024, prosecutors filed a motion to dismiss Khudainatov's claim, saying he didn't have legal standing after receiving 225 million euros for *Amadea* in 2021. At the same time, they were seeking testimony from Peter Lürssen, the owner of the German shipyard that built *Amadea*, *Crescent*, and *Scheherazade*. According to prosecutors, the real indication that Khudainatov is a mere straw owner: he claims to own a total of eight yachts or boats under construction.

The fate of *Amadea*—whether the Justice Department manages to sell it and transfer hundreds of millions of dollars of the proceeds to benefit Ukraine— could define whether the KleptoCapture task force is seen as a success or as a failure that took on the enormous cost of servicing a Russian superyacht in the rush to punish Putin's inner circle. KleptoCapture had other Russian billionaires apparently evading sanctions in their sights, with the prospect of seizing mansions and art on U.S. soil to be funneled to Ukraine. But aggressively going after Russian assets with their layers of ownership showed the difficulties of economic warfare. Russia's oligarchs had spent the last thirty years building their fortunes, and they weren't about to give up their billions without a fight.

PART II

FROM OLIGARCHS TO THE RISE OF PUTIN

CHAPTER 3

DEMOCRACY DERAILED

On a freezing dark evening in November 1996, I was in Moscow walking home along a quiet residential street north of the Kremlin when I stumbled upon a body. I had just entered a small tree-lined park when I saw a man in a dark coat splayed out on the side of the path ahead. As I got closer, I realized he'd been shot in the head. Blood seeped into the light dusting of snow that was still falling. Police had just arrived and gruffly shooed me away as I walked past. My heart racing, I scurried home, terrified.

When I turned on the news later that evening, I saw footage of the murder scene I'd chanced upon—a contract killing, allegedly. The man who lost his life that night was not a well-known figure. The details were still sketchy, but he was apparently just one of the many victims of gangland-style killings plaguing Moscow at the time, as rival factions battled for control of assets, big and small, after the collapse of communism. As I watched the news, I thought what a close call it had been. If I had left work a half hour earlier, I might have witnessed the shooting or, worse, been caught in the middle.

When I first arrived in Moscow as a young reporter earlier that year, Russia was in the midst of one of the biggest transfers of wealth in human history. The economy was in tatters. One in two workers had not been paid. Industrial enterprises were in such bad shape they'd resorted to medieval bartering—electricity for machinery, gas for metals. Russia's war in Chechnya was raging.

I was just one of the many expats who had flocked to the country. Russia's integration into the global economy was still nascent but well underway, only five years after the collapse of the Soviet Union. Many used their language skills to land jobs with Western companies pushing into the Russian market. I was working for Radio Free Europe/Radio Liberty, the U.S.-government-funded broadcaster. Since the fall of communism in 1989, it had transformed from a Washington influence operation aimed at piercing Soviet propaganda into an independent news outlet promoting freedom of the press and fact-based journalism in the region. I spent my days translating short dispatches from the war in Chechnya. I later also began working as a business reporter for the *Moscow Times*, the English-language daily, which gave me a front-row seat to an economic transformation like no other. I witnessed the birth of the country's crony capitalism, which is crucial to understanding Putin's rise and the West's present-day economic war against Russia.

The end of the Cold War gave rise to optimism that a new democratic Russia would emerge from the shriveled remnants of the Soviet command economy. The West was betting that Russia could peacefully transition to a market economy just as the former communist satellite states of Central and Eastern Europe had started doing in 1989. But the scale of the challenge Russia faced was unprecedented.

When Boris Yeltsin climbed on a tank outside the Russian parliament in August 1991 to fend off a communist hard-line coup against Soviet leader Mikhail Gorbachev, he denounced what he called reactionary forces trying to solve complicated political and economic problems by force. It was the defining image of the new Russia, throwing off the shackles of communism. As the country's first democratically elected leader, Yeltsin harnessed the frustrations of Russians with runaway inflation and rampant shortages as hundreds came out to defend democracy. He proposed abolishing central controls and moving toward private enterprise, positioning himself as the West's best hope for a peaceful end to the Cold War.

But an independent Russia was the largest country in the world by land-mass, almost twice the size of the United States. Moving it from central planning to a functioning market economy was a daunting project, unequaled in history. Given the arsenal of nuclear weapons spread across the disintegrating Soviet Union, the stakes for the West were enormous. Yeltsin needed to walk a fine line between advancing reforms without creating mass unemployment and further political upheaval.

Russia was starting from a much-worse position than the former communist states in Central and Eastern Europe. The Soviet Union's economy had been in decline for decades, only propped up by relatively high oil export prices in the 1970s and early '80s. By the mid-1980s, Saudi Arabia's decision to increase output caused the global price of oil to collapse, drying up a key source of revenue for the Kremlin and helping throw the Soviet economy into a tailspin. Growth had stalled, and the command economy had all but ceased to function. The shelves were empty. Russians stood in line for hours in the freezing cold for stale bread. Under Gorbachev, the authority of the party waned as bureaucrats took advantage of his reforms to profiteer.

Despite this bleak starting point, Western leaders held high hopes about the future of a new democratic Russia. Yeltsin, too, briefly enjoyed popular backing for his optimistic message about Russia's prospects for transforming into a market economy. Under Gorbachev, there'd been a split between the radicals, who wanted to jump into the capitalist deep end quickly to block a communist revanche, and the gradualists, who thought Russia wasn't ready to move so quickly after seventy years of a command economy. After the failed coup, Yeltsin sided with the radicals, led by the free-market economist Yegor Gaidar, who argued convincingly that the Soviet economy was bankrupt, facing the prospect of famine, and could only be saved by rapidly lifting controls. Faced with an economic crisis, Yeltsin didn't ask the communist-dominated legislature to dissolve itself and call for new elections during his honeymoon period when support for reforms was running high, something he later regretted.

With the help of Western advisers, including Harvard's Jeffrey Sachs, Russia embarked on "shock therapy," a radical plan launched in early 1992 that lifted import barriers and liberalized most prices after seventy years of controls. Sachs, who had helped Poland successfully carry out shock therapy two years earlier, compared his work to that of an emergency room doctor, helping economies bring hyperinflation under control. But Russia was a much-more complicated patient than Poland, with heavy debts built up by Gorbachev, oil production in steep decline, and runaway inflation. Spread across eleven time zones, Russia lacked the banks and market institutions needed to make capitalism work. Supply chains had effectively broken down. Shock therapy got goods onto empty shelves but almost immediately impoverished millions through hyperinflation. The breakdown of the central planning system had created a web of unpaid wages and fostered deep resentment among ordinary Russians about the transition to a so-called free market. The state of affairs led Strobe Talbott, President Bill Clinton's top Russia specialist, to quip that Russia needed "less shock and more therapy."

The United States and Europe placed a big bet on the Kremlin's ability to adopt free-market reforms in the belief that it would help Russia become a liberal democracy—the so-called Washington consensus of stabilize, privatize, and liberalize. But the reformers never managed to stabilize the economy. It didn't help that the price of oil began falling again after a brief spike during Iraq's invasion of Kuwait in 1990. The health of the Russian economy has always been tied to oil prices, the cornerstone of government revenues. The reformers were also continually frustrated by Russia's central bank, which was controlled by an old Soviet apparatchik named Viktor Gerashchenko, a man Sachs famously described as "the worst central banker in the world" for printing money that helped drive inflation up to 2,500 percent in 1992. At the same time, former Soviet republics—such as Ukraine and Kazakhstan—continued to use the ruble even after the formal collapse of the Soviet Union in 1991, adding to the lack of control. This baggage made an already difficult transition even more arduous.

Still, the West never stumped up the money Russia needed. Without large-scale financial support from the West, Yeltsin struggled to build public support for the reforms. Sachs advocated that shock therapy for Russia be accompanied by large-scale assistance—a kind of Marshall Plan—an infusion of Western grants and loans of around $15 billion a year for many years to bolster support for the transition.* But that didn't happen. In April 1992, President George H. W. Bush announced that the G7 would provide $24 billion to support Russia, but much of it never arrived, including a promised $6 billion ruble stabilization fund. In fact, the opposite happened, as the West demanded

---

* While Sachs might have been right years ago about the need for a Russian-style Marshall Plan, he's more recently sounded like a Putin apologist, blaming Russia's invasion of Ukraine on NATO enlargement. A Columbia University professor, he's been heavily criticized for appearing multiple times on Russian state-funded TV where he called for Kyiv to negotiate.

Yeltsin pay hundreds of billions of dollars of international debt run up by Gorbachev. While Russia was trying to pull off an economic miracle in 1992, Bush was fighting an election battle against a charismatic Bill Clinton. There was no appetite for large-scale financial support. As a result, Bush missed a key window to make a real difference to Russia's future by failing to match the historical moment with serious financial assistance. To be sure, given Russia's turbulent transition, there was undoubtedly a risk that Western funds would have been stolen; there was only so much Washington could do without Yeltsin embarking on deeper political reforms. But the West went on to take a badly calculated gamble on Yeltsin being able to maintain his grip on power.

*   *   *

Russia was roiled by constant turmoil. By October 1993, Yeltsin's standoff with the communists in the parliament over reforms brought Russia to the brink of civil war when he ordered the army to shell parliament, the country's biggest crisis since the Bolshevik Revolution. By the time new parliamentary elections were held later that year, Yeltsin won a referendum on a new constitution expanding his presidential powers, but the communists and right-wing populists captured the biggest share of the vote in parliamentary elections, frustrating his efforts to pass reform for years.

Yeltsin was decidedly unlucky: oil prices remained in the doldrums—averaging about $17 per barrel—for most of the 1990s, denying the Kremlin revenue that might have blunted the trauma of the reforms. With the country effectively broke and unable to collect taxes, the Kremlin depended on cash infusions from the International Monetary Fund (IMF), which lent it tens of billions of dollars over several years, but never enough to truly stabilize the economy. The IMF demanded Russia hit tough economic targets that included raising government revenues and reducing spending, pledges Yeltsin struggled to meet because of low oil prices and a recalcitrant Duma, the lower house of parliament. Michel Camdessus, the debonair French economist who served as IMF managing director, would fly into Moscow frequently, with markets hanging on his every word. If the IMF reached an agreement to release funds, it signaled to Russian bond markets that the economy, and government, were on track. If the IMF withheld funds, it was a sign of looming trouble.

As it doled out billions, though, the IMF was kept largely in the dark about a financial scheme being hatched behind the scenes. The idea was conceived by an emerging tycoon named Vladimir Potanin. Short and blue-eyed, Potanin was the son of a high-ranking Soviet foreign-trade official and spoke English. Having lived abroad with his father, he led a privileged existence under the confines of the communist system. Educated at Moscow's elite international relations institute known for training diplomats and KGB agents, Potanin had worked as a low-level trade official, so he knew his way around the corridors of power. Potanin had set up a trading company and a bank that profited handsomely from managing the accounts of the state customs agency and mining giant Norilsk Nickel, exploiting hyperinflation by converting funds into dollars and delaying payments as the value of the ruble slid. But he set his sights on Russia's vast natural resources as the real prize.

In 1995, he concocted a scheme that would later become known as loans for shares, an audacious program that allowed a clutch of tycoons to get stakes in some of Russia's most valuable state companies in exchange for loans to the government. Foreign investors were excluded. If the government didn't repay the loans by September 1996, the oligarchs could sell off the stakes, which were being held as collateral. The scheme was inherently corrupt; the oligarchs were entitled to organize the auctions themselves so they could favor their own bids, and they agreed in advance to stay out of one another's way. When Yeltsin agreed to Potanin's perverse plan, he effectively sold off some of Russia's best state assets for a fraction of what they were worth. The motivations for agreeing to the scheme were myriad. The reformers had already privatized thousands of enterprises by handing out vouchers to Russians, but Soviet-era red directors still ran many factories like their personal fiefdoms, siphoning off cash. Short of money, Yeltsin's economic advisers saw loans for shares as a quick way to get funding to pay pensioners and teachers and break the hold of communist-sympathizing directors on the economy. But it was also a way to enrich a circle of businessmen who would prop up Yeltsin's faltering presidency.

Up for grabs were some Russia's biggest natural resource companies—the country's crown jewels in the cash-rich oil and metals industries. Potanin was the biggest winner of this stitched-up sale, poised to deploy money he'd earned at the helm of a rapidly growing bank. His group loaned the government just

$170 million for a 38 percent stake in Norilsk Nickel, an arctic producer with rich deposits of copper, nickel, and palladium.

Russia's other emerging business moguls got in on the action. Roman Abramovich, the billionaire who would later rise to prominence by buying London's Chelsea Football Club, got a controlling stake in oil producer Sibneft for $107 million. To secure the deal, he needed a *krysha,* a Russian Mafia term for "protection," so he turned to another tycoon who was tight with the Yeltsin family: Boris Berezovsky, a short and balding mathematician who made his early fortune by setting up a car dealership. And there was Mikhail Khodorkovsky, now a staunch Putin critic exiled in London. He acquired 45 percent of oil producer Yukos for $159 million, before eventually gaining a controlling stake. By 2002, the stake was valued at $17 billion. Loans for shares has been called Russia's original sin, the episode that perverted the very genesis of the country's transition to capitalism. Voucher privatization had up to that point been relatively transparent and democratic, albeit plagued by unregulated firms preying on impoverished Russians to sell their vouchers. But with loans for shares, the tycoons were doing deals in secret with offshore shell companies.

The quest to consolidate control of enterprises sparked sometimes bloody battles. Nowhere was that more apparent than in the metals industry, where having a *krysha* was essential to survive. Murders and beatings were widespread as dozens died in shoot-outs at smelters in what became known as the aluminum wars, a sign of the criminalization of the Russian economy.

Just as the first stage of the loans-for-shares auctions were wrapping up at the end of 1995, the Communists won the biggest bloc of seats in the Duma, exploiting widespread discontent with the pain of the economic reforms. That gave their leader, Gennady Zyuganov, a good chance of winning the presidential election in the summer of 1996 and possibly renationalizing those very same assets.

By then, Yeltsin's drinking problem was well-known, and his health was deteriorating. He suffered a heart attack at the end of 1995, leaving a power vacuum that Russian tycoons exploited. Clinton had a starry-eyed belief that anything was worth the price of propping up Yeltsin. "Yeltsin drunk is better than most of the alternatives sober," he said. At the same time, Yeltsin's reformers convinced U.S. diplomats that they were picking the lesser of two evils: oligarchs were better than a communist comeback. Gaidar and other reformers told Talbott the oligarchs were just like the robber barons of the nineteenth century and would mature into captains of industry and philanthropists. "Our agreement with the reformers on the importance of a Yeltsin victory outweighed our disagreement with them over some of the methods they were using to ensure that victory, principally the enrichment and empowerment of the oligarchs," Talbott recalled in his book *The Russia Hand*. The warning signs were flashing, but Washington chose to ignore them.

When the world's elite convened in Davos, Switzerland, in February 1996 for the World Economic Forum, Yeltsin reneged on a promise to attend. Instead, Zyuganov became the star, swilling champagne and portraying himself as an unthreatening democratic socialist, in contrast to his hard-line communist talking points back home. He was looking like such a sure bet for president—but a threat to private property—that the oligarchs agreed to temporarily bury their feuds over control of state assets. On the sidelines of the forum, some of them banded together to back Yeltsin's reelection campaign in what became known as the Davos Pact. Berezovsky named seven tycoons who formed this group—including Potanin and Khodorkovsky—who later became known as the *semibankirschina*, the seven bankers who bankrolled Yeltsin's campaign. (The term stemmed from *semiboyarshchina*, the seven boyars who briefly wielded power in early seventeenth-century Russia.) To run Yeltsin's campaign, the group hired Anatoly Chubais, a tall, redheaded economic reformer from St. Petersburg whom Yeltsin had just fired from his post as deputy prime minister.

The prospects of the communists being back in power in Moscow frightened the G7, which piled pressure on the IMF to agree to a major new loan to Russia. Yeltsin asked Clinton to increase the proposed amount from $9 billion to $13 billion so he could "deal with social problems" in the run-up to the election. The IMF eventually agreed to another $10 billion lending facility in the middle of Yeltsin's campaign, in what some called one of the riskiest financial decisions the IMF has ever made. In exchange, Russia agreed to monthly—in practice continuous—monitoring of the government's precarious finances.

Aside from money, the *semibankirschina*'s control of the media helped boost Yeltsin's poll ratings and, crucially, shielded the public from his failing health. Hidden from view, Yeltsin had suffered another heart attack at the end of June, one week before the second round of voting. But by then, the oligarchs' hard work had already paid off. Yeltsin comfortably won reelection, which not only secured the fortunes of the tycoons but also gave some of them enormous power over Kremlin decision-making. Potanin joined Yeltsin's government as deputy prime minister, while Berezovsky became deputy head of his Security Council.

Still struggling to collect taxes and with oil prices depressed, the Kremlin didn't bother paying back the loans from the tycoons, even though the government could have sold those shares for much more after the communist threat had been vanquished with Yeltsin's reelection. But the Kremlin was broke. The oligarchs pushed through with the second stage of loans for shares to retain their assets just before Yeltsin underwent multiple-bypass heart surgery in November 1996. He didn't fully return to the Kremlin until March 1997, leaving the oligarchs free to plot and scheme to capture the next wave of state assets to be privatized.

*   *   *

After his heart operation, Yeltsin remained physically and politically weak. But Russia wouldn't have to face another election for four years, so it finally had an opportunity to try to put the economy on a more stable footing. In the spring of 1997, Yeltsin appointed a strong reform team that created enormous optimism that Russia was on a glide path to democracy and a market economy. Chubais came in as first deputy prime minister alongside a popular young governor from Nizhny Novgorod, Boris Nemtsov. The West welcomed Russia into the fold. The G7 club of industrialized democracies expanded to include Russia, making it the G8.

Foreign investors poured in as the political risk that had been holding back investment lifted. Western companies invested billions to get a piece of Russia's vast market of 150 million consumers. Russia was, at that point, a hot emerging market, with stocks surging more than 140 percent in 1996 and 98 percent in 1997. Moscow was booming. *Newsweek* ran a fawning cover story titled "Moscow Now—the Next World-Class City: It's Rich, Decadent, Dangerous and Fun," which featured a scantily clad Russian woman at a club.

Young Western bankers, who were making obscene amounts of money off trading Russian shares and debt, spent lavishly at the city's new restaurants and clubs. As expats and the wealthy partied at clubs called the Hungry Duck and Night Flight, tens of millions of Russians were experiencing crushing poverty.

The state was still practically bankrupt, unable to pay salaries or collect taxes because of widespread graft and the government's inability to take on politically connected enterprises. As oil output dropped precipitously due to mismangement and lack of investment, the state privatized the majority of its energy industry. Russia was in the midst of an economic depression much more severe than the American depression of the 1930s. Between 1992 and 1996, industrial output plunged 50 percent. Far away from Moscow, I met coal miners, factory laborers, and textile workers all over Russia who hadn't been paid for months but somehow continued to show up to work. In September 1997, I visited textile mills located in the wooded countryside around Ivanovo, 220 miles outside Moscow. One group of women, wearing cotton dresses and sipping tea on a break, told me they hadn't been paid for six months, but they kept showing up for work because there was nowhere else to go.

The depressed coal mining region of the Kuzbass, in southwest Siberia, was even bleaker when I visited in March 1998. Massive strikes by coal miners in 1989–90 had helped bring about the collapse of communism. Now they weren't getting paid. At the Kuznetskaya mine, desperate miners who hadn't received salaries in two years had recently taken the mine's director hostage. Tens of thousands of miners were being laid off. Some were living in ramshackle wooden huts separated by muddy paths blackened by coal. The houses had no running water or heat. "Yeltsin has driven us into poverty," Nikolai Suyazov, a hardened sixty-three-year-old miner who'd worked all his life underground, told me as we stood in the thick mud. "He's brought the country to a dead end, and he doesn't have a clue as to how to get us out of it." The leader of an independent mining union took me into his modest apartment, where he revealed he and his wife survived on black bread and *salo*, or lard, a traditional Slavic dish. They couldn't even afford to buy toilet paper. A few months later, thousands of miners went on strike, blocking highways and railways.

Meanwhile, the oligarchs grew even richer, a symbol of the corruption and insider deals that distorted the country's economic reform. They traveled around Moscow in their chauffeur-driven Mercedes with flashing blue lights that gave them special permission to cut through the city's notorious traffic, a glaring sign of the divide between rich and poor. They were partly responsible for huge tax arrears that led to pensioners, doctors, and teachers going unpaid. The oligarchs made fortunes by grabbing control of the financial flows of state agencies or enterprises, often delaying payments in order to profit from the currency market or investing in short-term debt. They weren't actually creating businesses but earning fortunes through corrupt relationships. As the oligarchs got rich quickly, feeding at the trough of the collapsing state, many Russians grew to equate economic reform with hyperinflation, quashing their faith in the wisdom of the transition.

The Asian financial crisis of 1997 eventually spread to Russia at the end of the year. At the time, investors told me Russia felt like a casino—a massive gamble on whether the government would be able to continue paying sky-high interest rates on its ruble debt, which was key to financing government spending. Yeltsin had the misfortune of watching the price of oil—the linchpin of the Russian economy and a vital source of government revenue—fall to as low as $11 a barrel. By June 1998, he brought his privatization guru, Chubais, back into government three months after he fired him, because he was the only one who commanded enough confidence in Washington to negotiate a bailout from the IMF. In July, the IMF released $4.8 billion; Russia ended up spending it all in a matter of weeks to defend the ruble and support the budget.

The oligarchs were pressing the government to slowly devalue the ruble to prevent a default, but a relatively stable ruble was seen as Yeltsin's signature achievement. It's rare for a country to default on debt in its own currency because it can simply print money to pay it off, but there was concern that such a move would cause inflation to skyrocket. By August, as Russia's debt markets spiraled out of control, everyone in power was on vacation. Camdessus was at his house in the south of France, Yeltsin was at his dacha outside Moscow, Chubais was in the Irish countryside, and U.S. treasury secretary Robert Rubin was fishing in Alaska. The U.S. Treasury sent David Lipton to Moscow to convey a stern message that the money spigot was closed, but he discovered that most officials were gone. The seriousness of the situation had yet to sink in. A run on several Russian banks was the first sign panic was spreading to the public at large. On Sunday, August 16, 1998, Chubais flew by helicopter to see Yeltsin at his dacha to get his approval to default on Russia's $40 billion of ruble-denominated debt and devalue the currency, to be announced on Monday. The impact was profound, transforming Russia's economy and politics overnight.

I had flown out of Moscow that Friday ready to start a new job at Bloomberg News in New York City on Monday. My first day in the newsroom was mayhem. Russia's default and devaluation triggered a crisis in global markets, forcing the then-unprecedented $3.6 billion bailout of the hedge fund Long-Term Capital Management from a group of banks under the guidance of the Federal Reserve. Clinton later privately told aides of his regret that the United States didn't provide more financial support to Russia. What the IMF had done, Clinton concluded, was like giving them a "forty-watt bulb in a damned big darkness." I got on a plane back to Moscow to help cover the fallout for a few weeks and was shocked to find the turmoil on the ground. Russia's grocery shelves were bare as the ruble's value plunged 50 percent. People lined up at banks desperately trying to withdraw their life's savings, often to no avail. Burned investors vowed never to return. "I'd rather eat toxic nuclear waste than invest in Russian securities," Adam Elstein, managing director of Bankers Trust's Moscow office, famously told the *Financial Times*. The financial crisis was a crushing blow to all the hopes for Russia after the end of the Cold War. The grand experiment in economic liberalism paired with democracy had failed, leaving Yeltsin's legacy in disgrace.

*   *   *

The 1998 financial crisis set off a political maelstrom that effectively ended Yeltsin's presidency and cleared the path for an authoritarian leader such as Putin to emerge. It forced out Nemtsov, the young populist reformer from Nizhny once considered Yeltsin's heir apparent, the one many hoped would put Russia firmly on the path to democracy. Yeltsin churned through three more prime ministers before finally settling on Putin in August 1999.

Born and raised in what was Leningrad, now St. Petersburg, Putin was an unspectacular agent of the KGB, serving in the East German city of Dresden rather than a high-stakes post in West Germany. When protesters descended on the villa overlooking the Elbe River where he worked in 1990 after the fall of the Berlin Wall, he was dismayed that his Soviet overseers failed to protect him. Soon after returning to St. Petersburg, he began working for Anatoly Sobchak, a charismatic law professor who became the city's first democratically elected mayor. Putin oversaw foreign economic activity as deputy mayor, a post that gave him the power to negotiate lucrative trade deals and court St. Petersburg's criminal underworld to control the city's gambling industry. In 1996, Putin got his first taste of why democracy couldn't be trusted when Sobchak lost his reelection bid amid accusations of corruption; Putin soon moved to Moscow to begin working in the Kremlin, where he quickly climbed the ranks and won the trust of Yeltsin. One way he did that was by helping his former boss, Sobchak, dodge a corruption probe, demonstrating he could do the same for Yeltsin. In November 1997, Putin helped spirit Sobchak out of the country. In 1998, Yeltsin appointed him to head the Federal Security Service (FSB), the successor to the KGB.

The president had been mulling the appointment of Putin as prime minister for a while. Berezovsky claimed he had persuaded Yeltsin and his advisers that Putin was a man who could be trusted to run the country and wouldn't rock the boat. They needed someone who wouldn't turn on Yeltsin after he left office, and Berezovsky thought Putin was their man. In July 1999, Berezovsky flew to Biarritz, the French resort town, where Putin was vacationing with his family to persuade him to become Yeltsin's successor. The next month, Yeltsin appointed Putin prime minister. The young tycoon Abramovich reportedly started helping Putin select members of his new government. In September of that year, explosions rocked four apartment blocks in Russia, which Putin used to justify launching the second war on Chechnya. But then Berezovsky had second thoughts about Putin. Alexander Goldfarb, a former adviser to George Soros in Russia, who was close to Berezovsky, told me that Berezovsky had dispatched Abramovich to St. Petersburg in October 1999 to attend Putin's birthday party to see what kind of people were around him. Abramovich reported back that Putin wasn't surrounded by old KGB types, despite having stepped down as head of the FSB six months earlier. At the end of the year, Yeltsin abruptly resigned, anointing Putin as his successor and setting him up to win the presidential election a few months later. His elevation was a sign of how the *siloviki*, former KGB agents and military officers, had captured the state. Putin and his *siloviki* viewed capitalism merely as a means to accumulate wealth and power as they stewed in the humiliation of a weakened Russia losing the Cold War.

After Putin came to power in 2000, he moved aggressively to try to reassert the power of the state and began filling the Kremlin with ex-KGB men. In July 2000, he called twenty-one of Russia's top businessmen into the Kremlin to agree to an implicit new deal. If they stayed out of politics, the government wouldn't overturn the 1990s privatization deals that had made them so rich. "I want to draw your attention to the fact that you have built this state yourself, to a great degree through political and quasi-political structures under your control," Putin told them. "So there is no point in blaming the reflection in the mirror. So let us get down to the point and be open and do what is necessary to do to make our relationship in this field civilized and transparent." What exactly Putin promised at the meeting isn't entirely clear, but the oligarchs believed they were protected if they stayed out of politics.

Not all of the original oligarchs were invited. Putin excluded anyone who dared to criticize his rule. Notably absent was Berezovsky, who accused Putin of "authoritarian" tendencies amid a probe into corruption at his businesses. A month later, Berezovsky, who controlled Russia's main TV outlet, Channel One, dramatically fell out of favor. After Russia's *Kursk* submarine sank in the Barents Sea in August 2000, killing 118 Russians on board, Channel One ran critical coverage of Putin's slow response to the disaster, showing clips of him ranting at relatives of the deceased. As Masha Gessen recounted in her book *The Man Without a Face*, Putin called Berezovsky into his office and demanded he hand over his shares in Channel One. Berezovsky refused. Fearing arrest, or worse, the oligarch fled Russia a few months later for France, and then London.

The West initially embraced Putin. After the 9/11 attacks, he was the first foreign leader to call President George W. Bush and offer him support. Two months later, Bush welcomed him to his ranch in Texas. "The more I get to know President Putin, the more I get to see his heart and soul, and the more I know we can work together," Bush said. The Russian leader talked up his efforts to push through reforms. Putin knew little about the economy, but he installed the liberal economist Alexei Kudrin as his finance minister. Russia finally pushed through a radical new tax code, introducing a flat tax of 13 percent and a reduced levy on corporations, which improved collection rates. The financial crisis in 1998 had forced the Russian government to start a serious crackdown on tax evasion because it couldn't borrow endlessly like before. Speculative foreign investors had run away. The IMF had stopped lending. Some argued the crisis was the best thing that ever happened to Russia. More expensive imports spurred domestic production of food and consumer goods.

Next in the line of fire was Khodorkovsky, then Russia's richest man. In a lengthy interview in his Moscow office in 2002, Khodorkovsky told me that his goal was to integrate his oil company, Yukos, with the West, an aim at odds with Putin's strategy of increasing state power over Russian energy. Khodorkovsky had undergone a makeover since the mid-1990s, shaving off his mustache and ditching his large-framed glasses for sleek rimless ones. He looked trendy and sounded supremely confident. Then just thirty-nine, he told me he wanted to retire from his CEO role at forty-five. Russian media later noted there was more to that aspiration than it appeared. He would turn forty-five in 2008, the year Putin would have to step down as president under the constitution.

In the spring of 2003, Khodorkovsky publicly admitted funding opposition political parties, including the Communists. He'd been spending more time on Open Russia, his philanthropic foundation, and calling on Putin to crack down on corruption. Khodorkovsky announced a merger with smaller oil rival Sibneft, controlled by fellow oligarch Abramovich. Behind the scenes, Khodorkovsky was in talks with ExxonMobil about buying a majority stake in the combined group, YukosSibneft. That could have put a chunk of Russia's strategic oil reserves in the hands of a U.S. oil major, a move that threatened Putin's goal to restore state control over strategic sectors of the economy.

For Putin, Khodorkovsky had gone too far. "I've eaten more dirt than I need to from that man," Putin told BP's then CEO, John Browne, during a private conversation in the spring of 2003. On October 25, armed commandos stormed Khodorkovsky's private jet as it refueled at the Novosibirsk airport. He was imprisoned and charged with fraud and tax evasion, less than two months before parliamentary elections. State-controlled Rosneft gradually took over Yukos's assets and went from Russia's eighth-largest oil producer to the country's biggest. Khodorkovsky remained in jail for a more than a decade, only to be pardoned by Putin and released at the end of 2013.

The arrest was widely seen as a declaration of war against the oligarchs, who hunkered down and mostly fell in line, fearful the same might happen to them. Putin was showing his willingness to openly use state power to attack the entrenched interests of the oligarchs who went against him. Indeed, Khodorkovsky's arrest was a brutal sign of how Putin had flipped the 1990s oligarchic system of capitalism on its head. The original oligarchs lost much of their sway over the government. They kept their wealth and assets only with Putin's blessing. If the Kremlin came calling with a "request," they had to obey, or else—kick in cash for this superyacht, that villa. "They are the tail, not the dog," one American investor in Russia told me. Putin had taken over national television channels, suppressed independent political parties, and driven oligarchs critical of him out of the country or into prison. After years of a weak state, Putin had centralized power in the Kremlin.

*   *   *

Unlike Yeltsin, Putin got lucky. Soon after he took over, the global price of oil started rising from around $25 a barrel to a peak of $146 in 2008 before the financial crash, giving him a tailwind as he consolidated power. Even as he attacked democracy, Putin's restoration of some semblance of order soon brought back Western investors and companies. To consolidate power, Putin was playing the long game, strategically positioning Russia to be able to weaponize its energy supplies. He set out to expand the Kremlin's control over the production of Russian energy *and* its distribution into Europe. He restored the government's control of Gazprom, the gas giant with a fifth of the world's natural gas reserves that had been partly privatized by Yeltsin. Having snapped up Yukos's best asset after throwing Khodorkovsky in jail, Putin soon expanded the state's grip on Russian oil. In 2005, he blessed state-controlled Gazprom's $13 billion takeover of Sibneft, a deal that allowed Abramovich to personally pocket a cool $10 billion. He was the first oligarch who'd made billions in the 1990s privatizations who was allowed to cash in his investment. The deal was part of Putin's long-term vision of rebuilding Russia as an energy superpower and helped turn Gazprom into what some viewed as a "state within a state"; it even got the right to create its own private army. The Kremlin now had control of 30 percent of Russian oil production. That same year, Putin and then German chancellor Gerhard Schröder agreed to build a new $6 billion, 750-mile gas pipeline connecting Russia with Germany under the Baltic Sea, bypassing Ukraine. It was later called Nord Stream 1.

Putin was not only strengthening the state's control over oil production but also setting a trap for Europe to get hooked on Russian gas.

While Putin laid the foundations for Europe's energy dependence on Russia, kleptocrats were flocking to London and embedding in the fabric of British society, giving rise to Londongrad. They hired public relations experts to launder their reputations in the West. London soon became a global hub for dirty Russian money and a nexus for layers of shell companies stretching from the British Virgin Islands to Cyprus. British lawyers and accountants helped Russia's emerging elite to squirrel assets out of the former Soviet Union. Many tycoons believed parking money in Western markets or offshore tax havens would offer some protection from the Kremlin and allow them to keep their fortunes in case the political winds in Russia shifted. London was so popular—for its top-notch schools, country piles, and direct flights—that it developed another nickname: Moscow-on-the-Thames. Russian companies were selling shares on the London Stock Exchange as oligarchs sent money surging through the London property market, buying mansions in and around the city's most exclusive enclaves.

But Putin had long been urging the oligarchs to bring their money back to Russia to shield it from Western governments. "Otherwise you'll be swallowing dust trying to get your property back through the courts," Putin warned in 2002. Few heeded his call. The West welcomed the Russian money amid a collective sigh of relief at the sight of some stability in Russia. Investors treated the Khodorkovsky arrest as a one-off. In a burst of optimism about doing business in Russia, the British oil major BP PLC agreed in 2003 to take a 50 percent stake in Tyumen Oil Company, known by its Russian acronym TNK, owned by a clutch of oligarchs, Mikhail Fridman, German Khan, Viktor Vekselberg, and Len Blavatnik. Putin traveled to London for the first state visit to Britain of a Russian leader in more than 125 years to seal the $8 billion deal. He even met the queen. After a signing ceremony with Putin, then prime minister Tony Blair hailed the joint venture as a sign of the U.K.'s "long-term confidence in Russia." It was the largest single foreign investment in Russia.

But then Putin turned on a Western businessman. In 2005, Bill Browder, who founded a hedge fund that was the largest foreign investor in Russia's stock market at the time, was barred from reentering the country when he landed at Moscow's Sheremetyevo Airport. The ban forced him to decamp to London as he fought a losing battle to be allowed to go back. He was just one part of an emerging divide in London between anti-Putin figures who'd been driven out of the country and wealthy Russians who remained in the Kremlin's good graces.

That rift blew into the open with the death in 2006 of Berezovsky's friend Alexander Litvinenko, a former KGB spy and staunch Putin critic. He'd been poisoned with polonium after meeting two former KGB officers at the Millennium Hotel in London. The pair ended up leaving a trail of the radioactive material around the city. The U.K. inquiry concluded Putin likely approved the poisoning. When I spoke with Berezovsky not long after Litvinenko's death, he sounded scared. He said that Litvinenko had told him before his death that he had received a tip-off that Putin was preparing to kill them both, along with the Chechen leader Akhmed Zakayev, who had secured political asylum in Britain. "I really don't feel safe like before," Berezovsky told me. "This is the responsibility of the government of Great Britain. Are they really able to protect this country from Russian attacks, in this case a radiation attack, or not?"

Despite Litvinenko's poisoning and Browder being run out of Russia, business as usual continued between Moscow and London and the rest of the world. Having defanged the original oligarchs, Putin created a new crop of tycoons beholden only to him. As Catherine Belton argued in her book, *Putin's People*, they were Putin's men. Unlike the Yeltsin-era oligarchs, who plundered from the state during the 1990s privatizations, Putin's cronies owed their wealth to him, having grown rich from lucrative state contracts or running state-controlled companies. The assets belong to the state—what some have referred to as Kremlin Inc.—but Putin acted kind of like a mob boss, demanding the new tycoons act in service of his rule. He was the final arbiter of any conflicts. Corruption was centralized and secretive; betrayal could never be forgiven. Putin knew many of the tycoons from St. Petersburg, where he'd grown up. They were instrumental in building Putin's brand of crony capitalism, and they've been among the first to be sanctioned by the West.

The most high profile of Putin's tycoons is Igor Sechin, who took over as chairman of the state-controlled oil giant Rosneft in 2004. With piercing blue eyes and arched eyebrows, Sechin has been nicknamed the gray cardinal of the Kremlin, the onetime leader of the *siloviki*, who had worked with Putin in the St. Petersburg's mayor's office. Unlike the other oligarchs, Sechin didn't appear to own major assets outright. Instead, his power was derived from executing Putin's strategy at the helm of a strategic state-controlled asset.

Others got even richer. A childhood friend of Putin's, Arkady Rotenberg trained with him at the same judo club in what was then Leningrad. Stocky and dark-haired, Rotenberg set up a bank in St. Petersburg with his brother, Boris, in the early 2000s. His coup came in 2008 when he bought five construction companies from state-controlled Gazprom, which he merged into one company, Stroygazmontazh. Rotenberg made billions from Gazprom contracts and building a bridge from Russia to Crimea across the Kerch Straight after Putin annexed the peninsula.

Perhaps the most important tycoon in Putin's inner circle is physicist Yuri Kovalchuk, who functions as his consigliere and played an important role in Russia's decision to invade Ukraine. The U.S. Treasury called him the "personal banker" for top Kremlin officials. After Putin became president, Kovalchuk's Bank Rossiya snapped up a series of key media assets, leading some to call him the Rupert Murdoch of Russia.

Russia's tycoons—both the surviving oligarchs and Putin's new men— sought to consolidate their assets at home while some went global, listing on international stock exchanges. Russia became one of the world's most important suppliers of aluminum and precious metals used in everything from cars to cell phones to planes. They all profited as the world underwent a commodity supercycle starting in 2000, when the global price of oil and metals began surging, fueled by demand from a rapidly industrializing China after it was admitted to the World Trade Organization. The West became hooked on Russian oil and metals as the tycoons ramped up output. Russia became the second-largest crude oil exporter after Saudi Arabia, turning Europe into one of its biggest markets. Having strong-armed the old and new oligarchs, Putin pulled off a restructuring that exploited Russia's asymmetric advantage as a natural resources superpower.

As Russia's economy surged, Putin made a point of paying off the country's Soviet-era debt in 2006, thanks to a windfall from high oil prices, eliminating the Kremlin's financial dependency on the West. That coincided with Putin's increasingly belligerent tone. He soon began objecting to NATO expansion eastward. While he initially expressed an interest in Russia joining NATO early in his presidency, by 2005 he began espousing nostalgia and hinting at his imperial ambitions, calling the collapse of the Soviet Union the "biggest geopolitical catastrophe of the century." Two years later, in a speech at the Munich Security Conference, Putin laid out his grievances in what some believe, in retrospect, was akin to a declaration of war. "It is obvious that NATO expansion does not have any relation with the modernization of the alliance itself or with ensuring the security of Europe," he said. "We have the right to ask: Against whom is this expansion intended?" One of the first to ring alarm bells about Putin was Yegor Gaidar, the principal architect of Yeltsin's economic reforms. In a book published in 2007, he warned about the creeping "post-imperial nostalgia" taking hold in Putin's Russia.

At a summit in Bucharest in 2008, NATO pushed ahead with vague promises to Ukraine and Georgia of membership in the future. Putin saw it as a direct threat against Russia. It was the worst of both worlds, stranding the two countries in a gray zone with no clear path to NATO membership. Putin responded by warning that the Soviet Politburo gave Crimea to Ukraine without "state procedures," implying the transfer was illegitimate. A few months later, Russian forces invaded Georgia and eventually occupied about a fifth of its territory. The Bush administration condemned the invasion but didn't impose any economic sanctions against Russia in response to a clear violation of an internationally recognized border. For Putin, it signaled impunity.

*   *   *

In the spring of 2008, Putin swapped places with his prime minister, Dmitry Medvedev, who became president. It was clear to everyone that Putin was still pulling the strings. In leaked U.S. cables, diplomats said Medvedev played "Robin to Putin's Batman." Obama, newly elected, embarked on his famous "reset" with Russia. It was not, as some assumed, about improving relations with Russia, but rather about finding common ground on big issues. Obama saw Medvedev as a flexible technocrat, in stark contrast to Putin. During Obama's first trip to Russia in 2009, Putin ranted at him for more than an hour, outlining a series of grievances. He was "like a ward boss but with nukes and a U.N. Security Council veto," Obama concluded in his memoir *A Promised Land*, comparing him to the men who once ran the Chicago machine. While Obama knew Putin still held all the power, the White House worked with

Medvedev to sign a new arms control treaty, cooperate on United Nations sanctions on Iran, and help Russia finally join the World Trade Organization.

Against the backdrop of the reset, Russian companies made an international push, deepening their integration with the global economy and making them vulnerable to later sanctions. Germany had an explicit strategy of *Wandel durch Handel*—"change through trade"—designed to foster ties with Moscow. In 2011 the first gas deliveries were pumped through Nord Stream 1, laying the bedrock of Germany's addiction to Russian energy supplies.

In September 2011, Putin announced he would again swap places with Medvedev. He would make another run for the presidency in the spring and proposed Medvedev stand for Putin's United Russia party in parliamentary elections slated for December so Medvedev could go back to being prime minister. United Russia won 53 percent of seats in the Duma, but widespread reports of ballot box stuffing and procedural violations plagued the vote. Allegations of voter fraud set off the biggest mass protests Russia had witnessed since the collapse of the Soviet Union as tens of thousands of people took to the streets in cities across Russia demanding fair elections and chanting, "Putin out." Putin accused Washington of fomenting the unrest.

After he won the presidential election that March, granting him a six-year term, massive protests resumed. Russian police arrested several hundred people, including the late opposition leader Alexei Navalny. The demonstrations continued throughout 2012 and into 2013, ending Obama's reset. It was the first time Putin confronted a democratic popular uprising that challenged his control of Russia. Many of the protesters were urban middle-class professionals who wanted basic democratic freedoms to accompany their rising standards of living, but the vast majority of Russians outside major cities continued to sit on the sidelines. While a kleptocratic state-led capitalism had taken root, Russia was a long way from the hopes of becoming a liberal democracy that had accompanied the end the Cold War. After returning to the Kremlin, Putin swiftly began a brutal crackdown on his critics.

Faced with flagging ratings in the polls and people taking to the streets, Putin moved quickly to consolidate the state's grip on the economy and create an undisputed national oil champion. To do so, the Kremlin intervened to settle a feud between the Russian billionaires and British oil giant BP, who had joined forces early in Putin's presidency. The joint venture—TNK-BP—had descended into squabbling. Bob Dudley, an American executive, ran TNK-BP in Moscow but repeatedly clashed with his Russian partners over strategy, eventually fleeing the country after saying he'd suffered "sustained harassment." "We're hung with labels like 'raiders' and 'Russian Mafia,'" Viktor Vekselberg, one of the billionaires who owned a stake, told me in an interview in 2008, calling it a simple corporate conflict. Dudley, who became CEO of BP in 2010, began trying to negotiate a way to exit the unruly joint venture.

The sharp-elbowed billionaires finally ended up agreeing to sell. Unlike Khodorkovsky, they had stayed in Putin's good graces. In 2013, Rosneft bought TNK-BP for $55 billion, Russia's largest takeover ever. The billionaires pocketed $14 billion, while BP ended up with a 20 percent stake in the state-controlled oil giant and around $12.5 billion in cash. The deal, which gave Rosneft control over 40 percent of Russia's oil output, created the world's largest listed oil company. The billionaires were among the few allowed to cash out from one of the biggest prizes of the 1990s privatization.

Mikhail Fridman and his partners moved to London, where they plowed the proceeds into an investment firm that took stakes in companies around the world. They set out to become more than just oligarchs. They wanted to be global businessmen with footholds in Russia and the West.

Just as they were completing the deal, Berezovsky, the exiled tycoon who had fallen out with Putin, was found dead, hanging in his bathroom at his former wife's home in Ascot, outside London. I recalled the fears he'd expressed to me six years earlier about his safety. A pathologist hired by Berezovsky's family concluded that the ligature marking on his neck was circular, instead of the V-shape mark found on hanging cases, suggesting he had been strangled. The cause of death was left open.

Berezovsky's death, whether by suicide or contract killing, signaled the end of the 1990s brand of oligarchic capitalism he'd created and the triumph of Putin's ominous kleptocracy. It was one of more than a dozen suspicious deaths of Russians in London, a symbol of the ever-rising stakes of Putin sitting in the Kremlin. After his full-scale invasion of Ukraine, the so-called oligarchs living in the West found themselves unable to straddle both worlds, hunted down by prosecutors acting as foot soldiers in a new kind of economic war.

CHAPTER 4

PUTIN'S CALCULUS

At the end of 2013, Ukraine was at a crossroads, faced with a choice of whether to tilt East or West. The country's pro-Kremlin leader, Viktor Yanukovych, had won the presidency in 2010 with the help of Paul Manafort (later Trump's campaign manager), who skillfully exploited divisions over NATO membership and the rights of Russian speakers in eastern Ukraine to secure votes. But some of the country's business elite had encouraged Yanukovych to look West. After years of talks, he was about to sign a trade and cooperation deal with the EU that would deepen Ukraine's ties with Europe. For Putin, it represented a threat to his ambitions to keep Kyiv firmly within the Kremlin's sphere of influence. Putin began twisting arms—threatening to cut off Russian gas supplies and imposing trade restrictions that would cost Ukraine billions of dollars. With Russian officials warning it would be "suicidal" for Ukraine to sign the EU deal, Yanukovych ditched it in favor of Putin's promises of billions of investment.

Yanukovych's decision to pivot East sparked domestic protests, but it was his order to the police to beat demonstrators that lit the flame for the Revolution of Dignity, bringing hundreds of thousands of people to the streets. They erected a tent city in Kyiv's Maidan Square, where they camped for months through a bitterly cold winter as the violence escalated. On February 20, 2014, just as Putin was wrapping up the Sochi Olympics, the protests against Yanukovych turned deadly. Ukrainian security services and police opened fire, killing forty-eight protesters in a single day, one of the bloodiest clashes since the Cold War ended. (The revolution ultimately claimed more than one hundred lives.) As the death toll mounted and dead bodies were dragged from the square, European officials held crisis talks with Yanukovych, who agreed to hold early elections and restore a constitution that limited his powers. Two days later, he fled Ukraine for Russia.

Back in Washington, Dan Fried, the U.S. State Department's sanctions coordinator, had been talking with Victoria Nuland, then the U.S. assistant secretary of state for European and Eurasian Affairs, for weeks leading up to the shootings about whether they could impose sanctions on Yanukovych's government. Russian media accused the United States of trying to engineer regime change because Nuland was photographed handing out cookies and bread to protesters, a claim she dismissed as "pure fantasy." At that point, sanctions were confined to the likes of Iran, North Korea, and Cuba, so deploying them against Ukraine's leadership would have sent a strong message. Fried, one of the State Department's top experts on the former Soviet bloc, had watched Russia's chaotic 1990s morph into Putin's kleptocracy, and he was worried that Yanukovych's decision to seek refuge in Russia meant Putin might escalate to keep Ukraine under his control. A Russia hawk, Fried remembered how Putin had questioned the status of Crimea as Ukrainian territory at the NATO summit in Bucharest in 2008. Fried and Nuland voiced their concerns at a meeting with then secretary of state John Kerry that Putin would move against Ukraine now that Yanukovych had fled.

Just days after the Sochi games ended, Fried and Nuland's hunch turned into reality. On February 27, 2014, Russian military in unmarked uniforms—the "little green men"—fanned out across Crimea. When Fried read the first reports, he immediately started talking about imposing sanctions against Russia with Nuland, an enthusiastic supporter. Troops dressed in unmarked fatigues— Putin's little green men—stormed the local parliament and government buildings in Crimea's capital, Simferopol, and hoisted a Russian flag. Russia initially denied involvement, even though the soldiers were carrying Russian equipment.

Despite Fried and Nuland's sneaking suspicion, Putin's first move against Ukraine caught most U.S. and European officials by surprise. As his little green men blocked roads across Crimea, the Obama administration scrambled for a response and was divided over how hard to hit back. Obama was the president who sought to end wars, not start them. But Putin's stealth takeover of Crimea, changing borders by force, threatened to set a dangerous precedent. The administration needed to hit back, uncertain if Putin would move beyond Crimea. Obama's National Security Council was split. Fried, a career diplomat, wanted to move quickly to impose sanctions but encountered pushback. "The U.S. doesn't have any serious security interest in Ukraine," one White House official told Fried one day in the basement of the White House's West Wing. The comment only stiffened his resolve to push for tougher penalties.

*   *   *

As U.S. officials scrambled for a response, they found themselves facing a dilemma that states have grappled with for centuries: How to coerce an opponent without the costs of direct military conflict? Using economic force hasn't always worked. One of the earliest examples of sanctions dates to ancient Greece. In 432 BC, Athens imposed a blockade of the city of Megara, which turned to its ally Sparta for help. Known as the Megarian Decree, the economic sanctions led Sparta to declare war against Athens, which eventually ended the Athenian age. In the twentieth century, the League of Nations, created after World War I, formalized the use of economic sanctions as a way of avoiding military conflict, but that did little to avert another world war. Starting in 1940, the United States banned the export of oil, iron, and steel to Japan and froze the country's assets. Faced with economic ruin, Japan attacked Pearl Harbor.

After World War II, the United States increasingly used economic sanctions as a tool in the Cold War. In 1962, it imposed an embargo on Cuba, which remains in place today and is often cited as an example to show the ineffectiveness of sanctions. But there are also plenty of examples of effective economic war. The most successful is perhaps the embargo placed on South Africa, which eventually helped end the apartheid regime in the early 1990s. That same decade, the United States and the United Nations adopted sanctions against Serbian leader Slobodan Milosevic and his regime in an economic pressure campaign that some say contributed to the end to the Yugoslav war and ultimately the overthrow of Milosevic.

As U.S. officials weighed the risks of imposing economic penalties on Russia, their sanctions playbook wasn't geared to the challenge. The United States sanctions programs against Cuba targeted a relatively small economy, as did the equally unsuccessful program against North Korea. After the September 11 attacks, Juan Zarate, then a top Treasury official, and his band of "guerrillas in gray suits" devised ways to blacklist companies and individuals to try to cut off money flows to terrorists in a way that fundamentally reshaped financial warfare. The most extensive U.S. sanctions program grew from Iran's efforts to develop a nuclear program and was considered the gold standard for how to isolate a rogue state. But Iran's economy and international financial ties were tiny compared to Russia's. The United States was able to put a full block on Iran's banking sector and its central bank without worrying about any significant blowback to the global financial system. Together with the EU, it also imposed an oil embargo on Iran, a much smaller exporter of crude than Russia, which helped bring Tehran to the table to agree to restrictions on the country's nuclear program in exchange for lifting oil sanctions. (Trump reimposed those sanctions in 2018.)

In the run-up to Putin's annexation of Crimea, Bill Browder, the American-born investor Putin had banned from Russia, persuaded the U.S. Congress to pass the Magnitsky Act, named after his lawyer, who died in a Moscow prison in 2009 after uncovering a vast $230 million fraud committed by tax officials. The 2012 act allowed travel bans and asset freezes to be imposed on Russian officials for human rights abuses, but its use was still fairly limited by 2014.

And the fact remained that the United States had never imposed sanctions on an economy as big as Russia's, or one with such extensive links to global financial markets. It was then the tenth-largest economy in the world, roughly the size of Italy's. As a major energy and metals exporter, Russia was deeply intertwined with global supply chains. Sanctions against Russia could backfire on the global economy in unpredictable ways. Soon after Putin moved on Crimea, Fried was at Whole Foods in Washington, DC, when he bumped into a top Treasury official working on sanctions. "He thought I was absolutely nuts to think we would sanction Russia," Fried recalled.

Then Putin escalated. On March 16, the Russian leader staged a sham referendum in Crimea where more than 95 percent voted to join the Russian

Federation, but there were multiple reports of widespread fraud, and the vote was widely condemned as illegitimate. Even with all its obvious defects, it gave Putin the ammunition he wanted to argue that Russia's annexation of Crimea was legal, feeding into his increasingly sophisticated hybrid warfare to control the narrative.

Russia's annexation of Crimea was a gross violation of international law. Yet the Obama administration's response was timid. The next day, it announced asset freezes and travel bans on less than a dozen Russian and ex-Ukrainian officials, including Yanukovych. The EU followed with similar penalties, but the sanctions were seen as a craven response to Putin snatching territory. The officials had played key roles in destabilizing Ukraine, but they didn't touch the nerve center of Putin's regime. Inside the White House, pressure was mounting for a bolder response. One of the key figures developing sanctions policy was Rory MacFarquhar, then a forty-two-year-old senior director on the NSC. Fluent in Russian, MacFarquhar had spent eight years at Goldman Sachs in Moscow following spells in the 1990s in Russia, working for the economist Jeffrey Sachs and then for a think tank, when I first got to know him. He knew his oligarchs better than most. "I didn't think it was right to be sanctioning all of Russia—I thought we should be going after Putin and sanctioning the people around him," he told me.

The day after Washington imposed the first round of sanctions, Putin gave a strident speech in the Kremlin's ornate St. George's Hall to the country's Federal Assembly, accusing the West of hypocrisy and for failed attempts to contain Russia, a policy he said stretched back centuries. He complained that many Cold War–era restrictions on the sale of technologies to Russia remained in place. "Today we are threatened with sanctions, but we already live under a number of restrictions, which are very significant for us, for our economy, for our country," he said. "They are constantly trying to drive us into some corner." He was frequently interrupted by applause, and, at the end, officials gave him a standing ovation, shouting, "Russia! Russia!" in unison. Putin had firmly rejected the U.S.-dominated post–Cold War order, declaring Russia would no longer submit to the West.

The pressure was on to come up with a more hard-hitting response. MacFarquhar wanted to take out Putin's cronies instead of random politicians. Two days later, the U.S. Treasury blacklisted some of Putin's closest confidantes. It was a recognition that Putin's regime was propped up by the oligarchs he'd created and the security forces he relied upon. Some were obvious targets, such as Sergei Ivanov, who was Putin's chief of staff, and Igor Sergun, head of Russia's military intelligence, the GRU. Drawing concentric circles around Putin, the oligarchs who got rich off state contracts or running government-controlled companies were also hit with travel bans and asset freezes. In addition to sixteen Russian officials, the sanctions targeted Bank Rossiya—the personal bank for Putin's inner circle—and four cronies, including the Rotenberg brothers; Yuri Kovalchuk, described as one of Putin's "cashiers"; and Gennady Timchenko, cofounder of the commodities trading company Gunvor. The U.S Treasury alleged that Putin had investments in Gunvor and access to its funds, which Timchenko has long denied. They were close in another way: Timchenko's Labrador retriever, Romi, was the daughter of Putin's dog Connie.

Timchenko, then worth almost $8 billion, may have heard about the sanctions ahead of time. A day before Washington blacklisted him, he sold his stake in Gunvor, the world's fourth-largest oil trader, to his Swedish business partner Torbjörn Törnqvist, enabling the company to escape the sanctions. The penalties upended Timchenko's charmed existence living in the upscale neighborhood of Cologny on the shores of Lake Geneva as he shunned travel in Europe, even though the EU hadn't designated him. Putin appeared to be personally offended by the targeting of his inner circle, saying the measures appeared to be aimed at him. "I'm not in any way ashamed for my friends," Putin said of the sanctions. He complained that Timchenko's wife had been unable to pay for surgery in Germany because her bank account and credit cards were frozen, calling it a "flagrant violation of human rights"—a brazen claim as unmarked Russian troops committed widespread human rights abuses in occupied Crimea. In reality, his friends were soon able to circumvent the restrictions. In the months that followed, shell companies linked to the recently sanctioned Rotenberg brothers close to Putin bought $18 million worth of art through an intermediary at a Sotheby's sale in New York, including works by Marc Chagall, Henry Moore, and Georges Braque—part of $91 million they shuffled offshore. The sanctions made it more difficult for the tycoons to do business, but they didn't change Putin's behavior.

"It was about trying to drive a wedge through the elite to say we're going to target people who are holding money on behalf of Putin or are only rich because of Putin," MacFarquhar told me. "We certainly didn't think they'd turn on him, but we did think he would care about what happened to them. We didn't think he'd lose a minute's sleep if the Yeltsin-era oligarchs were bankrupted."

When Obama traveled to The Hague for a nuclear summit later that month, he was forced to defend his response. Mitt Romney had claimed in the 2012 election that Russia was America's main geopolitical foe, an argument that Obama rejected. "Russia is a regional power that is threatening some of its immediate neighbors, not out of strength but out of weakness," Obama said. The remark was a clear dig at Putin, who was trying to reassert Russia as a global player, not a regional power. Years later he called Obama's remarks "disrespectful," lambasting U.S. attempts to dominate Europe and attacking the president's claims of American exceptionalism. In 2018, Putin informed Trump's national security adviser John Bolton that Obama had told him that the Ukraine confrontation could be contained if he went no further than annexing Crimea. Bolton acknowledges that would be an extraordinary thing for a U.S. president to say explicitly. "If he did say it, it was just another sign of weakness," Bolton told me. "We were displaying plenty of weakness across the board during that period."

*   *   *

Whatever was said, Putin clearly wanted more than just Crimea and was undeterred by the limited sanctions. In early April 2014, as Fried was trying to anticipate Putin's next move, the little green men joined Russian-backed fighters in eastern Ukraine to seize government buildings in Donetsk and Luhansk and declare a "people's republic." Among them were mercenaries led by Yevgeny Prigozhin, Putin's favorite caterer, who'd set up a private military company later known as Wagner. Putin was escalating faster than Obama officials could devise countermoves. Later that month, Washington stepped up its sanctions, targeting the boss of state-controlled oil giant Rosneft, Igor Sechin, and seventeen companies linked to Putin allies, including Timchenko. Washington also placed some restrictions on the export of high technology to Russia, but no major Russian bank was on the list, leading some to conclude the limited rounds of sanctions would do little to persuade Putin to change course.

Fried, meanwhile, was writing up a path to escalate sanctions, but the White House told him they could only go as far as the Europeans would agree. "The basic instruction was 'We're not going to do this unilaterally,'" Fried recalled. The White House believed U.S. sanctions alone would be far less effective than penalties coordinated with Western allies. Russia had a much more substantial trade relationship with Europe than the United States, and Europe had long been a playground for the country's oligarchs, who luxuriated in their villas and superyachts on the Mediterranean coast.

Fried began his tour of European capitals to try to get the EU on board, but he encountered resistance. The EU had only targeted a bunch of random Russian and Ukrainian officials. Anything that touched Europe's reliance on Russian energy was totally off the table. At the time, Europe was just coming out of the eurozone debt debacle, the U.S. recovery from the global financial crisis was anemic, the global price of oil was above $100 per barrel, and Obama was heading into midterm elections. The world economy was still fragile. There was no appetite for radical action that could spark another crisis.

MacFarquhar began brainstorming with two officials from Treasury's international affairs office, where the self-professed economic nerds reside: Singh, who would go on to lead Biden's 2022 sanctions, and Brad Setser, a tall, brainy graduate of both Harvard and Oxford. They weren't sanctions specialists but brought their expertise in economics and financial markets, where they wanted to tread carefully. Russia's largest banks were similar in size and complexity to Lehman Brothers before it collapsed during the financial crisis. "We started thinking about what we could do that would hurt Russia and have less blowback to the U.S. than a full block," Setser recalled.

Economists are generally focused on how to grow an economy. Now they were flipping that way of thinking on its head. There was some banter about the two being engaged in the "dark arts of economics." "It's basically causing market forces to damage an economy rather than support it," Singh recalled. Or, as Setser put it, "We know how to fight a financial crisis—can we cause one?"

As they explored new types of financial warfare, they quickly zeroed in on the battle for capital. They started bandying about ideas to stop the flow of funding to Russia, short of a full Iran-style block. It was a novel approach that grew from the lessons learned from the unprecedented collapse in capital flows during the 2008 financial crisis. "The answer that emerged was

'Why can't we just block new financing rather than block all transactions?'"
Sester recalled. The idea was partly about constraining big state-controlled
companies from borrowing from the rest of the world to pay dividends to the
government. Curtailing capital flows to Russia would be costly to the Kremlin
but contained because it had sizeable central bank reserves to cushion the
blow. Then treasury secretary Jack Lew wanted to make sure the sanctions
didn't rattle the stability of Western financial markets.

This more targeted approach opened up a new chapter in the playbook for
economic war. It meant the U.S. government could go after bigger companies
in the Russian economy to bleed them of resources over the long term without
pain being felt in the West. It might impact a few European or U.S. banks,
but it wouldn't affect Western economies the way a block on Russian natural
resources would. "Where did U.S. economic leverage intersect with Russia's
economic vulnerability?" Singh recalled thinking. "Financial capital was and
is an obvious choice." It had never been done before.

In July 2014, they unveiled the first of these pinprick sanctions, banning
two major state-controlled banks, VEB and Gazprombank, and two energy
firms, Rosneft and Novatek, from raising new debt of longer than ninety days
or new equity in American markets. The companies had multibillion-dollar
debts they needed to pay off in the coming months and years, so the financing
restrictions were aimed at blocking them from growing. The Europeans at
first refused to match the U.S. moves.

The next day, Obama was on a call with Putin, who said he'd just been
informed of a downed plane in eastern Ukraine. The reports were still sketchy
and they didn't discuss it further. It soon emerged that Malaysian Airlines Flight
17 had taken off from Amsterdam and was blown out of the sky over eastern
Ukraine by a Russian-made missile, killing all 298 people on board. The images
were gruesome. Charred dead bodies and open luggage were strewn for miles.
Militants kept international monitors away as they dragged bodies around or left
them rotting in the sun. Two-thirds of the passengers were Dutch, with citizens
of Australia, Malaysia, Indonesia, and the U.K. accounting for most of the rest.
Russia denied responsibility, but Kremlin-backed separatists were in control of
the area. Grieving and infuriated, Europe finally took a swing at Russia.

"The Dutch went from sanctions skeptics to sanctions champions," Fried
told me. Weeks later, the EU barred Russian state-owned banks from selling

bonds or shares in Europe and banned the export of equipment that could help modernize the country's oil industry. The moves were an attempt to destabilize the economy's anchor—hydrocarbons—while it killed the idea that Europe would be a strategic partner for Russia. The United States also cut off three more state-controlled banks from American capital markets—VTB, Bank of Moscow, and the Russian Agricultural Bank—and restricted exports of technology to help develop new sources of oil. The decisions marked a noticeable ratcheting up of sanctions, but were more a poke in the eye than a devastating blow.

The economic restrictions provoked a standoff. In a tit-for-tat move, Putin announced a ban on importing billions of dollars of U.S. and European agricultural products, including meat, fruit, and cheese, which only led to food inflation for Russian consumers. In September, Washington and Brussels tightened the noose further, announcing that Russia's biggest bank, Sberbank, would be barred from accessing Western capital markets for any borrowing longer than thirty days. The other five large banks already under sanctions were reduced to the thirty-day lending window, a step designed to attack Russia's financial plumbing.

The United States and the EU also took a shot at one of Putin's most ambitious strategic goals—developing Arctic oil as aging Siberian wells run dry. Washington and Brussels banned foreign oil companies from helping Russia develop new exploration for deepwater Arctic offshore or shale gas. The move eventually forced Exxon out of what it saw as its future: a joint venture with Rosneft to develop Arctic oil in the Kara Sea.

While the penalties went further than ever before, hope that the downing of a passenger plane would spur global action to end the war in eastern Ukraine soon fizzled. The drip-feed of sanctions were narrowly targeted. "We were trying to influence Putin's calculus," MacFarquhar told me. "Clearly it wasn't enough to make him pack up and go home. But maybe it influenced his decision to not go further back then."

It's impossible to prove a counterfactual, but by some measures, the penalties had a meaningful impact. For one, they combined with the falling price of oil to exacerbate a currency crisis in Russia at the end of 2014 as big companies targeted by sanctions struggled to roll over their foreign debts. By the end of January 2015, the ruble had plunged almost 50 percent against the U.S.

dollar from its pre-sanctions level while Russia's central bank burned through $160 billion by April 2015 trying to defend the currency. Even the sanctions architects thought the Russian central bank would manage the crisis better. "I was surprised by how badly the Russians handled it," Setser told me. The twin pressures—the sanctions and a lower oil price—hammered the Russian economy, which shrank 3.7 percent in 2015. "What we didn't anticipate was how little Putin seemed to care about the economy's decline," MacFarquhar told me. In 2015, Putin demonstrated how little he cared when he ordered the bulldozing and burning of hundreds of tons of food and cheese—despite rampant inflation—allegedly imported from the West in violation of his ban.

On another level, he clearly did care. After 2014, Putin began devising his Fortress Russia strategy to protect the country from future sanctions. Russia's central bank reserves started growing again. After Putin annexed Crimea, U.S. and European legislators threatened to cut off Russia from SWIFT, the financial messaging system that facilitates global payments. The proposals went nowhere, but Visa and Mastercard suspended services to some Russian banks to comply with sanctions. That prompted the Kremlin to build a homegrown payment system with its own card, Mir ("world" in Russian), to wean the country off Western companies that channeled most transactions inside Russia. After it got off the ground, Russia forced all Visa and Mastercard transactions onto it. In December 2014, Russia started to create SPFS, its own version of SWIFT, as part of its strategy to develop "payment sovereignty." It took another three years before it officially launched. The decisions prevented Russia's financial system from melting down in 2022 when Visa and Mastercard suspended operations in Russia and SWIFT kicked major banks off its platform. Securing independence from the West's financial architecture was central to Putin's efforts to fortify Russia's economic defenses.

By early 2015, the war in eastern Ukraine was at a stalemate, with Ukrainian forces and Russian-backed separatists digging in along a line of control. They agreed to an uneasy ceasefire in September 2014, known as Minsk I, which failed to halt the fighting. In February 2015, France and Germany helped broker Minsk II, a deal that called for elections in the war-torn Donbas and its reintegration into Ukraine with an autonomous status. But it never brought an end to the fighting, which rumbled on for years. The terms of the deal were disputed, and Russia claimed it wasn't responsible for implementing them even though its ambassador to Ukraine had signed the agreement. The dangled carrot of sanctions relief couldn't persuade Putin to uphold his side of Minsk II—another sign of how little he cared about the economy. Putin pursued his expansionist goals regardless of the limited economic costs Washington and Europe tried to impose. If the West wanted to change Putin's calculus, it needed to hit back much harder.

*　　　　　*　　　　　*

In the summer of 2016, the FBI began investigating Russian meddling in the presidential election. Paul Manafort had quit as chairman of the Trump campaign after reports about his work for pro-Russian political parties in Ukraine. Trump, meanwhile, was sounding like Putin's dream candidate, saying he would consider recognizing Crimea as Russian territory if he won.

Around this time, the FBI was trying to get oligarchs to cooperate with the investigation into Russian meddling in the election, believing their ties to the Kremlin might mean they would know of any outreach to Trump's team. In September 2016, FBI agents went to the one of the Manhattan homes of the metals tycoon Oleg Deripaska to ask him about reports of Russian meddling. Tall and lean, Deripaska had emerged victorious from the 1990s aluminum wars when so many had been killed in the battle to control the industry. As one of Russia's richest men, he was known for being both ruthless with his adversaries and extremely well-connected.

In early 2011, I spent more than four hours interviewing Deripaska at his home in Zhukovka, a wealthy suburb of Moscow, where his neighbors included Putin and Medvedev. It was the first time he'd let a journalist into his home, a sprawling compound with seven horses and six dogs surrounded by a fourteen-foot-high brick wall patrolled by beefy security guards. His young kids kept popping in and out of his home office as he sipped on green tea. With his deep-barreled voice and yoga-trained physique, Deripaska made an effort to come across as the cerebral physics graduate he was, rather than the bruising entrepreneur of media legend. I knew he hoped to reposition his image by inviting me into his inner sanctum.

Raised by his grandparents in a small village in southern Russia, Deripaska studied physics at the prestigious Moscow State University, where he began trading metals on the side. By 1994, he'd gained control of the southern-Siberian smelter of Sayanogorsk, one of Russia's biggest producers, but not without blood being shed. In the spring of 1995, Deripaska's deputy and a colleague were shot and seriously injured at the smelter, revealing the mobster climate that prevailed at the time. "I only had two guys injured in all those years," he told me. "It was a mistake when I didn't pay enough attention."

During our interview, Deripaska talked expansively about how powerful he was. "I'm very politically connected to every important figure in Russia," he told me in 2011. "There is no one in Russia whom I can't reach in less than one hour." That bold comment reflected the reality of the business he controlled, the aluminum giant Rusal. At the time, the company was the world's largest aluminum producer. "Rusal is not a company, it's an industry," he told me. In other words, Rusal *was* the Russian aluminum industry.

Deripaska had experienced problems getting a U.S. visa since 1998. "I traveled, then denied, traveled, then denied," he told me. Media reports cited U.S. government concerns that he may have had links to organized crime, an allegation that Deripaska has vociferously denied. But he had been granted entry on a diplomatic visa in 2015 and 2016, when the FBI sought him out for questioning. The agents approached Deripaska at one of his Manhattan homes in 2016, wanting to know whether Russia's interference ran through Manafort. Deripaska had worked with Manafort on a failed cable-television deal in Ukraine in the late 2000s, but the tycoon was suing him to get an accounting of what had happened to his money, which had disappeared. He told the agents he didn't believe Russia was colluding with the Trump campaign. It wasn't Deripaska's first encounter with the FBI, which had questioned him before, and it wouldn't be the last time the U.S. government set its sights on him.

Before Trump was sworn in as president, the U.S. Treasury dripped out some more sanctions, this time targeting the Wagner mercenary leader, Yevgeny Prigozhin, because of his dealings with Russia's Defense Ministry. After Trump took office, the Treasury continued by imposing sanctions on Prigozhin's companies and his mercenaries. But he operated largely outside the U.S. financial system—propping up dictators in Sudan, Syria, and the Central African Republic as part of Russian influence operations—so the moves did little to deter his operations around the world. (The Justice Department indicted him in early 2018 for funding an internet troll factory that sought to sway public opinion in the U.S. election.)

By 2017, U.S. and EU officials were trying to maintain a united front on sanctions against Russia, but Brussels was lagging. The EU failed to blacklist some members of Putin's inner circle, such as Sechin and Prigozhin, until years later, allowing them to operate freely in Europe. Sechin, one of Putin's closest allies, nicknamed Darth Vader, continued to cruise around the Mediterranean while under U.S. sanctions. He frequently used boats owned by secretive offshore companies, including the 280-foot *St. Princess Olga* (later renamed *Amore Vero*—Italian for "true love"—after Sechin divorced his wife, Olga.).

The greatest weakness of this emerging economic war was the lack of enforcement. Governments rely primarily on banks to report potential violations because they see the financial flows that officials don't. As the penalties became increasingly complex, Treasury agencies set up to police sanctions found themselves underfunded and overwhelmed. Since 2014, the U.S. Treasury brought only between seven and twenty-six enforcement actions per year, usually imposing relatively small fines. They don't have the staff to comb through all the suspicious financial reports flagged by financial institutions. Global banks fall into line out of fear of criminal prosecution or being blocked from the U.S. financial system. In a warning shot to financial institutions worldwide, the French bank BNP Paribas pleaded guilty in 2014 to criminal charges of violating sanctions against Iran, Cuba, and Sudan. It agreed to pay a record penalty of almost $9 billion to settle the case. These kinds of "public hangings" of banks rippled across the financial industry, forcing them to invest in extensive checks on their customers to avoid facing a similar fate.

*   *   *

In 2017, just after Robert Mueller launched the special counsel investigation into Russian election meddling, Congress voted with overwhelming bipartisan support to impose tougher sanctions on Russia. Worries about Trump's soft-pedaling on Russia spurred lawmakers into action. The legislation was dubbed the Countering America's Adversaries Through Sanctions Act, or CAATSA. Trump complained that Congress legislating on sanctions reduced the executive branch's ability to maneuver, but he was forced to sign the law because it passed with a veto-proof majority. CAATSA put existing sanctions against Russia into law and gave Congress the power to block efforts to water them down. One provision required the Trump administration to submit a report to Congress identifying oligarchs based on their closeness to the Russian regime, relationship to Putin, net worth, and "indices of corruption." CAATSA didn't require that the oligarchs listed in the report be sanctioned, but Russia's billionaires believed being tagged on the list put them at a higher risk of being sanctioned. Anxiety in Moscow ahead of the report's release was running high.

But when the report landed in January 2018, just before the congressionally mandated deadline, it was seen as a joke. Dubbed the Putin List, it included 96 oligarchs along with 114 senior Russian officials. The list was long and random, including billionaires already under sanctions, such as Arkady Rotenberg, as well as businessmen widely regarded as distant from the Kremlin. It looked as if the U.S. Treasury had copied and pasted the *Forbes* list of the richest Russians, an allegation that the U.S. Treasury didn't deny when it was later challenged in court. Putin joked that it was "offensive" that he wasn't included. "In effect, all one hundred forty-six million of us have been put on some list," he said at a campaign event, referring to Russia's population. Conspiracy theories mushroomed that Trump had watered it down to protect Putin. Treasury officials told me that was not true. "There was the unclassified list for public consumption, and then there was the classified version," one former U.S. Treasury official told me. "It's a report for the Hill, one of thousands of reports Treasury has to do for Congress."

The day after the report's release, Treasury Secretary Steve Mnuchin testified before the Senate Banking Committee, which skewered him over why no new Russia sanctions had been imposed yet.

"How can sanctions punish Russian interference in Ukraine and in American elections," asked Democratic senator Sherrod Brown of Ohio, "if these sanctions continue to sit on the shelf, unused by the president?" Mnuchin responded that considerable work had been done and promised that action would soon follow.

"This Congress and the American people don't trust the president on Russia, his closeness to Putin," Brown replied. "Your delay on this, your slow-walk, this just reinforces that."

Bolton told me CAATSA was a wake-up call for Mnuchin, who was a sanctions skeptic. "His business friends didn't necessarily think sanctions were a good idea," Bolton told me. But with Congress breathing down his neck, Mnuchin had to respond. In early April 2018, Mnuchin unveiled sanctions against seven tycoons in response to Russia's "malign activity around the globe," noting the occupation of Crimea and attempts to subvert democracy. "Russian oligarchs and elites who profit from this corrupt system will no longer be insulated from the consequences of their government's destabilizing activities," he said. The list landed like a bombshell. Unlike the Putin List, which didn't actually impose sanctions on anyone, these oligarchs were subject to asset freezes and travel bans. Among those targeted were Viktor Vekselberg, the oil and aluminum tycoon, and gold billionaire Suleyman Kerimov—both ranked among Russia's richest men.

But it was the blacklisting of the aluminum titan Deripaska that sent shock waves across the world. The U.S. Treasury threw everything it had against the oligarch, saying he acted directly or indirectly on behalf of the Russia state. "Deripaska has been investigated for money laundering and has been accused of threatening the lives of business rivals, illegally wiretapping a government official, and taking part in extortion and racketeering," it said. Deripaska denied the allegations, saying they were "groundless, ridiculous, and absurd." Treasury believed Deripaska was holding assets on behalf of Putin himself, and, on at least one occasion, was used as a cover to transfer funds for the Russian president's personal use, according to allegations later revealed in court filings. It said the billionaire had once canceled a share sale of Russian auto producer Gaz to hide Putin's money laundering through the company. The U.S. Treasury hadn't just imposed sanctions on Deripaska personally but also on his aluminum business. Unusually, the Treasury announced the sanctions on a Friday, so the full impact wasn't felt until the following Monday. The sanctions shaved billions from Deripaska's net worth in just one day. At the time, they were the most costly sanctions ever imposed on a businessman and his publicly traded companies.

The sanctions severed Deripaska's sprawling aluminum empire from the

U.S. dollar, sending shock waves through global markets. Shares in Rusal, listed in Hong Kong, fell 50 percent on the Monday after the penalties were announced, while the price of aluminum—used in everything from the auto industry to aircraft manufacturing—rose 20 percent in a panic over potential shortages. The sanctions threw a complex global supply chain into chaos. Non-U.S. entities couldn't deal with Rusal without running afoul of the restrictions if they had ties to the U.S. financial system. Rusal plants outside Russia suddenly faced an uncertain future, including an Irish refinery on the banks of the Shannon Estuary near Limerick that employed 450 workers and was one of the largest suppliers of alumina, used to make aluminum, to smelters in Europe. Multiple plants depended on the Rusal refinery in Ireland and another Rusal smelter in Sweden. European automakers faced supply shortages. Behind the scenes, European officials were lobbying the United States to lift the penalties.

Critics complained the U.S. Treasury had failed to consider the consequences. In reality, multiple arms of the U.S. government had to sign off on the sanctions, from Trump's National Security Council to the State and Justice Departments. The key part of the U.S. Treasury that draws up sanctions targets is the Office of Foreign Assets Control (OFAC). John Smith, the director of OFAC at the time and a seasoned sanctions lawyer, told me there was a view that the ramifications could be handled by issuing licenses to allow Rusal to operate. "The market reaction was anticipated," Smith told me. "Treasury was being called upon to consider sanctions on Russian oligarchs, some of the richest and most powerful people on the planet. Did Congress and the public expect Treasury to go after the least significant oligarchs? Or did they want Treasury to send the message that no oligarch was too big to sanction?" Even inside Treasury, some thought there wasn't enough attention paid to the potential fallout. "There was analysis saying this was maybe not a good idea," one Treasury official told me. "It did highlight the way the aluminum market is global, and some of the impacts would be on countries other than Russia. Mnuchin saw it."

After years of timid sanctions, the U.S. Treasury had overshot the mark, unleashing turmoil in the global metals markets to a degree few anticipated. The crisis served as a humbling lesson in how to use an economic weapon without shooting yourself in the foot.

Deripaska controlled Rusal through a holding company, En+, registered in the British Crown dependency of Jersey in the Channel Islands. He had installed Lord Gregory Barker as chairman of En+ in 2017, just before it raised $1.5 billion in an initial public offering in London. Barker was another example of "lords on boards," a long-standing strategy of Russians and other companies hiring the British elite to open doors and gain respectability. After the sanctions, Lord Barker thought about quitting Rusal, but he decided to stay on to try to broker a solution. It was an existential choice. A senior financier told him if he left the company in the lurch, he might never work in the City of London again, a person familiar with the discussion told me. "You can't just walk out the door," Barker recalled being told during a Bloomberg TV interview in 2019. "You've gotta be absolutely damn sure that you've tried everything in your power to try and rescue the minority shareholders." Barker would go on to pull off one of the biggest and most complicated multinational deals that set a precedent for how to lift sanctions. He shuttled between London, Washington, and Moscow, hiring a bevy of lawyers and lobbyists to craft a compromise that would satisfy not only the U.S. Treasury but also Congress.

After more than two weeks of market turmoil and political wrangling, Mnuchin threw a lifeline to Rusal by giving it a license to continue operating as the company petitioned to be taken off the list. "The U.S. government is not targeting the hardworking people who depend on Rusal and its subsidiaries," he said. "Our objective was not to put Rusal out of business." Barker realized the only way to lift the sanctions was to eliminate Deripaska's control of the company. "Initially when I started out, I thought there was no way that the man who'd actually sat at the helm of this group and founded it and controlled over seventy percent would actually consent to go back to being a minority shareholder," he recalled.

Over dinner at Deripaska's apartment in Moscow, Barker pitched his proposal to persuade U.S. officials to lift the sanctions on En+ if the tycoon relinquished control, according to a person with knowledge of the meeting. At the time Deripaska was distracted, plotting ways to retrench his aluminum empire to manage the U.S. penalties. Thinking it was unlikely to work, he gave Barker the green light to try. By the end of April, Deripaska agreed "in principle" to consider reducing his control of the business, but the deal took months to hammer out.

To win over U.S. Treasury officials, Barker's proposal called for Deripaska to reduce his ownership of En+ below 50 percent, but allow him to keep a significant stake in the business. Deripaska would step down and a majority of independent directors would join the board. Personal sanctions on Deripaska would remain, and he would be barred from receiving dividends. Dubbed the Barker Plan, it faced skepticism within Treasury.

Barker hired the lobbying firm Mercury on a $108,500-a-month contract to garner support from foreign governments for lifting the sanctions. The expensive lobbying campaign helped. Mercury solicited letters of support for the Barker Plan from ambassadors representing Germany, Sweden, Australia, and Jamaica, among others, to be sent to the State and Treasury Departments. "Rusal impacts thousands of manufacturing jobs, including our automotive industry and companies such as BMW, Daimler and Volkswagen," Germany's ambassador, Peter Wittig, wrote. Meanwhile, Barker and Andrea Gacki, the new head of Treasury's OFAC office, were wrangling over a compromise with lawyers.

In the middle of intense talks over the fate of a Kremlin-aligned oligarch, Trump sat down with Putin in Helsinki in July 2018 for one of the most controversial U.S.-Russia summits in history. After their meeting, Trump cast doubt on U.S. intelligence that Russia meddled in the 2016 election and said Putin's denial of the claims was "strong and powerful." Before the summit, Trump had agreed to impose sanctions against Russia in response to the Novichok attack on the Skripals in London, as required under a chemical weapons treaty the United States signed in 1991. Trump didn't want to go ahead with the sanctions. "'We've just pounded him with these CAATSA sanctions, we don't need to do it again,'" Bolton recalled Trump telling him after the summit. The sanctions went ahead anyway, limiting the export of sensitive U.S. goods and technology to Russia, including lasers, electronics, and some energy technologies. The restrictions caused the ruble to slide.

There was little appetite for doing a deal to lift sanctions on a Russian tycoon right after Trump's explosive comments at the summit with Putin. But in September, Barker put a proposal on the table: eight independent directors would be appointed to the En+ board, leaving Deripaska with only four on the twelve-member board. The tycoon kept insisting he needed to appoint half the board and was refusing to reduce his stake below 49 percent. Treasury was unlikely to agree to a plan that only barely pared back his control, so Barker persuaded Deripaska to cede more ground.

At the end of December, the U.S. Treasury finally agreed to lift sanctions on Deripaska's empire, portraying it as a deal that would steady the aluminum market. Deripaska ultimately agreed to a bigger haircut than he originally anticipated. He reduced his stake in En+ to 45 percent, with state-controlled bank VTB taking ownership of a block of his shares pledged as collateral for a loan. As part of the deal, the bank increased its stake in En+, reducing Deripaska's share and crystallizing a loss for the tycoon. Deripaska also pledged to donate some shares to a charitable foundation that he founded and transferred stock worth tens of millions of dollars to a trust fund for his two children, required under his divorce settlement with his wife. Deripaska's voting shares were slashed to 35 percent, with the rest controlled by independent directors.

The deal was unpopular in Washington. Many Democrats in Congress thought that it could allow the billionaire to still pull the strings at the company, but they failed to block the move. Barker acknowledged the deal wasn't perfect. "I am not pretending that Deripaska is removed from the company altogether, but we have removed control," he told Bloomberg TV.

Barker earned a small fortune—$7.8 million in 2019—after brokering the historic agreement. For all the turmoil, Treasury officials chalked this one up as a success. "It's generally considered a win if you can remove a global company from the clutches of a Russian oligarch," Smith, the OFAC director, told me. "The intent of the sanctions is not only to deter those who are put on the sanctions list from continuing to support malign activity." Whatever doubts about the deal, it showed the enormous power of the U.S. dollar to tie the hands of a Russian billionaire and limit his room to maneuver. And it taught U.S. officials a lesson about the cost of sanctions if they targeted markets heavily dependent on Russia.

Outraged by the sanctions, Deripaska sued the U.S. Treasury and Mnuchin, claiming a $7.5 billion loss from their actions. He asked the court to bar Treasury from calling him an oligarch and release all records underlying its decision to sanction him. More than two years later, a U.S. judge dismissed his claim, saying it lacked merit. He appealed all the way to the Supreme Court, but his petition was denied.

*   *   *

The 2018 sanctions had far-reaching consequences. For one, it accelerated Putin's strategy of hedging against future penalties. By the end of that year, Russia's central bank reserves were among the ten largest in the world, totaling $458 billion. In January 2019, Russia disclosed it had dumped $101 billion in U.S. dollar reserves, moving them into euros and Chinese renminbi in its biggest-ever move away from the greenback. Russia had dramatically cut its share of reserves held in the United States to just 10 percent, down from about a third when the Deripaska sanctions hit.

"We aren't ditching the dollar, the dollar is ditching us," Putin said in November 2018. "The instability of dollar payments is creating a desire for many global economies to find alternative reserve currencies and create settlement systems independent of the dollar. We're not the only ones doing it, believe me."

Failing to impose tougher penalties on Russia for meddling in the U.S. election and the continued occupation of eastern Ukraine was an invitation for Putin to go further. To be sure, the Trump administration had rolled out some of the toughest sanctions against Russia, but Trump himself repeatedly complained that the penalties were too harsh. The Trump administration's relatively tough stance on Russia was almost despite him. As Bolton remarked, "He barely knew where Ukraine was."

Zelensky's position had been weakened by his now-infamous July 2019 phone call with Trump, who asked for help digging up dirt on Hunter Biden, the son of then Democratic presidential candidate Joe Biden, setting off the second U.S. impeachment saga. It capped five years of Western governments dithering over how to respond to Putin's assault on Ukraine. Boris Johnson, who became the U.K.'s foreign secretary in 2016, expressed regret for not being tougher on Russia sooner. "We were all too weak following the invasion of Ukraine in 2014," Johnson told me. "That was the fundamental problem."

"We got through as many sanctions as we could during my seventeen months," Bolton told me. "It was Mnuchin who was increasingly the problem because of the secondary effect of sanctions. But that's part of the price of international political conflict. If you're not willing to assume any cost yourself, you're going to lose." When Putin decided to go all the way and launch his full-scale invasion, it was clear the West had not gotten the economic pressure right. It needed to figure out a way to isolate Russia in a more profound way—and be ready to swallow the costs.

CHAPTER 5

OLIGARCHS IN AMERICA

On a sunny morning in October 2021, FBI agents descended on a sprawling Renaissance-style mansion near Embassy Row in Washington, DC, one of the most exclusive neighborhoods in the nation's capital. After lifting the yellow police tape and passing through the iron gate, they entered the eleven-thousand-square-foot home carting backpacks and evidence boxes preparing to conduct an extensive search. The $15 million faux-limestone mansion was linked to Deripaska, the metals tycoon the United States had sanctioned in 2018. Simultaneously, agents marched into a three-story red-brick Greenwich Village town house in Manhattan also tied to the Russian billionaire. Police blocked the narrow street to allow the FBI to park several vehicles outside the nineteenth-century home, where agents were seen carting out boxes throughout the morning.

Questions swirled around the raids. Deripaska hadn't been able to visit the properties since Washington imposed sanctions on him in 2018, subjecting him to a travel ban. He said they were owned not by him but by his relatives. What evidence could the FBI agents possibly find that could aid a criminal case? Was the Justice Department investigating him for sanctions evasion or something else entirely? The day after the raid, Deripaska took to social media with an acerbic quip. "Did they find a load of Putin's money in those abandoned houses?" he asked on his Telegram channel. "Did they manage to refresh themselves with some sour jam from the pantries and a couple bottles of vodka?"

It's not every day that FBI agents get court orders to swarm the homes of a Russian billionaire in the United States. It turned out that the FBI, working with Adams's team at SDNY, had been running a sweeping investigation into Deripaska's clandestine activities in the United States for years, long before the war in Ukraine. The billionaire's tentacles in the United States stretched far and wide—from California to New York.

Adams's team at SDNY had been tracking Deripaska ever since April 2018 as part of Operation Accordable, the joint U.S.-U.K. effort to investigate blacklisted oligarchs. They soon discovered that Deripaska was unabashedly ignoring the ban on his doing business in the United States. While he hadn't set foot on American soil since being sanctioned, a cast of enablers was helping him transfer money in and out of the United States to manage his U.S. investments. It was a brazen violation of sanctions.

*   *   *

For years, Deripaska had sought a form of respectability in the United States that eluded him because of allegations he was tied to Russian organized crime—a charge he vehemently denied. Like many Russian billionaires, he was fascinated by the pulse of American life and free markets, perhaps because it was so different from Putin's Russia. People who know him say he loved to wander around New York City and saw U.S. business as a model to emulate. But more than anything else, he viewed doing business in the United States as a marker of his influence and success as a global, rather than just a Russian, tycoon.

His problems getting an American visa didn't stop him from assembling an unusual array of interests in the United States. Between 2005 and 2008, he bought three homes, including the mansion in DC, the Greenwich Village town house, and a five-story town house on the Upper East Side of Manhattan. I was told he bought the DC mansion because it provided a base to lobby the U.S. government on a range of issues, no doubt the possibility of aluminum tariffs being one among many interests. While he was the controlling shareholder of Gaz, the Russian vehicle manufacturer, he spent almost $1 billion buying just under 5 percent of General Motors in 2007, leading to speculation that he was looking to take over the company. He told me in 2011 that was never his plan.

Before the 2008 financial crisis, he was planning to plow $100 million into a private equity fund to invest in U.S. media and other assets even as Washington was denying him a visa to visit. In 2007, he decided to buy a music recording studio in Los Angeles and sent his lawyers out to find one. It was more of a personal pet project than a grand attempt to get into the U.S. music industry. He settled on the famed Ocean Studios in Burbank, California, where big names such as Crosby, Stills & Nash, Kanye West, and Avril Lavigne had recorded tracks. The sixty-four-hundred-square-foot brick building, dating back to the 1920s, had a vast recording room with skylights and twenty-one-foot ceilings. It was outfitted with vintage recording equipment, a pool table, a pink kitchen, leather sofas, and antique rugs. Freddie Piro, the music producer who owned it, was astonished that a Russian billionaire was trying to buy it sight unseen. Piro wasn't looking to sell, but lawyers for Deripaska kept pestering him. "I finally told them I wasn't going to do it because I just didn't feel as though I was ready to retire," Piro told me. "They said, 'We'll hire you as a consultant, and you can stay on. You don't even have to show up.' It was unbelievable. They made me an offer I couldn't refuse."

Companies controlled by Deripaska paid him over $3 million for the studio and a consulting fee. Piro never dealt directly with Deripaska, who, he says, never visited the studio. But the billionaire's decision to buy it stemmed from an unusual friendship he'd struck up. He'd gotten to know an American indie rock band called Ringside, which he'd brought to Russia half a dozen times to play at private parties and a few concerts. On one of their trips, the bandmates were complaining about the difficulty of getting recording contracts in the United States. "Why don't you just do it yourself?" Deripaska told them. "You need a studio," they replied. So Deripaska bought one for them, letting Ringside record tracks at Ocean Studios. Actor Joaquin Phoenix hung out with them as they recorded an album there, Piro recalled. So did Balthazar Getty, the American actor and musician, who was the great-grandson of oil tycoon J. Paul Getty, once the richest man in the world. Balthazar was part of Ringside, though I was told he never traveled to Russia with the band. Piro thought Deripaska just wanted the studio as a toy. "You couldn't find a much better place to have an incredible party," Piro told me. The 2008 financial crisis scuttled Deripaska's private equity plan to invest in the United States—the billionaire was drowning in debt—and the $100 million commitment was never funded, but he hung on to the studio as a favor to his musician friends.

In 2019, a year after the U.S. Treasury sanctioned Deripaska, he decided to unload the studio even though the sanctions had frozen his assets. To help him, he enlisted his U.S. fixer, a woman named Olga Shriki, who once worked at the Manhattan office of his aluminum company Basic Element, to sell it for about $3 million, according to U.S. prosecutors. Shriki, a naturalized U.S. citizen in her early forties with long blond hair, was described in emails as a "trusted contact for any assignments by OVD," Deripaska's initials. Without a special license from the U.S. Treasury, selling the studio violated the sanctions. It was an odd risk to take. The amount of money he would get was like loose change down the back of a couch for the billionaire. Shriki then tried to transfer the proceeds from a Wells Fargo account belonging to Ocean Studios to an account in Russia that belonged to a Deripaska-controlled entity. The billionaire and his aides seemed unaware that he and his assets were being monitored. He was also asking Shriki for help getting gifts in the United States, including sending flowers to a U.S. television host and getting iPhones and American Eagle–branded T-shirts for himself. "OV wants these t-shirts, 10 counts, size XL. Could you find them and urgently send them?" Natalia Bardakova, Deripaska's assistant in Russia, wrote to Shriki in December 2020, referring to Deripaska by his first and middle name, Oleg Vladimirovich.

In 2020, at the height of the pandemic, Deripaska again sought to cement his ties to the United States, despite the sanctions. At the time, Deripaska was divorced from his first wife and mother of his two children, Polina Yumasheva, the daughter of one of Yeltsin's top advisers, and was dating a Russian erotic model in her early twenties named Ekaterina Voronina, aka Ekaterina Lobanova. Voronina had been involved with Deripaska for several years and mixed in his high-level government circles. *New Lines Magazine*, working with the Russian investigative website the *Insider*, obtained a photo of her in Tokyo in 2018, sandwiched between Deripaska and Russia's sharp-tonged foreign minister, Sergei Lavrov. While Deripaska had long denied U.S. claims he was close to the Kremlin, here was evidence of him on a relaxed day out in Japan with one of Putin's closest confidants, the man who had served as Russia's foreign minister since 2004. (It wasn't the first time Deripaska was photographed with a young woman from the sex industry; in 2017, the late opposition leader Alexei Navalny released a video of Deripaska with a Belarusian sex worker known as Nastya Rybka on his superyacht in Norway.)

When Voronina became pregnant, Deripaska tapped Shriki again for help in the United States, a country that had for years worked to keep him at bay. Under Deripaska's direction, Shriki arranged for Voronina to fly by private jet to Los Angeles in July 2020 to give birth so the child could gain U.S. citizenship. At the time, hospitals were struggling with COVID cases. Voronina got a ten-day tourist visa but stayed for six months on a trip that cost Deripaska $300,000. Shriki had arranged everything: a two-story Beverly Hills penthouse, a nearby clinic, five nannies, a housekeeper, custom-made baby clothes, and cord blood and placenta preservation. Shriki sent regular updates to Deripaska's assistant in Russia, Bardakova. "Listen, it's so cool that you sorted out just about everything with her," Bardakova said in an audio message obtained by prosecutors. "The dad is happy." Through intermediaries, Deripaska paid Shriki $170,000, some of which she used to pay for Voronina's expenses. After she gave birth in August 2020, Deripaska asked Shriki and others to get the child a U.S. birth certificate and U.S. passport, altering the last name slightly so it didn't exactly match that of the sanctioned billionaire. Deripaska, blacklisted by the U.S. government, still wanted his child to have all the benefits of U.S. citizenship—the open economy, the rule of law, the top-notch health care.

While Adams's team at SDNY was running down tips on the tycoon's efforts to evade sanctions, a separate probe by the Justice Department and the FBI discovered something that sent shock waves through U.S. law enforcement: Deripaska had hired one of its own, Charles McGonigal, the FBI's former head of counterintelligence in New York—arguably the agency's most prestigious post—where he had led its investigations into Russian oligarchs, including Deripaska himself.

*   *   *

McGonigal spent more than two decades as a high-flying FBI agent working on major national security and counterterrorism cases, including the September 11 attacks. He later joined a special squad focused on terrorist threats in New York City. His stellar track record earned him a promotion in 2016. As New York's top special agent in charge of counterintelligence, he had access to the country's sensitive secrets and knowledge of probes into foreign spies operating in the United States. He was known for a certain arrogance. "He'd always been sort of a cowboy, you know, the smartest man in the room," one former colleague told me. Since 2017, he'd been having an affair with a woman named Allison Guerriero, who claimed he left a bag of cash at their Brooklyn apartment that year. When they ended the relationship at the end of 2018, she emailed the FBI about the mysterious cash, a tip that likely triggered the Justice Department and FBI investigation.

McGonigal's work for Deripaska was all the more surprising because of what he knew. He had seen a classified report stating that Deripaska was associated with Russian intelligence. In January 2018, McGonigal reviewed the list of oligarchs with ties to the Kremlin to be considered for sanctions. A few months later, through a mutual contact, McGonigal met Yevgeny Fokin, a former Russian diplomat who was working for Deripaska. McGonigal told a colleague Fokin was a Russian intelligence officer he wanted to recruit, but then he helped Fokin's daughter get an internship at the New York Police Department, where she got VIP treatment working in counterterrorism, an extraordinary position for the daughter of an alleged Russian intelligence officer. After McGonigal retired from the FBI in 2018, he introduced Fokin to a law firm to help get sanctions on Deripaska lifted and began working for the lawyers. McGonigal met the Russian billionaire at his home in London and also traveled to meet him in Vienna.

McGonigal's desire to enrich himself after two decades of relatively low pay in the FBI led him to violate the laws he'd spent his whole career enforcing. In 2021, Deripaska hired McGonigal to dig up dirt on his archrival, Russian billionaire Vladimir Potanin, in an attempt to get him sanctioned by the United States. The two oligarchs had feuded for years over control of the metals giant Norilsk Nickel, the world's biggest miner of palladium. Potanin held a larger stake in the company than Deripaska did, and the two men quarreled over dividend payments and strategy. McGonigal agreed for Deripaska entities to pay him through a Cyprus corporation channeling money into a New Jersey business account. To conceal the payments, neither of the companies were registed to Deripaska or McGonigal. Without a license from the U.S. Treasury, it was illegal for McGonigal to do business with a sanctioned billionaire. McGonigal accepted $17,500 from Deripaska, a paltry sum given the enormous risks involved. But a bigger payday awaited. Prosecutors said McGonigal was asking for as much as $3 million to provide Deripaska with compromising files about Potanin found on the dark web.

The FBI investigation of one of its own agents was incredibly tricky. McGonigal had worked in both the New York and Washington field offices, where he had friends and former colleagues. Part of the probe was handled by the FBI's office in Los Angeles to ensure secrecy. In addition to the Deripaska work, investigators also discovered that McGonigal had accepted a loan worth almost a quarter of a million dollars from a former Albanian intelligence officer while working for the FBI, concealing it from the agency. The FBI arrested McGonigal in January 2023, after he landed in JFK on a flight from Asia. "Mr. McGonigal betrayed his solemn oath to the United States in exchange for personal gain and at the expense of our national security," FBI assistant director in charge Donald Alway said after the arrest.

The announcement astonished McGonigal's former colleagues, many of whom were left dejected by the betrayal. "The more I learned, I got mad," one former FBI agent who worked on the case told me. "Since 2016, all we'd been doing is fighting one story after another about Russian influence, corruption, and oligarchs. To have one of our own feed into that was probably the most disappointing thing of all." McGonigal later pleaded guilty to sanctions evasion and money laundering. "I never intended to hurt the United States, the FBI, or my friends and loved ones," McGonigal told the judge. In December 2023, he was sentenced to four years and two months in prison (later extended another two years and three months for hiding payments from the former Albanian intelligence officer).

There was no indication McGonigal was a Russian spy while inside the FBI, but Deripaska had managed to recruit one of the FBI's most senior officials who access to sensitive U.S. intelligence. Deripaska was not only obsessed with getting the U.S. penalties lifted—he wanted to use the U.S. sanctions regime to get his fiercest rival blacklisted to undermine him *in Russia*. It was a sign that sanctions weren't just a U.S. foreign policy tool but had also become a weapon in internal mudslinging matches between Russian oligarchs.

* * *

A week after Russia's full-scale invasion, Deripaska called for an end to the war in Ukraine but failed to attack the man who started it all: Putin. "Peace is very important! Delaying negotiations is madness!" he said on Telegram. Deripaska's vague call for negotiations wasn't a call for Russian invading forces to withdraw. As the war in Ukraine intensified, prosecutors doubled down on the existing Deripaska probe. With the tycoon himself in Russia and out of their reach, they began focusing on Deripaska's enablers, the cast of fixers who helped him move money, maintain real estate, and assist his family members.

Not long after Deripaska's Telegram post, Adams and his team got a lucky break. Voronina, the erotic model who was Deripaska's girlfriend, got pregnant again. In mid-April 2022, less than six weeks after Russian troops invaded Ukraine, killing thousands, Voronina asked Deripaska if she could make arrangements for her second child to be born in the United States. Shriki, Deripaska's former office assistant in Manhattan, said she was busy on another project and couldn't help. In reality, she'd already received a grand jury subpoena at the end of September 2020 requesting her communications with Deripaska and his aides. In any investigation, cracking communications is key to proving "intent" to willfully commit a crime, in this case sanctions evasion. Appearing to panic, she deleted text and voice messages and searched for information on the consequences of withholding information, according to court documents.

But Shriki did not let slip that the Feds were onto them, given she was already under a grand jury investigation. Bardakova, Deripaska's assistant in Moscow, flew from Russia to Los Angeles in May to find another Beverly Hills house to rent for his girlfriend. "Hooray!" the billionaire responded to a message from Voronina when they found a place. Bardakova coordinated $229,000 in payments to intermediaries so that a U.S. entity could pay the rent. At the time, Washington was ramping up sanctions on Russia and widening the list of individuals and companies blacklisted from doing business in the United States. It was the height of hypocrisy for the girlfriend of a sanctioned oligarch to fly to Los Angeles to give birth to gain American citizenship for their child as missiles rained down on Ukraine.

On June 1, as Russian forces bombed Ukrainian bridges in Kherson, Voronina, her first child, and her nanny flew from Istanbul to Los Angeles by private jet using Cyprus and Swiss charter companies. When she arrived, she was hauled aside at LAX by Homeland Security and questioned for hours about her relationship with the sanctioned tycoon. She lied to them, saying the father of her child was "Alec Deribasko," according to court documents. She said she didn't know where the father of her child lived or what his occupation was and that her parents had paid for the private jet and her Beverly Hills rental.

Investigators seized her phones and discovered a gold mine for any legal prosecution: communications from Deripaska himself, which showed his intent to circumvent sanctions, and Shriki's knowledge that she was violating the restrictions. Bardakova, his assistant, arrived in LA the next day expecting to help Deripaska's girlfriend settle in and prepare to give birth. Instead, FBI agents grabbed her at LAX and took her to her hotel for questioning. Apparently unaware that Voronina had handed over her phone with all their communications, Bardakova lied, saying she never communicated with Deripaska directly and that she hadn't helped with his girlfriend's first trip to the United States. (Bardakova's lawyers sought to have the charges against her dismissed, arguing in a court filing that her actions weren't criminal and that her alleged false statements should be litigated in California where they purportedly took place, not New York.)

The FBI let the two women go, focusing on Shriki as the one closer to Deripaska's U.S. financial dealings. After combing through Shriki's phone, they'd gathered enough evidence of willful intent to evade sanctions, enabling them to arrest Shriki at the end of September 2022. At 6:00 a.m. on a crisp dry morning, FBI agents arrested Shriki at her six-bedroom, brown-shingled home in Jersey City. She was released after questioning on a $2 million bond secured by her Jersey City home. She pleaded not guilty to charges of sanctions evasion and destroying evidence in a federal investigation.

*　　　*　　　*

Meanwhile, Deripaska had also been working to safeguard his homes and art collections in the United States. With no U.K. sanctions in place against him, he leaned on Graham Bonham-Carter, a sixty-two-year-old British property manager, who is also a second cousin of the British actress Helena Bonham

Carter. Acting as a kind of concierge-cum-fixer, he'd worked for Deripaska since 2003, when the Russian billionaire bought 5 Belgrave Square, a six-story, stucco-fronted Regency home in one of London's most exclusive neighborhoods, held through a company registered in the British Virgin Islands. When squatters broke into the mansion after Russia's invasion, they revealed it was decked out with what looked like a Bösendorfer grand piano worth £80,000 and a sculpture by Barbara Hepworth. While the United States hassled Deripaska over visas, the U.K. welcomed him. Working from an office near St. James's Palace, Bonham-Carter was one of those under-the-radar "enablers" helping to grease the wheels of finance and real estate for one of Russia's richest men—arranging for security, insurance, and upkeep. Born in Zimbabwe to a South African mother and an English father, he had worked as the director of palaces for the king and queen of Jordan before parlaying his skills into a lucrative career catering to Russia's elite.

Prosecuting enablers of Russian billionaires such as Bonham-Carter was one of the most effective ways to enforce sanctions and cut off evasion networks. Soon after Washington slapped sanctions on Deripaska, he asked Bonham-Carter to set up a separate company to manage his Belgravia house in London and possibly others in Japan, Italy, China, and elsewhere. Bonham-Carter knew his boss's room to maneuver was limited. "Times a bit tough for my boss as sanctions have hit him from the USA so not an ideal time," he emailed a contact inquiring about Deripaska in June 2018.

Bonham-Carter set up a company in the U.K. called GBCM Ltd, which funneled money on Deripaska's behalf. In 2021, Bonham-Carter wired more than $1 million from Russia to bank accounts belonging to Gracetown Inc., a company managing Deripaska's U.S. properties, including the Washington mansion and the Greenwich Village town house, according to court filings. (The United States froze his five-story Upper East Side mansion in 2018.) The funds covered staff salaries, property taxes, and upkeep.

Bonham-Carter didn't stop there. In March 2021, he attempted to recover a collection of eighteen works of Russian art that Deripaska had bought in 2008 in New York, where they'd been stored at Christie's auction house ever since. Bonham-Carter knew the transaction was going to be difficult. A year earlier, he'd written to a financial services firm about the art collection, which was in the name of a company called Turcos Ltd. "No one now wants or maybe can deal with Turcos admin as it's seen as a very 'Hot cake' vis a vis OVD and the USA," he wrote, referring to the initials of his boss. Bonham-Carter paid the auction house more than $12 million to cover the cost of shipping the artwork from New York to London.

Christie's balked. It wrote to Bonham-Carter that it believed the artwork belonged to Deripaska and would block shipment in accordance with sanctions unless Bonham-Carter provided written confirmation that it wasn't the tycoon's property. Bonham-Carter showed the auction house that he'd paid for the shipping with his own credit card, but that wasn't good enough. In August 2021, the auction house notified the U.S. Treasury that it was treating the collection and the $12 million payment for shipping as the property of Deripaska, effectively freezing the artwork and the cash. Any transaction that touched the U.S. banking system for a sanctioned individual would be a violation, giving the Justice Department grounds to go after a U.K. citizen for facilitating evasion. (Christie's said in a statement it doesn't permit transactions with sanctioned individuals or companies.)

But the U.K. refused to act when SDNY requested help with warrants to search phones and interview witnesses. London's response was invariably, Deripaska's not sanctioned here, so we can't help unless he's also committed a crime on British soil. Even though American and British law enforcement had joined forces to pursue sanctioned Russian oligarchs under Operation Accordable, U.S. prosecutors weren't getting the cooperation they needed.

That all changed in early March 2022, when the U.K. added Deripaska to its own sanctions list after Putin's invasion, unlocking stalled cooperation. In October 2022, police arrived at Bonham-Carter's home outside London early in the morning to arrest him. The United States charged him with wire fraud and conspiracy to violate sanctions, seeking his extradition. Then it all went quiet—the court filings ceased. Lawyers looking at the case told me it's likely that Bonham-Carter was cooperating with U.S. authorities. He hasn't been convicted. His lawyers declined to comment. Whatever the outcome, a high-profile enabler to a sanctioned Russian oligarch had been stopped in his tracks, serving as a warning for others who might be tempted to facilitate evasion.

Once the KleptoCapture task force was up and running, the Justice Department threw resources at the existing Deripaska probe and secured international cooperation to fast-track a series of indictments. The United States charged Deripaska with relatively minor infractions of sanctions laws involving small amounts of money, but prosecutors want to forfeit his homes in DC and New York and the proceeds from the sale of his music studio. The moves could make tens of millions of dollars available for Ukraine.

Bonham-Carter is just one of a handful of foreign nationals the Klepto-Capture unit targeted for facilitating sanctions evasion. His indictment signaled a shift in strategy. With so many Russian oligarch assets out of reach—in Russia, Dubai, or Turkey—prosecutors focused on the professional facilitators who move Russian money and assets worldwide. Adams sees them as fair game, saying they're helping sanctioned tycoons "enjoy the privileges of life in a democracy." But the hunt for enablers sent some of them on the run.

*   *   *

Deripaska was the most high-profile oligarch indicted, but he wasn't alone. The Justice Department was prepared to take shots wherever it could, seeking to forfeit other Russian-owned assets in the United States for Ukraine and close down the route for sanctions evasion to make the restrictions bite. Next in the line of fire was Viktor Vekselberg, another sanctioned billionaire who used enablers to maintain his assets in the United States. One of Russia's richest men, who made his fortune in oil and aluminum, Vekselberg is a white-bearded tycoon who grew up in a small city in western Ukraine, born to a Russian mother and a Jewish father whose family was decimated by the Holocaust. Vekselberg moved to Moscow in the 1970s to attend engineering school before going on to cofound Renova Group, an oil and aluminum conglomerate, with his classmate Len Blavatnik, who moved to the United States and became an American citizen in 1984. Like Deripaska, the pair cobbled together ownership of smelters during the Russian aluminum wars of the 1990s.

Vekselberg was an attractive target for U.S. sanctions because he had so much at stake in the United States—property, powerful contacts, and even family. His children were educated at Yale, and his wife had lived mostly in the United States. Once a green-card holder, Vekselberg at one point spent nearly as much time in the United States as in Moscow working with U.S.

companies, institutions, and politicians on a variety of projects. He had even met three previous U.S. presidents—Barack Obama, George W. Bush, and Bill Clinton. In 2004, Vekselberg made headlines as the billionaire who bought nine imperial Fabergé eggs and other items from the collection owned by the late American media magnate Malcolm Forbes for $110 million. The jeweler Carl Fabergé made about fifty eggs for Russia's imperial family in the late nineteenth and early twentieth centuries, of which forty-three have survived. The Bolsheviks sold many to foreigners, and some went missing. Vekselberg touted his purchase as fulfilling his duty to return the lost treasures to their homeland.

Like Deripaska, Vekselberg was captivated by the United States, especially its West Coast. In 2010, he helped organize part of then president Dmitry Medvedev's state visit to the United States, including a three-day Silicon Valley tour headlined by meetings with Apple's Steve Jobs, Google's Eric Schmidt, and Cisco's John Chambers. He spent years overseeing the Skolkovo Foundation, Medvedev's project to build a tech incubator near Moscow, striking partnerships with Microsoft, Intel, Cisco, and Boeing. When then California governor Arnold Schwarzenegger visited Russia later that year to boost cooperation in high tech, Vekselberg showed him his Fabergé collection, which was then on display at the Ritz-Carlton in Moscow. After Putin annexed Crimea in 2014, Vekselberg's inroads into Silicon Valley raised a red flag with U.S. intelligence. In April that year, the FBI issued a rare public notice to the entire tech industry. Skolkovo, it warned, was a potential Trojan horse for espionage. "The foundation may be a means for the Russian government to access our nation's sensitive or classified research, development facilities and dual-use technologies with military and commercial applications," the alert said.

In January 2017, Vekselberg met Trump's then lawyer, Michael Cohen in Trump Tower with his American cousin, Andrew Intrater, who was investing some of the billionaire's money and had donated $250,000 to Trump's inaugural committee. (Vekselberg denied the donation was his money.) Cohen was shopping a business idea that went nowhere, but the two also discussed a desire to improve U.S.-Russia relations. After attending Trump's inauguration as a guest of Intrater, Vekselberg began telling Russian officials and fellow businesspeople he had influence in the White House, though his spokesman denied he tried to act as a go-between on securing sanctions relief for Russia.

In March 2018, Vekselberg was stopped at a New York airport by federal investigators working with Robert Mueller's probe into Russian meddling in the U.S. election. They asked about his ties to Cohen and whether Intrater's $250,000 gift to Trump's inaugural committee was really his money. A month later, the U.S. Treasury slapped sanctions on Vekselberg. Michael Carpenter, a former Pentagon official who oversaw Russia for the National Security Council in the Obama administration, viewed Vekselberg as cause for concern. "Vekselberg was deeply implicated in efforts to influence leaders and politicians here in the U.S.," he told me in 2018.

Vekselberg was shocked by his blacklisting. "I always believed that I understood the Western world well, much better than many," he told the Russian edition of *Forbes*. He said he had more than $1.5 billion in U.S. and Swiss bank accounts frozen due to the sanctions. The U.S. Treasury never permitted him to use the funds. Without a license to unlock the cash, he wasn't able to spend money in the United States without running afoul of sanctions.

The task force began drilling down into the surreptitious steps Vekselberg allegedly took to maintain his extensive U.S. real estate portfolio. There was the split-level Park Avenue apartment on the twenty-first floor. There was the nine-bedroom home on Duck Pond Lane in the Hamptons, set on two acres, with a pool and a tennis court. And then there was a penthouse and another apartment on Fisher Island, the exclusive members-only island off Miami for billionaires, where the likes of Oprah Winfrey and Julia Roberts have owned homes. Altogether, the properties were worth around $75 million, which he owned through layers of shell companies in Panama, the Bahamas, and the British Virgin Islands. The sanctions froze his assets and barred him from paying for their upkeep, but he found ways around those restrictions.

A longtime associate, Vladimir Voronchenko, stepped in to help him maintain his real estate portfolio. A Russian national who was a permanent resident in the United States, Voronchenko was a childhood friend who had helped Vekselberg broker the deal to buy the Fabergé eggs. When Vekselberg set out to create a museum in Russia to house the collection, he put Voronchenko in charge. The billionaire leased the grand eighteenth-century Shuvalov Palace on the banks of the Fontanka River in St. Petersburg and spent $40 million to renovate the neoclassical building. With his round John Lennon glasses and gray beard, Voronchenko, who once owned several luxury shops in Moscow, was always immaculately turned out, with crisp suits adorned with a pocket silk square. He lived off and on in some of Vekselberg's properties, including the nine-thousand square foot home in Southampton.

When the sanctions hit, Voronchenko began paying for the upkeep of Vekselberg's real estate holdings—property taxes, insurance, and other costs—through a company he set up in the Bahamas and a Russian bank account in the name of one of his relatives. It's illegal to make payments on behalf of a sanctioned individual without permission from the U.S. Treasury. He didn't pay it directly. Instead, in a sign of how convoluted sanctions evasion can become, he used another middleman: Vekselberg's old New York attorney, Robert G. Wise, a University of Michigan–educated lawyer who worked from an office in midtown Manhattan. Between 2018 and 2022, he facilitated almost $4 million in payments to cover taxes and insurance on six homes owned by Vekselberg, even though they both knew about the sanctions. They even tried to sell two of the properties—the Park Avenue apartment and the estate in the Hamptons—listing them with brokers without success.

In May 2022, Voronchenko was at one of Vekselberg's Fisher Island apartments when the FBI served a grand jury subpoena calling for him to testify and produce documents by the end of the month. Instead, he fled. He booked a flight to Dubai and was due to return a week later, but he flew on to Moscow the next day. Investigators got what they needed anyway. In September, U.S. Homeland Security and FBI agents swooped in on Vekselberg's apartments on Park Avenue and Miami's Fisher Island. Dressed in dark blue jackets, federal agents were seen carting away boxes and a heavy white safe. The same day, agents arrived in the Hamptons in a green armored vehicle—an over-the-top show of force for the luxury beach town—to search his home. While Voronchenko escaped, the Justice Department snagged Wise, the American lawyer.

Wise pleaded guilty in April 2023, admitting he should have questioned the transactions. "I then ultimately made a conscious decision not to press the issue and failed to confirm what was very likely the case, namely that Vekselberg was still the beneficial owner of the properties," Wise told the judge. "I understand that by continuing to make these payments on these properties despite realizing the high probability that Vekselberg was the beneficial owner of the properties, I was tacitly agreeing with others to use overseas funds to promote the violation of U.S. sanctions." When Wise appeared in court in

December 2023 for sentencing, the eighty-three-year-old real estate lawyer cut a sad figure, taken out by his son in a wheelchair after being punished with a year of home detention followed by a year of probation. He admitted he avoided learning who the beneficial owner of the properties was even though he had suspicions. "That was the worst mistake I ever made in my years of practice," he told the judge.

It's extremely rare for the U.S. Justice Department to go after lawyers for facilitating illicit money flows, but prosecutors had the evidence they needed to indict Wise. Going after an American lawyer for helping an oligarch evade sanctions sent a warning shot to the U.S. legal community that transgressions would no longer be tolerated. "The task force has targeted those enablers of money laundering and sanctions evasion who aim to hide crime behind a veneer of professionalism," Adams said announcing the plea deal. "Admission to the bar carries with it a public trust that attorneys will act with honesty and integrity—a trust that Robert Wise chose to betray in exchange for an easy, illicit paycheck."

While Adams's team pursued Vekselberg's sanctions evasion in the United States, the KleptoCapture task force was supporting prosecutors at the U.S. Attorneys' office in the District of Columbia who were closing in on Vekselberg's 255-foot superyacht, *Tango*, moored in the Spanish port of Palma de Mallorca. Despite the U.S. sanctions in 2018, Vekselberg could operate with relative freedom in Europe, where he wasn't sanctioned. He cruised around the world in the $90 million white-hulled superyacht, big enough for fourteen guests and at least twenty crew. DC prosecutors had traced *Tango* to a shell company in the British Virgin Islands, Arinter Management Inc., with Panamanians tied to Vekselberg as directors. Moreover, bank records showed that Vekselberg had made U.S.-dollar payments from his accounts to the company prior to being sanctioned, proving he owned it. In early April 2022, FBI agents boarded *Tango* together with Spain's Guardia Civil police force to seize the yacht with the aim of forfeiting it for Ukraine in a case based on bank fraud, money laundering, and sanctions evasion.

Prosecutors alleged Vekselberg had used intermediaries to make hundreds of thousands of U.S.-dollar payments for *Tango* under false names to evade sanctions. Once again, a British national, Richard Masters, allegedly helped orchestrate the evasion in a glaringly obvious scheme. Masters owned a yacht management company in Mallorca and channeled payments to maintain *Tango* under the fake name Fanta to disguise any connection to Vekselberg. Tango is the British brand name for an electric-orange soft drink; Fanta is the American name of a similar bright orange soda. It didn't take long for prosecutors to crack the setup.

The superyacht industry is saturated with uncharacteristically bronzed Brits such as Masters, who earn big money working in management companies and brokerages throughout the Mediterranean. A wine-loving entrepreneur, Masters is alleged by Spanish authorities to have made 800,000 euros ($867,000) from managing Vekselberg's yacht. In January 2023, at the request of the task force, Spanish police arrested Masters at Madrid's Barajas Airport, releasing him under house arrest. But the High Court, in Madrid, rejected a U.S. request to extradite him, saying Masters had not committed a crime and the United States had not proven the money used to maintain the yacht came from unlawful activity. It was yet another example of Europe's judicial system failing to line up with Washington.

The *Tango* remains at Mallorca's Club de Mar, and the United States has not formally filed to forfeit it yet. Justice Department officials and lawyers for Vekselberg entered protracted negotiations for a settlement to head off a court battle. As with *Amadea*, prosecutors appear to be betting that Vekselberg wouldn't risk a U.S. court fight to block a forfeiture claim. The U.S. government ultimately wants to put it up for sale, with net proceeds going to Ukraine. Together with Vekselberg's U.S. real estate, which the Justice Department has already moved to seize and sell, his property potentially subject to forfeiture for Ukraine totals more than $165 million. But the *Tango* saga was another reminder that seizing a superyacht for sanctions evasion is much more complicated than anyone could ever have imagined.

*   *   *

There had long been calls for a crackdown on the middlemen facilitating Russian illegal money flows, but the war in Ukraine was finally beginning to force at least some change. The growing pressure for action in the face of Russian atrocities created an appetite to make the economic penalties inflict meaningful pain in the hopes it could bring about behavior change. By the end of 2022, the KleptoCapture task force had succeeded in cutting off at least some of the backdoor channels for illicit Russian money entering the West. But the scale of Russian illicit finance was clearly so huge that the fight would require more than just the Justice Department running down targets with uneven support from other countries.

In 2022, the U.S. Congress considered a bill called the Enablers Act, which would require trust companies, art dealers, and lawyers to make sure their clients weren't laundering money, closing a loophole that had once allowed dirty Russian money to ping from offshore havens around the world to established financial centers. U.S. national security adviser Jake Sullivan backed the bill, but Senate Republicans blocked it at the end of 2022 after intense lobbying from lawyers. Even though the bill had bipartisan support with three Republicans pushing for its passage, it was all but dead. Without a legal requirement for lawyers or art dealers to flag suspicious transactions by their clients, the fight against Russian illicit finance would be capped by the limited resources of the Justice Department to root out cases.

But with so many Russians on the sanctions list, showcases such as Bonham-Carter and Wise put accountants, real estate agents, and art dealers on notice about the risks of acting for sanctioned individuals. Prosecutors have only scratched the surface of potential illegality among enablers working for blacklisted Russians.

Since 2022, Justice Department staffers have fanned out across Europe, from Monaco to London, to get more cases over the line. "We simply cannot do this work without building international cases against the targets we're going after," Adams told me in Paris at the end of 2022, when he was visiting French Justice Ministry officials. In a sign of the new zeal to stamp out evasion, the Justice Department said it was hiring twenty-five new prosecutors to work on sanctions and export controls in 2023. Through the KleptoCapture task force, the United States has helped kick-start a global campaign to flush out tainted Russian money, helping European and British law enforcement adopt U.S.-style tools to pursue oligarchs tied to Putin's regime.

But Europe will have a harder time because its legal system isn't set up to seize and forfeit assets. In March 2022, the EU created a "freeze and seize" task force to coordinate the actions of member states. The EU alone froze 21 billion euros in Russian assets, with six European countries doing most of the work. But some EU officials thought substantial Russian assets were slipping through undetected. The use of complex corporate layering makes the money trail hard to follow. Without proving a crime, such as money laundering or corruption, has been committed, European countries won't be able to confiscate assets. Because the EU only started aggressively issuing sanctions in February 2022, it will be harder to prove sanctions laws have been broken.

*   *   *

Two years after the KleptoCapture task force was formed, it had frozen or seized roughly $700 million of Russian assets and indicted seventy individuals along with five corporate entities. The actual forfeiture of the assets is a complex and lengthy process not without its critics. In the eyes of some, attempts to seize the assets of Russian oligarchs make a mockery of property rights and do little to put pressure on Putin.

In May 2023, at a roundtable with Adams at the New York Bar Association, Tom Firestone, a lawyer working for sanctioned tycoons, likened the seizures of boats, planes, and mansions to a populist push. Firestone isn't your average American sanctions lawyer; he studied Russian at Harvard and worked as the Justice Department's resident legal adviser at the U.S. embassy in Moscow. Russian intelligence tried to recruit him on the street in Moscow one evening, but he spurned them, an episode he says is for the reason he was expelled from the country in 2013 after he joined a private law firm. "Putin doesn't care when people get their yachts seized," Firestone said during the panel discussion. "Seizing them is not necessarily going to have any effect on Russian policy." Adams responded coolly, stating that the Justice Department was focused on sanctions evasion rather than influencing Putin's behavior. "The purpose, of course, is to stymie and slow the Russian war machine more than it is to get inside Putin's head," Adam said.

For those arguing that forfeiture claims against sanctioned oligarch assets violate property rights, the lengthy court battles show that the rule of law is being upheld. Michael Khoo, who succeeded Adams as cohead of KleptoCapture in 2023, told me the drawn-out litigation is part and parcel of any forfeiture. "The government can't just go out and grab property because you're Russian and support President Putin," Khoo said. "We have to show to the satisfaction of a U.S. district court that the property we're forfeiting is in fact connected to some kind of criminal activity."

There are historical examples of much more sweeping asset seizures during times of war. In World War II, the British government confiscated assets owned by residents of "enemy countries," such as Germany, under the Trading with the Enemy Act 1939. Even if the sanctions against oligarchs can't influence the political process in Moscow, they might provide some cash for war-torn Ukraine. But finding money to repair the damage in Ukraine was only part of the economic war. Beyond the scenes of the high-profile seizures of yachts and mansions, an even more consequential battle was going on: blocking Russia's ability to get Western technology for use on the battlefield, a fight that was playing out in unsuspecting neighborhoods in America.

PART III

LOOPHOLES, DIVESTMENTS, AND THEIR DISCONTENTS

CHAPTER 6

MICROCHIP MONTE

In July 2023, more than a year after Putin's invasion, I drove to the quiet community of Meadowoods in Merrimack, New Hampshire, about an hour north of Boston, looking for a man purported to be shipping sensitive U.S. technology to a Russian intelligence officer. After passing through quaint New England towns, I arrived to find a quintessential American suburb: pretty two-story timber houses lined by manicured grass and clipped hedges. Kids rode their bikes, kicked soccer balls in backyards, and practiced basketball in driveways. I found it hard to believe that Russia's war in Ukraine had somehow reached this unassuming corner of America.

I was searching for Alexey Brayman, a man who was allegedly shipping sophisticated U.S. electronics and components to a web of companies supplying Russia's military and intelligence services. An Israeli citizen who claimed on Facebook that his hometown was Kyiv, Brayman, thirty-five, had close-cropped dark hair and brown eyes. His wife, Daria, looked like any mother with a young child but hailed from Chelyabinsk, a city more than a thousand miles east of Moscow known for its military production facilities. A white Honda SUV was parked in the driveway, and toys were scattered about the yard. To outsiders, the Braymans were immigrants running a small business from their home selling customized night-lights, pushing their products at local arts-and-crafts fairs, vacationing in Florida, and attending Celtics games.

But secretly, the Braymans' home served as a crucial transshipment point for technology destined for Russia's military in violation of U.S. export bans. Or at least that's what federal prosecutors believed when they indicted Alexey Brayman and six others at the end of 2022 as part of a sweeping probe into an international smuggling ring. The U.S. government was hunting down legions of intermediaries illegally funneling technology to Russia using chains of front companies. However, Brayman's actions stood out. He was allegedly sending illicit shipments *directly* to a suspected colonel in Russia's Federal Security Service, the successor agency to the KGB, from his New Hampshire home to the Baltic state of Estonia. It's unusual to find a U.S.-based middleman with a direct line into the FSB. Prosecutors alleged the supplies included "advanced electronics and sophisticated testing equipment used in quantum computing, hypersonic and nuclear weapons development and other military and space-based military applications."

When the charges were first filed, media reports were quick to compare Brayman and his wife to characters in the TV spy drama *The Americans*, about undercover KGB officers posing as a normal American couple living with their children in an unsuspecting suburb of Washington, DC. But unlike *The Americans*, the Braymans didn't bend over backward to make friends in the neighborhood. I was told they mostly kept to themselves, even avoiding Ukrainians who lived on their street.

Prosecutors never accused Brayman of being an actual spy. Even still, evidence suggested he might have been a key functionary in the FSB's elaborate efforts to get its hands on crucial Western components. Trying to stop the flow of U.S. technology to Russia was one of the most important fronts in the economic war, which made my quest for answers from Brayman feel all the more pressing.

*   *   *

The extent of Russia's dependence on Western technology has been laid bare on the battlefields of Ukraine. In Kyiv, when the sirens wail, it's sometimes a warning that Russia is firing its hypersonic Kinzhal missiles, which Ukrainian officials have dissected to reveal are made with forty-eight foreign electronic components, many of which are produced by American semiconductor giants.

Researchers at the Royal United Services Institute (RUSI) who examined Russian weapons systems on the ground in Ukraine early in the war discovered more than 450 foreign-made components, the vast majority from U.S. companies known for producing microelectronics for the American military. Texas Instruments and Analog Devices accounted for a quarter of components in Russian weapons, including ballistic and cruise missiles. According to a Ukrainian government report, those two companies were the largest single Western suppliers of components in the Kinzhal missiles. Both companies stopped sales to Russia in 2022, but trade data showed their semiconductors continued flowing to the country in 2023 through chains of distributors in locations such as China and Hong Kong. (Texas Instruments said it requires its customers to comply with export control laws and that it conducts an in-depth internal review if the company learns its parts have been diverted to Russia.)

Western-designed inputs found on the Ukrainian battlefield included microprocessors and transceivers. Some were lower-technology components that could easily be purchased—and small enough to be stuffed into a backpack even—while others had been subject to export controls since 2014. Production dates varied. While some parts may have been sourced decades ago, others had been made more recently. RUSI found a Kalibr cruise missile that had Western-made components that appeared to date from 2018 to 2019, after some export controls were imposed.

As the war dragged on, Western components kept turning up in Ukraine. On August 19, 2023, Russian forces fired an Iskander-K cruise missile that hit the center of the Ukrainian city of Chernihiv, about ninety miles northeast of Kyiv. Residents were out on a warm sunny afternoon celebrating the Feast of the Transfiguration, a major Orthodox festival. As people were returning from church, the missile soared through the air and landed on the central theater in the city, which was hosting an exhibit on consumer drones. The attack killed 7 people, including a six-year-old girl, and injured 144 others. When Ukrainian officials dissected the remnants of the missile, they found several satellite navigation components from U.S. companies, including Analog Devices. While it was not certain when the components were shipped, they believed the missile was produced no earlier than March 2023, more than a year after stringent export controls were put in place. It appeared to be yet another sign that U.S. efforts had failed to wall off Russia's defense industry from Western inputs. (Analog Devices said it had instructed distributors to halt shipments of its products to Russia and doesn't condone their use in Russian military equipment.)

Smuggling rings have been trying to get their hands on critical technology for Russian military and intelligence agencies for years. During the Cold War, the KGB regularly targeted Western companies to improve its ability to produce the microelectronics used to design smaller, lighter, and more powerful computers. As Chris Miller explains in his book *Chip War*, the Soviet Union churned out steel and coal in vast quantities but lagged in advanced manufacturing needed to produce the semiconductors that fueled the U.S.-led technological revolution. In the early 1960s, the KGB set up a new division to lead the effort to try to acquire and copy Western technology called Directorate T, which stood for *teknologia*.

In the fight against the communist bloc, the United States and its allies restricted the export of technologies to the Soviet Union through an organization called the Coordinating Committee for Multilateral Export Controls, or CoCom. Some controls were loosened during détente and tightened again after the Soviet Union invaded Afghanistan in 1979. CoCom barred a wide range of items from being shipped to Soviet satellite states without special licenses, such as computers to East Germany. These measures kept the Eastern bloc technologically backward. By the 1980s, the KGB employed some one thousand people to steal and copy Western technology, but that strategy left the Soviet semiconductor industry constantly trying and failing to catch up with the West. Soviet microprocessors—used in everything from telephone switching systems to computers and radios—lagged half a decade behind the United States.

Following the collapse of the Soviet Union in 1991, the restrictions were relaxed, and CoCom was dissolved as the Russian economy opened up. Still years behind the West's advanced manufacturing expertise, Russia became increasingly reliant on buying components from the United States, Europe, and Japan as Putin embarked on a multibillion-dollar effort to modernize the country's military. Russia turned to Western inputs to produce more sophisticated tanks and cruise and ballistic missiles. In the 1990s and the 2000s, the West considered Moscow a reliable partner that could be brought into the fold of an international export control system. The focus was on nonproliferation to restrict items that could be used in nuclear, chemical, and biological weapons. The easing of the restrictions reflected newfound trust between Washington and Moscow.

After Putin sent his little green men into Crimea and eastern Ukraine, the United States and its allies began imposing restrictions on certain choke-point technologies, such as components needed for shale and arctic oil extraction. They also expanded prohibitions on consumer items if they were going to the Russian military. The moves reversed two decades of openness with Russia, but its defense industry was still able to source the Western components it needed.

When Putin invaded Ukraine in 2022, Washington imposed a blanket ban on the export of a broad swath of U.S. technology—components, tools, and software—to Russia in a bid to degrade its economy and stymie the defense industry, even if the components were made outside the United States. They were the most stringent restrictions ever imposed on a major economy. By some measures, the post-invasion export bans surpassed even Cold War–era constraints. One of the main aims was to hinder Russia's ability to produce the precision-guided weapons that have been so devastating to Ukraine's infrastructure. The rules opened up new possibilities to criminally charge individuals around the world for shipping U.S. know-how to Russia.

Among the many curbs, the augmented rules targeted Russia's ability to service planes, after its airline industry had become increasingly dependent on Boeing and Airbus. That forced the Russian government to advise its airlines to use some planes for spare parts and to ban foreign-owned air-craft from being returned to their owners, stranding around four hundred jets leased to Russian owners in the months following the invasion. Russia's civil aviation gradually began collapsing, with spare parts in short supply and accidents rising.

Cutting Russia off from technology was urgent. Putin's defense and intel-ligence services were figuring out how to circumvent Western restrictions and smuggle crucial components into the country to support Russia's production of precision-guided weapons. Western allies were spending billions on military aid to Ukraine, only to face Russian weaponry made with U.S. semiconductors and electronic circuits. Leaving the trade unchecked meant not just money wasted but lives lost.

The effort to block Russia's access to chips has the hallmarks of an old Cold War–style struggle: Russian intelligence operatives using clandestine networks to get the technological edge. But this time the task is much more complex thanks to Russia's ability to exploit the openness of Western economies. Globalization over the past thirty years has led to an enormous expansion of international trade and the creation of complex supply chains that aren't easy to control. U.S. officials have tried to block technology shipments to third countries such as Kazakhstan, Armenia, and Turkey, which were funneling illicit goods to Russia, but the problem was also homegrown.

* * *

Federal prosecutors in Brooklyn, part of the Eastern District of New York, had been investigating the illicit shipments of Western technology to Russia even before Putin's 2022 invasion. They could see Russian networks trying to use shell companies to buy advanced semiconductors from U.S. companies. When the KleptoCapture task force was set up, it boosted resources to support export control cases: translators, travel, and help to unlock international cooperation. Federal law enforcement officials saw the tech battle as the most important way of degrading Putin's war machine.

B. ayman in New Hampshire was just one thread in a much-larger web spun by Russian intelligence. The ringleader appeared to be a fifty-two-year-old Russian national named Boris Livshits, a former Brooklyn resident living in St. Petersburg. Livshits, an electrical engineer, looks like a Russian gangster out of central casting. His FBI "wanted" notice shows a bald middle-aged man, sporting a black T-shirt, a graying goatee, and a menacing squint.

Starting in 2017, Livshits worked for two Russian companies that supplied the FSB and various arms of the country's defense industry. One was a Moscow company called Serniya Engineering, which kitted out Russia's top security organizations: Rostec, the state-owned defense conglomerate; the Ministry of Defense; the Foreign Intelligence Service; and Directorate T. The other company was Sertal, licensed by the FSB to carry out work using "top-secret level" information. It ran a sprawling procurement network for the intelligence agency, which had been forced to deploy underhanded methods to get the Western components needed for its military-industrial complex as the United States started to erect a new technological Iron Curtain with Russia.

The scheme was breathtaking in its flagrant use of forged documentation and phony companies. Livshits would get orders from two Sertal employees in Russia, who in turn got instructions from an operative at a research institute that was part of Roscosmos, the state space corporation that develops satellites and military spacecraft. Livshits set up an array of companies to place orders with leading technology companies in the United States, from Texas to Illinois and Colorado, and shipped products to Russia through circuitous routes. To disguise the end users, they layered transactions through shell companies and shipped components to fictitious addresses belonging to the Serniya network. Money pinged rapidly from company to company, making it difficult to trace. The Serniya network exploited the U.K.'s lax rules around corporations by establishing two entities in London with Russian directors that channeled payments to U.S. companies controlled by Livshits.

Livshits sometimes operated under the alias David Wetzky to confuse compliance departments; he occasionally broke up large orders into smaller ones to avoid detection. Intermediaries such as Brayman in the United States helped him set up companies, open bank accounts, and ship goods to Europe. Livshits also enlisted the aid of another Russian national, a naturalized U.S. citizen named Vadim Yermolenko, who lived in the wealthy suburban neighborhood of Upper Saddle River, New Jersey, and played a similar role. They allegedly forged invoices and sent some components to Europe or Hong Kong before repackaging items to go to Russia.

The shipments were flowing long before Russia's full-scale invasion of Ukraine. In October 2019, Livshits emailed Brayman about a shipment to Germany with instructions to conceal its origins. "It is necessary to cut off all old labels and remove all invoices and packing lists from the boxes that came with them originally," he wrote. It was a "low noise cesium frequency synthesizer"—used in everything from radars and to telecommunications—that Livshits purportedly bought from a Colorado company for $44,965, using the alias David Wetzky and his company, Strandway LLC, registered at Brayman's home, as the end user. The equipment was subject to U.S. export controls, but the U.S. companies appeared to have done nothing to check who the buyer was.

After the war began, Livshits and Brayman intensified their efforts. In early

March 2022, they agreed they would send items to Russia through Germany "by hook or by crook." By then, the website of Sertal, the FSB contractor, bragged that it supplied semiconductors from Texas Instruments and Analog Devices, among a host of other Western companies. (Texas Instruments said it had no record of sales to Sertal in the past five years, but middlemen could have supplied them. Analog said it has complied with export controls.) On May 9, 2022, less than three months after Russia invaded Ukraine, Brayman shipped a package from his home in New Hampshire to a residence in Hamburg, Germany, labeling it OSCILLOSCOPE—USED, NO WARR [*sic*] and listing the value as $2,482, even though the value was roughly ten times more. (The military uses oscilloscopes to test avionics and radar.) Once again, Livshits had used the alias David Wetzky and his company Strandway LLC as the end user to order the dual-use oscilloscope from a company in Illinois, which shipped it to Brayman's New Hampshire home.

The U.S. government's efforts to tackle the illegal flow of technology was an interagency effort using shared intelligence. While federal prosecutors in Brooklyn were investigating the web around Livshits and Brayman, the U.S. Treasury announced sanctions on the Serniya network at the end of March 2022, revealing an interlocking chain of companies and operatives working globally to facilitate the trades. The disclosure was designed to warn tech companies and telegraph the way suspicious Russian networks operate, in a bid to shut down shipments. One company was struck off the U.K. register, but another, Photon Pro LLP, remained active more than two years after the indictment was unsealed, with Evgeny Grinin, a Russian charged by the United States as part of the scheme, listed as its active director. Its registered address in central London is at a virtual office available for rent for just £39.99 per year—yet another example of the U.K.'s continued failure to prevent London from being used for illicit trades of all kinds.

But Strandway was not on the Treasury's list. It appeared relatively easy for Livshits to fool the technology companies into believing the end user was David Wetzky in New Hampshire. But at times, Livshits got cocky. At the end of April—while the war in Ukraine was raging—he emailed an employee at a Florida-based electronics company that had shipped him a military-grade spectrum analyzer, which measures signals in missiles and defense avionics and can be used for countersurveillance operations. "I've finally received the [spectrum analyzer] I purchased from you in February, here in Russia," he wrote. He went on to complain it hadn't been calibrated correctly. The employee at the Florida company wrote back to say he couldn't speak to him because of the sanctions: "I have been strongly cautioned not to speak with you anymore or have any dealings with your associates in the U.S." Livshits shot back, "I purchased this unit from you not as myself, but as a U.S. company, with U.S. shipping address. Hence this transaction has nothing to do with Russian related sanctions." Whether it was a sense of invincibility or a lack of understanding of export controls, Livshits didn't seem to realize that admitting he was in Russia might raise red flags.

One day in October 2022, as residents in Merrimack, New Hampshire, were preparing for the school run and walked their dogs, federal agents descended on the Braymans' blue-shuttered home with a warrant to seize documents and cell phones. The raid on the Braymans' home unearthed a trail of emails and text messages showing how the Serniya network operated, through companies and operatives stretching from the U.K. to Spain and the Baltics. The search helped propel a global investigation into the vast network of companies operating under the direction of Russia's intelligence services. It became clear that Brayman was connected to a Russian intelligence operation thousands of miles away in Estonia, a country that was more than willing to help the Justice Department.

Brayman was just one spoke in the wheel. Weeks later, Estonian authorities caught Vadim Konoshchenok, a colonel in Russia's FSB, crossing the border into Russia at the city of Narva. With his buzz cut and five-o'clock shadow, forty-eight-year-old Konoshchenok looked every inch the part of an FSB agent. He identified himself in emails as an FSB colonel, used FSB.ru domains, and even shared a picture of himself in uniform. In his car, he had thirty-five kinds of semiconductors and electronic components, including U.S. items banned from export to Russia. Brayman had recently sent a prototype for a circuit board made by a software company in Texas to Konoshchenok at an address in Tallinn, Estonia's capital. Estonian authorities also found, hidden in the FSB colonel's car, thousands of 6.5 mm bullets used as sniper rounds that were manufactured by a company in Nebraska that thought it was shipping them to buyers in Germany, Finland, Luxembourg, and Latvia. He'd been communicating frequently with Livshits about the runs across the border, making it clear his fee was 10 percent: "[c]an't do less. Sanctions. . . . Sanction item for 10%."

A month later, Konoshchenok made another run at the border, this time with twenty cases of U.S.-made bullets, including sniper rounds. The Estonians once again let him go, believing they had another chance to nab him. "Sometimes you let a bad guy be a bad guy for a little bit longer so you can get the bigger catch at the end of the day," one investigator familiar with the case told me. While the Estonians had been keeping the Justice Department in the loop, back in Washington there was a high-level debate over whether to ask the Estonians to arrest and extradite Konoshchenok. Picking up a Russian intelligence officer as part of a U.S. criminal prosecution set off alarm bells in diplomatic circles. After all, the CIA has agents in foreign countries who might be targeted in retribution.

The KleptoCapture task force eventually got the green light from Washington to move against a sensitive international target. In early December 2022, toting guns, FBI squads swooped in to arrest Brayman in New Hampshire and Yermolenko in New Jersey, a jarring experience for two unsuspecting suburban communities. Federal authorities released Brayman and Yermolenko on bail pending a potential trial. The Estonians quickly moved to arrest Konoshchenok. Afterward, they searched a warehouse held in the name of his son and found 375 pounds of ammunition, likely headed straight to the front line in Ukraine. In July 2023, the Estonians extradited the FSB colonel to the United States to stand trial. "Far from the battlefield, Konoshchenok will now face justice in an American courthouse," Adams, the head of the KleptoCapture task force, said when the extradition was announced.

*   *   *

I set out to find Brayman and Yermolenko, the two U.S.-based operatives charged in the case. Could they really be living a quiet suburban life in America while secretly feeding Russian intelligence with Western technology? Were they "useful idiots," credulous foot soldiers recruited to unwittingly advance Putin's war, just out to make a fast buck? Or were they knowingly working for the FSB? I wasn't sure I'd be able to find them, and I was doubtful that they would talk to me, but I needed to give them an opportunity to tell me their side of the story.

I arrived in Upper Saddle River, New Jersey, on a hot day in July 2023 to find Yermolenko's four-bedroom beige home set back behind an overgrown lawn. The leafy neighborhood was just off the state highway, a commuter route into Manhattan. When I knocked, Yermolenko, sporting a beard and a white T-shirt, opened the front door. I saw kids in the background and a baby in the black-tiled foyer. He looked different from the pictures I'd seen. After I introduced myself in Russian, he asked me to come around to the garage at the side of the house. I told him I just wanted to get his side of the story. His first question: "Are you pro-government or antigovernment?" I wasn't sure which government he was talking about, but I figured it was the United States, not Russia. I didn't answer, stressing I just wanted his version of the events. He didn't want to talk on the record without his lawyer's permission, and his lawyer declined to comment on the case. He seemed like a typical East European immigrant, living under the radar in suburban New Jersey.

A month later, I drove to Merrimack, New Hampshire, to look for Brayman. I didn't think he would talk on the record given the criminal case against him, but it was worth a shot. Door-stepping people, as it's called in journalism, is notoriously low-yield work. I wasn't even sure he was still living in the same house he'd used to ship components to the FSB. I walked up the open driveway to the porch and rang the doorbell. I could see a camera above the door pointed at me. I was wearing a flowery summer dress, hoping I didn't look threatening. I rang again, but the house looked dark and quiet on a hot summer's day. I saw an Amazon package addressed to Brayman on the front porch. Thinking maybe the Braymans were out back and couldn't hear the doorbell, I walked to the side of the house, where I could see an empty pool with toys scattered about behind a gate. Ready to give up, I spotted a neighbor outside and began speaking with her. She knew little. "You realize there's a camera pointed at you, right?" she told me. "It's following you."

Brayman suddenly appeared in his driveway, as if from nowhere. "What are you doing?" he barked in English with a Russian accent. I introduced myself as a writer and told him I was researching a book that mentioned his case. I said I just wanted to give him a chance to comment and get his side of the story. His lawyer, I explained, wasn't responding to my messages. Wearing a gray

T-shirt and sunglasses, with his hair cut short, he accused me of trespassing and threatened to call the police and have me arrested. "I'm just trying to do my job," I told him. I had rated my chances of getting him to talk at less than 5 percent, but I certainly didn't think he'd accuse me of trespassing. It was the ultimate irony: a Russian indicted for illegally shipping technology to the FSB invoking U.S. law enforcement to intimidate me.

He didn't appear to be a useful idiot. He had cameras all around the outside of his house and had apparently been filming me talking to his neighbor. I gave him my card and told him to call me if he ever changed his mind and wanted to talk. I approached a handful of people on his street, and a few told me the Braymans didn't mix with others in the neighborhood. Others clearly didn't want to mess with him. "We'd love to talk to you, but we just can't," one friendly couple, standing in their driveway, told me with a knowing smile. It was hardly surprising. If I thought that someone on my street might be working with the FSB, I wouldn't want to talk about them either. Almost a year after my visit to New Hampshire, Brayman, Yermolenko, and Konoshchenok were continuing to fight the charges, another drawn-out legal battle sparked by Russia's invasion.

*　　　　*　　　　*

U.S. efforts to shut down Russian networks to procure technology faced unexpected resistance. Even with the largest land battle raging on the Continent since the Second World War, European authorities sometimes frustrated U.S. efforts to prosecute sanctions evaders. The United States and Europe had embarked on an unprecedented level of cooperation and synchronized sanctions, but they didn't always share the same will to pursue targets. The differences between the American and European legal systems were one factor, but U.S. prosecutors would sometimes build an indictment only to see their suspect in Europe slip through the net on some technicality or merely because of a lack of attention. As a consequence, Russia was able to continue feeding its war machine.

One case in particular came to symbolize the reluctance of European law enforcement to crack down on Russian illicit activity in their backyard. As the U.S. Attorney's office in Brooklyn began investigating the illegal export of technology to Russia, it wasn't just focused on the Serniya network. Prosecutors were also following two Russians in Europe allegedly shipping sensitive dual-use components from the United States to Russia, hiding their tracks by using a network of shell companies. One of the men under investigation was Artem Uss, the forty-year-old son of a former governor who was a member of Putin's United Russia party. He was politically connected by virtue of his father's links to the Kremlin. With a brown beard and shaggy brown hair, Uss operated from Italy, where he owned a home in an exclusive part of Milan, a stake in a luxury hotel in Sardinia, and a vineyard. His business partner was Yuri Orekhov, a Russian national who lived in the UAE and the German port city Hamburg. They were buying advanced semiconductors and microprocessors used in fighter aircraft, missile systems, and smart munitions from U.S. manufacturers and shipping them to Russia.

When placing orders, they claimed the end user was a Malaysian company called NDA Aerospace. In reality, it was just a shell. Other businesses occupied addresses for the company, and one consisted of an empty room in a Malaysian strip mall. In fact, federal prosecutors believed Uss and Orekhov were running a much-broader international smuggling and money-laundering operation under the noses of German authorities. They weren't just funneling sensitive dual-use technologies to Russia, they were also smuggling embargoed oil from Venezuela to Russia. They used a German company to buy $32 million in fuel oil from Venezuela in breach of sanctions, channeling funds through the U.S. financial system and processing the transactions in dollars. Because the Venezuelan state oil company was under U.S. sanctions, its crude was being sold at a discount to the world price, allowing for a sizeable profit margin. They allegedly used the German company as a front for Deripaska, the metals billionaire, to source cheap oil for his aluminum empire. Yet again, U.S. law enforcement had found evidence of Deripaska apparently involved in sanctions violations.

By October 2022, federal prosecutors in Brooklyn had enough evidence to ask Italian and German authorities to arrest and extradite the pair to the United States. Germany arrested Orekhov in Hamburg, while Italian police arrested Uss at the airport in Milan on his way to Istanbul. The U.S. Attorney for the Eastern District announced their arrest by describing them as "criminal enablers of oligarchs." The Germans kept Orekhov in custody, but Italian judges ignored the U.S. request to keep Uss in prison awaiting extradition. Italy's overextended justice system is known for letting criminal cases drag on for years, so it often lets defendants avoid jail while awaiting trial. The next month, a court in Milan allowed Uss to leave prison and go under house arrest at his home on the outskirts of Milan with an ankle bracelet.

Justice Department officials were exasperated, knowing Uss was a flight risk. "Anyone who has ever dealt with an ankle monitor system knows it's roughly worth the battery that's in the thing," said one person familiar with the case. The DOJ wrote letters to Italy's Justice Ministry explaining why Uss was a high-value asset for Russia who was likely to flee. He held a senior position at a subsidiary of state-controlled Rosneft, which was also under sanctions. Putin had appointed his father, Alexander Uss, as acting governor of the oil-rich region of Krasnoyarsk Krai in Siberia in 2017, setting him up to win an election the following year. Italian prosecutors didn't challenge the court's decision to let him go under house arrest. The Italian Justice Ministry could have requested Uss remain in prison awaiting extradition, but it didn't.

Italian police checked on Uss regularly but weren't parked outside his house 24-7. Uss soon began plotting his escape. In January, he hired a gang based in Serbia affiliated with organized crime to get him out if the Italian court approved his extradition to the United States. The group's leader was a fifty-two-year-old Bosnian national named Vladimir Jovancic. Their plan resembled the outline of a bad Hollywood script. Jovancic met Uss's wife at a hotel in Milan, where she gave him a cell phone and a 10,000 euro deposit for his efforts. The Bosnian would secretly help Uss escape by pretending to deliver groceries to their home. She later gave him a key card to enter their home directly.

In March, an Italian judge approved the U.S. extradition order for Uss, who faced up to thirty years in a U.S. prison. But instead of moving him into an Italian jail cell to await extradition, the Italians let him stay under house arrest. The next day, Uss launched his elaborate getaway. The Serbian gang arrived, stuffed Uss into a car, and gave him bolt cutters to snap off his ankle monitor, which he threw out the window.

By the time Italian authorities received an alert from Uss's ankle monitor, he was gone. The Serbians sped him out of Italy with a fake passport, crossing into Slovenia, Croatia, and Bosnia before eventually arriving in Serbia, a Slavic nation that retains friendly relations with Russia. From there, Uss flew on to

Russia. There was widespread speculation that Russian intelligence operatives were involved, given his father's Kremlin connections, but the lax conditions of his house arrest meant he didn't need a sophisticated operation to extract him.

"I'm in Russia!" he announced after his escape. "In the past few particularly dramatic days, I had strong and reliable people by my side." He said he was forced to escape because he didn't believe he could get a fair trial in the United States. His father personally thanked Putin for assisting his son's return: "Special words of gratitude go out to our president. He is not just the head of our state, he is a man with a big and open heart."

U.S. prosecutors were "apoplectic" at Uss's escape. For Italy, it was an embarrassing episode. Italy's prime minister, Giorgia Meloni, a vocal supporter of Ukraine, called the decision to keep him under house arrest an "anomaly," especially after the ruling to extradite him. The Justice Department demanded a probe into what had happened and began pressing Italian officials on more than a dozen pending requests for cooperation on other Russia-related sanctions cases to which they had yet to respond. Italy's justice minister began an investigation of the judges, while the government froze Uss's assets. The U.S. Justice Department indicted Jovancic, who earned 50,000 euros for the extraction, but he resided in Serbia. Meanwhile, the United States offered a $7 million reward for information leading to Uss's arrest. "We are not giving up," David Lim, the new cohead of the Justice Department's KleptoCapture task force, told me. "We will continue to pursue him. It may not be a lot of money to the son of a Russian oligarch, but it certainly is a lot of money to people out there who know his whereabouts."

Meanwhile, Germany let his partner, Orekhov, go after a court in Hamburg blocked his extradition; Orekhov is now reportedly living in Dubai, alongside hundreds of other Russians escaping sanctions. "We knew from the get-go there would be challenges and setbacks," Lim told me. "That's just the reality when you're dealing with different types of legal systems."

*   *   *

The Kremlin is acutely aware of its dependence on Western technology. In the run-up to the full-scale invasion in February 2022, Russia was building up enormous stockpiles of weapons and microelectronics, clearly planning for the war against Ukraine. Russian imports of critical components surged at the end of 2021, only to fall sharply as sanctions began to bite in the months following the invasion. By the end of 2022, Russia's imports of these components recovered, a sign it had succeeded in finding alternative routes. Mainland China and Hong Kong together accounted for 87 percent of Russian semiconductor imports in the last three months of 2022, up from just 33 percent in 2021. Those semiconductors were not all produced in China but were shipped through Chinese and Hong Kong intermediaries.

Russia's ability to backfill from China and exploit loopholes in the global supply chain for sophisticated technology was no accident. It was a strategy led from the very top. Just weeks before the full-scale invasion in 2022, Putin traveled to Beijing for the Olympics, where he agreed with Chinese president Xi on a "no limits" partnership. "There are no 'forbidden' areas of cooperation," they agreed. In early September 2022, as Chinese intermediaries were funneling semiconductors to Russia, Putin trumpeted this anti-Western alliance in the Far Eastern Russian city of Vladivostok, where he presided over an annual economic forum focusing on his country's ties to the Asia-Pacific region. Dressed in a dark suit, looking characteristically puffy faced, Putin stood for thirty-five minutes giving a defiant speech bashing the West for declaring economic war on Russia with its "frenzy" of sanctions. "We have not lost anything, nor will we lose anything," he said. The West will be the real loser, he declared. He went on to herald Russia as the champion of a new fast-growing Asia-Pacific alliance, with China at its center, that "rejects the destructive logic of sanctions."

At that point, Russia's losses already were enormous as it fought a grinding war of attrition in Ukraine. Tens of thousands of Russian soldiers had been killed or injured, and the military was burning through stores of tanks and missiles. Russia started the full-scale invasion with almost 3,000 main battle tanks, but by April 2024 it had lost more than 2,900, according to estimates from Oryx, an open-source research group. The losses forced the Kremlin to pull older Soviet-era tanks from storage for refurbishment, but often without advanced targeting systems because of export controls and sanctions. Defense Minister Sergei Shoigu announced that Russian ground forces received more than 1,500 new and upgraded tanks in 2023. According to estimates from the International Institute of Strategic Studies, roughly 1,200 of those were old, repaired tanks delivered with the most basic domestically produced thermal imaging systems because of Russia's difficulty sourcing Western components.

Russia was prioritizing other weapons systems that are more reliant on sophisticated Western technology. It had been churning through its stockpiles of long-range missiles with relentless attacks on Ukraine's military, civilian, and energy infrastructure. The sheer scale of the assault was staggering. By the end of 2023, Russia had fired 7,400 missiles into Ukraine since the start of the invasion. In the first three months of 2024, it unleashed another 1,000 missiles. Russia's Defense Ministry said it had received more than 1,400 missiles during 2023, a sign that the military-industrial complex was still humming but not at a replacement rate that could keep up with the Kremlin's persistent attacks. It wasn't clear if those missiles were simply reconditioned old stock or new missiles. Russia's production volumes, if the figures are to be believed, won't allow the Kremlin to return to pre-invasion stocks. Sanctions and export controls were hindering, but not completely stopping, Russia's ability to produce advanced missiles such as the Kh-101, along with hundreds of domestically made military drones that rely on Western electronics and cameras. The head of Russia's Tactical Missiles Corporation (KTRV) said in January 2023 he was actively looking for substitute imports because of sanctions. By September 2023, he claimed to have doubled the production of precision weapons. But labor shortages—from mobilization, frontline casualties, and the brain drain—are further hampering Russia's military production.

According to a U.S. intelligence assessment, it will take Russia up to ten years to rebuild its military capability given the drawn-out war and export controls. Other Western officials believe Russia's army has been set back twenty to thirty years. While Russia had managed to get around the restrictions to import semiconductors and other components from the West, the country's defense manufacturers couldn't keep up with the demand from the front. As a result, the Kremlin turned to Pyongyang in early 2024 for supplies of ballistic missiles, an allegation the Kremlin has denied despite evidence of North Korean missiles being found on the battlefield in Ukraine.

Partly because of export controls, Russia has turned to other autocracies—China and Iran—for supplies. China's Da-Jiang Innovations (DJI) supplied

Russia with millions of dollars worth of commercial drones through intermediaries, while Iran began sending combat drones in late 2022 that have been
used to attack both civilian and military targets across Ukraine.

The Kremlin's ability to source and produce drones on a massive scale
has allowed it to terrorize Ukrainian civilians. At the end of 2023, Moscow had
launched 3,700 Shahed drones since the war began, and stepped up the drone
attacks in early 2024. Aware of Russia's dependence on Western technology,
Putin announced in April 2023 a plan to invest 1 trillion rubles ($11 billion)
into developing domestic drones without foreign components. Russia began
to mass-produce Iranian Shahed-136 kamikaze drones at a new factory in
Alabuga, Tatarstan, a republic about six hundred miles east of Moscow.
Russia agreed to pay Iran $1.6 billion to build six thousand Shahed-136
drones under license through 2025, according to hacked documents leaked
by the Prana network. There were apparent delays getting the factory up and
running. Iranian drones rely heavily on Western electronic inputs made by
companies such as Texas Instruments and Analog Devices procured through
countries not subject to sanctions. Even with Putin's push to produce components domestically, Russia will have to continue playing elaborate games
to circumvent the restrictions.

Russia's ability to find third-party intermediaries in China, Turkey, and
the UAE to supply crucial microchips has revealed the leakiness of the West's
economic war. Moscow was able to increase its imported supply of microprocessors and semiconductors to $2.45 billion in 2022, up from $1.82 billion the
previous year. Turkey's exports to Russia surged 61 percent in 2022. Even the
tiny island state of the Maldives in the Indian Ocean, known for its luxury
resorts, got in on the action, shipping four hundred thousand U.S.-made
semiconductors worth almost $54 million to Russia in the year after the
invasion, making it one of Moscow's biggest suppliers, according to Nikkei
Asia. By 2023, China was playing the central role of supplying Russia with
the microelectronics needed for weapons production, with overall trade
between the two countries soaring to a record $240 billion. Still, Russia often
struggled to source advanced optical systems, bearings, engines, and machine
tools for the defense industry—a sign the export controls are at least making
it harder for Russia to rearm. But enforcement has turned into a cloak-and-
dagger chase, with new companies cropping up all the time to facilitate trade.

*   *   *

Biden's national security adviser, Jake Sullivan, likes to talk about America's asymmetric advantage of being a magnet for the world's top technical talent, unlike Russia, which has suffered from an outflow of skilled workers. Clamping down on Russia's access to technology turned into one of the most crucial fronts in the economic war. "Technology export controls can be more than just a preventative tool," Sullivan explained. "They can be a new strategic asset in the U.S. and allied tool kit to impose costs on adversaries, and even over time degrade their battlefield capabilities."

But the Kremlin's strategy of trying to duck U.S. export controls by running these kinds of illicit networks quickly turned into a never-ending game of Whac-A-Mole for U.S. law enforcement. While prosecutors in Brooklyn led many criminal probes, the strategic command post of this new war is a rather obscure U.S. federal department called the Bureau of Industry and Security, or BIS. It's housed in the Commerce Department's Herbert Hoover headquarters in Washington, a sprawling building that's the length of three football fields with a maze of long dark corridors and art deco elevator doors. BIS is one of the smallest bureaus within Commerce, with only around 350 agents and officers to track trillions of dollars worth of transactions worldwide.

If there were ever a sign of a return to a Cold War footing, it's at BIS. Before the fall of the Berlin Wall, strict export controls to the Communist bloc gave the Commerce Department a largely administrative role denying technology exports as part of a broad strategy to counter the Soviet Union. After the collapse of communism, the bureau was considered a regulatory backwater, torn between protecting national security and promoting U.S. business abroad. Historically, it tended to side with industry.

"The scope of the controls and the items restricted now are far broader than they were during the Cold War," Kevin Wolf, the assistant secretary of commerce for export administration under Obama, told me. "Back then, there was a strategic containment objective. The urgency of the current controls is different. Now there's a specific catalyzing event."

With the rise of China, and Russia's invasion of Ukraine, BIS turned into a central tool of the Biden administration's economic war against Putin. Just as it used the power and reach of the U.S. dollar to enforce sanctions, Washington is now weaponizing the dominance of U.S. technology. The United States has gone further than ever before to prohibit companies anywhere in the world from selling products to Russia if they're made with U.S. semiconductors or machinery. The curbs, known as the Foreign Direct Product Rule (FDPR), were used by Trump to block Huawei from accessing American technology because of concerns that the Chinese telecoms giant threatened U.S. national security.

For the first time, the Commerce Department used the rule against an entire country's economy, restricting an extensive class of technologies from going to Russia. The export controls were so broad that even sunglasses got added to the list of restricted items. Because of the ubiquity of U.S. software or machinery at chip factories globally, the FDPR allows the United States to assert jurisdiction over almost every semiconductor globally. If just one piece of U.S. equipment is involved—even if 99 percent of the inputs are foreign—Washington claims the right to block it from going to Russia. BIS rules would ban, for instance, a company in Malaysia from shipping anything made with any U.S. software or testing equipment to Russia. Some companies are trying to come up with designs that don't need U.S. inputs to avoid being subject to U.S. export controls.

But compelling companies all around the world to follow those controls has proved incredibly difficult. The semiconductor industry produces roughly 1 trillion chips every year, using a complex global supply chain. Chips are ubiquitous, found in everything from washing machines to televisions and weapons systems. Most semiconductors are designed in the United States but produced and packaged overseas before going for testing and snaking their way through daisy chains of distribution companies. As a result, U.S. export controls rely on customs officials in third countries, who are more often used to checking what's coming into their countries, not what's going out.

The head of enforcement at BIS is Matthew Axelrod, a Yale Law School grad who was a top DOJ official working for then acting attorney general Sally Yates during the Obama administration. He joined BIS right before Putin's invasion, putting him on the front line of the economic war against Russia. At Commerce, Axelrod's office looks as if it hasn't been remodeled since the Cold War; the furniture has a distinctly 1980s vibe. On the wall is a photograph of him with Yates in a helicopter from a few years back (he declined to say where they were going). Axelrod cut his teeth as a federal prosecutor in Florida, where he prosecuted Colombian drug cartels. At Commerce, Axelrod can impose civil penalties on companies for violating the restrictions, but a lot of his work involves supporting the Justice Department's efforts to bring criminal charges against middlemen squirreling products to Russia.

It might seem like an odd career path, from top Justice Department official to a little-known corner of Commerce, but Axelrod views his job to keep sensitive technology out of dangerous hands as the single most important fight facing the United States. "Our tools are at the center of the most pressing national security issues of our time," Axelrod told me. "The use of export controls has been unprecedented."

For all his expertise, Axelrod looks outgunned compared to Russia's ability to bypass Commerce's restrictions. Washington spearheaded the formation of a coalition of almost forty countries that have banded together to adopt similar export controls to respond to Russia's full-scale invasion in an attempt to plug the leaks. It was the first time since the collapse of the communist bloc that a group of allies came together to impose restrictions on a specific country outside the post–Cold War nonproliferation regime.

But for some weapons, Russia's defense industry doesn't need sophisticated chips and can use components harvested from home appliances. Ukrainian officials told Commerce Secretary Gina Raimondo in 2022 that they found Western semiconductors stripped from dishwashers and refrigerators in Russian tanks they captured on the battlefield. Trade data revealed suspicious patterns with even low-grade equipment thought to be cannibalized for the defense industry. The EU's exports of electric breast pumps—many powered with semiconductors—to Armenia, for instance, nearly tripled in the first half of 2022 compared to the previous year, Bloomberg reported. Kazakhstan's imports of electric breast pumps from the EU surged more than 600 percent in the same period.

Busting Russian procurement networks requires the painstaking investigative work of digging deep into the Russian cutouts that keep popping up. Lim, the new cohead of KleptoCapture, stressed the importance of going after middlemen even as Russian entities are constantly mutating. "These are highly complex and sophisticated networks," he told me. "By picking them off, will they be replaced by somebody else? It's possible. But it will take time to replace the skillset, connections and knowledge they possess at a level that will meet the demands of the Russian government."

One of the biggest challenges is stopping the flow of technology through Hong Kong and China. The trade is huge and cooperation is scant, but Washington managed to shut down one notable front operation. Working with the FBI and the Commerce Department, the Justice Department arrested a Russian national, Maxim Marchenko, in Hong Kong in September 2023 for creating a clutch of shell companies to purchase military-grade microelectronics from a company in New York State that had stopped all trade with Russia after the war began. The companies claimed the microdisplays were going to end users in China for "medical research," when in reality the devices were going to Russia. An unidentified Russian national posed as a fictitious woman named Amy Chan to communicate with the U.S. company and throw them off the scent. From May 2022 to August 2023, Marchenko funneled $1.6 million to the United States to buy the microdisplays, which could be used for everything from rifle scopes to thermal optics. He was charged with multiple counts of fraud and money laundering. Even though Marchenko was caught, the damage was done: Russia had gotten millions of dollars of equipment to power its war effort, and new shell companies to facilitate the trade likely took over to do it all over again.

In this long, drawn-out fight, the chances of having a meaningful impact depend at least partly on resources: more money and people would help. The 2024 budget for BIS was $191 million, unchanged from 2023 and hardly enough to turn it into the critical hub to fight a new Cold War in technology. Front companies are constantly shape-shifting to facilitate the trade. Axelrod's team is conducting more checks around the world than ever before, but it's like trying to stamp out a cockroach infestation. In April 2023, Axelrod traveled to Kazakhstan and Kyrgyzstan, two countries that have been major transshipment points, to warn them that companies there would face U.S. sanctions if the trade didn't stop. By the end of the year, exports of sensitive technology from those two countries to Russia had dropped significantly. The scope for smuggling continued to narrow. In November, the UAE agreed to restrict the re-export of senstive goods for Russia's military. At the end of 2023, Biden issued an executive order threatening sanctions on banks that facilitate the trade of goods with Russia's military industry, which spooked the financial industry from Central Asia to Turkey and the UAE, causing trade to fall further. No bank wants to get cut off from the U.S. dollar.

But no major Western technology company has been held accountable for violating export controls, despite their components being found in Russian weapons recovered in Ukraine. The question now is whether major tech companies should be ordered to thoroughly vet their supply chains the way banks are required to police their money flows. Companies argue that diversions of their products to Russia are unauthorized, and they are monitoring their sales networks. At the same time, the semiconductor industry argues it's impossible to police such a vast, $600 billion global market. In reality, it's convenient for the industry to not have visibility into their supply chain; unless a company knowingly sells to a banned end user, it can't be held legally liable.

Whether the United States and its allies can succeed in denying Russia access to Western components could determine whether Putin wins on the battlefield in Ukraine. Axelrod sees the battle to control the export of American technology as the inevitable evolution of the threats facing the United States. "Twenty years ago, the primary national security threat was terrorism, and our role in that fight involved preventing U.S. parts from going into IEDs" he told me. "But now the primary threat comes from state actors who are trying to obtain advanced U.S. technology to modernize their military. We're in the midst of a shift in recognition of the power and importance of export controls." Tech giants may finally be forced to wake up to this new reality and figure out ways to make sure their products don't end up in Russian weapons. But other Western companies with business in Russia faced a more immediate choice: whether to continue doing business under Putin's rule or get out, leaving billions on the table.

CHAPTER 7

CORPORATE HOSTAGES

Pressure on Western companies to leave Russia began mounting as soon as Putin's troops crossed the border into Ukraine. Outraged by the images of attacks on civilians across Ukraine, consumers quickly took to social media, threatening to boycott companies that continued doing business under Putin's regime. Just days after the invasion, a poll found three out of four Americans wanted corporations to cut ties with Russia.

Thousands of Western companies with operations in Russia had to quickly decide whether to stay or go, relinquishing billions of dollars of investment built up over decades. In a flurry of video calls and C-suite huddles, executives had to weigh the reputational risk of staying and being seen to indirectly help fund the war. In the first week, a parade of global brands announced plans to withdraw, suspend operations, or temporarily close stores in Russia, from consumer giants such as IKEA and Nike to oil majors BP and Shell.

But at first, the biggest symbol of American capitalism—McDonald's—carried on with business as usual. It had blazed the trail for countless other Western companies in Russia ever since opening its first restaurant in Moscow in 1990 in what was a powerful symbol of the easing of Cold War tensions. In the days after the invasion, McDonald's shut restaurants in Ukraine but kept its Russian operations going.

CEO Chris Kempczinski, a clean-cut Harvard Business School grad, was initially slow to react to the realities of continuing to do business in Russia. In early March 2022, McDonald's top global executives gathered for their annual meeting in Cascais, a chic coastal resort town in Portugal just west of Lisbon. An anxious Oleg Paroev, the newly appointed CEO of McDonald's Russia, asked Kempczinski and CFO Kevin Ozan if the company was considering leaving Russia or suspending operations. "They both looked at me and said, 'Are you insane? Do you think we would ever exit Russia? Of course not,'" Paroev told me. The stakes were enormous. The company directly owned almost all its 850 restaurants in Russia—only about 15 percent were franchised. It employed sixty-two thousand people in Russia; another one hundred thousand worked for McDonald's local supply chain companies. Russia accounted for around 7 percent of the burger chain's global revenue, or roughly $1.6 billion. McDonald's had a vast network of physical assets in the country.

But public pressure on companies to leave Russia was building. McDonald's announced financial support for Ukraine, but its decision to remain silent on operations in Russia led #BoycottMcDonalds to start trending on social media. The outcry was impossible to ignore. On March 7, 2022, Jeffrey Sonnenfeld, a Yale professor, wrote a column in *Fortune* and appeared on CNBC, calling it disappointing that McDonald's remained in Russia. The next day, Kempczinski emailed the company's employees and franchisees announcing it would temporarily close all its Russian restaurants. Kempczinski said McDonald's would continue to pay employees as well as leases on restaurant sites. He cited the motto of the legendary former McDonald's CEO Fred Turner, who was responsible for launching the company's global expansion: "Do the right thing."

Back in Moscow, Paroev was shocked, having been reassured by Kempczinski just days earlier that the company would continue with business as usual. "We had no idea what was going to happen to the business, whether it would stay suspended or whether it would be completely shut down," he told me. The McDonald's announcement left more than a hundred thousand jobs in limbo. Whether the restaurants reopened or not, there would be a massive price to pay.

*   *   *

McDonald's foothold in Russia was the product of fourteen years of schmoozing the Soviet elite by the late American-born Canadian businessman George

Cohon. His ancestors had fled Ukraine in the pogroms of 1906, so he had a connection to the region, and he became captivated by the idea of starting a McDonald's in Russia after meeting a Soviet delegation visiting Montreal for the 1976 Olympics. He'd lent the Canadian government a bus for the group and managed to steer them to a nearby McDonald's, where he fed them Big Macs, fries, and milkshakes. They were astonished. He realized the USSR was a vast untapped market. "Their diet is largely made up of meat, bread, potatoes, and milk," he recalled in his memoir, *To Russia with Fries*. "McDonald's provides meat, bread, potatoes and milk of the highest quality. At an affordable price."

After countless fruitless trips to Russia, Cohon finally clinched a deal in 1988 after Gorbachev allowed joint ventures with foreign partners as part of *perestroika*, the Soviet leader's restructuring reforms. The deal, struck with the City of Moscow, was to open a single restaurant in an old café on Pushkin Square just north of the Kremlin. The most iconic American brand opening up a gleaming new restaurant in the Soviet Union symbolized warming relations between Washington and Moscow. The only other Western consumer brand in the Soviet Union was Pepsi, which had been selling its soda since 1973 in partnership with the communist government.

The first golden arches in Russia went up in January 1990. It was a Herculean project: Russia didn't produce the large potatoes required for french fries or enough high-quality beef for hamburgers, let alone any of the processing facilities designed to provide a steady stream of supplies. Initially, Cohon had to import 80 percent of the restaurant's ingredients because the Soviet Union's agricultural and logistics systems couldn't cope. McDonald's started importing potato seeds from the Netherlands and taught farmers how to raise cattle for its hamburgers. Cohon also built a new processing center called the McComplex, located on the edge of Moscow, at a cost of $21 million. The McComplex produced everything from the Big Mac sauce to sesame buns and hamburger patties. Building a supply chain from scratch in the Soviet Union had never before been done, and McDonald's encouraged others to follow suit.

The interest in this symbol of the West was off the charts. When McDonald's advertised to hire 630 people, it got 27,000 applications. The first day it opened, McDonald's served thirty thousand people and stayed open until after midnight. Long lines of people had waited from the early-morning hours in the freezing snow, eager for a taste of the West. The restaurant proudly hung a sign out front that said RUBLES ONLY, in stark contrast to the stores that had popped up in Moscow offering Western goods for the Soviet elite in "hard currency only." The opening came to symbolize Gorbachev's reforms. "Many people talk about *perestroika*, but for them *perestroika* is an abstraction," Khamzat Khasbulatov, McDonald's Russian manager at the time, told a TV crew on the opening day. "Now me, I can touch my *perestroika*. I can taste my *perestroika*. Big Mac is *perestroika*." Cohon celebrated that evening at a gala party with champagne in St. George's Hall in the Kremlin.

McDonald's success in expanding in Russia distinguished it from its competitors, some of whom initially struggled. By 2010, twenty years after its first opening, McDonald's had 235 restaurants in Russia and was rapidly growing. It flourished in part because it invested in developing local supply chains and retained direct control over the vast majority of its restaurants instead of turning them into franchises, a strategy that left some other fast-food outlets vulnerable to shakedowns by Russian organized crime. The first sign of trouble came in 2014 when Putin annexed Crimea and Washington began imposing pinprick sanctions on Russia, prompting a political backlash. Russian authorities temporarily shuttered a dozen McDonald's restaurants, including the Moscow flagship. Putin retaliated against the sanctions by banning imports of food such as meat and dairy products from Western countries. By then, the company was already sourcing most of its ingredients locally, so the impact was minimal. In 2019, the company accelerated its expansion plans in Russia, vowing to increase investment by 40 percent and open sixty new restaurants.

When the war began and McDonald's executives began deliberating whether to stay or go, they conferred with that other symbol of American capitalism: the Coca-Cola Co. The two companies have been closely aligned globally for decades, helping each other grow their worldwide footprint, including in Russia, where McDonald's sold Coke products. After watching Cohon battle it out to open the first McDonald's in Russia, his son, Craig, then a young executive at Coca-Cola Co., persuaded the board to invest millions to build the first Coke factory in the Soviet Union and dislodge rival Pepsi. At the end of 1991, he broke ground on the first Coca-Cola factory in the Soviet Union, a week before the collapse of the USSR. Unlike Pepsi, Coca-Cola didn't partner with the government. "We had total ownership and lease on the land for the first time," Craig told me. "Once we built the first factory, then we had all the bottlers from around the world come in and say, 'Wow, you could actually do this.' That's when it really exploded." Coke soon surpassed Pepsi as the most popular brand in Russia. In 2021, Coca-Cola sold more than 2 billion liters of branded soft drinks in Russia. In the post–Cold War consumer battle for dominance, Coke had won.

Putin's invasion of Ukraine put an end to that legacy. Senior U.S. officials were telling McDonald's and Coca-Cola that they should leave Russia. Executives at both companies were soon on the phone strategizing how to respond to make sure that they—the biggest American brands in Russia—were on the same page. On March 8, 2022, McDonald's and Coca-Cola Co. each announced they were suspending their business in the country. News of McDonald's decision to close restaurants created havoc. Long lines formed at outlets around the country, including cars backed up to get into a drive-through McDonald's in Moscow. Some Russians started hoarding burgers. One man stuffed his refrigerator with more than fifty burgers, displaying the image on Reddit. When Paroev ordered all McDonald's restaurants in Russia to close, some franchisees refused to shut.

McDonald's was hemorrhaging money from the shutdown, but executives indicated they thought they could reopen. CFO Ozan told an investor conference in March that staying closed would cost $50 million a month. "We expect this to be temporary," Ozan said. "We think it's the right thing to do, both for the global business and for our people locally." But as the weeks passed and the war intensified, more Western companies said they planned to leave Russia or suspend operations.

It soon became clear to McDonald's executives that the Western sanctions would make it difficult to keep operating in Russia. The United States had put full blocking sanctions on Sberbank, due to take effect on March 26, 2022, which barred U.S. citizens from dealing directly or indirectly with Russia's largest bank. Payroll suddenly became questionable. Most McDonald's employees had personal accounts at Sberbank, which was often the only bank in town in rural areas. That made it extremely difficult, although not impossible, for McDonald's to continue.

Then, in early April, just days after the massacre in Bucha came to light, the Biden administration banned new investment in Russia and prohibited the supply of services "by a U.S. person, wherever located." It was a purposefully ambiguous move designed to cause companies to exit Russia, and it worked. Global executives with businesses in Russia panicked. "The investment restrictions were about methodically ejecting Russia from the international economic order, which included multinational companies," Daleep Singh, Biden's sanctions architect, told me.

Not long after the April investment ban, Kempczinski and the McDonald's board concluded it was game over. They decided to take the radical step of selling the Russian operations outright. "For the first time in our history, we are 'de-Arching' a major market and selling our portfolio of McDonald's restaurants," Kempczinski wrote in an email to employees and suppliers worldwide. "The Golden Arches will shine no more in Russia." The "de-Arching process" spelled the end of an era, a hugely symbolic move that encapsulated the reversal of more than three decades of Western investment into Russia. It was a sign that business with Russia would never again be the same.

Watching Putin destroy so many lives along with the corporate legacy of both companies in Russia wasn't easy for the Cohons, father and son. "One side of the family is from Ukraine, the other side is from Russia," Craig told me. "As an executive who spent his life on burger diplomacy, my dad was very, very upset by the war. I feel sad. It was a hopeful era. But that era is now over. I do think Coca-Cola had to make the decision to leave. It's the right decision."

McDonald's had the contours of an exit path mapped out. Even before the war, the company had decided it wanted to sell down directly owned restaurants in Russia and expand the number of franchises to bring it more in line with how McDonald's operates in other countries. Executives had already drawn up a short list of prospective buyers of the outlets as they contemplated selling out to franchisees. In early May, McDonald's executives flew to Dubai to meet with a handful of Russian bidders. The Gulf financial center was one of the few cities where Russians could travel with ease, making it a natural venue to hammer out a deal. The company ensured the contenders stayed at different hotels to prevent them from bumping into one another.

Among the interested buyers was a thickset, gray-haired former coal miner and entrepreneur named Alexander Govor, one of McDonald's rebellious franchisees. Govor had operated twenty-five restaurants in Siberia and defiantly remained open during the closures. The talks with Govor lasted hours. On May 9, McDonald's executives in Chicago held a video call with Govor in Siberia, telling him he'd won and they'd decided to "entrust" him with the business. Govor said he'd paid a "token fee" that was "well below the market" for the business in a deal that required him to retain all sixty-two thousand staff for two years. The contract gave McDonald's the right to buy back the business within fifteen years on market terms. It prevented Govor from using the McDonald's name, logo, colors, and menu, but the rest of the terms remained undisclosed. McDonald's said it would take a charge of as much as $1.4 billion to exit Russia, a sign it was unlikely to have taken much money from the deal. The fire sale had made one wealthy Russian businessman even richer overnight.

In late May 2022 at a branch outside Moscow, a large crane helped lower the giant M onto the parking lot. This was repeated at over eight hundred restaurants across the country, where the legendary golden arches were taken down, recycled, crushed, and thrown away. "Everything that could remind anybody of McDonald's had to be destroyed," Paroev told me. Elaborate efforts got underway to erase the McDonald's brand or logo, with sandpaper even deployed to remove the name from food trays and black markers to cover up the M on stockpiles of ketchup packets.

At the suggestion of the Russian Ministry of Industry and Trade, Govor scheduled the reopening of the still-unnamed flagship restaurant on Pushkin Square and more than a dozen others on June 12. That happened to coincide with Russia Day, a national holiday marking the anniversary of Russia's declaration of autonomy from the USSR. The timing of the relaunch was designed to display Russia's ability to not just withstand but thrive in the face of international sanctions and the exodus of Western companies. Ministries fast-tracked the paperwork to get the new business up and running on time. On the eve of the reopening, the new name was still a mystery. Some were hoping it would be called McDuck, the nickname Russians use for McDonald's, while Govor dismissed a suggestion to rebrand as McGovor as "immodest." In reality, they couldn't use Mc-anything. They had to run the proposed names and new packaging by McDonald's to make sure it didn't compromise their agreement. McDonald's rejected around twenty suggested names, Paroev told me.

At the last minute, Govor finally decided to rebrand as Vkusno i tochka, which means "Tasty and that's it," replacing the golden arches with a new logo—two lines and a circle meant to symbolize fries and a burger. Some Russians hated the new name, but the opening was a major event. With a new menu, Paroev boasted they'd sold 120,000 burgers on opening day, claiming better sales than McDonald's had ever achieved, driven by pent-up demand and curiosity. But within a month, Vkusno started running out of french fries at some restaurants, citing import restrictions in the wake of the invasion and a poor potato harvest in Russia. Parts of McDonald's supply chain were owned by foreign businesses, which were also frantically trying to get out after the invasion. A U.S.-Dutch joint venture producing fries sold out to a local investor, who refused to work with Vkusno.

Perversely, the exodus forced Russians to be more self-reliant. "Those things which were imported or where Russia was very much dependent on foreign technologies now will be replaced with Russian solutions," Paroev told me. To ensure a smooth-running operation, Govor bought out the Russian business of the U.S. logistics company Havi, which had supplied McDonald's with food. Govor borrowed from state-controlled Sberbank to buy the Russian operation of the Finnish paper company Huhtamaki, for 150 million euros, which produced the chain's packaging.

After some initial hiccups, the fries soon returned, and Vkusno boasted that 99 percent of the ingredients were Russian. Govor replaced the Big Mac with the Big Hit, using a new special sauce. By the end of 2023, Vkusno had 860 restaurants, serving more than 1.8 million customers daily. Paroev told me sales are now bigger than they were under McDonald's. At a press conference celebrating Vkusno's one-year anniversary, Govor, dressed in a bright purple blazer, T-shirt, and tight white pants, said the business was growing faster than anticipated. He plans to expand the number of restaurants to one thousand within three years and has already started producing toys for the children's menu based on Russian cartoon characters, replacing the Disney ones McDonald's once sold with its Happy Meals.

McDonald's exit from Russia was a microcosm of the moral and business dilemmas created by Putin's invasion of Ukraine. Staying would have meant paying taxes to the Russian government, indirectly supporting the war. The company would have had to cooperate with Russian authorities if any of its employees were called up to serve on the front line. Doing business in Russia as it waged indiscriminate attacks on innocent civilians in

Ukraine would have damaged the standing of its brand globally in the eyes of millions of customers. And running a business in a heavily sanctioned economy would have been risky. Yet the company lost not just financially—an estimated $300 million annually in operating income—but strategically too. A Russian copycat brand easily took over the McDonald's concept, assets, and systems, which had been built up over decades. Russian buyers had figured out a way to prosper, on their own, in a newfound self-sufficiency. And unintentionally, the exit of Western companies created fertile ground for a slew of brands aping well-known American or European names. But U.S executives and shareholders were no longer supporting a business in Russia as it waged war. There was a moral imperative driving the decision, with all the costs it entailed.

Russia witnessed the largest withdrawal of multinational companies from a single country since the mass corporate boycott of South Africa to protest apartheid in the 1980s. Some of the most powerful global symbols of Western capitalism, including Visa and Mastercard, announced they were leaving Russia, not just because of sanctions but because of the global public outcry. The economic war had effectively gone private. More than fifteen hundred companies, big and small, announced they would exit or curtail their operations in one way or another, according to the Kyiv School of Economics. But more than two thousand Western companies continued operations, profiting in Russia as the global outcry over Ukraine subsided.

In hindsight, McDonald's decision to cut and run relatively early after the invasion looks smart because it could choose who took over the business and on what terms, even if those terms may ultimately be unenforceable. Other Western companies that later sold businesses to Russians at knockdown prices weren't so lucky as their trademarks were hijacked by suspiciously similar logos. During Soviet times, Levi's jeans were traded on the black market and came to symbolize Russia's hunger for American-style capitalism. A few months after the invasion, Levi's decided to leave, selling its inventory to the company's local franchise partner, which rebranded several stores as JNS with a similar red logo. Levi's said it hasn't shipped jeans to Russia since the beginning of the war, but JNS is still selling Levi's online, either from inventory or imports from other countries. After Pizza Hut owner Yum! Brands announced it was pausing operations in March 2022, it sold the Russian business to a local buyer, who renamed it Pizza H, just lopping off the last two letters. Russia had become a surreal theme park of local companies producing copycat Western brands.

One of the most glaring examples of a Western business being cloned by a Russian takeover was Starbucks, which suspended operations at its 130 cafés in early March 2022. Two months later, it announced it would leave after fifteen years in the country. The following July, a pro-Putin Russian rap artist, Timati, teamed up with entrepreneur Anton Pinskiy to buy the business for $6 million. Timati is known for his 2015 song "Vladimir Putin Is My Best Friend" and a 2019 music video that praised the Kremlin-backed mayor Sergei Sobyanin and touted Moscow as "the city that doesn't hold gay parades" (which he later deleted after getting more than 1 million dislikes on social media). The two owners began reopening the cafés in the summer of 2022 under the new brand Stars Coffee. The Stars circular logo features a woman with long hair, not unlike the Starbucks mermaid, but they gave her a *kokoshnik*, a traditional Russian headdress (with a star for a communist retro flair). Pinskiy, who lost the bidding war for McDonald's in Russia, saw buying Starbucks and its ready-made infrastructure as a "chance that could not be missed."

Some Western companies remained under the cover of Russian brands. In August 2022, Coca-Cola Hellenic, Coke's European bottler, said it was renaming its Russian business Multon Partners, ring-fencing it from the rest of the company to focus on producing existing local brands at its bottling plants. While the original branded Coke was still being trafficked in from neighboring countries such as Kazakhstan or Poland and sold online, Multon Partners began pushing its replacement, Dobry Cola, or Good Cola, a knockoff sold with a similar red label. Many say it's indistinguishable from the real thing.

The exodus of Western capitalism could be seen just off Red Square inside Moscow's most iconic shopping arcade—the GUM department store. Christian Dior, Chanel, and Burberry boutiques have been closed since just after the invasion began, but they were still displaying bags in lit-up front windows in early 2024. Europe banned the export of luxury goods to Russia, but the elite could still fly to Dubai for shopping or rely on items being smuggled into the country. And in the rival TsUM department store in Moscow near the Bolshoi Theatre, brands such as Gucci and Tom Ford were on sale in early 2024, though it was unclear if this was old stock. Dolce & Gabbana was there too, one of eighteen outlets it lists as still open in Russia on its website. Even Putin's preferred luxury label, the Italian fashion house Loro Piana, part of LVMH, remained open in Moscow in early 2024. (Putin wore a $13,000 Loro Piana jacket to a pro-war rally in Moscow in March 2022.) More than eighteen months after LVMH said it was suspending operations in Russia, a Loro Piana saleswoman told me over the phone that they're still selling old stock, but it sounded as if she could get me anything I wanted.

In early 2024, stores in Moscow were selling Mars bars, Jack Daniel's whiskey, and Heinz ketchup—all made by companies that had announced they would suspend operations or halt imports and exports. PepsiCo Inc. said it would stop selling brands like 7Up and Pepsi, but it continues to sell potato chips and dairy products, while its branded sodas continue to make their way into Russia via other countries. Even though Apple announced it would suspend sales in Russia on March 1, 2022, iPhones were also widely available at electronic stores, which imported them from Turkey, the UAE, and China, albeit costing at least 25 percent more than in the United States. New companies cropped up to serve rich consumers. An online retailer called CDEK, established in May 2022, can search, purchase, and deliver almost anything from abroad to Russia—iPhones from Hong Kong, new Yves Saint Laurent handbags from UAE. For now, Russian consumers can enjoy real and copycat Western goods and services—coffee, burgers, banking—even if the substitutes may not be as good.

On one level, little had changed for Russian consumers as long as they had deep pockets. The well-off could get what they wanted, but for ordinary Russians on lower incomes, the sanctions and corporate exits were feeding into high inflation, which remained above 7 percent in late 2023 and early 2024.

*　　　*　　　*

For Ukrainians, it's not just immoral for Western companies to stay in Russia. It's foolish for them to even think they can stay and do business as usual. Since the invasion, Andrii Onopriienko has spent his days and nights at the Kyiv School of Economics tracking more than fifteen hundred Western companies in Russia, using a small army of researchers and volunteers, posting in-depth research on the website Leave-Russia.org. As an ex-financier who's worked at Western banks and consulting firms in Ukraine, he's been asked by foreign executives what they should do. "They say, 'If we leave, we'll lose everything, and if we wait, we won't be giving away our know-how and technologies,'" Onopriienko told me, referring to concerns among Western executives about leaving behind factories kitted out with proprietary equipment to produce goods. "I tell them they are already hostages, and they are not in control of their assets or technologies in Russia. Just accept that fact."

Under pressure from the public to exit Russia, many European and U.S. executives agreed to deals with politically connected oligarchs who profited from the exodus. In April 2022, Russia's richest man, Vladimir Potanin, scooped up the French bank Société Générale's Rosbank unit for what looked like nothing. At the time, Potanin, who used to play ice hockey with Putin, wasn't under sanctions in the EU or the United States, enabling the agreement to go ahead (Washington later imposed sanctions on him but Brussels never did). The French bank wrote off 3 billion euros from its exit, which meant Potanin suddenly added billions to his fortune. Other Western banks defiantly stayed, profiting from the dislocation and paying taxes to the Russian government, notably Austria's Raiffeisen and Italy's UniCredit.

Within a year, it became almost impossible for Western companies to sell, even to Kremlin cronies at knockdown prices, proving Onopriienko's point. Instead, foreign companies that tried to agree to orderly sales had their assets seized by Putin's acolytes. In April 2023, Putin signed a decree that allowed the state to take "temporary control" of assets of companies or individuals from "unfriendly" countries. While some saw it as a tit-for-tat response to the sanctions that froze the assets of Russian companies and billionaires, most Western countries haven't confiscated Russian property without court proceedings. Putin used the decree to legitimize the Russian government's "temporary" takeover of the subsidiaries of German energy giant Uniper and Finland's state-owned utilities company Fortum. Both companies took multibillion-dollar hits after losing control of their Russia operations. The Kremlin had threatened to seize the assets of foreign companies in 2022, but many executives naively believed Putin wouldn't go ahead. Now the threat of arbitrary confiscation was real.

Some Western companies in advanced talks with buyers weren't worried by the decree, but they should have been. The Danish beer manufacturer Carlsberg A/S had spent the year following the invasion preparing for a sale by ring-fencing its Russian unit to wall off its finances from the rest of the company. It had whittled down a long list of interested bidders. The business was huge, worth around $3 billion before the war: it accounted for almost 10 percent of Carlsberg's global revenue and employed more than eight thousand people at eight breweries in Russia.

In June, Carlsberg announced it had found a buyer for its Russian business, subject to regulatory approval. The Russian Finance Ministry had given the company an informal nod to sell it to Arnest, a Russian producer of metal cans that Western sanctions hadn't touched. A month later, Carlsberg executives were shocked to find out from Russian news reports that Putin had signed a decree to seize control of the business, along with the Russian subsidiary of French yogurt maker Danone SA, by transferring their shares to the Russian government for "temporary management." To lead Carlsberg's Baltika subsidiary—one of Russia's top two brewers—the government picked seventy-year-old Taimuraz Bolloyev, an old friend of Putin's from St. Petersburg. Bolloyev is chairman of the St. Petersburg judo club board where Putin is the honorary president. Bolloyev had set up a clothing company that became the sole supplier to the Russian army. Russian authorities didn't consult or inform Carlsberg about the change of management.

Some Western business executives speculated the government takeover may have been an attempt by Putin to shore up support among the Russian elite after the failed mutiny by the Wagner mercenary leader, Yevgeny Prigozhin, a few weeks earlier. "There's no way around the fact that they have stolen our business in Russia," Carlsberg CEO Jacob Aarup-Andersen said. "We are not going to help them make that look legitimate." Carlsberg wrote off $2.5 billion, while Danish executives were left guessing whether the Russian business would be permanently handed to someone else. The Kremlin turned up the pressure on Carlsberg in November 2023 when Russian authorities arrested two of its top local executives on charges of fraud, a move the Danish company branded "appalling." Putin's friend Bolloyev proposed nationalizing the company, an idea Russia's finance minister, Anton Siluanov, shot down, saying there were "no plans" for such a step. Meanwhile, a court in Russia ruled Baltika could continue to use Carlsberg brands, such as Kronenbourg, in Russia, even though the Danish company had revoked licenses to do so.

The same fate appeared to await French yogurt maker Danone, one of the earliest investors in Russia after the breakup of the Soviet Union. Like Carlsberg, Danone had found a buyer for its Russia business pending regulatory approval before the Kremlin swooped in to take control. The Russian government named the thirty-two-year-old nephew of Chechen leader Ramzan Kadyrov, a close Putin ally who had deployed forces in Ukraine, as the general director of Danone, the producer of Activia yogurt and Evian water. Danone had a dozen production facilities and employed around eight thousand people in Russia. It booked a loss of 1.2 billion euros from its Russia subsidiary, which its Kremlin handlers have rebranded as H&N, which stands for Health & Nutrition. In March 2024, Putin halted the seizure of Danone, clearing the way for its sale to Vamin Tatarstan, a Russian dairy company owned by a businessman close to Kadyrov, at a heavily discounted price. Both Danone and Carlsberg are profitable businesses with huge cash flows, which had been taken over through opaque backroom deals.

Carlsberg and Danone are just two examples of how Putin enriched a new crop of elites to keep them onside, creating a new kind of crony capitalism. For Western companies, staying in Russia had gone from a game of Russian roulette to an almost-certain corporate death. The common thread throughout all these Western exits: Russian tycoons, big and small, have grabbed Western-owned assets at bargain prices, blunting the effect of sanctions by enabling these businesses to continue operating, and paying taxes, at least in the short run.

The biggest mistake of Western companies was clinging to their assets and waiting to get out, thinking the political situation might improve. The companies that quickly exited on their own terms and swallowed the losses fared better, without all the legal uncertainties around "temporary control."

*   *   *

Consumer goods could be copied and rebranded, but the exodus of Western companies providing technical expertise or foreign-made components has

hurt Russia much more. The economic war against Russia has been devastating to one of its key manufacturing sectors: auto production.

Russia's car industry has been set back decades by the imposition of
Western sanctions and foreign companies leaving en masse. Auto production
relied heavily on Western technology and just-in-time global logistics. Major
U.S. and European auto manufacturers, including Renault, Ford Motor Co.,
and Volkswagen AG, entered the Russian market by forming alliances or
taking stakes in local manufacturers. They built world-class car plants and
tried to increase the number of parts produced locally.

But the reality of the automotive industry is that producers need an unin-
terrupted supply of components from all over the world; no one country can
do it all. After the full-scale invasion, suppliers began halting shipments of
critical components after the United States and Europe started rolling out
sanctions. The exodus of Western automakers paralyzed the industry because
Russia was suddenly cut off from global supply chains. Russia's car industry
collapsed. Its biggest automaker, AvtoVAZ, started producing cars without
crucial parts, such as airbags and antilock brake systems. It began installing
airbags again six months after the invasion, but the sanctions hit to Russia's
automotive industry was profound. Russia's new car sales plunged almost
60 percent in 2022.

In May 2022, French car giant Renault SA agreed to sell its 68 percent
stake in AvtoVAZ for one ruble to the city of Moscow in a deal that gave it
the option to buy it back within six years. It also surrendered its factory in
Moscow to the city government for another symbolic sum. After announcing
a write-off of 2.2 billion euros ($2.34 billion), the French car giant described
the deal as the "responsible choice" given its forty-five thousand employees in
Russia. It left behind a high-tech factory that, at its peak, was able to produce
around two hundred thousand cars a year.

To save some five thousand jobs, Sergei Sobyanin, Moscow's Kremlin-
backed mayor, took over the Renault factory and renamed it Moskvich, an
old Soviet car brand that disappeared more than two decades ago. It was
another example of a resurgence of Soviet-era nostalgia. "This is a historic
event," Sobyanin said at the launch in November 2022. "Many thought that
this would be the end of the Russian auto industry, but in fact this became
another incentive to revive production." However, the cars rolling off the

production line were not Russian cars and looked nothing like the boxy Moskvich model of the Soviet era. Cut off from Western components, the Moskvich factory had merely started reassembling a Chinese car called the JAC from knockdown kits.

China's creeping takeover could be seen elsewhere. Ford Motor Co. transferred its 49 percent stake in a joint venture with Russian car producer Sollers to its local management in October for the nominal value of 1 euro. To replace Ford, Sollers began assembling JAC commercial vehicles from China at the end of 2022 at its plant in Tatarstan, more than 600 miles east of Moscow. Meanwhile, Volkswagen sold its operations to the Russian car dealer Avilon, including its plant in Kaluga, a city some 125 miles southwest of Moscow, for as much as 125 million euros. Soon after, reports emerged it was negotiating to assemble kits from Chery, the most popular Chinese carmaker on the Russian market. By the end of 2023, China accounted for about 80 percent of Russia's new-car imports.

The increasing dependence of the Russian automotive industry on China has left it vulnerable to the tightening noose of Western sanctions. In September 2023, the U.S. Treasury dealt another hammer blow to the Russian auto industry by imposing sanctions on AvtoVAZ, Moskvich, and Sollers. As Chinese automakers embark on a global expansion pushing electric vehicles, they may be reluctant to risk losing crucial export markets by running afoul of U.S. sanctions and doing business in Russia. Chery alone sold almost five hundred thousand cars in 2022 outside China. Global markets are more valuable to China than Russia. China helped Russian car sales bounce back to prewar levels by the end of 2023, but the U.S. sanctions on major Russian automakers make the industry susceptible to a sudden Chinese exit.

*   *   *

No company had more to lose, financially at least, than the British oil major BP PLC. It held a 20 percent stake in state-controlled oil giant Rosneft, making it one of the biggest foreign investors in Russia. BP had a tortured but extremely profitable three decades of investing in Russia. As Putin's troops massed on Ukraine's border in early February 2022 preparing to invade, BP's CEO Bernard Looney signaled he wouldn't abandon the alliance. "Russia is a large member of the energy system," he told Bloomberg TV after reporting the company's highest quarterly profit in a decade. "We avoid the politics—that serves us well in many countries around the world."

That all changed less than three weeks later. Hours after Russia invaded, Looney gathered his senior team to review their options. He soon realized Russia's invasion was not a blip. The only option was to sever ties. If the company didn't, employees would quit in protest and it would likely have trouble hiring; other entities might not work with a company taking profits from a Russian state-controlled oil major. It quickly became clear that oil sales would directly fund Putin's war. The day after the invasion, Looney held a lengthy Zoom call with Kwasi Kwarteng, then the U.K.'s business and energy secretary, who was urging Looney to exit. Kwarteng, with his deep voice, black-rimmed glasses, and PhD from Cambridge University, didn't hide that he was putting pressure on BP to leave. "We couldn't force them to do anything, but they're a big British business, and we wanted them to be aligned to our policy. We said, 'You've got to get rid of these assets,'" Kwarteng told me. "He was very understanding of our position. He realized they didn't have a leg to stand on, but he said it's going to be challenging."

In reality, Looney's claim that BP avoided politics didn't reflect the company's tumultuous history of trying to make money in Russia; the company had former British intelligence officers and political consultants on its payroll to navigate tricky calls all around the world, not only in Russia. Looney, a blue-eyed Irishman with salt-and-pepper hair, had made radical decisions before. Soon after becoming CEO in 2020, he embarked on an ambitious plan to move the British oil giant to clean energy much faster than its rivals. On Sunday, February 27, the board met and agreed that BP would write off $25 billion from its Russian investments, more than a quarter of the company's market value. Besides the cash, BP took an enormous hit by exiting Russia, wiping out a third of its production and half of its oil and gas reserves. "No other company has had the financial impact we had," a senior BP executive told me. "It was an incredibly difficult decision and easy decision at the same time. It was a values-based decision."

But writing off the investment is different from legally exiting. Technically, BP still owned the stake. The announcement caused BP's share price to plunge more than 14 percent—less than the value of the write-off—indicating that some investors thought BP might be able to get something for the stake in the future. In the weeks after the war began, BP went hunting for buyers, sounding out state-backed firms such as China National Petroleum Corporation and Sinopec Group. It also gauged interest from India's Oil & Natural Gas Corporation and the Indian Oil Corporation in taking over some of its Russian projects. Those talks went nowhere, with prospective buyers choosing to wait until the war's outcome became clear. Because it still legally owns the stake, BP was owed more than $1.5 billion in dividends from Rosneft in 2022 and 2023, which it didn't recognize as income. Under Russian regulations, payments to a company in an "unfriendly state" such as the U.K. would go into a restricted Russian bank account that requires Russian government approval to be transferred.

Ukrainian president Zelensky's top economic adviser, Oleg Ustenko, wrote to Looney in December 2022 urging him to outline a plan to ensure the company doesn't profit from the war, calling the accrued dividends "blood money." "We haven't taken a penny," a senior BP executive told me. "We're trying to do the right thing. We're not hanging around and waiting for things to change." Judging by Putin's actions since then, chances are high that the Russian state could end up formally seizing BP's stake. Looney steered BP out of its financial entanglements in Russia, but he resigned in September 2023 after admitting a lack of transparency over past personal relationships, leaving his successor to sort out what to do with the company's legal stake in Rosneft.

Major Western oil and gas companies leaving Russia could have the biggest economic impact, depriving the country of technical expertise to extract hydrocarbons. The big oil services companies such as Baker Hughes and Halliburton sold their Russian operations to local management six months after the war began. But SLB, formerly Schlumberger, the world's largest oilfield contractor, controversially chose to stay in Russia, increasing its market share. It initially promised to not deploy new technology and later halted shipments of all products in July 2023 in response to expanding sanctions.

Some companies followed BP's path and ate their losses. European oil giant Shell PLC wrote off $4.2 billion after deciding to pull out of Russia. It had a 27.5 percent stake in Sakhalin-2, one of the world's largest liquefied natural gas (LNG) projects, in Russia's Far East, which it had been developing for decades with state-controlled Gazprom. Shell started talking to China's key state-run energy companies about buying the stake.

Then Putin pounced. In June 2022, he signed a decree citing Russia's economic security that created a new state company to seize control of Sakhalin-2, giving Shell and two other Japanese firms a month to ask the Russian government whether they would take a stake in the new company. The Japanese firms, Mitsui & Co. and Mitsubishi Corp., were approved to stay, even though Japan had imposed sanctions on Russia. Shell chose to walk away from its investment rather than risk entanglement with the Russian state. It was the first time Putin snatched control of an energy project from a foreign company since the invasion, but it wouldn't be the last. For Putin, grabbing Russia's energy assets was just one maneuver in a much-bigger battle with the West as it tried to crimp the Kremlin's oil and gas profits, which were soaring because of the very war he'd started.

Shell had provided years of technical advice to help get Sakhalin-2 up and running, which limited the effect of the company's exit in the short term. Sakhalin-2 returned to full operations in September 2023. Six months later, Russia "sold" Shell's former stake in Sakhalin-2 to state-controlled Gazprom, tightening the Kremlin's grip on LNG production. (Shell, meanwhile, came under criticism for continuing to trade Russian LNG; the company maintained it was fulfilling long-term contracts after committing to a phased withdrawal.)

The lack of Western technology could undermine future production. Russia is struggling to replace Western oil and gas extraction technology by using Chinese or domestically produced alternatives, with mixed success. Russia was aiming to triple its exports of LNG by 2030 as a way to shift away from its reliance on piped gas to Europe. The Kremlin was betting on a new LNG plant above the Arctic Circle being able to ramp up supplies to China. But in November 2023, Washington imposed sanctions on Novatek, the major shareholder in the Arctic LNG 2 plant, throwing those plans into disarray. France's oil giant TotalEnergies and Japan's Mitsui & Co. suspended their participation in the project after the restrictions. It needed specialized icebreaker ships to cut through the frozen Arctic waters to transport the gas through the Northern Sea Route, but the South Korean shipbuilding company that was supposed to supply the vessels balked because of the sanctions.

Putin's grand plan to develop the Arctic region as part of Russia's new economic alliance with China looked in peril.

*   *   *

Western businesses played an important role in the Russian economy before the full-scale invasion. Some fifteen hundred foreign companies in Russia generated $300 billion in revenue in 2021, or about 17 percent of Russia's gross domestic product. By the end of 2023, more than half of them remained in Russia, according to the Kyiv School of Economics. They paid roughly $5 billion in only corporate profit tax in Russia in 2022—or an estimated $20 billion in total taxes—money that Putin desperately needed to fund the war.

Plenty of major Western companies have reduced their footprint or stopped investing but retained some business in Russia. There are no sanctions on basic consumer goods, but remaining in the country means indirectly feeding into the war economy. Consumer giants such as Procter & Gamble and Nestlé continued to sell key brands, attracting criticism from Ukrainians and other antiwar activists. The fast-food chain Subway kept more than five hundred franchised restaurants open (the company said it had no corporate-owned outlets in Russia). Alan Jope, the outgoing CEO of Anglo-Dutch conglomerate Unilever, which sells Dove soap and Cornetto ice cream, said he didn't want the company's four production sites in Russia to fall into the hands of the government or pro-Kremlin tycoons. The company has pledged to not take any profits from Russia, but it more than doubled its earnings in Russia in 2022—which means a higher tax take for the Kremlin—and resisted calls to leave. Tobacco giant Philip Morris, the seller of Marlboro cigarettes, said soon after the war it was working on options to exit Russia, but by February 2023, its CEO, Jacek Olczak, told the *Financial Times* he would rather keep the business than sell it on the Kremlin's strict terms. At the end of 2022, Putin started narrowing the exit doors. Any sale of a company must be at a steep discount of at least 50 percent of the market value, and 10 percent of the proceeds must go to the federal budget.

Companies that want to leave are now effectively forced to pay ransom to Putin's regime. Curiously, it was oil majors entangled with the state or other oligarchs that were among the first to decide to cut ties at enormous costs. Despite some high-profile exits such as McDonald's and Starbucks, consumer goods companies, normally more sensitive to boycotts, account for most of the corporations that have decided to remain in Russia. A barrage of corporate public relations statements has made it difficult for most consumers to track who actually followed through on their promises to leave. A few Russian oligarchs grumbled that Western companies that stayed ought to be sanctioned like they were. Some executives continue to justify their decision to stay by saying they're selling items such as food or diapers far removed from the war effort. But they're still paying taxes to the government, indirectly funding the Russian military, and they could be taken over by the Kremlin any day.

CHAPTER 8

HOW TO SELL A SOCCER CLUB

Billionaire Roman Abramovich was long known as an oligarch with rare direct access to Putin. Before the full-scale invasion, he met with the Kremlin leader one-on-one roughly twice a year, and they addressed each other in Russian with the informal *Ty* (ты), or you, used with familiar friends, rather than the formal *Vy* (вы).

Despite this relationship, Abramovich didn't know about the invasion beforehand—few but a handful around Putin did. In the weeks running up to the war, Abramovich and his inner circle were convinced the Kremlin leader was bluffing, according to three people familiar with their discussions. "It's never going to happen," one said. "This is classic Putin." He's got all the troops on the border, and he'll get a deal that Ukraine will never join NATO, they thought. "The troops will all melt away, and he'll have gotten something for nothing," another said. Abramovich told one worried friend thinking of leaving Russia during the troop buildup not to panic and to stay put.

Slim, with a gray beard and blue eyes, Abramovich is known to be quiet and secretive. Worth as much as $20 billion before the full-scale war, a fortune built from steel and oil, Abramovich knew the invasion put all his investments in the West at risk of being frozen. He'd begun to transfer some of his assets to his children in the weeks before the war began in what some believed was evidence he knew Putin would invade, but the one asset he really cared about remained firmly under his ownership as Russian troops crossed into

Ukraine: Chelsea, the West London soccer club that had millions of fans around the world. Since buying the club in 2003, he'd poured more than $2 billion (£1.5 billion) into Chelsea, transforming European soccer in the process. Over the years, he'd strategized on the club's future with Joe Ravitch, a globe-trotting American banker who made a name for himself cutting mega sports and media deals.

The day Russia invaded Ukraine, Ravitch was scuba diving in Mexico and returned to his hotel room to find fifty missed calls, some from Eugene Tenenbaum, a director of Chelsea. Ravitch immediately called back. "Sell the team as fast as possible," Tenenbaum told Ravitch, according to people familiar with their conversation. "The invasion is going to make things a lot worse." It was clear that Abramovich was likely to be sanctioned given his high profile. Facing the prospect of a freeze on the club's assets and activities, he quickly concluded selling was the only option. Ravitch suddenly found himself in the middle of one of the biggest and most complicated deals in sporting history.

At the same time, Abramovich threw himself into the unlikely role of an informal mediator between Moscow and Kyiv. Always on the move, the billionaire that day happened to be on the French Riviera, where he owns Château de la Croë, a sprawling $120 million villa on Cap d'Antibes. The estate, once the home of Edward VIII and his wife, the American socialite Wallis Simpson, is located down a narrow lane, behind a high stone wall, with a wrought-iron-gate entrance flanked by conical cypress trees. It sits on a rocky coastline overlooking the Mediterranean known as Billionaire's Bay, a nickname earned after many of Russia's richest men bought luxury homes there.

That morning, Abramovich got a call from a Ukrainian film producer, Alexander Rodnyansky, asking him if he'd try to help broker a peace deal. Zelensky's chief of staff, Andriy Yermak, wanted the magnate's help. The Ukrainians wanted a "full-fledged intermediary," Rodnyansky would later recall, someone who could contact key figures in Russian politics. The same day, Putin had called a summit of the country's top oligarchs in the Kremlin's St. Catherine Hall. Putin was late and kept three dozen assembled tycoons waiting. "Why is Roman not here?" one oligarch in the room texted a friend. Abramovich hadn't planned to attend, but he was on his way to Moscow for his own meeting with Putin.

The summit with the oligarchs had already begun when Abramovich's private plane landed in Moscow. He had arranged to see Putin privately later that day one-on-one after the other tycoons had left. Abramovich quickly changed into a suit and headed to the Kremlin, where they discussed how he could mediate with the Ukrainians. As the war intensified, Abramovich took on an increasingly tricky and often mysterious role behind the scenes, all while the fate of his soccer club, Chelsea, hung in the balance.

*   *   *

When Abramovich bought Chelsea in the early 2000s, he paved the way for many Russians to follow in his footsteps to London and embed in the fabric of British society, accelerating an influx that began in the 1990s. Russian cash was pulsing through the city as billionaires listed their companies on the London Stock Exchange, hiring bankers, lawyers, and PR agents. London became a magnet for the world's kleptocrats, a place where they could launder their money and their reputations by buying a stucco mansion in Mayfair, or using British courts to settle long-running scores back home. The Russian elite was uniformly enamored with the trappings of the British class structure and eagerly snapped up crumbling English historic homes and Scottish castles.

But Abramovich stood out from the other Russians flooding London. Buying Chelsea, one of England's Premier League clubs, out of near bankruptcy for about $220 million, immediately put him in the headlines of the British tabloid press, which started calling the team Chelski. At the time, Chelsea was struggling to keep up with the big English soccer teams and hadn't won a top domestic trophy since 1955. In 2004, he brought in one of the era's hottest coaches, José Mourinho, who turned Chelsea into a winner. When Abramovich sold his stake in Russian oil company Sibneft in 2005 to state-controlled Gazprom, he pocketed roughly $10 billion in what was the biggest takeover in Russian history at the time. He was one of the first oligarchs allowed to cash out of 1990s privatizations in a deal that gave him even more cash to pump into Chelsea.

Under his ownership, he splashed money on expensive players, kept seat prices on the low side, and subsidized buses for Chelsea fans to watch away matches. His big spending sparked an arms race in European soccer. The strategy had the hallmarks of American sports franchises, then relatively new to English soccer: buy talent, win titles, and sell merchandise and media rights. With his deep pockets, he could afford to run the business more as a trophy asset rather than a commercial enterprise, and fans loved him for it. Other teams had to up the ante to keep apace. Abramovich became a regular at matches, using his multimillion-dollar property portfolio as a base, including a mansion in Kensington purchased for more than $100 million and a penthouse in Chelsea. His investments in Chelsea fed into a sophisticated image-making exercise that positioned him as less Russian oligarch, more international sports magnate. It wasn't just about soccer, but offered the billionaire an entrée into the British establishment and the global elite.

Questions about the origins of Abramovich's wealth intensified in 2011, when his former ally, the exiled anti-Putin critic Boris Berezovsky, sued him in London for $5 billion. In what was billed as the biggest private litigation battle in British history, Berezovsky claimed he had an unwritten agreement that he would get half of the oil company Sibneft. He claimed Abramovich "coerced" him into selling his stake at a fraction of its true value. Abramovich denied he had any such agreement, arguing he'd made substantial cash payments to Berezovsky as protection money to serve as his *krysha*. Berezovsky lost in 2012, but not without exposing how Abramovich paid for political influence, pulling the curtain back on how corruption worked in Russia.

*   *   *

In March 2018, the British mood toward Russia darkened dramatically after Sergei Skripal, a former Russian military intelligence officer, and his daughter were poisoned in Salisbury, England. British officials concluded that Putin likely approved the poisoning. In response, the U.K., United States, and two dozen other countries expelled more than 150 Russian diplomats, and the EU later sanctioned four Russians suspected of carrying out the attack. The U.K. overhauled its "golden visa" scheme, which sold residency to the ultrawealthy in return for an investment. The program had drawn in a parade of Russian kleptocrats, with few checks. Almost seven hundred Russians had received golden visas between 2008 and 2014 in exchange for plunking down an investment of only £1 million, a threshold later raised to £2 million because the program was so popular. As part of the new scrutiny in 2018, British officials demanded Abramovich answer certain questions about his finances before renewing his visa amid calls for Russia's elite to explain the sources of their wealth and how they paid for British property. Stonewalling the billionaire's visa was one way for the British government to show that it would no longer welcome Russian money, no questions asked. Abramovich could no longer travel to the U.K. to watch Chelsea play. When he stopped coming to games, Chelsea fans unfurled a forty-foot blue-and-red banner with his image that said THE ROMAN EMPIRE.

Politically, Abramovich chose to weather the storm over Skripal and find other ways to eventually return to the U.K. At the end of May 2018, his Gulfstream G650 touched down in Tel Aviv, where he was a major donor to Jewish causes and where he owned a home in the exclusive Neve Tzedek neighborhood. He left two days later with an Israeli passport, which enabled him to travel to the U.K. visa-free for up to six months. The next day, Chelsea announced it had put a £1 billion plan on hold to develop Chelsea's Stamford Bridge stadium, citing "the current unfavorable investment climate."

For his part, Putin urged Russia's billionaires such as Abramovich to bring their money home. "Some say we need to help Abramovich and other Russian businessmen who have ended up in a difficult situation," he said in his annual phone-in with the Russian public in 2018. "I warned them that this situation which we see today could develop. I warned them about this and recommended at the time that our business keeps capital in Russia, in the motherland. To keep capital in the place where it was earned and to use it to develop the Russian economy."

In 2018, Abramovich turned to his adviser Ravitch as he considered Chelsea's future and began toying with selling a stake in the club, in part because of his visa problems following the Skripal poisoning. Abramovich had known Ravitch since they met in the mid-2000s while on vacation in St. Barts, the Caribbean island where the billionaire has a sprawling estate. A white-haired, blue-eyed, fast-talking Yale Law School grad, Ravitch was fluent in Russian. In the early 1990s, he helped set up the Moscow practice of the white-shoe firm Cleary Gottlieb Steen & Hamilton, which advised the Russian government led by the reformer Yegor Gaidar. Ravitch went on to become a senior partner at

Goldman Sachs, advising on major global sports transactions, including the spin-off of the National Basketball Association in China, before cofounding his own boutique advisory firm, Raine Group. From there, he facilitated many complex international deals, including a Chinese investment into the soccer team Manchester City.

Ravitch had been helping Abramovich develop a strategy to grow the West London club as a business, even though the billionaire didn't seem to particularly care if it made money. In 2018, against the backdrop of his visa troubles, they began discussing options for Chelsea, everything from strategic partnerships in Asia to selling a stake in the club to an American buyer to reduce the political heat on Chelsea, sources familiar with the talks told me. The club had plenty of supporters in the U.K., but scores of Chinese fans followed it too. Sovereign wealth funds in Asia entered early-stage talks about investing in Chelsea. There were also discussions about marketing deals and setting up Chelsea academies abroad.

Abramovich agreed to consider doing a deal, but only if he could get a higher valuation than had ever been achieved for a soccer club. At the time Chelsea was riding high. After more than a dozen trophies in the previous fifteen years, it had just won the Football Association Challenge Cup. That year, Ravitch found an American buyer willing to stump up a record sum for an eventual 51 percent stake, valuing the club at £3 billion.

But then Abramovich decided he didn't actually want to sell. He was starting to get excited about the European Super League, a proposed grouping of roughly a dozen top English and European clubs that would create a new elite competition. Chelsea was among the "founding members" of the proposed league, and Abramovich thought the club would be even more valuable once the league started. The idea was to rival the Champions League, Europe's top soccer competition, but the new grouping faced overwhelming opposition from politicians and sports bodies because the plan would shut out smaller clubs, threatening the health of domestic competitions. Despite repeated attempts, the Super League never got off the ground.

Abramovich had been looking for a legal place to reside in Europe even before his U.K. visa troubles. He withdrew his application for residency in Switzerland in 2017, but the reason only came out a year later, when a court in Lausanne allowed the media to publish a police report that described

Abramovich as a "danger to public security and Switzerland's reputation" because of suspicions of money laundering and connections to organized crime. His lawyers called the allegations "defamatory," denying he had links to organized crime.

Abramovich's ability to travel eased when he got a Portuguese passport in April 2021. He took advantage of a program in Portugal that enabled descendants of Sephardic Jews expelled from the Iberian Peninsula centuries earlier as part of the Roman Catholic Inquisition to get citizenship. Even though Abramovich is a common Ashkenazi last name, Alexander Boroda, a Russian rabbi, had vouched for his Sephardic heritage. His application breezed through unusually quickly, granting him the right to live in the European Union. The late Russian opposition leader Alexei Navalny criticized Portugal's decision to grant Abramovich citizenship. "He finally managed to find a country where you can give some bribes and make some semiofficial and official payments to end up in the EU and NATO—on the other side of Putin's front line," Navalny wrote. In January 2022, Portuguese authorities began investigating how Abramovich secured citizenship.

In the run-up to the invasion that February, Abramovich was reshuffling his assets on paper, making it look like a precautionary move to shield his wealth from possible sanctions if Putin invaded. According to the FBI, Abramovich reorganized his assets in February 2022 to make his children—all Russian nationals—the beneficiaries of two trusts that owned his private jets, yachts, and a helicopter. The *Guardian* newspaper, which later got files from an offshore administrator through a leak, estimated that the sweeping shake-up transferred more than $4 billion in assets to his children. In fact, the reorganization was much bigger. In early February, Abramovich transferred beneficial ownership of a Jersey-registered company with investments worth more than $7 billion to five of his children, according to a lawsuit filed by the U.S. Securities and Exchange Commission. Putting the assets in the hands of his children made them less susceptible to Western sanctions, in theory. However, the company that owned Chelsea was not part of this restructuring. It's unclear why, but any change of ownership or control of Chelsea would have needed the approval of the Premier League and could not have been done quietly.

*   *   *

Within days of the invasion, Abramovich announced he was placing the club under the "stewardship" of Chelsea's charitable foundation, which ran community programs for young people focused on sport and education. Behind the scenes, he was preparing to sell Chelsea outright and put the proceeds into a new charity. "We were hoping to preempt any kind of sanctions around it," one person close to the deal told me. "We thought it would let Chelsea continue to operate."

Abramovich continued his asset reshuffle the day the war began, transferring his British Virgin Islands company, Norma Investments Ltd., which held stakes in several start-ups, to his partner David Davidovich, who told me a few months later that he bought it as a "core business" for himself. Meanwhile, Abramovich threw himself into what turned out to be fruitless peace talks, fraught from the start, while the scrutiny over his ties to the Kremlin led to calls in the U.K. parliament for the billionaire to be sanctioned immediately. "The danger is that Mr. Abramovich will have sold everything by the time we get round to sanctioning him," the MP Chris Bryant said. The Russian billionaire quickly sent his superyachts, *Solaris* and *Eclipse*, worth more than $1 billion, to safe waters in Turkey, out of the reach of Western governments.

Within a week of the invasion, Abramovich was en route to Kyiv for secret peace talks in a bid to end the war when he announced he was selling Chelsea. "This has never been about business nor money for me, but about pure passion for the game and club," he said, adding he would donate the proceeds to a foundation "for the benefit of all victims of the war in Ukraine." That wording led some to conclude he meant Russians as well as Ukrainians, but few paid attention in the scramble to sell the club. Regardless of his role as a mediator in the emerging peace talks, Abramovich and Chelsea could be sanctioned at any time.

A day later, Abramovich was in Kyiv for talks, first with Zelensky and then with fellow Ukrainian negotiator Rustem Umerov, who would later become Ukraine's defense minister. Abramovich and Umerov went on to a dinner that lasted late into the night, after which the two men began suffering from symptoms consistent with poisoning: peeling skin, headaches, red eyes, and loss of their eyesight for a few hours, say several people close to Abramovich. They didn't know how it had happened.

Abramovich and Umerov traveled out of Kyiv via Poland and flew on to Istanbul, where they were seen at a military hospital, but the doctors couldn't determine the cause of their symptoms. They recovered relatively quickly and soon returned to the negotiations, undaunted. While some assumed it was the work of the Kremlin, Abramovich didn't think it was a targeted attack on him or an attempt to derail the peace talks, but rather that he was collateral damage in some intrigue playing out in Kyiv at the war's outset, a person familiar with his thinking told me. No one ever figured out who was behind the alleged attack. Putin's spokesman, Dmitry Peskov, denied that Abramovich had been poisoned at all, calling it "part of information sabotage," deepening the mystery over Abramovich's role.

Behind the scenes, Abramovich jetted around the globe for weeks trying to help broker some kind of peace accord or ceasefire. Was he merely doing Putin's bidding? Rival Russian oligarchs privately concluded the nature of Putin's rule meant he could do little more than collect information like an errand boy for the Kremlin. Khodorkovsky, the exiled Russian tycoon and outspoken critic of the regime, told me Putin was helping Abramovich avoid U.S. penalties by publicly confirming his role as a negotiator. "It's very important for Roma that American sanctions were not imposed on him," he said, referring to Abramovich by his nickname. Mykhailo Podolyak, a top aide to Zelensky who participated in the talks, also thought Abramovich was using the negotiations to try to avoid sanctions. "I think his motive was exclusively selfish, to minimize the personal costs of this war," Podolyak told me. "He did not want to be perceived by Western countries, primarily Britain, as the same type of person as Putin." But David Arakhamia, who headed the Ukraine negotiating team, has said Abramovich played a "positive" role. Ironically, his attempts to broker a deal with the Kremlin made it impossible for him to argue that he was *not* close to Putin and therefore shouldn't be penalized. (Abramovich's representative said there was no basis for saying he had a "close relationship" to Putin.)

Ukrainians who worked with him downplayed his influence on Putin's thinking. "He helped smooth over and establish communication somewhat, but it was very informal," Alexander Rodnyansky, an economist at the University of Cambridge whose father first reached out to Abramovich, told me in the spring of 2022. "That was useful, but he's not really a game changer or someone who can make or break a deal." Zelensky asked Western nations not to sanction Abramovich while he was acting as an unofficial peacemaker.

President Joe Biden honored that request, but U.K. prime minister Boris Johnson did not. On March 10, 2022, the U.K. slapped sanctions on Abramovich,
calling him a "pro-Kremlin oligarch." That same day, Portuguese authorities
swooped in to arrest the Daniel Litvak, the Portuguese rabbi in Porto on
suspicion of money laundering and falsification of documents connected to
his role signing off on paperwork that helped Abramovich get citizenship.
He denied wrongdoing. (An appeals court later criticized how prosecutors
handled Litvak's case, saying there was a lack of evidence, but the investigation is ongoing.)

The EU followed with sanctions on Abramovich five days later. The
sanctions meant Chelsea was frozen: Abramovich couldn't sell without the
government's permission, broadcast fees were blocked, and new ticket sales
were suspended.

Sitting in a hotel in Istanbul not long after, surrounded by Turkish government security guards, Abramovich told a friend he was downbeat about
Chelsea but optimistic about a possible breakthrough in the peace negotiations. But he wasn't giving much away and didn't reveal why. "He's not a
man of many words," his friend told me. "He was distraught about Chelsea."
But the club, after all, was just a sports team. As the fighting in Ukraine
claimed thousands of lives, the stakes for the peace talks were much higher
and became all-consuming.

On March 29, 2022, as the fighting around Kyiv still raged, Russian negotiators sat down in Istanbul with their Ukrainian counterparts, as Abramovich
sat on the sidelines, an unusual move for the secretive oligarch. Kyiv negotiators proposed a framework: Ukraine would accept neutrality and promise not
to join NATO in exchange for a clear path to EU membership and security
guarantees from Western allies and Russia. They fudged the tricky issue of
Ukraine's borders, calling for the status of Crimea to be negotiated in the
future. Ukrainian negotiators knew they would have to change the country's
constitution to agree to any deal that touched on NATO, an unlikely prospect
in the middle of a raging war. Later that day, Russia's deputy defense minister
Alexander Fomin announced beleaguered troops would begin withdrawing
from around Kyiv to "increase mutual trust" in the talks. In reality it was a
ploy. Russian forces were suffering huge losses and had failed to capture any
major city. It continued to bomb Ukrainian cities as troops retreated. The role

of the Western allies in these talks was unclear. On March 30, British prime minister Boris Johnson wasn't focused on peace but economic penalties against Russia. "We should continue to intensify sanctions with a rolling program until every one of his troops is out of Ukraine," he told a parliamentary committee.

Not long after the Ukrainian delegation returned to Kyiv, reports of Russian atrocities in Bucha emerged, where dead bodies were left strewn on the streets. "If Russia remained in the occupied territories, or even had the right to control Kyiv, which was part of its ultimatum, we would be facing genocide," Podolyak, Zelensky's adviser, told me. When Johnson visited Kyiv in early April, he expressed doubt that any deal with Putin could be trusted and said the U.K. would continue backing Ukraine. Many saw his intervention as a decisive turning point, but the Ukrainians continued talks for weeks. As outrage over the atrocities in Bucha intensified, the negotiations fizzled, as did Abramovich's furtive role.

*   *   *

Against the backdrop of apparent war crimes emerging in Ukraine, Abramovich watched more of his assets get frozen as a result of U.K. and EU sanctions. A court in Jersey, a U.K. Crown dependency, froze $7 billion in assets it said were linked to Abramovich, the same assets that had been transferred to his five children in February 2022. One of his biggest holdings, a stake in Russian steelmaker Evraz PLC, listed on the London Stock Exchange, was suspended and later sanctioned. The U.K. government said Evraz, which produces 97 percent of the country's rail tracks, is of "vital significance as Russia uses rail to move key military supplies and troops to the front line in Ukraine." (A representative for Abramovich said Evraz's production in Russia has only been for civilian projects.) By June, the U.S. government issued a warrant to seize the two planes Abramovich had been using for his globe-trotting—a $350 million Boeing 787-8 plane and a $60 million Gulfstream G650 jet.

But it was Chelsea that faced an existential crisis, with legions of fans wondering if the club would survive the unprecedented restrictions. There were real fears Chelsea might run out of money. Abramovich still technically owned it, but because he was sanctioned, the club could only continue to operate under the strict conditions spelled out in a U.K. government license, which at least initially banned it from selling new tickets or shirts to fans. It had a huge monthly bill to pay staff wages but no incoming revenue. It couldn't sell or buy players either. Every time Chelsea wanted to spend money, it had to clear the plan with the U.K. government, which initially imposed unrealistically low caps on expenses for such things as travel to Champions League away matches. Operating under those conditions meant the club was on the verge of bankruptcy; Ravitch had to sell it as quickly as possible to lift the government restrictions hampering its finances. With the license expiring at the end of May, Chelsea was living on borrowed time. Another month under the government's strict licensing rules wasn't possible financially. They had until June 1 to sell, or the club could go under.

Abramovich was still spending most of his time working on peace talks and wasn't focused on the sale. The sanctions meant he couldn't be involved in picking the winner. His trusted lieutenant, Tenenbaum, a director of Chelsea, took the lead, but in mid-April, the U.K. imposed sanctions on Tenenbaum too. Ravitch, who was racing to compile a list of bidders before time ran out, suddenly found himself formally without a client he could talk to. Standing outside Milos, the Greek restaurant in midtown Manhattan, he called Tenenbaum and asked, "Who the fuck do I talk to who can make decisions about who to sell this team to?" "You figure it out," Tenenbaum replied. "Go save Chelsea."

The economic war against Russia had forced the auction of one of Europe's most high-profile soccer teams. The deal was unlike any other in sporting history. Not only did it need to be completed under extreme time pressure, but it also involved behind-the-scenes political machinations that took both dealmakers and officials into unchartered waters. Never before had such a valuable asset subjected to sanctions been sold under stringent terms imposed by a government.

The interest in Chelsea was off the scale. After getting two hundred and fifty inquiries, there were thirty potential bidders, which Ravitch whittled down to an eclectic mix of four, including private equity firms, hedge fund billionaires, and U.S. sports investors. Four consortia emerged: the Los Angeles Dodgers investor Todd Boehly, backed by the California-based private equity firm Clearlake Capital; another led by British businessman Martin Broughton, with money from tennis champion Serena Williams and Formula 1 driver Lewis Hamilton; a third from the NBA's Boston Celtics co-owner Steve

Pagliuca; and a fourth from the Ricketts family, which controls the Chicago Cubs baseball team.

It wasn't about the highest bidder but rather who would be the best owner, and one who would be welcomed by both the British government and the public. After all, British authorities needed to approve the sale because of sanctions. The Ricketts bid soon fell out after Chelsea fans cried foul. Leaked emails from 2012 had revealed racist and anti-Muslim sentiments of the father, Joe Ricketts, who had later apologized. His son Tom, chairman of the Cubs, tried to distance himself from his father, but the scandal led them to be ruled out as a potential buyer. With three bids left, it came down to who would agree to the stringent terms Ravitch outlined, which included limits on debt and investments in the women's team, the stadium, and the academy.

As the June 1 deadline drew closer, obstacles kept popping up. Even though Abramovich had agreed to put the proceeds from the sale into a foundation to benefit "all victims of the war in Ukraine," reports surfaced in early May that the U.K. government was considering diverting some of the funds into grassroots soccer. There were concerns that Abramovich might not agree to sell at all if the money went to U.K. youth soccer instead of being earmarked for the foundation. After Ravitch called some senior British officials to warn them the deal might not happen if the bickering over the proceeds continued, the rumors stopped. No one wanted the club to go into liquidation. It was the first inkling that there would be a fight over how to use money from the sale.

In the end, the Boehly-Clearlake consortium won the bidding after agreeing to pay £2.5 billion plus investing an additional £1.75 billion into the club. At the time, it was the most expensive deal in sports history. The new owners thought of it as a beachhead to invest in other clubs, but they might have taken on more than they bargained for. Six months after clinching the deal, Behdad Eghbali, the cofounder of Clearlake, called Chelsea "a business that was not terribly well managed on the football side, sporting side, or promotional side." More than a year after the sale, Chelsea ended up paying a 10 million euro fine to regulators for "submitting incomplete financial information" during Abramovich's ownership that breached Financial Fair Play rules, but it could face more trouble. The Premier League was also investigating millions of pounds of payments made by Chelsea under Abramovich's ownership between 2012 and 2019 to offshore companies, which Boehly discovered after he took over, according to the *Times of London*. For all Abramovich's big spending, off-book payments appeared to be happening behind the scenes. Leaked documents from Cyprus obtained by the International Consortium of Investigative Journalists and Paper Trail Media suggested Chelsea had failed to follow Financial Fair Play rules designed to prevent clubs from spending beyond what they earn. (Abramovich's representative said there was no evidence showing the club spent above the limits of the Financial Fair Play rules during his tenure and that suggesting otherwise would be false.)

Abramovich's efforts on peace talks and promise to donate Chelsea proceeds to Ukraine didn't convince Navalny, the jailed Russian opposition leader. He unleashed a Twitter tirade from prison in August 2022, attacking the United States for letting oligarchs in Putin's inner circle like Abramovich escape sanctions. "From Day 1, Western leaders firmly stated that Putin's oligarchs and bribe-takers would face imminent sanctions and wouldn't get away this time," he tweeted. "But they did."

*   *   *

The Chelsea sale was precedent setting in another way: £2.34 billion from the deal was earmarked for the independent foundation. It was the first time that proceeds from the sale of a sanctioned asset were allocated to set up a humanitarian charity. Sanctions had suddenly made several billion dollars potentially available to victims of the war in Ukraine. The funds were put into a frozen bank account, pending approval of the charity by the British government. U.K. officials wanted to ensure Abramovich didn't benefit in any way and issued a unilateral declaration when the sale completed that said permission would hinge on assurances that the "proceeds are used for exclusively humanitarian purposes in Ukraine." This wording differed from Abramovich's original statement, referencing "all victims of the war in Ukraine." People close to Abramovich later accused the U.K. government of changing the terms of setting up the charity. U.K. officials denied altering their position.

Chelsea picked Mike Penrose, the former U.K. UNICEF chief, to set up the new foundation, independently of Abramovich. Penrose brought more than twenty-five years of experience in humanitarian work to the project, including at the U.K.'s Department for International Development. In November 2022, he told me the foundation could serve as a model for how frozen assets stemming from sanctions might be deployed to aid people suffering from conflicts. "This will be a remarkable precedent we could set," he said. "It could possibly be the largest purely humanitarian foundation in the world." Amid all the costs of economic warfare, here was a demonstrable gain. He said the focus would be on Ukrainian victims, including refugees who had fled. "We would certainly not be looking to put money inside Russia," he told me.

Penrose said he completed all the paperwork needed to set up the foundation and recruited a chairman of the board, the respected head of the Norwegian Refugee Council, Jan Egeland. The provisional name for the organization: Foundation for the Victims of Conflict. He drew up a short list of candidates to join the seven-member board and investment managers to oversee the money. "We're ready to go," Penrose told me in April 2023. He even offered a seat on the board to the U.K. government to make sure all spending complied with sanctions and Abramovich wasn't pulling the strings. "I have no dealings with him whatsoever," Penrose said.

But the release of the funds required the go-ahead from both the EU and the U.K. British officials wanted iron-clad assurances that the funds wouldn't flow to Russia or Belarus. Apparently they weren't getting them. Without an explicit promise the funds would only be spent in Ukraine, the U.K. government indicated it would refuse to approve the release of the money. "He doesn't want the foundation to be politicized," said one person close to Abramovich. "Most victims would be Ukrainians, but a small proportion could be Ukrainians in Donetsk. They also suffered a lot of casualties, with lost kids." One person familiar with the foundation said they had proposed various formulations to the government: "It would be for people inside Ukraine, refugees fleeing Ukraine, and people everywhere suffering because of food and fertilizer shortages because of the war."

That wasn't good enough for U.K. officials. They wanted Abramovich to agree to spend the money in Ukraine only and indicated they would not grant a license for the frozen funds to be used until that was spelled out in the foundation's mandate. (A representative for Abramovich said he had not sought to impose any conditions in relation to the donation and that it is false to allege he was intentionally frustrating or delaying the foundation.) With no agreement on how the charity can spend the money, the $2.95 billion was just sitting in a frozen bank account.

Meanwhile, there are more than 6 million Ukrainian refugees globally, and almost 4 million displaced internally. Some 15 million Ukrainians need humanitarian assistance. The billions could make a real difference as Putin pursues his scorched-earth strategy in Ukraine. Amid the blame game, Ukraine is once again the real loser.

For Abramovich, losing Chelsea, a multibillion-dollar trophy asset, was a financial blow. For Putin, it was water off his back. The sanctions may have spurred Abramovich to offer to donate the Chelsea proceeds to charity—a potential win in the economic war for Ukrainian victims—and perhaps provided another incentive for him to continue his back-channel diplomatic efforts. In the two years following the invasion, Abramovich continued to work secretly to persuade the Kremlin to agree to prisoner swaps between Russia and Ukraine. At the end of August 2022, he shuttled to Saudi Arabia for a meeting with Crown Prince Mohammed bin Salman, who helped broker an exchange that led to some 215 Ukrainian fighters held by Russia being swapped for 55 prisoners held by Ukraine. The detailed prisoner swap work was all-consuming. "It's impossible to discuss business with him now," one person close to him said. "What's driving him now is Ukraine."

Abramovich even got involved in one of the most sensitive proposed prisoner swaps since the invasion. In February 2024, it emerged he was part of negotiations to exchange Navalny, along with two jailed U.S. citizens—the *Wall Street Journal* reporter Evan Gershkovich and the U.S. businessman Paul Whelan—for Vadim Krasikov, an FSB agent jailed in Germany for killing a Chechen dissident in Berlin. Maria Pevchikh, a top Navalny aide, said she'd been told that Abramovich was the one who delivered the proposal to Putin. But then Navalny died in an Arctic prison on February 16. Pevchikh accused Putin of ordering Navalny's murder because he didn't want to release him. Abramovich met with U.S. government officials in the Middle East about the swap just before Navalny's death, a person familiar with the talks told me. After securing his record sixth term as president in March 2024 in a sham election, Putin confirmed that "certain colleagues not from the (presidential) administration" told him about the proposal to swap Navalny and that he supported the idea, as long as Navalny promised to never return to Russia.

"The person talking to me didn't even finish their sentence when I said 'I agree,'" Putin said. But the full story behind Navalny's death and Abramovich's role in a possible prisoner exchange remains shrouded in secrecy.

By the summer of 2023, Abramovich appeared to be more distant from Putin, who started addressing the billionaire with the formal *Vy*, instead of the usual informal *Ty*, according to a person familiar with their conversations. It was a sign that Abramovich's efforts on peace talks and prisoner swaps might have led to a certain distrust from Putin. The asset freezes and travel bans against the country's elite were finally removing Russian influence in the West, but driving some of them back to Russia, where they were becoming more dependent on the whims of the Kremlin.

Abramovich, for his part, was splitting his time between Moscow, Istanbul, and Tel Aviv. This was just what Putin had long wanted, for the oligarchs to come back to mother Russia where he could control them. "Before the war, they all tried to be international to diversify risks," said one source close to the Kremlin. "Now all of them are here in Russia and extremely dependent on Putin. From time to time, he tells them, 'Look, guys, I told you, you should invest in Russia, not in the U.S. or Europe.' So he's happy with that, and his power is much stronger because now they're in his hands."

PART IV

FOLLOW THE MONEY AND THE OIL . . . IF YOU CAN

CHAPTER 9

CYPRUS: THE TROJAN HORSE

Over two decades, Christodoulos Vassiliades had made such a killing advising Russian billionaires from his base in the Mediterranean island of Cyprus that he had expanded his father's small vineyard to a sprawling compound of 370 acres. Nestled in the mountains of southern Cyprus, Domaine Vassiliades Oenou Yi (which means "land of wine") has all the trappings you might expect at a top-notch vineyard. A luxurious three-story white stone building boasts tasting rooms, an indoor pool, cellars with oak barrels, and a high-end restaurant with terraces overlooking manicured vines in the shadow of Mount Olympos.

Founded in 2017, the winery quickly attracted the Cypriot elite. In 2018, Vassiliades held a lavish wedding reception for his daughter in the vineyard's main courtyard, overflowing with flowers as a Greek pop star entertained hundreds of guests. Vassiliades regularly hobnobbed with Cypriot power brokers, including then president Nicos Anastasiades, who came for a ribbon-cutting ceremony at the vineyard in 2019.

A bald, plump lawyer in his sixties, Vassiliades was renowned for his long list of Russian clients, notably the metals-and-telecoms billionaire Alisher Usmanov, who once led the investment arm of gas giant Gazprom and helped Putin restore state control over its assets in the early 2000s. Usmanov had transferred most of his real estate and other property, including his $600 million superyacht *Dilbar*, into an irrevocable trust of which he was no longer the beneficiary, which made it complicated to enforce the sanctions against him. As a lawyer, Vassiliades set up nests of shell companies and trusts for clients in offshore tax havens around the world that artfully concealed ownership of assets. Cyprus was home to many accountants and lawyers who helped wealthy plutocrats navigate the shell-company game, but Vassiliades took it to a new level. He had expanded his law firm in the capital, Nicosia, to include branches in Moscow, Belize, the Seychelles, and, of course, London. He had the closest ties to the Kremlin of any law firm on the island, according to the Center for the Study of Democracy, a respected Bulgarian think tank.

For decades, Russian money had been pouring into Cyprus, a small island divided between Greeks and Turks at the crossroads of Europe, Africa, and Asia. With its sandy beaches wrapped by crystal-blue waters, Cyprus became a favorite destination for Russian companies to register an outpost, facilitating billions of dollars in capital flight. Over the years, Limassol, the Cypriot resort town on the southern coast, had attracted so many Russians—fifty thousand by some counts—that it was nicknamed Limassolgrad, replete with shop signs in Cyrillic and restaurants serving pelmeni, Russian dumplings.

Russians used Cyprus like a Trojan horse to stealthily infiltrate Europe and the wider global financial system. Even though Cyprus was a member of the European Union, it had ignored the Continent's anti-money-laundering rules for years in the rush to welcome Russian cash. Most Russian billionaires had companies registered on the Mediterranean island, which made it a central battleground in the quest to freeze Russian assets following the invasion of Ukraine. A year into the war, the West shifted from sanctioning Russia's oligarchs to finally trying to crack down on professional enablers helping them dodge the penalties.

In April 2023, accountants and lawyers in Cyprus panicked when the U.K. and the United States simultaneously imposed sanctions on Vassiliades. The U.K. said Vassiliades was at the center of a web of trusts and offshore companies that linked Usmanov, the sanctioned metals oligarch, to Sutton Place estate, a sixteenth-century Tudor manor in Surrey, south of London, which British authorities sought to freeze. Coordinating with London, Washington also sanctioned Vassiliades, citing his work for the Cyprus subsidiary of Russia's state-controlled Sberbank; it also imposed asset freezes and travel bans on his daughter and son. After Vassiliades was placed under sanctions, other Cypriot lawyers and accountants told diplomats in Cyprus, "It took you long enough."

At the same time, the U.K. also imposed an asset freeze and travel ban on another high-powered Cypriot enabler, Demetris Ioannides, who had founded the Cyprus branch of the accountancy Deloitte. His most famous client was the billionaire Chelsea owner, Abramovich. The U.K. said Ioannides crafted "murky offshore structures" that Abramovich used to hide $960 million worth of assets before he was sanctioned. (The United States did not target Ioannides.)

Sanctions against Vassiliades and Ioannides spooked the Cypriot enabler community. Any company or trust they were associated with suddenly became toxic. The website listing companies registered in Cyprus crashed as lawyers, accountants, and financial advisers rushed to log on to check exposure to the two men, who had helped set up countless companies. I was told some were logging on to change details on shell companies to shield themselves from future sanctions. A parlor game quickly began among the island's tight-knit elite to try to guess who would be next in Washington and London's renewed zeal to target professional fixers.

*　　　*　　　*

When I visited Cyprus in June 2023, I was hoping to talk to Vassiliades myself. He wasn't answering my emails, and his sandstone office building in Nicosia appeared shut, so I decided to see if he'd retreated to his vineyard. When I got there, I thought I might see some sign that the sanctions were making it hard for him to continue to operate the business. After all, a high-end restaurant he owned in Nicosia had been closed since the sanctions were imposed. Instead, I saw a group of Russian tourists sitting down to a lavish lunch. I asked the young Russian man working behind the cash register if Vassiliades was available, but he told me his boss was in Nicosia. I found his card with his cell phone number on the desk next to bottles of olive oil and jars of honey for sale.

I made my way to the nearby village of Omodos, where his daughter had been married in one of the island's oldest monasteries and Domaine Vassiliades had its own store selling wine down one narrow lane. Among a smattering of tourists, I sat down to lunch in the cobbled square and pulled out my phone to call Vassiliades, expecting he wouldn't answer an unknown number. To my surprise, he picked up. I told him I was writing a book about sanctions and wanted to ask about the allegations against him. He sounded agitated and distressed. "I don't want to talk to you," he told me gruffly, and hung up. Vassiliades told the *Cyprus Times*, "We have not offered any assistance or service to any person included in the relevant sanctions lists." It soon turned out Vassiliades had bigger problems. In July 2023, two men on motorcycles shot at Vassiliades's house in an upscale neighborhood in Nicosia at around 1:00 a.m. and sped off. No one was injured. A few months later, a court in Moscow issued an arrest warrant for him in absentia in connection with an investigation into 1 billion euros stolen from the Russian bank Promsvyazbank.

Vassiliades was just one of many fixers in Cyprus who had been helping to steer illicit Russian cash for decades. Cyprus had a reputation for washing dirty money going back to the 1990s, when the regime of Serbian leader Slobodan Milosevic evaded United Nations sanctions during the Yugoslav wars by stashing funds in Cypriot banks. The island was uniquely suited to hiding money because of laws that kept ownership of companies secret. A former British colony, Cyprus uses an English common law system, enabling nests of shell companies to seamlessly operate across London and U.K. overseas territories with similar rules, such as the British Virgin Islands. After Cyprus joined the EU in 2004 and adopted the euro as its currency four years later, lawyers, accountants, and bankers became the engine of the local economy and a nexus for corruption. Lax banking regulation meant few questions were asked. Cyprus had the lowest corporate tax rate in the eurozone, at 10 percent.

The island's close ties with Moscow go back centuries, partly due to their shared Orthodox Christian religion. Since Turkey's invasion of the north of the island in 1974, Cyprus has been divided, with a buffer zone resembling the Berlin Wall running through Nicosia, part of a 112-mile line splitting the island into an ethnically Greek southern part of the country and the Turkish-controlled northern region. The Soviets exploited the island's division as Cyprus looked to Moscow for support in its conflict with Turkey.

The influx of Russians began in the 1990s, when they started registering companies and opening bank accounts in Cyprus to dodge taxes and park their cash to hedge against the possibility of a communist resurgence. They often set up secretive trusts and nominees to shield ownership. Cyprus was technically the largest foreign investor in Russia for decades because so many Russian companies were based on the island, "round-tripping" their money in and out of banks and companies in Nicosia and Limassol. Cash pumped into and out of Cyprus, greasing the wheels of Putin's crony capitalism.

The American-born British investor Bill Browder was one of the first to expose dirty money flowing through Cyprus, as he recounted in his best-selling books *Freezing Order* and *Red Notice*. When Interior Ministry officials raided Browder's company offices in Russia in 2007 after he'd been barred from entering the country, they took stamps and documents to file false tax returns, claiming a fraudulent $230 million refund. They proceeded to launder the money through shell companies, with some of the funds channeled to a Cyprus-based real estate company, Prevezon Holdings Ltd., which in turn bought luxury real estate in Manhattan with the proceeds of the fraud.

Russian money in Cyprus turned into a problem for Brussels when the island's banks began to melt down during the European debt crisis of the early 2010s. In 2011, the financial crisis in neighboring Greece spilled over into Cyprus. The island's banks had devoured Greek debt, exposing them to massive losses. Meanwhile, the wealthy Russians who had deposited money in Cypriot banks were clamoring for aid. Unable to borrow as its credit ratings sank to junk, Cyprus turned to the Kremlin for a lifeline—a 2.5 billion euro loan from the Russian government. But the island's banks needed much more to stay afloat. The following year, Cyprus went cap in hand to Brussels to ask for a multibillion-euro bailout. But some EU leaders worried that rescuing the island's banks would aid Russians and facilitate money laundering—by the beginning of 2013, a third of the total deposits at Cypriot banks were from nonresidents, most of them Russians—and so the EU dragged its feet on a deal.

When the EU finally agreed to the bailout at the end of March 2013 per-versely ended up giving wealthy Russians more control over the island's largest financial institution, the Bank of Cyprus. The 10 billion euro package, almost half the size of the entire Cypriot economy, protected all deposits under 100,000 euros, while wealthy depositors, many of them Russians, with more than 100,000 euros, were forced to write off 47.5 percent of their holdings to prevent the collapse of the banking sector. The deal, which made account holders contribute to the bank bailout, was dubbed a "bail-in."

While many Russian depositors lost out, others exploited the situation to secure even more power and deepen their ties with the island. Existing shareholders in the Bank of Cyprus were mostly wiped out, while bailed-in depositors—mostly Russians—converted their losses into equity. Local law firms representing major Russian investors with their new shares began wheeling and dealing to secure seats on the board of the Bank of Cyprus, against the wishes of the European Central Bank. Six Russians were elected to the sixteen-member board, giving the key post of vice chairman to Vladimir Strzhalkovsky, an ex-KGB agent from St. Petersburg who had served alongside Putin. Strzhalkovsky was also a client of the Cypriot president's old law firm, which Anastasiades had handed to his daughters when he took office, saying he was no longer involved even though it still bore his name. Vassiliades also acted as a proxy for Russian investors in the Bank of Cyprus, helping to elect Russians to the board. Russians with ties to Putin now had enormous sway over a large European bank.

A year later, the Bank of Cyprus was still teetering on the edge. In 2004, raised 1 billion euros in a share sale to shore up its finances. That's when U.S. billionaire (and later Trump's commerce secretary) Wilbur Ross became a cornerstone investor. Other Russians came in during the share sale, including Russian billionaire Viktor Vekselberg. Ross ended up sharing the vice chairman role with Strzhalkovsky for several months, until the American vulture investor forced out Putin's old friend, replacing him with Vekselberg's representative. For all the reshuffling, Russians were still calling the shots at a major European bank. After Ross exited in 2017, Vekselberg remained the single largest shareholder, a position he has retained—despite having his 10 percent stake and dividends frozen due to sanctions. More than two years after Putin's invasion, Russian influence had drained away, but they still held sizeable stakes in the Cypriot economy.

*   *   *

One of the main tools for Russian fraud and money laundering in Cyprus was a scheme known as citizenship by investment, which allowed individuals to get passports in exchange for depositing funds in local banks or buying real estate. Tiny island states, such as Saint Kitts and Nevis, offer similar programs. While citizenship by investment is legal, calls to crack down on so-called golden passports and revoke those granted to sanctioned individuals began growing after Putin's invasion out of concern Russians were using them to launder money and evade the restrictions.

Cyprus kicked off its first citizenship-by-investment program in 2007, which allowed individuals who deposited roughly 17 million euros into local banks to get citizenship and thereby an EU passport, granting the right to work and travel across Europe. But the system was rife with abuse. RCB Bank, the Cyprus-based subsidiary of Russia's state-controlled VTB, was one of the first to pounce on the scheme, obtaining citizenship for eight of its executives in the program's first three years. Some described RCB as the "private pocket" for top Kremlin officials. The 2016 Panama Papers leak of offshore corporate records revealed how RCB had been used to channel hundreds of millions of dollars to a Russian cellist, Sergei Roldugin, a close friend of Putin's who is suspected of holding some of the Kremlin leader's wealth as a straw man. RCB provided letters to the government confirming the deposits required under the passport scheme, but there were signs they'd been falsified, indicating that passports were likely being handed out in violation of the rules.

After the so-called bail-in of 2013, President Anastasiades relaxed the requirements for obtaining citizenship. Whereas Cyprus's first citizenship-by-investment program required applicants to deposit 17 million euros into Cyprus banks, the president's new scheme allowed nonresidents who lost at least 3 million euros from the deposit haircut to apply, opening it up to more wealthy Russians who became ensnared in the 2013 banking crisis. The island's new supercharged citizenship-by-investment program also lowered the threshold for others to qualify, handing golden passports to anyone willing to plunk down more than 5 million euros. That was later reduced to 2 million if the money was invested in real estate. The program quickly became another backdoor route for rich Russians with questionable sources of money to get all the rights of EU citizens, including the right to vote and free movement across the continent.

Ostensibly, the scheme was about boosting economic growth after the banking crisis, but the impact on Cyprus was negligible. In most cases, investors paid heavily inflated prices for villas or luxury apartments as high-end projects mushroomed around Limassol. Profits went to developers and lawyers facilitating the citizenship applications. The law firm founded by President Anastasiades and run by his two daughters while he was in office processed more than sixty citizenship applications, while a company founded by his son-in-law became one of the biggest developers in Limassol. Between 2007 and 2020, almost three thousand Russians received Cypriot passports, thereby becoming EU citizens.

The muckraking Cypriot author Makarios Drousiotis, a former adviser to President Anastasiades, turned against his boss and has written scathingly about past abuses on the island in a series of controversial books, titled *Mafia State: How the Gang Abolished the Rule of Law in Cyprus* and a new volume in English called *Putin's Island*. In February 2024, Cyprus's Independent Authority Against Corruption announced an investigation into the corruption allegations contained in *Mafia State*. Two months later, Anastasiades sued him for defamation in Cyprus, seeking 2 million euros and an order preventing him from distributing content. With his gray beard and exaggerated hand gestures, Drousiotis has all the hallmarks of a cranky, opinionated investigative journalist. Though critics tried unsuccessfully to ban his book when it came out on the island in 2022, it was nevertheless a bestseller in Cyprus. "The Cypriot state had set up a passport-selling racket motivated by fast and easy money," Drousiotis told me. "It was exploited by a large number of politically exposed persons and international crooks who were trying to escape the arms of the law in their home countries."

Former government officials told me there was no due diligence at all in the early years of the citizenship scheme, with no checks on whether individuals held political or public posts in their home countries. No one monitored whether applicants immediately flipped properties after getting their passports, violating the rules. "It was systemic corruption," one former senior Cypriot official involved in the program told me. "Lawyers, enablers, accountants, property developers—it was a whole system built around it." Vassiliades was among the many lawyers who helped clients gain citizenship through the scheme.

Among the cohort receiving Cypriot passports were some of Russia's richest men aligned with Putin, including Deripaska, the aluminum billionaire.

Despite a number of red flags, Deripaska breezed relatively quickly through the citizenship application process. Using the local branch of Pricewater-houseCoopers (PwC), one of the world's biggest accountancy firms, Deripaska applied in 2016 on the basis of plunking down 2.55 million euros to buy three units in the Oval, a distinctive spherical tower in Limassol overlooking the water, and a villa in the Aphrodite Hills, a luxury residential development west of Limassol. Deripaska's application didn't include the sales contracts for the properties and had other missing or incomplete paperwork. Cypriot authorities had no information on the source of his funds. An investigation by Interpol into Deripaska for money laundering initially held up his applica-tion, but once it ended, he got his passport. Cyprus granted him citizenship in March 2017, along with his two children, Petr and Maria.

Efforts to revoke passports from people who'd obtained citizenship under questionable circumstances faced entrenched opposition. In 2019, U.S. offi-cials raised concerns with their counterparts in Nicosia that Deripaska could use his Cyprus passport to avoid U.S. sanctions and asked for assistance with a probe into his alleged money laundering. (Deripaska has denied being involved in money laundering.) Cypriot officials proposed revoking his passport along with those of twenty-six others who got citizenship with few checks, but other government ministers held up the proposal.

In 2020, the TV network Al Jazeera sent undercover reporters to Cyprus posing as representatives of a fictional Chinese client to expose the corrup-tion plaguing the citizenship program. Sitting down to a lunch of lobster by the Mediterranean, the reporters secretly filmed a lawyer who offered to help their client get a passport, despite his past conviction for bribery and money laundering. They also covertly recorded high-ranking Cypriot officials willing to help criminals get a passport. Documents they uncovered showed convicted fraudsters, money launderers, and political figures from all over the world bought golden passports, with Russians the biggest applicants from 2017 to 2019, years after Putin annexed Crimea. The explosive report was a watershed moment, sparking an outcry from European officials. Just days after Al Jazeera's undercover film was released, Cyprus ended its golden passport scheme, though it continued to process pending applications until mid-2021.

The government set up an independent commission to investigate what went wrong. It was headed by the former head of the Cyprus Supreme Court,

Myron Nicolatos, a soft-spoken, bespectacled lawyer, who told me that the extent of the problem was much bigger than he had originally thought. In 2021, the commission released a 780-page report detailing the abuses, but with the names redacted. It found that more than half of the passports issued were outside the framework of the law simply because the rules didn't allow for citizenship to be granted to family members or company executives. It recommended the government consider revoking the citizenship of eighty-five people who might have committed criminal or other offenses to get a passport.

Nicolatos told me over coffee on the beachfront in Limassol that the whole affair had been deeply damaging to Cyprus and Europe as a whole. It was easy enough to document the wrongdoing, but taking away citizenship is far more complicated. "Once nationality is granted, it creates vested rights and is not so simple to revoke," he said. "Now the West considers us the Trojan horse in the European Union because so many Russians are here."

By the time Putin launched his full-scale invasion, Cyprus had little choice but to follow the EU sanctions against Russia. Over the previous decade, the number of bank accounts in Cyprus belonging to Russians dropped from more than a third of all deposits on the island in 2013 to roughly 2 percent, as banks closed the accounts of thousands of Russians because of either sanctions or compliance checks. But thousands of Russians still held passports obtained through the corrupt government scheme. Finally, in April 2022, the Cypriot government announced it would revoke the passports of eight sanctioned Russians, but didn't name them. Annuling citizenship has to be approved by the Council of Ministers, the government's executive branch, and sources told me in the summer of 2023 that the Interior Ministry hadn't been officially informed that Deripaska's passport had in fact been canceled. The status of others' passports, including those of suspected or convicted criminals, also remains shrouded in secrecy because of EU data protection rules. As of January 2023, Cyprus said it had rescinded the citizenship of 222 people but their names were not released.

The passport scandal was just part of a broader mystery around what happened to Russian money in Cyprus. Within a month of Putin's invasion, RCB, the Russian bank in Cyprus, shut its retail business. Six months later, it surrendered its banking license. Russian money had drained quickly from the bank to who knows where. By January 2023, officials in Nicosia had frozen only 105 million euros of Russian deposits in the wake of sanctions. The amount was so small that officials in Brussels began asking what was going on. "It's a real concern," the EU's commissioner for justice, Didier Reynders, said, citing a report that the island received 96 billion euros in Russian investments in 2020 alone. Cyprus later disclosed it had frozen an additional 1.2 billion euros in Russian assets managed by companies on the island, mostly in European banks. Cyprus was beginning to crack down on Russian illicit money, but there were signs that potentially billions of dollars had escaped the ever-widening net of sanctions.

*   *   *

The pressure from Western governments on Cyprus began ramping up a few weeks after Washington and London blacklisted Vassiliades and Ioannides, the island's two most prominent Russian enablers. First, the United States sent an eight-hundred-page dossier to the government in Nicosia dissecting sanctions violations by local individuals or entities. The evidence was mostly produced from simple Google searches, leaving some Cypriot officials embarrassed they'd failed to take action. British officials traveled to Cyprus in May 2023 to help the country build a sanctions enforcement unit.

Under pressure from the United States and the U.K., the Cyprus government tried to show it was taking action. The central bank governor said the island had closed 43,000 shell companies and 123,000 suspicious bank accounts in recent years. Then, in a move that went above and beyond what was required under EU law, the Bank of Cyprus announced that 10,000 accounts belonging to about four thousand non-EU Russian passport holders would be shut down.

Six months later, in November 2023, a massive leak of 3.6 million files obtained by the International Consortium of Investigative Journalists underscored how Cyprus had played an outsize role for years in moving dirty Russian money. Among the leaked documents were those showing that Ioannides's firm, MeritServus, handled the day-to-day business of more than one hundred Cyprus companies and trusts owned or controlled by Russian oligarchs. The leak also revealed how Cyprus staff at PwC had tried to help

Russian steel billionaire Alexei Mordashov transfer a $1.4 billion stake in TUI, Europe's largest travel operator, to his third wife just as the EU was announcing sanctions against him. Cyprus authorities said they were conducting a criminal investigation into the share transfers. If it had happened after sanctions took effect, the transfer would have been illegal, raising the possibility that PwC and Mordashov could be prosecuted for sanctions violations. While the transfer was publicly known, the role of PwC Cyprus was not. (In a statement, PwC said it takes the application of sanctions seriously. Mordashov denies sanctions violations.)

The island's new president, Nikos Christodoulides, who took office in February 2023, pledged to investigate and tighten controls, admitting mistakes were made. "We should be done with this matter," he told reporters in mid-November 2023. "No one is above the reputation of our country." After a lack of action, the United States sent twenty-four FBI agents to Cyprus in December 2023 to assist the police in their investigations into sanctions breaches.

*   *   *

But the island's Russia connection is so deep that it may take years to unravel. When I was in Cyprus, just after Christodoulides declared a "zero tolerance" policy on Russian sanctions evasion, I made my way to the Limassol Marina to attend an event billed as a one-hour evening yacht cruise of networking and cocktails to discuss "Sanctions: How to recover assets and profits." I had seen the cruise advertised online and registered, listing my profession as a writer. When I arrived around 8:00 p.m. on a Thursday in June, I had a hard time finding the yacht. The setting seemed wrong. Tourists were out in flip-flops eating ice cream, kids were playing in the square, and the bars were packed. I spotted a trickle of people in business-casual attire walking along the marina and figured my best bet to find the yacht was to follow them. After a year of chasing luxury superyachts, I was disappointed to find only a hundred-foot vessel that looked more like a tourist party boat full of Russian yuppies.

Around thirty people were on board, a mix of men in button-down shirts and women wearing pastel pantsuits clutching expensive handbags. The young man on the gangway cheerily checked me off his list, welcoming me with a neon-colored cocktail. I sat on a white bench on the upper deck and looked around, trying to figure out who had decided to spend a summer evening in 2023 learning about navigating sanctions. It was an odd crowd—a mix of lawyers, accountants, and fixers, mostly Russian but with a smattering of Cypriots. The firm hosting the event was based in Moscow and led by young Russian lawyers who had clearly spotted a gap in the market. They had recently worked for Western firms in Russia, most of which closed shop after Putin's invasion.

As the yacht finally pushed off to cruise along the coast, the speakers revealed how Cyprus remained a weak link in the West's economic war against Russia. After a few minutes at sea, one lawyer offered an obvious solution to get around sanctions: re-domicile! In other words, Russian companies and individuals should get out of jurisdictions following Western sanctions. "For example, the Seychelles do not comply with any sanctions regime, except maybe the U.N.," one female Russian lawyer told the group, adding Mauritius and Hong Kong as other possibilities. "It's quite an easy, straightforward process to register there.

"A second passport is also very helpful," she said.

"You don't show the first!" a Russian woman in the audience chimed in.

"Exactly, especially in the bank," the lawyer responded.

Another Russian woman working for an "offshoring" business in Cyprus and the UAE agreed. "A lot of our clients are relocating businesses to different regions," she said. "Not only in Dubai, but now very often it's about Latin America—Brazil, Argentina—or it's Asia, or even Saudi Arabia."

The discussion moved on to cover cases of Russians who successfully had their sanctions lifted, including the mother of Yevgeny Prigozhin, the leader of the Wagner mercenary group. She'd recently won her appeal to remove the EU sanctions, despite her owning shares in companies controlled by her son between 2011 and 2017. The warlord's mom was held out as an example of how it's possible to successfully overturn sanctions. As the boat cruised back and docked at the marina, I left, but many stayed on board, no doubt discussing other ways of navigating the economic war. I decided to head to Dubai, which from all the talk sounded as if it had become—for Russians—the new Cyprus.

CHAPTER 10

A GLITTERING MOSCOW-ON-THE-GULF

After hearing stories about Russian money flooding into the United Arab Emirates after Putin's invasion, I decided to travel to the place that had come to epitomize this new Moscow-on-the-Gulf: Jumeirah Bay, a secluded man-made island shaped like a seahorse connected to the Dubai mainland by a bridge. Locals call it Billionaires Island, where villas were fetching as much as $50 million in 2023. Opened in 2017, the island is home to the Bulgari hotel and residences, an Italian-branded luxury development with a yacht club, beach resort, and spa that has been a magnet for Russians. The gated community boasts a mix of low-rise apartments and modern mega-mansions with private beaches and views of the Dubai skyline.

Asiya Khasnutdinova, a Russian-born real estate agent at Sotheby's International in Dubai, offered to show me around. As we stood in the foyer of one of the Bulgari apartment buildings, Victoria Lopyreva—a onetime Miss Russia picked as ambassador for Russia's 2018 FIFA World Cup, undoubtedly with Putin's approval—swanned by in killer heels and floating long blonde hair as the overwhelming scent of Bulgari perfume seemed to be pumped through the air-conditioning shafts. She sells the Russian way of life in Dubai to her 6 million Instagram followers. I'd never heard of her, but when I looked her up, there she was, big lips and all, clad in a string bikini sitting in an infinity pool overlooking the city's skyscrapers or dining at the Bulgari yacht club.

She'd been flogging Dubai to Russians long before the 2022 invasion, paving the way for the influx that followed.

Many Russians looking to move to Dubai scouted Billionaires Island for properties, from the ex-wives of sanctioned Russian tycoons to tech bros, according to developers and real estate agents there. Russian foreign minister Sergei Lavrov stayed there in early 2023 when he was house hunting. Many prefer it to the Palm, an older man-made archipelago of dredged sand that is Dubai's most famous development and has historically attracted Russians. It, however, lacks the privacy of Billionaires Island. "Some clients say, 'Anywhere but the Palm,'" Khasnutdinova told me.

I wasn't surprised when a developer casually mentioned that Billionaires Island is home to the wife of sanctioned Russian oligarch Andrei Skoch, who has used Dubai to shelter from Western restrictions. In 2018, the United States sanctioned Skoch for what it called his "long-standing ties to organized crime." The U.K. and the EU followed with penalties against him in 2022. With a fortune from metals and telecoms, Skoch was a member of Russia's parliament and voted to officially recognize the occupied Ukrainian regions of Donetsk and Luhansk as independent states on the eve of Putin's invasion.

On a blistering-hot day in mid-June 2023, I arrived at Dubai's Mina Rashid Marina, looking to see if a superyacht linked to Skoch was still docked there, long after a few media reports had flagged it was hiding from sanctions in the UAE. A smattering of superyachts bobbed in the water, baking under the sun. It felt eerily quiet. The retired ocean liner *Queen Elizabeth 2*, now a floating thirteen-deck hotel with art deco interiors, loomed at one end of the dock. Not far away, I spotted the distinctive shark-blue hull of *Madame Gu*, a 324-foot superyacht with a helipad that converts into a squash court. The United States listed *Madame Gu* as blocked property because of its ties to Skoch.

For much of the year, Dubai draws the superrich from all over the world, some of whom sail their superyachts into the Arabian Gulf for the winter. But when summer approaches, and temperatures in Dubai soar above 110 degrees Fahrenheit, the wealthy elite usually flee with their superyachts to more temperate climates in the Mediterranean such as Saint-Tropez or Monaco. For Russia's tycoons, Putin's war changed all that. Russian yachts were suddenly in danger of being impounded if they strayed into European waters. Dubai, on the other hand, had ignored Western penalties, making it perhaps one of the safest places in the world to keep a sanctioned superyacht. As a result, Skoch may have decided it wasn't worth the risk of moving it out of the Gulf's grueling temperatures.

The sanctions mean that U.S., U.K., and EU citizens and companies are barred from receiving payment from Skoch in dollars, euros, or pounds. Those that did so ran the risk of getting hit with sanctions themselves. In August 2022, the Justice Department showed its willingness to go after the billionaire's assets when it issued a seizure warrant for his $90 million Airbus jet, grounding it in Kazakhstan, saying it was involved in sanctions violations. The same fate seemed to await his superyacht.

None of that stopped *Madame Gu* from being maintained in top-notch condition at the Mina Rashid Marina. When I peered through the metal fence protecting the dock, I saw crew wearing white T-shirts on board carefully washing the side of the boat in the sweltering heat, while a large red generator on the dock powered the air-conditioning to preserve its interior. The Dubai-based company that operated the generator, Rental Solutions & Services, was run by two British executives, despite Skoch being under sanctions. (A person close to the company said it did not interact directly with *Madame Gu* or its owner.) The Mina Rashid Marina itself, meanwhile, was operated by DP World, a vast multinational logistics company owned by Dubai's royal family that has business in the United States. Allowing *Madame Gu* to dock at the marina could open up DP World to being punished by Washington or elsewhere. But few in Dubai seemed worried by that prospect.

Madame Gu is just one of many symbols of Russians—and their money—flooding into Dubai after Putin's invasion. The EU and the United States shut their airspace to any Russian-owned or Russian-registered aircraft, which ended direct flights. Rapid-fire sanctions were closing Russian money flows to the West, including its long-standing enabler, Cyprus. But the Emirates became a glittering safe haven for Russians of all kinds, from ordinary citizens fleeing Putin's conscription to some of the country's wealthiest and most politically connected tycoons escaping Western sanctions. Direct flights from Moscow to Dubai made it an easy-to-reach getaway. In contrast to many European capitals, Dubai didn't have Ukrainian flags flying in solidarity. Foreigners, many of them now Russians, outnumber locals by nine to one in this glitzy city-state in the desert. The UAE pitched itself as a new kind of

Switzerland—neutral in the economic war, open and eager for business, and marked by the kind of secrecy that led illicit money to gurgle through its financial system.

The UAE was thumbing its nose at Washington, Brussels, and London when it came to sanctions enforcement by allowing billions of dollars' worth of Russian assets to flow into the country. The Gulf state is a prime example of the yawning gaps in the West's economic war against Russia. Dubai has replaced Cyprus as the new artery of Putin's regime, an outlet for Russian money that functioned as a valve to release the pressure of Western sanctions.

I wanted to see for myself how Dubai had turned into a sanctuary for illicit Russian finance. There were superyachts aplenty, oligarchs buying luxe waterfront villas, and a burgeoning class of middlemen facilitating the sale of oil and technology to prop up Putin's war. And there were more sanctioned enablers for me to try to hunt down in what was turning into an almost comical quest to talk to shady people suddenly shut out of the Western financial system.

*   *   *

On paper, the oil-rich UAE is a key partner of the United States, cooperating on defense, energy, and foreign policy in the Middle East. In addition to buying American surveillance technology, it hosts five thousand U.S. military personnel at its Al Dhafra Air Base. But in reality, the UAE has an uneasy relationship with Washington, chafing at lectures on everything from sanctions to human rights. UAE officials have long rejected accusations of facilitating sanctions evasion and maintain they're protecting the integrity of the global financial system.

But the Gulf state has clearly been tilting East. At the United Nations in 2022, the UAE refused to condemn Russia's invasion and did not match Western sanctions. In April 2023, Pentagon leaks revealed that U.S. spies had caught Russian intelligence officers bragging about how they'd convinced the Emiratis to work against U.S. and British intelligence, an allegation the UAE dismissed as false, according to the Associated Press. But months later, in June 2023, UAE president Mohamed bin Zayed Al Nahyan—best known by his initials MBZ—arrived for talks with Putin in St. Petersburg, where he was the guest of honor at Russia's annual economic forum, one of the few international leaders to attend the event. It wasn't just a one-off. He'd already met with Putin in Moscow in 2022 eight months after the invasion, a sign that the UAE would not let the war get in the way of their close ties. And in one of his rare trips abroad since facing an international arrest warrant over the war in Ukraine, Putin traveled to the UAE in early December 2023 to meet with MBZ to discuss energy cooperation, the conflict in the Middle East, and Ukraine.

As Putin sought to strengthen ties with the Gulf to offset isolation from the West, more than a million Russians visited the Emirates in 2022, a 60 percent rise from the year before, with tens of thousands making it their home. Like London in the 2000s, lucrative businesses cropped up to serve this new wave of Russian expats, from private schools to medical facilities and flashy restaurants selling tiny $500 plates of beluga caviar. There's even Russian ice cream on sale at waterfront kiosks.

Soon some of Russia's wealthiest elites were making Dubai their base. The high-profile fertilizer billionaire Andrey Melnichenko started spending more time in Dubai after coming under Western sanctions in March 2022, penalties which he called "absurd and nonsensical." After Italy froze his $530 million sailing yacht in the port of Trieste, he moved a smaller $300 million boat to Ras Al Khaimah, one of the poorest Emirates in the north. For a while, he kept his yacht anchored off the Al Hamra Marina & Yacht Club, known locally as the Moscow Cluster. After being sanctioned, he stepped down from the coal and fertilizer companies he founded, and they soon opened trading units in the Gulf nation. That followed a pattern of Russian-backed oil and metals companies setting up shop in the UAE's free zones.

In 2021, with the help of the leader of Ras Al Khaimah, Sheikh Saud, Melnichenko even obtained a UAE passport. Citizenship by investment—schemes that allow individuals to get passports in exchange for plunking down cash—was still new and rare in the UAE, but the Gulf state had just introduced new rules that allowed it under secretive conditions. More often, Russians used UAE's golden visa program, which provides long-term residency to investors willing to invest $2.7 million.

The influx of Russian money enabled property developers and real estate agents to rake in huge profits. In 2022, Russians were Dubai's biggest international real estate buyers.

For years, buying houses or apartments in Dubai was a relatively easy way to launder money. Until the middle of 2022, there were no checks on sources of wealth for people purchasing property or requirements to report suspicious transactions. Some brokers told me about buyers arriving with bags of cash, with the whir of counting machines frequently heard in real estate offices. As the ruble crashed in the immediate aftermath of the invasion, there was a sudden urgency for Russians to move their money out. I heard tales from multiple sources of cash being smuggled into the UAE on private jets. Meanwhile, some sanctioned tycoons converted rubles to dirham—the UAE's currency, with an exchange rate pegged to the U.S. dollar—in Moscow, then found smaller banks to transfer the money to Dubai.

Using cryptocurrencies was another way to buy real estate to get around sanctions and banks wary of Russian transfers. Agents and expats told me many Russians were using the cryptocurrency Tether, a so-called stablecoin pegged to the U.S. dollar and known as USDT, to move millions into Dubai. Russians didn't need a bank account to buy real estate in the UAE if sellers or middlemen were willing to accept USDT for a deal at the right price. Moreover, USDT was easy to convert into dirhams at one of the many exchanges operating across the Emirates, which was turning itself into a cryptocurrency hub. "Everything is possible," one real estate agent told me.

*   *   *

This free-for-all climate didn't go unnoticed by international regulators. In March 2022, not long after Putin's invasion, a Paris-based global watchdog called the Financial Action Task Force added the UAE to its "gray list"— countries that need closer monitoring because of deficiencies in countering money laundering and terrorist financing. Being put on the gray list was a bad look for a country such as the UAE, which prides itself on becoming a hot new global financial center. It placed the UAE in the same company as the likes of Syria, Nigeria, and South Africa. Gray listing gums up the wheels of finance by triggering extra checks from international banks to ensure they aren't doing business with money launderers. To try to get off the gray list, the UAE began enforcing anti-money-laundering rules that had been on the books for years but had largely been ignored. One of the government's first targets: Dubai's booming real estate market. In July 2022, the UAE government began requiring real estate brokers to run identity checks on buyers and file reports on transactions using physical cash and cryptocurrencies.

Even with these new regulations, Dubai continued to offer plenty of loopholes for Russian money to be laundered. Real estate brokers told me they won't automatically turn away buyers because of sanctions, unless they're imposed by the United Nations. As long as the transactions are in the local currency rather than dollars, euros or pounds, doing business with a sanctioned individual isn't technically against UAE law. "If they're sanctioned by one country, it doesn't mean we can't do business with them," Khasnutdinova told me. The increased scrutiny following the UAE's gray listing led to other creative approaches to getting money into the country. Some wealthy Russians trying to transfer cash to Dubai with no questions asked were able to pay developers directly for properties still under construction. Private developers not listed on stock exchanges were allowed to accept money for "off plan" real estate without the checks and reporting requirements that banks and agents must now do. These off-plan purchases surged in 2022. A financial adviser told me one former Russian government official transferred $30 million into the UAE that way. With so many new skyscrapers going up, many were willing to take Russian money, no questions asked, to ensure buildings were sold.

By the end of 2022, it became clear that the UAE's bid to become a global cryptocurrency hub had helped facilitate more sanctions evasion and money laundering, even as it was trying to get off the gray list. As other jurisdictions began tightening digital currency regulations, Dubai granted a license to Sam Bankman-Fried's crypto firm FTX. It was one of the first digital currency shops allowed to set up an exchange in the Gulf state after regulators boasted it had gone through a rigorous evaluation. Just months later in 2022, FTX imploded in one of the biggest financial frauds in history. That same year, Dubai gave a provisional license to Binance, the world's largest crypto exchange, and welcomed its founder, Changpeng Zhao, as a resident. In 2023, Dubai gave Binance a full license to operate an exchange and as a broker-dealer. However, data showed Binance users were converting rubles at sanctioned Russian banks into digital currencies through layers of intermediaries, even as the company said it was adhering to Western sanctions, according to the *Wall Street Journal*. In September 2023, amid a probe into sanctions evasion, Binance announced it had sold its Russia business to a new crypto exchange. Two months later, the United States charged Binance with facilitating transactions with users in sanctioned jurisdictions, including Iran and Russian-occupied regions of Ukraine. Among the many violations: more than $100 million was transferred to Binance wallets from the Russian dark-web market Hydra, used by criminals for everything from money laundering to stolen data. Binance reached a plea deal with the U.S. Justice Department, agreeing to pay over $4 billion. Its founder, Zhao, pleaded guilty to violating U.S. money laundering laws and was sentenced in May 2024 to four months in prison.

* * *

Illicit money exploited the UAE's unique dynastic structure. The country is a loose federation of seven competing emirates, each ruled by different sheikhs trying to outbid each other to attract investment. It has more than forty self-governing "free zones"—half of which are in Dubai—that exempt companies from taxes and customs duties.

Dubai gets all the headlines, but the capital, Abu Dhabi, a separate emirate, began an aggressive pitch for new wealth starting around 2021. From Dubai, I took a taxi eighty miles south along an accident-prone four-lane highway through the desert and along the Persian Gulf to Abu Dhabi. Once the center of the pearl trade, it's a quieter, more traditional city than its flashier neighbor, though it still has plenty of soaring skyscrapers. On the streets, there are more men dressed in the dishdasha, or long white robe, while most women wear the abaya, an ankle-length black dress. Despite this traditional feel, Abu Dhabi had gone out of its way to try to turn itself into one of the world's largest financial centers, eager to lure investors from all over the world. Some are merely investments on paper. For example, two companies registered in Abu Dhabi in the name of Arkadiy Abramovich, the eldest son of Roman Abramovich, the sanctioned former Chelsea owner, were nowhere to be found at their listed addresses—sparsely populated coworking spaces where employees had never heard of him.

One morning, I had breakfast with a senior Abu Dhabi official to hear why so many wealthy Russians were coming to this corner of the world. He didn't want to be named because of the sensitivities involved, but he was acutely aware that Abu Dhabi was the beneficiary of an elaborate global reshuffling of wealth as Russians sought somewhere "neutral" to park their cash. "Wealth sits easily in Abu Dhabi," he said. Only United Nations sanctions would automatically stop the authorities from registering a business. "Everything else is a gray area," he told me. As Western governments continued to add more names to sanctions lists, Russian tycoons began setting up companies in Abu Dhabi. Billionaire Vladimir Lisin transferred his stakes in Russia's biggest steelmaker, Novolipetsk, and a rail freight operator to Abu Dhabi from Cyprus, though he's only subject to sanctions in Australia and Ukraine. It was yet another sign of how the UAE was replacing Cyprus as a nexus for Russian money. Well-known tycoons prefer low-key Abu Dhabi because they can walk around unnoticed, unlike in Dubai, and the more relaxed regulations enable them to set up flexible holding companies for their assets. "My quip is, 'Millionaires go to Dubai. Billionaires come to Abu Dhabi,'" the official told me.

In June 2022, a few months after the UAE was added to the gray list, Deputy Treasury Secretary Wally Adeyemo touched down in Dubai. Concerned about the flood of Russian money into the Emirates, Adeyemo was there to warn officials and bankers about the dangers of allowing sanctioned individuals to use the UAE's finance sector. "The UAE—and other global financial hubs—continue to face the threat of illicit financial flows," he told bankers at a roundtable in Dubai. "Financial institutions must be exceedingly cautious in handling any Russia-related business." He said that Washington wouldn't hesitate to target non-U.S. citizens for supporting sanctioned individuals or entities. The implicit warning: bankers couldn't plead ignorance as a defense.

Adeyemo reminded them that Russian banks continued using shell companies to hide who is behind transactions. Money launderers and sanctions evaders often try to trick banks by layering transactions through multiple cross-border payments or splitting transfers into smaller amounts to avoid detection. The bankers assembled assured Adeyemo they had robust compliance systems to check for illicit money—most major UAE banks are terrified of being cut off from the U.S. dollar for violating sanctions. But Adeyemo pushed them. If your compliance systems are so good, he asked, then how is Russian money getting into the UAE? Do they come in with cash? Buy real estate? Gold? Diamonds? "His message was 'Try to make sure there isn't leakage,'" one banking CEO at the dinner told me.

According to three people who attended, many of the bankers began to feel frustrated. Some complained the Western sanctions and export controls were a maze to navigate. "We told him, 'Be reasonable. Make it clear what you're prepared to allow.'" Another said that Adeyemo displayed an arrogance that didn't go down well with his audience. "The tone was very directive. It was, 'We are the U.S., we're it,' attitude."

While the bankers claimed they were following Western sanctions, it was clear business with Russia was booming. Russian exports to the UAE surged 71 percent to $8.5 billion in 2022, mostly precious metals, making it into Russia's largest trading partner in the Gulf. Meanwhile, reexports of electronics to Russia grew fifteen times, a sign that the country was being used as a conduit to sell technology banned under Western export controls. Some seven hundred Russian companies registered in the UAE in 2022. At the end of that year, after heavily sanctioned Sberbank, Russia's largest lender, closed its representative office in Abu Dhabi, the UAE quietly issued a license to MTS Bank, a subsidiary of Russia's largest mobile phone operator, to open a branch. No announcement was made, but it was the first foreign bank in the UAE to get a license in several years. The country's central bank framed it as an attempt to serve the Russian community in the UAE and support trade between the two countries. But at that point, about 80 percent of Russia's financial sector was subject to Western sanctions, so trade would inevitably go through blacklisted banks.

In January 2023, the United States tried again to convince the UAE to cooperate. Brian Nelson, the Treasury's undersecretary for terrorism and financial intelligence, arrived in Dubai to highlight the "dangers of countries being permissive of dark money flowing through their financial systems." Nelson, a lean, tall lawyer from California, brought his diplomatic skills, honed while working for the organizing committee for the Los Angeles 2028 Summer Olympics. During his visit, Nelson expressed concern to officials about the UAE's deepening financial ties with Russia and its decision to allow MTS Bank to operate there. His trip got off on a bad foot when Reuters

▲ Vladimir Putin and Joe Biden met in June 2021 for a historic summit at Villa La Grange on the shores of Lake Geneva, Switzerland. Biden wanted to use the summit to build what he called a "stable and predictable" relationship with Russia. "This is not a 'kumbaya' moment," Biden told Putin. Three months later, Russian troops began to build up on the border of Ukraine.

▲ In the White House situation room, Biden convened a meeting of his national security team on February 24, 2022, to discuss how to respond to Russia's unprovoked invasion of Ukraine. Left to right: Chairman of the Joint Chiefs of Staff Mark Milley, Defense Secretary Lloyd Austin, Secretary of State Antony Blinken, Vice President Kamala Harris, President Biden, National Security Adviser Jake Sullivan, Chief of Staff Ron Klain, and Treasury Secretary Janet Yellen.

▲ Signs requesting funds to rebuild a destroyed building in Irpin, Ukraine, which was liberated from Russian forces on March 28, 2022, after fierce urban warfare that destroyed or heavily damaged almost 70 percent of the city.

◀ Daleep Singh, Biden's deputy national security advisor for international economics, speaking during a news conference at the White House on February 22, 2022, after the United States unveiled sanctions against Russia's elite and two major banks. Singh played a leading role devising U.S. sanctions against Russia following Putin's full-scale invasion.

▶ Andrew Adams meeting with Attorney General Merrick Garland in March 2022 soon after accepting the role as the head of the KleptoCapture task force, an interagency body set up to enforce sweeping sanctions against Russia. Deputy Attorney General Lisa Monaco, who oversaw the task force, looks on.

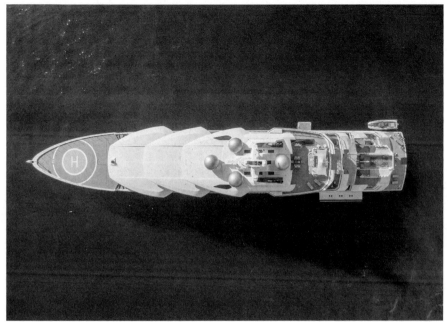

▲ The U.S. Justice Department seized the 348-foot superyacht *Amadea* in Fiji just months after Putin's full-scale invasion, alleging it was involved in sanctions evasion. The Justice Department wants to sell the boat, which has been docked in San Diego since June 2022. It's costing the U.S. government almost $1 million a month to maintain the yacht, including dry-docking fees.

▲ The Justice Department alleges the Russian tycoon Suleyman Kerimov, a senator in the country's upper house of parliament, owns *Amadea* and violated sanctions imposed on him in 2018 by using the superyacht. He denies buying the ship, but prosecutors unearthed evidence on board that indicated he owned it through a front company.

▲ Eduard Khudainatov, the former CEO of state-controlled oil giant Rosneft, came forward claiming he was the real owner of *Amadea*, setting off a protracted legal battle with the Justice Department. He maintains *Amadea* was not involved in sanctions evasion and the U.S. government has no grounds to seize it. The EU sanctioned him in 2022, but the United States has not.

▲ *Madame Gu*, a 324-foot superyacht linked to Russian parliamentarian and sanctioned billionaire Andrei Skoch, was docked in Dubai from March 2022 and listed as blocked property by the U.S. Treasury. Valued at $156 million, it boasts an elevator and a helipad. Dubai served as a safe haven for superyachts owned by sanctioned oligarchs after more than a dozen Russian-linked vessels were frozen in Western ports.

▲ Matthew Axelrod, the Commerce Department's assistant secretary for export enforcement (far right) and Matthew Olsen, U.S. assistant attorney general for national security (second from right), in Kyiv in November 2023, examining drones and electronic components used by Russia to attack Ukraine. Axelrod and Olsen have led efforts to stop the flow of U.S. technology to Russia's defense industry.

◀ A digital signal processor made by Texas Instruments found on the battlefield by Ukrainian investigators in an Iranian-designed Shahed-136 kamikaze drone, rebranded by Russia as Geran-2. Small and cheap, these microprocessor chips are used in a broad range of products, such as charging stations and other industrial applications. It was just one of thousands of Western components found in Russian weapons systems in Ukraine.

▶ Estonian authorities caught Vadim Konosh-chenok, a colonel in the Federal Security Service, the successor to the KGB, trying to cross the border into Russia with thirty-five different types of Western semiconductors and electronic components and American-made ammunition. They arrested him in December 2022 and extradited him to the United States in July 2023 to stand trial on charges of violating U.S. export control laws. He pleaded not guilty.

WANTED BY THE FBI

BORIS YAKOVLEVICH LIVSHITS

Conspiracy to Defraud the United States; Conspiracy to Violate the International Emergency Economic Powers Act (IEEPA); Bank Fraud Conspiracy; Wire Fraud Conspiracy; Wire Fraud; Money Laundering Conspiracy; Money Laundering; Conspiracy to Violate the Export Control Reform Act (ECRA); Smuggling Goods from the United States; Failure to File Electronic Export Information

DESCRIPTION

Aliases: Boris Levitan, Boris Livshitc, David Wetzky

Date(s) of Birth Used: May 9, 1970	Place of Birth: Leningrad, Russia
Hair: Black / Bald	Sex: Male
Race: White	Occupation: Electrical Engineer
Nationality: Russian	Languages: Russian, English

▲ Boris Livshits is wanted by the FBI for his alleged involvement in a procurement network backed by Russian intelligence to obtain military and sensitive dual-use technologies used in Russian weaponry. The Justice Department alleged that he directed Konoshchenok on smuggling U.S. technology into Russia.

▶ British prime minister Boris Johnson speaking with Italian prime minister Mario Draghi at the G7 Summit at Schloss Elmau, a German castle in the Bavarian Alps, in June 2022. G7 leaders agreed to explore imposing a price cap on Russian oil to try to limit Putin's hydrocarbon revenues. A month earlier, Draghi had proposed creating a "cartel" of buyers to limit Russia's energy revenues.

▲ The international waters of the Laconian Gulf off the coast of Greece became a busy hub for Russia's oil trade after Putin's invasion of Ukraine. Russia's shadow fleet of rusty tankers were frequently seen engaged in risky ship-to-ship transfers at sea to hide the origin of the oil traveling to global markets. In September 2022, *Simba* (pictured left) was emptying Russian fuel into *Turba*, which was transmitting a fake AIS position to hide the transfer.

◀ Russian billionaire Roman Abramovich was forced to sell Chelsea Football Club in 2022 after he was sanctioned by the U.K. and the EU. He pledged to put the proceeds—£2.35 billion—into a foundation to benefit "all victims of the war in Ukraine." Disagreement with the U.K. officials over how the money would be spent prevented the foundation from being set up. Pictured here in Porto, Portugal, on May 29, 2021, with then-captain César Azpilicueta and Abramovich's sons Aaron (left) and Arkadiy (right) after Chelsea won the UEFA Champions League final. Abramovich had received Portuguese citizenship just a few weeks earlier.

18

▲ In December 2022, British law enforcement raided Athlone House, the $125 million mansion in north London belonging to Fridman, alleging he was involved in sanctions evasion. The investigation was dropped after his lawyers successfully argued the authorities had bungled the raid.

▲ Russian billionaire Mikhail Fridman lived in London for eighteen months after Putin's full-scale invasion of Ukraine trying to get U.K. and EU sanctions lifted while battling a criminal probe into alleged money laundering, which he denied. In September 2023, he left London for Israel; after the October 7, 2023, Hamas attacks, he left for Russia and has been splitting his time between Moscow, Israel, and other countries in the Middle East. Pictured in Madrid, Spain, on October 21, 2019, arriving for a court hearing over allegations he helped undermine Spanish technology company Grupo Zed in a bid to buy the company. A Spanish judge closed the case in 2023, citing a lack of evidence.

▲ Russian billionaire Oleg Deripaska (far right) standing next to his girlfriend, a Russian porn model, and Russian foreign minister Sergei Lavrov (third from right) in Tokyo in 2018 in a photograph obtained by *New Lines Magazine* and the *Insider*. The U.S. Justice Department indicted Deripaska in 2022 after a long-running probe into sanctions evasion that included paying for his girlfriend to give birth in the United States so their child could get American citizenship. Washington believed Deripaska was holding assets on behalf of Putin.

◀ Ukrainian volunteers carrying an elderly man from an evacuation boat in the city of Kherson after Russian explosions caused the Nova Kakhovka dam to collapse on June 6, 2023, flooding dozens of villages and towns along the Dnipro River. The dam's destruction caused Ukraine's worst environmental disaster since Chernobyl.

▶ Pipes being laid in Ukraine to provide clean water to 1.5 million people affected by the flooding and destruction of the reservoir at Nova Kakhovka. It was just one of many reconstruction projects happening in Ukraine while Russian attacks on critical infrastructure continued.

◀ Putin shakes hands with China's president Xi Jinping in Beijing on October 18, 2023, during the opening ceremony of the Belt and Road Forum to reinvigorate what Xi called the "project of the century," aimed at increasing China's geopolitical influence by investing in infrastructure in more than 150 countries. China's backing of Russia through deepening trade ties has helped Putin to fund his war in Ukraine.

reported that he was planning to "warn" officials about the consequences of sanctions evasion. Not wanting to listen to what they believed would be another reprimand, some private sector leaders and officials refused to meet with Nelson. But his message to other officials was clear: the United States was prepared to impose sanctions on individuals and companies in the UAE unless the Emiratis enforced Washington's restrictions.

Despite the kerfuffle over Nelson's trip, Washington eventually scored a win. A few weeks after he returned home, the United States and the U.K. imposed sanctions on MTS, which banned it from conducting dollar or pound transactions and effectively hamstrung its ability to operate. At the end of March 2023, UAE's central bank relented and announced it was canceling the MTS license because of the "sanctions risks." It soon began winding down operations.

There were other signs Washington's pressure was beginning to work. By the middle of 2023, Russian individuals and companies started having a harder time opening bank accounts and transferring funds as the UAE stepped up its efforts to get off the gray list and satisfy calls from Western allies to enforce sanctions. Banks began asking more questions and blocking transactions. After introducing stricter checks on money laundering, the UAE succeeded in getting crossed off the global watchdog's gray list in late February 2024. But sanctioned Russian businessmen were still using it as their base, even if they couldn't open up a bank account. One told me the trick was to use a Russian travel agency in Moscow to pay for everything—hotels, restaurants, taxis. "You can transfer cryptocurrency here without banks, so it's much easier to transact in Dubai than in any other place," he told me.

U.S. officials had been monitoring Dubai's booming crypto market and finally made good on their threats to start people in the UAE. In its never-ending game of Whac-A-Mole, the U.S. Treasury also began targeting fixers based in the UAE who were helping Russians circumvent the rules. In May 2023, the United States imposed sanctions on John Hanafin, an Irish citizen living in Dubai and the founder of Huriya Private, a firm Washington said was helping wealthy Russians open UAE bank accounts and get fraudulent passports under assumed names. With Russians barred from traveling to many countries following the full-scale invasion, demand for second passports skyrocketed. Hanafin boasted online in a Russian post about his services providing "citizenship by investment," in island states, such as the South

Pacific archipelago of Vanuatu. It wasn't just UAE; he was allegedly procuring fraudulent passports from other golden passport schemes to help Russians hide their nationality. In designating Hanafin, the U.S. Treasury listed a digital currency address associated with him that had received almost $5 million worth of mostly Tether stablecoins since January 2022, indicating, officials believed, he was using the cryptocurrency to open bank accounts or procure passports for Russians.

Hanafin was more than an obscure middleman. His company had funded scholarships for the London-based Cherie Blair Foundation for Women, set up by the wife of former U.K. prime minister Tony Blair. Hanafin's wife, Huriya's chief operating officer, Katerina Pawlowska Hanafin, who was also later sanctioned, appeared with Cherie Blair at an event a year after the full-scale invasion. Washington also imposed sanctions on Georgios Georgiou, a Cypriot citizen who worked with Hanafin, for what it called his "money laundering globally for criminal organizations, corrupt businessmen and Russian oligarchs."

In mid-June 2023, I went to Hanafin's office on the eleventh floor of an office tower in Dubai's Business Bay, hoping to speak with him. At the entrance, I waited on a green velvet sofa, bizarrely set against a large black-and-white photograph of the Eiffel Tower on the wall, which made little sense in downtown Dubai. His assistant came out to tell me he wasn't in and seemed alarmed I'd even gotten past the front door. His lawyer later emailed me accusing me of taking pictures—I hadn't—and saying his client had been "the subject of various inaccurate media articles," but Hanafin never responded to my request to speak to him about his sanctions designation. A few months later, he changed his LinkedIn profile picture to that of a Middle Eastern man wearing a traditional red-checkered headscarf, his face partially cropped out of the photo. It looked as if he'd gone to ground.

About a week after I left Dubai, Washington began to target the Dubai middlemen facilitating the flow of Russian commodities. Russia is the world's second-biggest producer of gold and was once one of its biggest exporters until the invasion. After London's bullion market closed its doors to Moscow, the UAE became a nexus for trading Russian gold. At the end of June 2023, the U.S. Treasury imposed sanctions on a Dubai-based entity called Industrial Resources General Trading, based in a glass tower in the city's commercial district, for providing financial support to Yevgeny Prigozhin, the founder of the Wagner mercenary group. The Dubai company had done business with a Prigozhin-controlled company in the Central African Republic, selling huge amounts of gold for U.S. dollars—just one spoke in a vast financial wheel funneling cash to the warlord. But the penalties likely had little effect, coming just a few days after Prigozhin's failed mutiny against the Kremlin and long after Wagner forces began fighting in Ukraine. Prigozhin himself died two months later in a suspicious plane crash north of Moscow. The U.K. followed with blocks on gold traders in the UAE channeling cash to Russia, but new companies keep popping up to fill the gaps.

Some engaged in the illicit trading of Russian gold operate out of Dubai's old souk in the northern district of Deira, the historic commercial trading neighborhood. It's about as far as you can get from the sanitized streets and Western malls of Dubai. The area had been used for centuries to trade spices and fabrics from India, Africa, and Asia along the Silk Road. In the early 1900s, jewelers gathered on a bend in the Dubai Creek and began trading gold in what has now become the city's most famous bazaar, with retail shops overflowing with extravagant necklaces and bracelets.

One day, I wandered down a busy narrow street to the roof-covered souk, trying to see how much money I could launder if I wanted to buy gold jewelry. In other words, how much cash would dealers take without any checks on my identity? And could I turn around and sell the piece to make the cash look legit? Dealers kept haggling me to come into their shops, so I figured it would be easy. At one store manned by a father and son, I found a gaudy necklace that I could have bought on the spot for $100,000 cash—no forms to be filled, no IDs needed. "No limits," the father told me. Next door, I asked a man wearing a dishdasha behind the counter if they'd be willing to buy a gold necklace, showing them a picture of the piece from the father-son shop. After some questions about karats and weight, he told me he'd buy it for an agreed price per kilo if I brought it in. He said he'd give me a receipt with a stamp, which, theoretically at least, I could use to deposit the cash in a UAE bank, allowing the money to enter the financial system clean.

Clearly, one could only launder so much cash at retail shops in the souk. But the bigger operators were in the nearby Gold Centre, a six-story building where traders toiled in a maze of offices. One of the biggest Russian gold traders at the time, an obscure company called Al Bahrain Jewelers LLC, operated from the fourth floor behind a frosted-glass door with a high-tech keypad security system. It had taken over $50 million in gold from Russia in just six months of 2022. I rang the bell and was greeted by several men behind a white counter. If I had to imagine what a shady front for laundering gold from Russia would look like, this would have been it. They wouldn't say where they sourced their gold and shooed me out. (In December 2023, Al Bahrain issued a statement saying it has had no business dealings with Russian entities and it currently didn't accept materials from Russia.) I went looking for another notorious trader of Russian gold called Paloma Precious, with an office in the souk, but after a few hours of looking and asking around, I couldn't find it.

My attempts to document Russian money laundering and sanctions busting in the UAE were as amusing as they were deeply disturbing. There were signs of it happening everywhere, but the very ubiquity of dodgy schemes made me realize how hard it is to enforce sanctions on Russia globally.

Six months later, the U.K. sanctioned Paloma as part of a network channeling more than $300 million in gold revenue to Russia. Paloma was probably just one of many helping Russia smuggle gold out to international markets. Dubai has long been known as the City of Gold, but that's only part of the story. Dubai was morphing into the central trading center for Russia's other key commodity: oil. Obscure companies were coming out of nowhere to set up in Dubai and help Russia keep the petrodollars flowing.

CHAPTER 11

CAPPING PUTIN'S WAR PREMIUM

When leaders gathered for the G20 summit in Rome at the end of October 2021 for their first face-to-face gathering since the pandemic, Biden decided to share U.S. intelligence with some European allies revealing for the first time Putin's plans to invade Ukraine. Behind the scenes, U.S. officials were trying to build a coalition to counter Putin if he did invade. They quickly realized the West's biggest weakness in the event of a war: its dependence on Russian oil and gas.

Russia is the world's second-largest crude oil exporter behind Saudi Arabia. The late U.S. senator John McCain once called Russia "a gas station masquerading as a country." The strength of the Kremlin, going back to the Soviet period, has always relied on the global price of oil, its principal source of hard currency. During his twenty-four years in power, Putin has enjoyed a relatively high price for oil, which has, in turn, enabled him to pour money into the Russian military. Western leaders had to figure out some way to put a lid on Russia's profits that would hinder his ability to fund the country's military-industrial complex without causing a global energy price spike. But the United States and Europe had two very different pressure points. Americans were sensitive to higher prices for gasoline—a byproduct of oil—to fuel their cars; Europeans cared more about natural gas piped in from Russia, used widely to heat homes and power industry. Those divergent interests made it all the more unlikely that Washington,

Brussels, and London would find the political willpower to counter Russia as an energy superpower.

Energy prices were already running high as economies reopened after the pandemic. A short-term fix was available. A network of underground salt caverns in Texas and Louisiana known as the Strategic Petroleum Reserve (SPR) holds the world's largest supply of emergency crude oil. Set up in 1975, after the Arab oil embargo caused gas prices to spike, the reserve is one tool the U.S. president can use to release oil to cool prices.

"Energy was the one area where Russia had an asymmetric advantage over the West," Daleep Singh, Biden's deputy national security adviser, told me, recalling the discussions around the G20. "We were trying to get ahead of what we knew might be a supply disruption in the aftermath of a war. If Russia were to press its advantage by weaponizing its supply of energy, we needed to be ready to respond in kind with a collective release of our own reserves."

In November 2021, Biden announced the release of 50 million barrels of oil—enormous by historical standards, but it was equal to only about two and a half days of U.S. demand. The drop in prices was short-lived, and by December, concern about the buildup of Russian troops on Ukraine's border, combined with pent-up demand after Covid, was causing oil prices to shoot up again. As a Russian invasion looked ever more likely, the price of natural gas also began to spike. Europe relied on Russia for about 40 percent of its imported natural gas, raising the prospect of thousands of people dying from the cold because they couldn't afford to heat their homes if Putin ordered his troops into Ukraine.

Once Russia invaded, the global price of oil and natural gas skyrocketed. Initially, Western leaders consciously decided *not* to go after Russia's energy exports, fearing any move would simply cause prices to spike even further. As one senior Biden administration official put it, "We wanted to put pressure on Russia, not cause a global recession." The administration refrained from blocking Gazprombank, Russia's third-largest bank, which serves the energy sector, apart from restrictions on its ability to raise funding in the West. As a result, Putin continued to enjoy a steady stream of petrodollars, with Gazprombank serving as the main conduit. It was a gaping hole in the otherwise sweeping package of financial sanctions. Oil and gas revenues comprised 45 percent of Russia's federal budget in 2021. Pressure to attack those revenues began to build.

Canada was the first to go after Russian energy, which set off a chain reaction. On February 28, 2022, just four days after the invasion, Canadian prime minister Justin Trudeau announced a ban on Russian crude oil imports in what was a symbolic move—the country exports oil and hadn't imported crude from Russia since 2019—but efforts to block Russian oil snowballed from there. In Washington, members of Congress started asking why the United States wasn't as firm as Canada. "The message we were getting was 'Either you ban Russian energy imports or we'll legislate,'" Singh recalled.

In a video address in early March, Zelensky piled on the pressure for a full boycott, likening buying Russian energy to "giving money to a terrorist." Ukraine's foreign minister, Dmytro Kuleba, called out Shell for buying Russian oil. "Doesn't Russian oil smell [like] Ukrainian blood for you?" he tweeted. Days later, Shell announced its plan to withdraw from Russian hydrocarbons, including an immediate halt to spot oil purchases, a historic shift for a company that was such a major player in the market. Shell's decision accelerated the withdrawal of Western energy companies from Russia, but it also raised concerns about how the global market would replace Russian barrels.

Soon after, Washington announced a ban on Russian oil and gas, which Biden said would "deal another powerful blow" to Putin's "war machine." For the United States, it was a relatively painless move. Only 8 percent of U.S. oil imports came from Russia. The United States is a net exporter of petroleum products, meaning it could easily replace supply. After Biden's announcement, global worries about Russian supplies mounted, causing the price of oil to peak at $139 a barrel, the highest since just before the financial crisis of 2008. Gasoline prices in the United States jumped to a then-record high of $4 per gallon. The U.K. followed with a more gradual phaseout. Like the United States, the U.K. relied on Russia for 8 percent of its oil demand, but it was not a major oil producer and relied heavily on imports, meaning it would have to source other supplies.

While the United States fretted about oil, Europe was more worried about the skyrocketing price of natural gas. But in reality, the Continent was facing a full-blown energy crisis because of its heavy dependence on Russia. Unlike the United States or the U.K., Europe relied on Russia for about a third of its oil imports before the war, making talk of an outright ban a nonstarter, at least initially. At the end of March 2022, Biden met with European Commission president Ursula von der Leyen and agreed they needed to work together to reduce the continent's dependence on Russian energy broadly. To help Europe wean itself off Russian gas, Biden offered to supply the EU with an extra 15 billion cubic meters of liquefied natural gas shipped via special tankers, aiming to raise that to 50 billion per year—or about a third of what Russia piped into the EU every year. Meanwhile, Italy's prime minister, Mario Draghi, was traveling the world trying to drum up additional supplies of natural gas from Algeria, Egypt, Angola, and the Republic of the Congo to reduce Italy's dependence on Russia.

Biden simultaneously tried to flood the market with oil. At the end of March, he announced the largest-ever release of U.S. oil reserves to fight what he called "Putin's price hike": 1 million barrels of oil per day for the next six months, or 180 million barrels in total. But it barely made a dent. By April, Putin was earning almost $1 billion a day from energy sales and looked set to earn more than $320 billion in exports in 2022, a third more than the previous year.

Wars involving major producers often cause oil price spikes because of worries about supply disruptions, and this time was no different. Many buyers were steering clear of Russian oil because of public outrage, which caused prices to surge. Russia's hydrocarbon revenues were helping neuter the effects of the other Western restrictions and causing the ruble to rebound. While the West was penalizing Putin with one hand, it was bankrolling his war machine with the other. It revealed the heart of the dilemma facing the West. If it cut off Russian energy supplies to punish Putin, prices would only increase further, enabling him to profit even more. The West needed to find a way to limit Russia's revenues without causing an oil supply shock that would push Europe and the United States into an economic downturn.

*　　　*　　　*

Singh had been brainstorming ways to cap Russia's oil profits for months with Deputy Treasury Secretary Wally Adeyemo and David Lipton, an international affairs counselor to Treasury Secretary Janet Yellen. Singh told me some of their early thinking had been inspired by Draghi, the former ECB president, who had been trying to persuade Europe to impose a price cap on natural gas from Russia. "At that point, we started thinking about the analogy to oil," Singh told me. For decades, a group of oil-producing nations led by Saudi Arabia had clubbed together through a cartel—OPEC—to agree on production quotas. Now the idea was for consumers to band together to demand lower prices. "Why don't we try to use our collective bargaining power as the world's largest block of consumers to limit any price spikes?" Singh recalled the thinking at the time. "There's already a sellers' cartel, so why not create a buyers' cartel?" It was a radical step that flipped the idea of OPEC on its head.

But that effort only gained momentum when officials in Washington got wind of a plan being hatched in Brussels to ban Russian oil from Europe altogether, a move that threatened to plunge the global economy into a downward spiral. The proposal set off alarm bells in Washington. U.S. Treasury officials were growing increasingly worried that an EU embargo could blow up global energy markets and cause U.S. gasoline prices to spike ahead of crucial midterm elections.

For Europe, it was a sudden about-face. In the first month after the invasion, Germany's Olaf Scholz warned that an immediate ban on Russian energy would trigger a recession. Greece was balking, saying its shipping industry would be upended. But the Baltic states and Poland were pushing hard for an embargo. After the atrocities in Bucha emerged in early April, once unthinkable policies became acceptable. Attacks on innocent civilians in Ukraine made continued imports of Russian oil politically untenable, and Germany dropped its opposition.

After the U.S. ban on Russian oil, there was now an unstoppable momentum for a similar move in Europe. "In the beginning, getting agreement on sanctions was sort of rolling a ball up the hill," von der Leyen's head of cabinet, Björn Seibert, told me. "Once the war started, the ball was rolling down the hill, which was much more complicated to control because everybody wanted more sanctions."

In mid-April, Biden's top economic brains got on a virtual call to hash out ways to limit Putin's energy windfall and persuade the EU to change course.

Singh joined the call with Biden's trusted confidant Jared Bernstein and David Kamin, another senior White House economic adviser. Adeyemo hopped on with his colleague Ben Harris, Treasury's top economist. Catherine Wolfram, a Treasury energy economist who had worked with Yellen at the University of California, Berkeley, logged in from home, recovering from a case of COVID. "It was clear that the Russians were minting money on energy markets and benefiting from a war premium—a war they'd started," Wolfram told me. "It was the ultimate irony."

They knew the numbers were scary. Russia was too big for an oil embargo. It accounted for about 11 percent of global oil production. Treasury's initial models indicated that if all Russian oil was removed from the market, prices would go up by 100 percent, causing a global recession. Even taking half of Russia's oil off the market could cause prices to jump 50 percent.

In other words, Russia was not Iran. In 2012, the United States sought to freeze Iran out of global oil markets over its nuclear program. But Russia's oil exports were much bigger than Iran's. "You couldn't do nothing because Russia was profiting from the war, and you couldn't do what we have usually done to bad actors that are big oil exporters—an embargo—because you would suffer these big price increases," Wolfram recalled. "We realized we needed to try something new."

As they sought to head off an EU embargo, they batted around ideas. Imposing a punitive tax or tariff on Russian oil was one option. Tariffs are widely used by countries around the world to protect domestic products, like cars or metals, from competition; there was growing pressure to impose a tax or tariff on Russian oil and use the proceeds for Ukraine. But European officials shot down that idea because it raised the risk of increasing prices for Western consumers since importers would shoulder the costs of the tariffs.

The other idea was to use a price cap on Russian oil to restrict the Kremlin's revenues. Trying to limit the price of oil from one country had never before been attempted, so there was no model to follow. The basic concept was simple—a coalition of countries would band together and agree to only buy Russian oil under an agreed price—but devilishly complex to implement. It was an exercise in thinking outside the box. They had to map out market assumptions—what would be the impact on Russia's revenues, would Moscow reduce production, how would the market react. They asked Wolfram to crunch the numbers, and she wrote the first of many memos outlining the pros and cons. A few days later, she came back with an analysis arguing that a tariff or tax option and a price cap would have broadly similar effects. But the cap amounted to an unprecedented attempt to manipulate the global oil market.

They spent several weeks trying to convince the Europeans to drop the idea of a Russian oil ban. Forging consensus on sanctions among the twenty-seven EU member states was always a tough grind, and there were some doubts such a radical policy to impose an embargo would survive diplomatic squabbles. Divisions within Europe were why Brussels mustered only a weak response to Putin's 2014 annexation of Crimea. This time, Seibert used "confessionals"—so called because the small gatherings of EU ambassadors were frequently held on Sundays—to find enough common ground. In early May, von der Leyen announced a proposal to completely block Russian crude oil imports within six months. "Let us be clear, it will not be easy," she told the European Parliament. "But we simply have to." At this stage, it was just a draft that had to win the support of all the EU member states, with their competing economic interests.

Crucially, von der Leyen's proposal included barring all EU companies from offering insurance, brokerage, and financial services for the transport of Russian oil anywhere in the world. The London-based International Group of P&I Clubs, the insurance group that covers 90 percent of the world's maritime fleet, relied heavily on European members and contracts; the planned EU ban on services raised the prospect of millions of barrels of Russian oil suddenly disappearing from world markets because shippers couldn't get insurance.

Ben Harris, then Treasury's top economist and a longtime Biden adviser, told me he spent weeks on Zoom calls trying to convince EU officials to back a price cap instead of the embargo, to no avail. He thought the EU ban would cause Russia to withhold at least some oil from global markets, generating a price shock. With his earnest delivery and multiple economics degrees, he made a strong pitch, but it wasn't landing. "There was skepticism from our counterparts in Brussels," he told me. "It was maddening at times. The shipping nations were worried about their own economic interests and told us,

'We can't disrupt this trade.' And others told us, 'We're fully happy to drive up the price of oil by 30 percent if that means hurting Russia.'"

For months, U.S. officials were getting pushback from everyone. "I can't tell you the number of times people told me this is a moronic idea, or unworkable, or both," Singh told me. "They said, 'You'll never build a coalition for it, you'll never be able to enforce it. It's just way too complicated to explain.'" Another former Biden official said plenty of U.S. and European officials hated the concept when they heard about it: "They said it's never going to work, it's economically inefficient, it's a crummy idea." The proposal even had detractors inside the U.S. Treasury, who thought it could backfire. "There was a faction that did not like the word *price cap*," Wolfram recalled. "It had negative associations in economic circles." After all, free-market economists generally like the market to set prices, not Washington policy wonks.

Even in London, there were doubts the idea could work. "I'm a free market person, so I thought how can you have a price cap for a commodity coming out of one particular country when there's a global price? We were quite skeptical," Kwasi Kwarteng, the U.K.'s business and energy secretary at the time, told me. "I got the sense it was all about the midterms. The one thing the American administration was totally paranoid about was the price of gasoline in the U.S. I could hear it in their voices, like 'we've got to sort this shit out. We can't have spiking prices.'"

Others pushed back, echoing Winston Churchill's famous phrase that democracy is the least bad form of government. The oil price cap was the least bad option they had. Yellen liked the oil price cap idea because she thought it would help rein in inflation and give other countries bargaining power to pay less to Moscow for oil. As an economist, Yellen understood the modeling and asked tough questions throughout to test the assumptions about how it would work. "This was Janet Yellen's baby," Elizabeth Rosenberg, the Treasury's assistant secretary for terrorist financing and financial crimes, told me.

In Kyiv, Zelensky's top economic adviser, Oleg Ustenko, viewed the price cap idea as a breakthrough when he first heard about it. He'd held fruitless calls with Greek officials trying to persuade them to clamp down the country's shipping companies trading Russian oil, telling them it might not be illegal, but it was immoral given the bloodshed in Ukraine. "I thought, 'With the price cap, now we have the real solution,'" Ustenko told me.

The horse-trading in Brussels over the proposed Russian oil embargo began immediately after von der Leyen proposed it. One of the most vocal holdouts was Hungary, led by the irascible Viktor Orbán, a young communist dissident turned strongman leader and Putin ally. Landlocked Hungary, fed by the Druzhba pipeline from Russia's heartland, was unusually dependent on Moscow for oil. The Hungarian oil company MOL had refineries that were designed to process Russia's Urals oil blend, and it was a huge cash cow for Orbán's government. Von der Leyen knew Hungary's dependence on Russian oil would make an EU embargo a hard sell. In early May, she flew to Budapest to meet with Orbán. Diplomats familiar with the talks told me she was convinced she could persuade him to agree if Hungary was given a grace period to implement it.

Von der Leyen has one of those anything-is-possible CVs that led her to be dubbed a *Wunderfrau*: seven children, a degree in medicine, and fluency in three languages. She had defied criticism over her weak track record as Germany's defense minister by navigating the EU's Byzantine ways with surprising diplomatic skill. Over dinner in his office in the city's historic Buda Castle, Orbán stubbornly refused to sign up to the embargo, and diplomats told me that von der Leyen almost walked out in frustration. She left empty-handed. "We made progress, but further work is needed," she tweeted diplomatically. Hungary, with a population of less than 10 million, was holding up a policy pursued by other EU states representing some 440 million people. Orbán got his way in the end. After a month of negotiations, EU leaders approved the planned embargo but carved out an exemption for pipeline oil. That meant Hungary could continue to import Russian crude via the southern section of the Druzhba pipeline, enabling its refineries to continue to profit.

*   *   *

U.S. officials watched the situation in Europe unfold with dismay. Figuring out a way to undercut Russia's oil revenue without a total embargo was becoming urgent. The EU's plan, approved by member states in early June, banned the purchase of crude oil delivered by sea starting December 5 and barred EU firms from providing insurance for ships carrying Russian crude to other countries outside the EU. Because European companies played such a big role in shipping insurance, the decision threatened to spike oil prices by taking Russian supply off the market. That set the clock ticking. U.S. officials had six months before the ban came into force to persuade the EU to back an alternative.

In June 2022, Harris, Wolfram, and Rosenberg hopped on a plane for a whirlwind European tour to persuade their counterparts to allow some Russian oil to flow with European insurance and financing under restricted pricing. If Russian tankers carried oil above the agreed price, they would be barred from using Western insurance and shipping services. They were facing enormous skepticism. After racing through meetings in London, Brussels, Paris, and Berlin over just three days, they left feeling dejected. "We came out of there thinking we probably wouldn't get a deal," Harris recalled.

At the end of June, G7 leaders convened at Schloss Elmau, a German castle deep in the Bavarian Alps, for their first summit since the war began. Putin's continued enrichment from energy overshadowed the talks. A lot of sweeping sanctions had been rolled out, but Putin's hydrocarbons were the last big target. With U.S. gasoline prices at the pump now topping $5 a gallon, Biden argued for the G7 to endorse the cap.

Draghi was willing to back the oil price cap as a way to convince a reluctant Scholz to back a cap on the price of natural gas too, hoping the German leader would see similarities between the two proposals. An oil price cap was an easier sell to Germany, which was far more worried about Russian natural gas. The G7 agreed to "explore" the idea of an oil price cap without committing to it. Even that weak statement was viewed as a victory given the overwhelming resistance. G7 leaders asked ministers to figure out the details, giving them plenty of wiggle room.

British officials were drawn into devising the plan because the U.K. is home to so much of the world's shipping insurance, giving it a choke point for enforcement. "We just didn't quite know if it was going to work in practice," Jonathan Black, the U.K.'s G7 sherpa, told me. "It's probably one of the most complicated pieces of international policy I've ever been involved in, with different regimes interacting with each other across multiple jurisdictions." There were conversations with companies about the impact on the market, debates about how the insurance ban would work, and political wrangling over the ripple effects on different industries.

The critics piled in immediately. "This is going to fail," tweeted Adam Posen, president of the influential Peterson Institute for International Economics, a Washington think tank. "The G7 won't enforce it on India, and China will retaliate until a workaround is reached."

Nonetheless, Harris flew with Yellen to Bali in July for the G20 finance ministers' summit, where they met leaders from Asia and Africa to explain the price cap idea and build support for it. The feedback was lukewarm. "We realized it was going to be really hard to get buyers to commit to this," Harris said. "We figured out we didn't need to because we could have enough of an impact by using the G7's dominance of shipping services to enforce it."

But they needed to set a price that would ensure Russia kept oil flowing to avoid a supply shock. During months of behind-the-scenes negotiations in Washington and European capitals, leaders debated what level to set the cap. Everyone wanted a different number. The nagging worry throughout was that if the cap was set too low, Putin would "shut in" Russian oil in response to Western penalties. In other words, he would just leave Russian oil in the ground, thereby driving up global prices exponentially.

Harris was betting Putin couldn't afford to do that because of the unique vulnerabilities of the Russian oil industry. Russia can't easily flip a switch and turn its West Siberian oil wells on and off. Unlike Saudi Arabia, many of Russia's oil wells are deep underground and operate under a delicate pressure system that can't be shut down without the risk of losing long-term capacity. "We understood pretty quickly they probably weren't going to weaponize oil," Harris said. "We realized *we* had the leverage rather than Russia." But they couldn't be completely sure. In July 2022, Russian deputy prime minister Alexander Novak, the bespectacled former energy minister, warned that Moscow would not sell oil if the cap was too low. "We will simply not pump oil at a loss," he told Russian TV. "If the price cap they're talking about is lower than the cost of crude oil production, naturally Russia will not supply that crude on global markets."

That got Yellen worried. Rationally, Russia would cause itself more harm by leaving oil in the ground, but Putin's invasion of Ukraine itself was a massive act of self-harm. As the United States midterm elections approached, U.S. officials grew concerned that Putin might strike for maximum effect, spiking U.S. gasoline prices to hurt Biden at the polls. "One view was that

Putin saw this as an impingement on his sovereignty and that he would try to test the price cap by shutting in oil in October when he had all the leverage," Harris told me.

In Kyiv, Ustenko, Zelensky's economic adviser, was talking to Adeyemo in Washington. "I told him the cap should be set at ten to twenty dollars a barrel," Ustenko recalled. "We had the statistics. We knew Russia sold oil at this level before." In 1998, after Asia's financial crisis, Russia continued selling even as the global price of oil fell to as little as $11 a barrel. Treasury officials drew up intricate modeling to find a kind of "Goldilocks" number—not too high that it would have little effect on Russian revenues, but not so low as to cause Putin to withhold supply. Russia's cost of oil production was below $10 a barrel for most wells before taxes and transport costs. Levies ratcheted up when producers fetched higher prices. Wolfram and a small team crunched the numbers and came up with $60 as the best balance between those twin goals of incentivizing Russia to keep oil flowing while curtailing the Kremlin's profits. But there was still no agreement.

Many analysts and traders thought it was foolhardy to try to put a lid on Russian prices in a highly complex multitrillion-dollar oil market. But in a virtual meeting in September, G7 finance ministers announced they'd agreed to go ahead with the oil cap in December. The price would be formally agreed later. The idea had gone from a nonstarter among some leaders to an accepted policy of the world's biggest economies, albeit with the details to be hammered out.

Just hours later, Putin weaponized natural gas. The state-controlled gas giant Gazprom suspended supplies indefinitely through the Nord Stream 1 pipeline that connects Russia with Germany under the Baltic Sea, claiming it found a technical fault that couldn't be fixed because of Western sanctions. The move plunged Europe into an even deeper energy crisis and piled pressure on the EU to find alternative supplies ahead of what was expected to be a difficult winter. It left just two major routes supplying gas to the EU: one through Ukraine, which had been curbed because of the war, and another through TurkStream, via the Black Sea. Putin's gas war cannibalized his biggest market. Weeks later, someone finished the job for him. A series of mysterious bombings of the Nord Stream 1 and 2 pipelines deep undersea—since blamed on everyone from Ukraine to the United States, and even Russia itself, without any definitive proof—choked off any temptation to restart supplies. Nord Stream 2 wasn't even operational at that point, but the attacks were lethal corporate warfare. Ukraine accused Russia, Putin blamed the CIA. Whoever was behind it, the end result was a devastating blow to Gazprom as its profits tumbled.

Putin thought he could force Europe to freeze. Speaking a few days later in the Far Eastern Russian city of Vladivostok at an annual economic forum focusing on his country's ties to the Asia-Pacific, the Russian president railed against the price cap and compared the energy battle to a well-known Russian fable about a fox who tricks a wolf into believing it will capture fish by dipping its tail into an ice hole. The wolf is trapped when his tail freezes, and villagers take their revenge by beating the animal. In Putin's reading, the West is the foolish wolf and Russia is the sly fox who will stop supplying energy to Western countries, trapping them in an inflationary spiral. "The only thing we can do is keep on saying the line from a Russian fairy tale, 'Freeze, freeze the wolf's tail!'" he said.

Putin's folklore was wishful thinking. Draghi's proposed price cap on natural gas hadn't been agreed yet but Europe had managed to find other supplies. By October 2022, Russia's 40 percent share of Europe's piped natural gas imports had shrunk to about 9 percent. In December, Germany completed its first liquefied gas shipping terminal off its North Sea port of Wilhelmshaven in less than two hundred days, enabling the United States and others to replace Russia's pipeline gas supplies. "Putin thought he could blackmail us by cutting off our gas supplies," Scholz said at the opening of the terminal. "We will not be blackmailed."

But Russia was making more money from oil than natural gas; the G7 price cap posed a greater potential threat to Putin than the loss of Europe as his biggest gas customer. Talks among the G7 on where to set the cap took months, with protracted negotiations in Europe. As talks on the price cap dragged on, Harris raced around the world attempting to persuade doubters in the oil market. In the fall, he flew to Houston to meet with executives from the global commodities firm Trafigura, which was one of the largest traders of Russian oil. After the invasion, Geneva-based Trafigura had said it would wind down its trade of Russian oil and end projects with state-controlled oil giant Rosneft. When Harris walked into the conference room, he could feel the anxiety; Trafigura had terminated long-term contracts with Russia but there were worries about how to navigate such a major intervention in the global oil market. "I had to repeat several times, 'We don't want to ban Russian oil, we want to keep it flowing,' until the tension in the room went out and we could start talking about how to make it happen," Harris recalled.

In early October, OPEC+, the enlarged cartel that includes Russia, surprised markets by announcing a steep cut to oil production, equal to 2 percent of global supply, in a bid to keep prices high. Saudi Arabia was clearly willing to help Russia as the price cap loomed. OPEC+ members viewed the cap as a dangerous precedent that could be turned on them in the future. Putin trolled U.S. officials on the price cap in an October speech at a Russian energy conference when he cited Milton Friedman. "If you want to create a shortage of tomatoes, just pass a law that retailers cannot sell tomatoes for more than two cents a pound," he said. "Instantly you will have a tomato shortage. It's the same with oil or gas."

Detailed talks on the cap level were delayed until after the U.S. midterm elections. Some in Europe wanted to set the price as high as $70, but that was well above the roughly $52 a barrel that Russia was getting in November. Big shipping nations such as Greece and Malta were haggling for an even higher price. Poland was holding out for $30 a barrel, throwing the EU into a deadlock in the run-up to the EU's December 5 deadline. Officials in Washington were trying to break the impasse during talks that dragged into the night. Yellen called Poland's prime minister, Mateusz Morawiecki, and her diplomatic charm offensive worked: Poland finally agreed to $60.

Even though the price was higher than what Russia was fetching at the time, getting this novel policy over the line was viewed as a victory. Harris, Wolfram, and other U.S. Treasury officials who'd worked on the plan gathered in Rosenberg's office to celebrate with Polish pierogi and kielbasas. Yellen and Adeyemo stopped by to thank them. In Kyiv, the mood in Zelensky's office was very different. "We were all extremely disappointed," Ustenko told me. "We immediately started to discuss ways to squeeze the price cap lower."

When the cap on crude oil went into force on Monday, December 5, after months of doubt and criticism, uncertainty hung over the whole policy.

Putin immediately threatened to withhold Russian oil. He branded the move "stupid, ill-conceived, and poorly thought-out" and vowed to refuse to sell oil to any country that imposed it: "All this will lead at some stage to a catastrophic surge in prices and to the collapse of the global energy sector." But Putin's own finance minister, the long-serving Anton Siluanov, was more gloomy, warning the price cap could widen the country's budget deficit in 2023.

At first, what was a grand experiment to manipulate one of the biggest markets in the world appeared to be actually working. Prices for Russian oil at Baltic ports slumped after it came into force, while a Russian pipeline to China couldn't handle the volume that once went to Europe. The Kremlin was forced to raid the National Wealth Fund, its rainy-day oil fund to plug holes in government finances. Russia's oil export revenue plunged by almost half in June 2023, to $11.8 billion compared to the same period in 2022. Russia's budget deficit was bigger in the first four months of the year than it was supposed be for all of 2023. The Kremlin was forced to alter the way it taxed oil production to plug what was becoming a yawning hole in government finances. Russia's foreign minister, Sergei Lavrov, labeled the price cap "nothing short of a theft" of its "natural resources."

Critics of the cap argued Putin would "weaponize" oil supplies in much the same way he did with gas. Indeed, at the end of December 2022, Putin signed a decree banning the supply of oil to countries following the price cap starting February 1. But the West only tightened the noose more. In February 2023, G7 countries extended the price cap to diesel and refined oil products. Putin's threats turned out to be empty. The cap forced Moscow to offer deep discounts to a smaller universe of buyers, reducing its profits.

For the Treasury officials who spent months sweating out the details and facing down the doubters, seeing the cap working was sweet satisfaction. Even critics who feared that the mechanism might set off a scramble for oil admitted it was hitting Russian revenues as intended. "It's been a remarkable reshuffling of world oil supplies," Daniel Yergin, the celebrated oil expert and historian, told CNBC.

The cap and the embargoes forced one of the most profound transformations of global trade in decades as Russia redirected oil supplies from Europe to Asia. China and India combined accounted for 90 percent of Russia's seaborne crude oil exports by the end of 2023. India in particular turned into a nexus for Moscow's oil trade, getting as much as 45 percent of its supplies from Russia, up from just 1 percent before the war began. But the loss of European buyers was costly to the Kremlin. Shipping oil longer distances is more expensive, eating into Russia's profits. There were other problems with the rerouting of supplies to Asia. Lavrov, Putin's foreign minister, complained in 2023 that Russia was sitting on billions of Indian rupees from the oil trade that it had no way of using. Russia would need to spend those rupees by buying goods from India, which doesn't produce what the country needs. Perversely, India also turned into one of the biggest loopholes of the policy. Once Indian refineries transformed the oil into gasoline, it was no longer deemed "Russian" and could be reexported freely at market prices on to Europe without breaching sanctions. While Russia had to sell at a discount to India, it effectively provided a backdoor route for Russian hydrocarbons to Europe.

The cap represented the kind of unorthodox policymaking Washington was pursuing in response to Putin's aggression, effectively opening up a new front in the economic war. It flew in the face of the free-market ideology Western leaders had preached to Russia for thirty years following the collapse of the Soviet Union. The story behind this attempt to undermine Putin's petrodollars also reveals a broader tale of how the policy sausage gets made in Washington and other world capitals. It involved a mix of economists inside and outside the U.S. government trying to figure out how to hit Putin where it really hurt without inflicting pain on the rest of the world. But their success was only fleeting.

Moscow quickly figured out ways to dodge the price cap and reshuffle trade routes. It had been assembling a shadow fleet of tankers to transport oil without G7 shipping services, often with the help of Greek shipping tycoons willing to sell aging vessels to Putin's cronies. A murky network of roughly six hundred mostly old and rusty tankers with mysterious owners and dubious insurance emerged to ship Russian oil. Adeyemo, Yellen's number two, defended the policy by saying it was forcing Russia to shell out cash on elaborate workarounds, which was precisely what they wanted. "Russia invested a bunch of money in buying tankers, not tanks," Adeyemo told me. "Their costs are up significantly."

But Russia's revenues also rebounded. New trading companies emerged in Dubai to trade Russian oil outside the price cap coalition. The entities often masked their ownership structure, making it difficult to trace who was profiting. Middlemen were making fortunes off the dark trade, some with murky ties to Moscow. There were growing suspicions that money was making its way back to Russia through the padding of freight and shipping costs, masking the actual price paid for the crude. Calls grew for the price cap to be slashed to squeeze the Kremlin's revenue. By July 2023, the price of Russia's Urals crude traded above the $60 limit for the first time since the cap came into force in December. Urals, named after the oil-rich mountainous region east of Moscow, had been trading at a deep discount to Brent, the leading global benchmark, because of the war and the price cap, but that gap began shrinking.

Over the summer of 2023, with the shadow fleet of rusty tankers cruising international waters, Russia's revenue from oil began climbing again, cushioning the Kremlin's finances. By October, the average price of Russian oil from the Baltic and Black Sea ports was almost $82 a barrel. The price jump was a tactical win for Russia because it had managed to assemble the dark fleet. But it wasn't a surprise for U.S. officials, who knew that Russia would try to find ways to bypass the restrictions. "We anticipated that prices would move back upward," Rosenberg told me. "We knew there would be vessels migrating into the Russian fleet."

But for almost a year, U.S. and European officials did little to enforce the policy they'd so carefully crafted during months of diplomacy. The rules required insurers to get an "attestation," a document from traders promising that the oil was sold under $60 a barrel, but Western governments weren't checking. Insurers poked holes in the system early on. "We're reliant on a piece of paper," Mike Salthouse of insurer NorthStandard told an industry gathering in Singapore. In other words, the attestations were just a bunch of emails going back and forth from buyers claiming they'd paid below the price cap. Without governments investigating, it was impossible to know what prices were really being paid. By October 2023, almost all of Russia's seaborne crude exports breached the cap. About a third of the shipments were covered by Western insurers, which signaled widespread insurance fraud was occurring as Russian tankers sold oil above $60 a barrel. It was sanctions evasion on an industrial scale. The EU failed to crack down on Greek tycoons for helping Russia assemble its fleet.

Washington's innovative policy had worked only briefly. Russia had outsmarted the U.S. Treasury's creative economic modeling by building its own oil shipping and insurance ecosystem, shoddy though it was. Vessels carrying Russian crude were often taking elaborate steps to evade detection in order to dodge the sanctions.

But the high-seas antics of Russian ships didn't stay hidden for long. Plenty of maritime spies were tracking their every move. Prominent among them was Samir Madani, then a forty-four-year-old half-Jordanian, half-Croatian Swedish entrepreneur, who had seen it all before. Russia wasn't the first to use a shadow fleet to dodge sanctions. Madani had watched Iran do it for years from his base in Stockholm soon after he cofounded his business, TankerTrackers.com, in 2018. After dabbling in oil trading himself, he set out to shed light on the opaque end of the oil shipping industry to feed the huge demand from insurance companies and regulators for information about how much oil is flowing where. Like others, he began tracking the flow of oil by following tankers through their automatic identification systems (AIS), transponders designed to help ships avoid collisions at sea. But he and his partner layered AIS data with satellite images of tankers transporting oil to reveal a disturbing new trend.

After Trump reimposed sanctions on Tehran in 2018, Madani noticed Iranian tankers would enter the Persian Gulf, switch off their transponders, and reappear a week or two later. Madani quickly began zeroing in on Iran's furtive oil trade. He realized the tankers were loading up Iranian oil, turning off their AIS, and heading to China. In 2020, he stumbled on an even bigger con. He spotted one VLCC—a very large crude carrier—with a red deck. "I called it the ART, or the Annoying Red Tanker," he told me. "It was pinging from the Gulf of Oman, but it was physically located north of Lavan Island, almost halfway up the Iranian coastline," more than a hundred miles away, according to satellite imagery. He soon tracked a dozen other tankers doing the same thing, in what's called AIS spoofing. "They were falsifying their latitude and longitude positions," he said. "That's when I realized this is now a thing." Foreign vessels were using a new technique to relay fake AIS data using secondary transponders, which showed them in another location. It enabled them to stage a series of secret rendezvous to be loaded with oil from Iranian state-owned ships, evading restrictions. Venezuelan tankers started doing the same thing to dodge U.S. sanctions. Spoofing had become widespread. Merely turning off a ship's transponder to hide transfers could void a vessel's insurance, but spoofing solved that problem.

By the start of the war in Ukraine, Madani and his partner had built up a database of forty-three hundred tankers based on satellite images, including what he calls the "naughty fleet": some six hundred vessels engaged in dark oil trading. Madani's clients were, by then, mostly governments and insurers that wanted to know about sanctions dodging in international waters. Until then, Madani wasn't tracking Russian oil, but when Putin invaded, Madani thought, "Dammit, we have no option but to do it."

Madani quickly realized that Russia was using Iran's playbook. On January 26, 2023, less than two months after the price cap was imposed, a Panamanian-flagged, Greek-owned tanker named *Pollux* switched off its transponder as it cruised south from the Messenian Gulf southwest of Athens in the Ionian Sea. Two days later, Madani spotted a tanker called *Sakhalin Island*, which had traveled from the Russian port of Primorsk north of St. Petersburg to Greece's Laconian Gulf, not far from where *Pollux* was headed before it went dark. On board were seven hundred thousand barrels of medium-sour Russian crude oil, which was siphoned into the Greek *Pollux* tanker while it was off-line. According to AIS data, *Pollux* wasn't there, but satellite images showed the ships side by side. The next day, *Pollux* reappeared cruising south from the direction of the Laconian Gulf, through the Suez Canal to the Red Sea and headed for Kochi, India, where the government owned a refinery. "Why would the tanker go dark inside a tiny gulf in Greece while the Russian tanker was still transmitting?" Madani asked. "It's likely that Russia was selling crude above the G7 price cap."

Surrounded by mountains, the Greek Gulf of Laconia became a busy hub for Russia's oil trade. Millions of barrels of oil each month are smuggled through risky ship-to-ship transfers. Massive rusty tankers sidle up to each other for days to transfer the crude in open waters visible to anyone who goes looking. In one classic case of spoofing captured by my Bloomberg colleague Alaric Nightingale in September 2023, a corroded black tanker called *Simba*, known to be carrying Russian oil, anchored next to another rusted red vessel called *Turba*, which was beaming an AIS signal that indicated the ship was seven kilometers away. There was no other reason to engage in a risky ship-to-ship transfer unless it involved sidestepping sanctions.

Turba was the symbol of a looming problem. Built in 1997, it should have been scrapped years ago. A Marshall Islands front company ironically named Shadow Shiptrade SA owned *Turba*, sailing it under the blacklisted flag of Cameroon. According to *Lloyd's List*, the twenty-seven-year-old ship hadn't been inspected in port since 2010. Like *Turba*, many of the rickety tankers in the hastily assembled Russian ghost fleet were an accident waiting to happen, sailing under flags from countries, such as the Cook Islands or Liberia, not known for their rigorous vetting of insurance companies, which might be mere brass-plate offices with nothing behind them. If one of Russia's shadow tankers ran aground, spilling hundreds of thousands of barrels of oil, there might be no company to hold responsible for the cleanup.

European countries on the Baltic Sea were at risk of a major environmental disaster. Tankers leaving the Russian port of Primorsk have to travel through waters near Finland's capital, Helsinki, and on through the narrow and busy Danish straits up to the North Sea en route to global markets. Russia's ghost tankers were known to have anchored off Denmark's Skagen harbor. In May 2023, disaster almost struck as a notorious oil tanker from the shadow fleet called *Canis Power*, laden with 340,000 barrels of Russian crude, lost power and drifted into shallow waters off the coast of a picturesque Danish island. After several hours, the vessel regained power and moved to deeper waters. Sailing under a Cook Islands flag, it didn't have recognized insurance. Had there been an accident, much of the cleanup costs would likely have ended up with Danish or EU taxpayers. About 80 percent of Russia's seaborne oil passes through maritime choke points in European and British waters, theoretically giving their governments leverage to demand that aging Russian tankers be fully insured in case of accidental spills. But international maritime rules mean Denmark can't interfere with a ship in transit unless there's concrete evidence of a threat to the marine environment.

In October 2023, ten months after the price cap came into force, Washington finally started cracking down. Under attack that its signature policy of depriving the Kremlin of oil revenues was failing, the United States Treasury, for the first time, began rolling out sanctions on specific oil tankers and trading companies for violating the price cap. The United States blacklisted ships owned by companies in the UAE and Turkey. It fired off a flurry of notices to ship management companies around the world asking about more than one hundred vessels suspected of violating the cap. Washington and London also began imposing sanctions on oil trading companies based in the UAE, where half of Moscow's shadow vessels were thought to be registered. The impact of the penalties could be seen at ports around the world. Some tankers performed U-turns or abandoned planned deliveries. The number of Greek-owned ships carrying Russian crude plummeted after the U.S. Treasury began asking owners how they complied with the price cap while the Greek navy carried out drills in the Laconian Gulf to halt the risky transfers. Russian oil deliveries to India slumped because of the stepped-up enforcement. Russian crude was still hovering just above the price cap, but it was a sign that Washington's sanctions could have real teeth if they were enforced. Just before the two-year anniversary of Putin's mass invasion, Washington imposed sanctions on Sovcomflot, Russia's state-owned shipping company, and blacklisted more of its oil tankers, bringing the number to twenty-one. Some switched their flags from Russia to Gabon. In total, the United States had blacklisted forty tankers for transporting Russian oil, putting a sizeable dent into Russia's shadow fleet. "Russia has decided they're going to try and build an alternative ecosystem to get around the price cap," Adeyemo said, after announcing the sanctions. "We want to increase the cost of building that ecosystem."

The price cap didn't deliver a knockout blow to Russia's oil trade, but it succeeded in draining the Kremlin of billions of petrodollars it could have earned. The government's revenues from oil fell 29 percent to $100 billion in 2023 as it was forced to sell at a discount to world prices. In the first three months of 2024, Russia was selling its Urals oil blend for an average of $66 a barrel using the remainder of its shadow fleet. The Kremlin's oil and gas revenues bounced back compared to the previous year. Russia added new vessels to its ghost fleet to replace sanctioned ships. In April 2024, Russian government revenue from oil more than doubled from the year earlier, helping to finance continued defense production. As the U.S. presidential election loomed, the Biden administration appeared to back off from continuing to sanction Russian vessels as the global price of oil ticked up.

The G7's novel policy could have been more hard-hitting. If the West wanted to meaningfully drive down Putin's revenues, governments should have blacklisted more tankers and trading companies for violating the price cap.

One trend might help sap Putin's hydrocarbon power: the OPEC cartel that has controlled prices for decades is beginning to lose its grip on the global oil market. Bumper output from non-OPEC+ countries such as the United States, Brazil, Guyana, and Canada is shrinking the ability of the cartel to influence global prices. If those four countries can maintain that output, or better yet, increase production, Putin might finally face difficulty funding his war against Ukraine. But lowering the price cap is the obvious way to make the West's newfangled economic weapon really hurt. For Oleg Ustenko, Zelensky's economic adviser, it's the only coherent solution. "We're still letting the Russians earn all this money so they can destroy my country while at the same time the West is spending huge amounts on assistance to Ukraine," he told me. "It's completely illogical."

PART V

WAITING FOR
THE END GAME

CHAPTER 12

FREEZING LONDONGRAD

At around 7:30 a.m. on December 1, 2022, Russian billionaire Mikhail Fridman was sitting in his study at Athlone House, a sprawling $125 million neo-Gothic mansion in north London. On a Zoom call with his partners from Alfa Group, a Russian banking and retail conglomerate he cofounded, he was discussing how the business was doing amid the expansive Western sanctions (relatively well). At the time, most of his partners were subject to asset freezes and travel bans in the U.K. and Europe as a result of Putin's invasion.

Unbeknownst to Fridman, a team of around fifty officers clad in black jackets and masks from the U.K.'s National Crime Agency (NCA) had erected ladders to climb over the brick wall surrounding his manor home before the security guards opened the front gate. Officers scurried along the winding stone driveway, past the clipped grass and manicured gardens, to the entrance of the thirty-five-thousand-square-foot house.

When they entered his study right off the main foyer, the call kept running. His partners, sitting in Moscow and elsewhere, watched in shock as the whole raid unfolded for several minutes. The NCA claimed Fridman jumped out the study window and attempted to run away. Fridman denied that allegation and said he'd walked toward the officers. Either way, police handcuffed him to bring him to a central-London police station for questioning.

While Fridman was being arrested, Nerijus Kuskys, a Lithuanian immigrant who managed the estate, was panicking. He hurriedly took cash from a safe in the guardhouse, stuffed tens of thousands of pounds into a plastic bag, and handed it through a window to a Polish security guard who also worked for Fridman, but NCA officers caught and arrested him. Kuskys said it was his life savings, stored in the guardhouse safe because his bank had closed his account, ostensibly because he was working for a sanctioned Russian oligarch. Officers spent most of the day turning the enormous property upside down, opening safes and carting away documents and digital devices as part of a probe into alleged money laundering, conspiracy to defraud the Home Office, and conspiracy to commit perjury. Fridman's girlfriend and their young child were not home during the raid, but officers tracked down her ex-boyfriend in West London and arrested him on suspicion of money laundering. He too was hauled in for questioning. They were all released later that day on bail.

It was the most high-profile action by the NCA's Combatting Kleptocracy Cell, a new unit formed in the wake of Russia's invasion of Ukraine. The agency bragged about the raid by posting a photo on social media of officers inside the home of an unnamed fifty-eight-year-old wealthy Russian businessman, but the media quickly worked out it was Fridman. The NCA's director general, Graeme Biggar, said the unit was having "significant success investigating potential criminal activity by oligarchs."

But it turned out the NCA had bungled the raid. The search warrant left on the premises was unsigned and had the wrong date. After months of legal wrangling, the NCA admitted the search was unlawful and dropped the probe. It later agreed to pay the billionaire damages for trespassing and to cover his lawyer's bill. For all their tough talk on enforcing sanctions, the U.K. authorities showed they were incapable of conducting a basic search. The NCA had been given more funding over the preceding few years, but it still lacked the capacity to conduct complex investigations, especially against one of Russia's cleverest billionaires.

*   *   *

Like many Russian tycoons, Fridman dismissed warnings from Western intelligence that Putin would launch a full-scale invasion in early 2022. He'd been telling colleagues in London at his private equity firm LetterOne that he didn't think it was possible. He just couldn't imagine Russians and Ukrainians actually fighting each other. When the Russian army first crossed into Ukraine early on February 24, Fridman was in Moscow for meetings and had already planned to fly back to London that evening, but decided he couldn't wait. Anything might happen. He gathered his things and hightailed it out of Moscow on a rented jet at 2:00 p.m., not knowing when, or if, he might return. He spent the next few days fielding frantic calls from colleagues in Ukraine. He told them to use whatever company money they needed to ensure the safety of employees and their families. The day after the war began, he sent a letter to his staff at LetterOne, decrying the conflict as a "tragedy" that would cost lives and saying, "War can never be the answer." It was a rare political statement for Fridman, but he stopped short of directly criticizing Putin. Any pointed attack on the Kremlin leader might have risked trouble for his colleagues and assets in Russia, but the comments stood out given how few billionaires had said anything at all.

The European Union had already announced initial sanctions, including high-profile Russian officials and bank executives, but held off from prominent billionaires. The moves might have served as a warning sign, but Fridman remained convinced his years of lobbying and networking in Western capitals would protect him. The following Monday, his charity organization, the Genesis Philanthropy Group, announced it would donate $10 million to Jewish organizations supporting refugees in Ukraine.

His guarded denouncement of the war didn't help him. That afternoon, his lawyer pulled him out of a meeting at his office in Mayfair, London's posh central district, with news that the European Union had sanctioned him and his longtime partner, Petr Aven, for being close to Putin. The lawyer started to rattle off what it meant: travel bans, frozen accounts, words that seemingly floated over Fridman's head. "I was in shock," Fridman told me. "I almost didn't understand what he was saying."

Just days after the sanctions hit, Fridman arrived at a North London café to meet me, looking frazzled, wearing a blue cashmere sweater, a T-shirt, and jeans. The world as he knew it—as we all knew it—had changed overnight. I wanted to learn what happens to a Russian billionaire who suddenly gets cut off from his cash. I'd met him several times before and knew he was a bit wary of me. He complained about a story I'd written a few years earlier about his decision to postpone plans to invest in the United States during the Mueller probe into Russian election interference.

Fridman's relationship to the Kremlin suddenly came under intense scrutiny. He told me he'd met Putin in groups, never one-on-one. His partner, Aven, did meet with Putin alone, but Fridman said those meetings meant little. "The power distance between Mr. Putin and anybody else is like the distance between the Earth and the cosmos," Fridman told me. "Mr. Aven was just approaching this like 'Thank you very much for taking the time.' To say anything to Putin against the war, for anybody, would be kind of suicide."

Over two hours, Fridman and I discussed the war, Putin, Ukraine, and Russia's future, much of which he didn't want to say on the record. He was adamant about one thing: his inability to persuade Putin to change course. "If the people who are in charge in the EU believe that because of sanctions I could approach Mr. Putin and tell him to stop the war, and it will work, then I'm afraid we're all in big trouble. That means those who are making this decision understand nothing about how Russia works. And that's dangerous for the future."

At the time, many people assumed blacklisting Russia's elite would make them turn on Putin. It was an indirect approach that some in the U.S. Treasury in 2014 and 2018 thought had a decidedly mixed record. "The success of that strategy is spotty, both in terms of whether targeted oligarchs have clearly moved away from Putin, and to the extent that they have been materially harmed by the U.S. measures," Adam Smith, a former U.S. Treasury official who advised on sanctions until 2015, told me. Some U.S. officials denied to me that the goal of sanctions was to get the oligarchs to turn on Putin, but that perception persisted. If all the oligarchs had their toys taken away and were barred from Russian haunts in Saint-Tropez and Courchevel, some of the thinking went, they'd get fed up and stage a coup.

That belief ignored how the role of Russia's billionaires had been turned on its head since the 1990s. The Yeltsin-era oligarchs kept their fortunes only if they adhered to the rules of Putin's regime and lived with the real possibility that the Kremlin would seize their assets any day if they stepped out of line. The other tycoons had gotten rich only because of their connections to Putin, so they were unlikely to turn on him. The sanctions against Russia's business leaders made sense as a way to undermine the Russian economy and help degrade Putin's war machine, but so far they have failed to set in motion regime change.

The United States initially refrained from sanctioning Fridman or his partners, but in April 2022 it blocked their main holding, Alfa-Bank, from the U.S. financial system. That reflected two schools of thought on sanctions. Washington initially held back from sanctioning some of the country's top tycoons as individuals and focused on government-owned assets and oligarchs linked to criminal activity or profiting from state companies. The EU and the the U.K. moved earlier to blacklist a wider range of Russian tycoons, often lumping together the kleptocrats who got rich because Putin had awarded them state jobs or contracts with those billionaires whose fortunes were cemented before Putin came to power. Fridman was in the latter camp.

Fridman originally thought he could fight the sanctions and salvage his business empire in the West, all while keeping some assets in Russia and refraining from directly criticizing Putin. In other words, he wanted to maintain the status quo, an impossible juggling act once Russia invaded Ukraine. No one as prominent as him had managed to do it. But Fridman had battled poor odds before and won, which made him confident he could pull it off. Stocky and blue-eyed with a pudgy face, Fridman was a first-wave oligarch who started out washing windows and selling computers before prospering in the rough-and-tumble 1990s at the helm of a rapidly growing bank. Born and raised in the western Ukrainian city of Lviv to a Jewish family, he always considered himself an outsider, but he clawed his way to the top of Russia's business elite through a combination of smarts and ruthlessness. He was one of the original seven oligarchs who bankrolled President Boris Yeltsin's reelection campaign, but he missed out on the infamous loans-for-shares schemes that handed Russia's most valuable assets to a clutch of tycoons.

Even so, he played hardball like the rest of them, if not more so, and was quick to pursue lawsuits against business rivals and journalists alike. (Fridman was one of the Russian billionaires who sued Catherine Belton for her book *Putin's People*, which they eventually settled out of court.) His long-running battle with Norway's state-controlled Telenor telecoms company, in which Fridman and his partners owned a stake, ended up in a New York court in 2008, when a judge ruled that his Alfa Group had a "brazen history of collusive and vexatious litigation . . . used to avoid compliance with their legal obligations." In 2010, before Russia's relations with the West turned ugly, he gave a speech in his Ukrainian hometown titled "How I Became an Oligarch," in which he compared his life to a thriller. "It's very difficult to convey in words the excitement of the story that unfolds in business," he told the audience. "When you get used to living in this genre, life without it becomes very boring."

At his level, business was less about money for its own sake, but more a signifier of how successful he was. He prided himself on never having worked directly for the government or a state company, but making a multibillion-dollar fortune in Russia inevitably required dodging and weaving the Kremlin's edicts. His Alfa Group empire, which included banking, insurance, telecoms, and retail, was just one of the many building blocks that made up the DNA of Putin's Russia. Fridman sat on the board of the Russian Union of Industrialists and Entrepreneurs, an oligarch lobbying group that regularly holds large roundtable meetings with Putin. Fridman sometimes skipped those summits, leaving Kremlin relations to Aven, the smooth-talking, bespectacled economist who had been Yeltsin's reformist minister of foreign economic relations in the early 1990s. Unlike Fridman, Aven, worth almost $7 billion before the full-scale invasion, did meet regularly with Putin one-on-one. He was one of fifty oligarchs who met with him quarterly, a fact he disclosed in the Mueller investigation; he recounted a December 2016 meeting when the Kremlin leader raised the prospect that the United States would impose additional sanctions on Russia, including Alfa, and Aven said he would establish a "line of communication" with the incoming Trump administration to try to protect the group. Aven told Mueller he understood that any suggestions or critiques that Putin made during these meetings as "implicit directives," with consequences if he didn't follow through. Aven told me he'd been misinterpreted. "Putin just gave his opinions," he told me. "I never had any direct orders from Putin."

While Fridman tried to steer clear of direct involvement with the Russian state, his Alfa Group used Putin's politicized legal system to its advantage. He and his partners used Russia's notoriously weak courts to secure and retain their assets. They brawled for years with BP, the partner in their mega oil joint venture TNK-BP, once Russia's third-largest crude oil producer. During the height of the battle in 2012, the *Wall Street Journal* asked Fridman if he'd been in touch with Putin or Igor Sechin, the head of state-controlled Rosneft. "We're always in touch with everyone, that's our job," Fridman said. He and his partners came out on top when they pocketed $14 billion from the sale of oil company TNK-BP to Rosneft in 2013, a deal that required the Kremlin's approval. The next year, Putin annexed Crimea, triggering the first wave of Western sanctions against Russia.

It looked as if Fridman and Aven had gotten out just in time by taking such a huge pile of cash off the table in Russia. They moved to London and set up their private equity firm, LetterOne, to plow the proceeds into a string of European assets such as health-food retailer Holland & Barrett and Spanish supermarket chain Dia. They recruited some powerful advisers, including Lord John Browne, the former head of BP PLC, and made regular trips to Washington for roundtables with the Atlantic Council, the foreign policy think tank. Fridman and Aven were often sought after for their insight into Russia's ever-changing political landscape. They had set up a fellowship program to fund more than two hundred U.S., British, and German citizens to work and travel in Russia to "advance knowledge of Russia in the West." Fridman told me he thought those deep relationships, carefully cultivated over the years, would protect him. "We sincerely believed we are such good friends of the Western world that we couldn't be punished," he told me. When the invasion happened, Western governments saw those Washington trips as examples of the pair doing Putin's bidding to lobby against sanctions, an allegation they denied.

But Fridman and his partners had more invested in the West than other Russian tycoons and attempted to straddle London, Moscow, and Kyiv in a strategy would prove unsustainable. As they sought to establish themselves as global business magnates investing around the world, they kept their Russian assets, including Alfa-Bank, the country's largest privately held bank, and X5, Russia's biggest supermarket chain. Fridman and his partners also owned one of Ukraine's biggest banks and held a stake in its largest telecoms operator, Kyivstar. Following a well-worn path, they chose to manage their Russian bank through a parent company in Cyprus.

* * *

After Brussels blacklisted Fridman, U.K. officials debated whether to follow suit under intense public pressure for a clampdown on Russian oligarchs, with emails flying between the Foreign Office and the Home Office. Initially Foreign Secretary Liz Truss resisted designating him—it's unclear why—but the Home Office and Johnson's Cabinet Office supported sanctioning him, according to Foreign Office emails. The back-and-forth reflected a degree of randomness in deciding when and whether to designate individuals, with some Foreign Office staff even resorting to Wikipedia as they did their research.

When the U.K. announced sanctions against Fridman on March 15, 2022, it called him a "pro-Kremlin oligarch" who was benefiting from or supporting the Russian government. He called me in a state of despair, denying the allegations. "I just don't know what to do. I just don't know." It was odd to watch a titan of Russian business descend into desperation. Like many of his fellow billionaires, he assumed his assets would be safer in the West than in Russia, where property rights notoriously depend on shifting political winds. (The U.K. later dropped the "pro-Kremlin oligarch" wording after he denied being part of Putin's inner circle.)

Once he was sanctioned, U.K. officials had to figure out what to do with him now that he was in London rather than Moscow. The U.K. sanctions regime had never faced such a dilemma: a sanctioned billionaire living on British soil. Long before Putin's invasion, Fridman had submitted an application for British citizenship, which the Home Office planned to refuse because it claimed he didn't meet the "good character requirement." But he had permanent residency, which gave him the right to live and work in the U.K. indefinitely. After imposing sanctions, U.K. officials canceled his residency permit and planned to tell him he had twenty days to leave the country. "Our approach should be for him to physically leave the country as quickly as possible under his own steam," a Foreign Office official wrote to the Home Office on March 11, 2022.

But Fridman didn't leave the U.K. for eighteen months. Instead, he tried to use the British legal system to fight back. He appealed the order to revoke his permanent residency, allowing him to stay while the decision was under legal review. He held an Israeli passport, but didn't own a home or have a bank account there. So he stayed in London, unlike other Russian tycoons subjected to asset freezes and travel bans, who'd long since gone. He thought he could get the sanctions lifted, and the only way to do that was to stay. For a long time, he was the last Russian oligarch in London.

Fridman created a conundrum for British officials eager to show they were extinguishing all remnants of Londongrad. To continue living in London under sanctions, he had to apply for a license from the U.K. government for permission to use his frozen funds for anything. The Treasury initially gave the billionaire an allowance of roughly £2,500 a month for living expenses and £24,000 a month to pay security staff guarding his estate 24-7. Over roughly eighteen months, the U.K. allowed him to use £1 million in frozen funds for his "basic needs," including contractually owed back pay for staff such as cleaners and his estate manager. But it denied him permission to keep paying staff on the grounds that it would enable him to "continue enjoying the lifestyle he had prior to being designated." In July 2022, Fridman applied for a license to donate £10 million to the Federation of Jewish Communities of Ukraine for humanitarian assistance, but permission was never granted.

Before targeting Fridman, the NCA homed in on his partner, Aven, in one of its first probes into alleged sanctions evasion. In May 2022, around thirty NCA officers descended on Aven's neo-Palladian mansion set on eight and a half acres in Surrey, south of London, seizing cash from his house manager. They were investigating around £3.7 million that he'd transferred from a trust in Austria to the U.K. in the hours before the EU imposed sanctions on him. The exact timing of when the EU sanctions took effect would determine whether the transfer was legal. A billionaire living in a gated mansion outside London needs amounts of money that ordinary people might find hard to comprehend. Initially, he needed to cover roughly £140,000 in monthly expenses, mostly for security and to protect and insure his art collection, which included works by Wassily Kandinsky, Henry Moore, and Louise Bourgeois, along with what he said were pieces from the largest private collection of Russian art in the world. (The monthly expenses were later reduced to about £60,000.) The U.K. froze about £1.5 million linked to Aven as the billionaire battled the NCA, which believed he was using accounts held by his wife and estate management firms as his personal "piggy bank."

After the raid, Aven decided to leave England. He realized his position was untenable. In July 2022, Aven and his wife checked in at Heathrow for a flight to New York and were standing in line to board the plane when five policemen with guns, part of an anti-terrorist unit, ran toward them. The policemen took their passports and phones, forbade them from speaking Russian, and marched them through the airport to a side room, where police interrogated them for more than three hours. The billionaire didn't have a sanctions license allowing him to leave. Aven told me that every twenty minutes the officer ducked out and came back with more questions. "What's your attitude towards the war? Who are your friends in Russia?" Aven said the police asked him why he and his partners had invested billions of dollars in Europe from their head office in London.

"By mistake!" Aven shot back. "We were just wrong!"

British law enforcement eventually let them go, returning their passports and most of their devices. Because Washington had not imposed sanctions on Aven, he was able to travel to the United States, where he spent the summer at his wife's home in Amagansett in the Hamptons. Aven intended to move to Latvia, where he had acquired citizenship in 2016. Aven's departure left Fridman as the last major oligarch still living in London. "My suspicion is the NCA switched to Fridman after I left," Aven told me.

While the NCA continued investigating Fridman for alleged sanctions busting, he was working behind the scenes trying to get off the EU and U.K. blacklists by soliciting support from some surprising allies: Russia's political opposition, known for its intense squabbling. It might seem odd that such a prominent Russian oligarch would turn to staunch opponents of Putin for backing, but Fridman had a number of ties to well-known Kremlin critics. He was close friends with Boris Nemtsov, the Russian opposition activist who was gunned down outside the Kremlin in 2015. A year after his death, Fridman appeared in a Russian documentary about Nemtsov alongside other opposition leaders—an unusual move for such a prominent Russian billionaire—and expressed regret that he'd spent less time with Nemtsov in the years before his death because of concerns the friendship would be toxic to his business.

Fridman had also once employed Vladimir Ashurkov, who went on to become a key aide to the late Alexei Navalny, Russia's most famous opposition leader, who was killed in an arctic prison in February 2024 while serving a sentence on politically motivated charges. Ashurkov was a top executive at Fridman's Alfa Group when he first started working with Navalny, but Fridman asked him to resign in 2012. "Fridman said that they had to deal with authorities on a daily basis and they didn't want to be involved in politics," Ashurkov told me. "If you run a big business in Russia, even if you don't agree with what the government does, you still need to be on good terms with them to avoid raiding or some other kind of punishment."

At the time, Navalny was leading street protests against election fraud, calling Putin's United Russia bloc the "party of crooks and thieves." Navalny was poisoned in Russia in August 2020, an attack that he and Western governments blamed on the Kremlin, and only barely survived after being treated in Germany. In 2021, he returned to Russia, and Putin promptly imprisoned him. Navalny's team continued producing hard-hitting investigations into Putin's corruption, while Navalny himself endured harsh conditions in a penal colony, where he was eventually sentenced to a nineteen-year term.

Working from exile under the umbrella of his Anti-Corruption Foundation (ACF), Navalny's team was lobbying for the West to impose more sanctions on the Russian elite in response to his imprisonment long before the invasion, but Washington, London, and Brussels weren't listening. ACF had done more to document Russian corruption than almost anyone, giving Western governments a road map to follow. In early 2021, it sent a list to the Biden administration and 10 Downing Street of thirty-five Putin associates it wanted to be blacklisted, including Chelsea owner Abramovich and metals billionaire Alisher Usmanov. Fridman and his Alfa Group partners were not on the list. Western governments failed to respond to the Navalny 35, as it was called.

After the Ukraine invasion, Navalny's team drew up a list of some six thousand state officials and businessmen connected to the Russian government that it argued should be sanctioned. While Western governments had targeted thousands of Russian officials and oligarchs, they didn't go as far as Navalny's team wanted. Even two years after the war, only Canada has sanctioned all thirty-five on the group's original list.

Leonid Volkov, who was chair of Navalny's Anti-Corruption Foundation, wanted Western governments to target more cronies but also draw up a clear list of criteria for lifting sanctions on individuals. Volkov told me he met with British officials working on sanctions in July 2022 and offered to pare down the six thousand to a short list of two hundred Russians that his group felt were priority targets. "This subset that will be the most painful to sanction for Putin and will send a very clear signal to all the others, your turn is next,"

Volkov told me in September 2022. "The U.K. is by far the most important jurisdiction for sanctions because London is a mecca for Russian oligarchs and their money."

At the start of the war, the U.K. had a lot of catching up to do. Until the U.K. officially left the EU in January 2020, London followed Brussels on sanctions. The U.K. had to build a sanctions regime almost from scratch and had to quickly change legislation to make it easier to impose penalties. In the first six months of the war, the number of Foreign Office staff working on sanctions tripled to almost 150 from about 40 before the invasion. But they were still understaffed compared to the gush of restrictions they'd unleashed. The sanctions had turned into a new bonanza for British lawyers, who had made small fortunes for years representing Russian oligarchs suing journalists for defamation and exploiting the U.K.'s weak libel laws. In May 2023, I attended what was billed "Sanctions Soiree" in the august surroundings of the Royal Society of Arts in London that featured some Treasury and Foreign Office officials; so many lawyers showed up looking for guidance that there was an overfill room. The U.K. had frozen more than £22 billion in private Russian assets, but it introduced some head-scratching policies. For instance, the U.K. announced a new mechanism that would allow sanctioned Russians to donate frozen funds to Ukraine, but explicitly said donations would not be tied to sanctions relief. Unsurprisingly, the mechanism raised no funds for Ukraine.

The U.K. ended up being among the most aggressive at blacklisting individuals, but Volkov thought the U.K. had missed some obvious targets—including corrupt Russian Defense Ministry officials and their families. At the same time, Volkov told U.K. officials it made little sense to go after businessmen not connected to the government. As an example, he told me he'd raised the case of Oleg Tinkov, a brash self-made billionaire who made his money in retail and online banking rather than off state contracts. The U.K. sanctioned Tinkov in March 2022. Before the war, Tinkov had suggested Putin should be made czar, a remark Tinkov later dismissed as a mistake. But after being sanctioned by the U.K. in March, Tinkov was the only prominent Russian billionaire to publicly attack the Kremlin for launching what he called an "insane war." He'd gone on to describe Russia as a "fascist" state and criticized Russia's business elite for refusing to speak out against Putin's war.

Tinkov was recovering from leukemia while living in Europe and no longer held any management position at his eponymous bank, Tinkoff. Nonetheless, Russian government officials contacted Tinkoff executives in Moscow and threatened to nationalize the bank if it didn't sever ties with him. He sold his 35 percent stake to Russian metals billionaire, Vladimir Potanin, the country's richest man, in what Tinkov described to the *New York Times* as a "fire sale." Potanin was quickly becoming the biggest beneficiary of all the post-invasion forced exits.

When I contacted Tinkov in May 2023, he expressed outrage that the U.K. was still keeping him under sanctions. "I have lost nine billion dollars due to my clear stand against Putin and the war," he told me. "I dropped my Russian citizenship and lost friends and a home and I'm sanctioned." He'd even enlisted the support of British entrepreneur Richard Branson, who wrote to the U.K. government calling for sanctions on the Russian billionaire to be lifted. Tinkov's plight served as a warning to other oligarchs: even if you denounced Putin and lost the bulk of your fortune, you could still remain stuck on the sanctions list. "The ultimate goal is to stop the war, not to punish people," Volkov told me at the end of 2022. "It's about increasing the costs for Putin, to make his team members leave him, to make it harder for him to operate the country, to increase turbulence. Only with an exit strategy will sanctions be efficient. Otherwise, people have nowhere to run but back to Moscow, where they get more dependent on Putin. They have to be presented with a clear option—do this and this and sanctions will be lifted."

*   *   *

As Fridman tried to get EU sanctions on him and his partners dropped, he approached Volkov and other Russian opposition figures to write him letters of support. In October, Volkov wrote to the EU asking for sanctions to be lifted from businessmen who condemn the war and "are not connected to the crimes committed by Putin's regime." Volkov cited Fridman, Aven, and their other partners, German Khan and Alexei Kuzmichev, as examples of tycoons who deserved sanctions relief. "We do not believe they were somehow connected to Putin's regime or that they should be held responsible for his crimes," Volkov wrote. The sanctions sometimes "target businesspeople acting in good faith, often simply because they hold Russian passports, while the real criminals, who have enriched themselves through their close relationships to Putin's regime, have once again escaped scot-free."

Putin, in his state-of-the-nation address in February 2023, called on Russia's wealthy to come home in words that seemed eerily addressed to Fridman specifically. "Some may choose to live in a seized mansion with a blocked account, trying to find a place for themselves in a seemingly attractive Western capital," he said. "Running around with cap in hand, begging for your own money makes no sense, and most importantly, it accomplishes nothing, especially now that you realize who you are dealing with."

Ten other Kremlin critics signed appeals similar to Volkov's on Fridman's behalf addressed to EU leaders. Nobel Peace Prize winner Dmitry Muratov, the editor in chief of *Novaya Gazeta*, an independent newspaper shuttered by the Kremlin, called for the EU to reconsider sanctions on the tycoon, citing his investments in Ukraine and friendship with Nemtsov. "It's hard to imagine a 'person close to Putin' who would befriend a furious opponent of the Kremlin," Muratov wrote. Ilya Yashin, an opposition politician who worked with Nemtsov, signed a similar letter, handwritten from pretrial detention center No. 4 in Moscow, where he was being held for denouncing the war in Ukraine (and was later sentenced to eight and a half years). Anyone entertaining fantasies of a liberal government taking over in Russia might include all these figures.

I called Volkov in February 2023 to ask him about why he'd thrown his support behind such a prominent Russian oligarch, thinking the letters were newsworthy but unlikely to help Fridman get sanctions lifted. The letter wasn't public yet. He initially denied signing the letter, but I had a copy of it on the Anti-Corruption Foundation's letterhead. On March 1, 2023, I wrote a story for Bloomberg that revealed for the first time the unusual array of letters from Russia's opposition supporting the lifting of sanctions on Fridman, but my story didn't get picked up in Russia.

At the time, not everyone in Russia's fractured opposition believed Fridman deserved sanctions relief. Mikhail Khodorkovsky, the exiled former oligarch who spent more than a decade in prison, believed Fridman hadn't gone far enough. The two had worked together to bankroll Yeltsin's 1996 reelection campaign, but they were intense business rivals in the late 1990s and early 2000s. In Khodorkovsky's mind, lifting sanctions should be clearly linked to a condemnation of the war and a public denouncement of Putin, and Fridman had only met the first requirement. "I believe Fridman and Aven are scared of falling into the gap between the two chairs on which they have been sitting for many years," he said. "Russia will block the way for them, and the West will not open it."

A week later, Alexei Venediktov, the prominent former head of the liberal and now shuttered Ekho Moskvy radio station, shared one of the letters on his social media channels, where he has more than two hundred thousand followers, including members of Moscow's elite. His decision to reveal the letters was designed to undermine the Navalny foundation, which had just published an investigation that alleged Venediktov received millions of dollars from the mayor of Moscow to voice support for Russia's electronic voting system, which opposition figures believe Putin uses to falsify election results. Fridman's efforts to get sanctions lifted had set off a mudslinging match between some of Russia's leading anti-Putin forces, deepening rifts that had split the opposition for years.

The reason for Volkov's nervousness with me soon became clear. It turned out Volkov was freelancing. Soon after the story spread within Russia, Volkov took to social media to label his October letter supporting Fridman a "big political mistake" and said he'd signed it without consulting his colleagues at Navalny's foundation. "I had a feeling that the situation at that time (against the backdrop of the defeats of Putin's army and discord in the Russian elites) was critical, and that it was possible, by creating a precedent, to start a chain reaction of public condemnations of the war and the split in the Russian elites," Volkov wrote on his Telegram channel. Volkov announced he was "taking a break" from his public activities as chair of Navalny's Anti-Corruption Foundation. But he went on to reiterate his message on the need to rethink personal sanctions in an opinion piece in the *Economist* magazine in March 2023. A few weeks later, Navalny replaced him as chair of the foundation with Maria Pevchikh, who led his investigative department presenting high-profile reports on corruption. But Volkov remained active with the Navalny team. (In March 2024, he was brutally attacked with a hammer outside his home in Vilnius, which Lithuanian officials blamed on Russian special services.)

Alexander Rodnyansky, an economist at the University of Cambridge and adviser to Zelensky, told me about his frustrations with Russian oligarchs lobbying against sanctions. "They're part of the problem," he told me. "We need to dismantle the oligarchs, seize the assets that they've been criminally holding, and make sure they're available for our reconstruction." The oligarchs, he argued, destroyed the judiciary to protect their businesses and were complicit in Putin's corrupt regime.

Indeed, it is almost impossible to run a major business in Russia without some form of state entanglement. Fridman repeatedly insisted he never worked for state companies, but that didn't mean his companies necessarily cut themselves off from the security state. Russian investigative journalists at Proekt Media revealed in July 2023 that one of Alfa Group's insurance companies worked for the Ministry of Defense and Russia's National Guard (Rosgvardia, Russia's internal military force), while a report by Radio Liberty showed documents and pictures of Alfa insured trucks returning from Ukraine. Fridman told me Alfa did provide third-party liability insurance to cars used by Russia's National Guard but only in regions far from Ukraine. Either way, any business entanglement with the Russian security state undermined his case for sanctions relief.

In July 2023, the Ukrainian government nationalized Alfa Group's bank in Kyiv and later charged Fridman with helping to finance Russia's war against Ukraine, an allegation he denied. Around the same time, the United States finally imposed sanctions on Fridman and his partners for operating in Russia's financial services sector. Washington had clearly decided Fridman and his partners hadn't done enough to avoid personal sanctions. Alfa's parent company later filed a $1 billion claim against Ukraine in an international arbitration tribunal for what it called the "unlawful expropriation" of the bank, a brazen move against a country that had suffered devastating damage by Russian forces. Authorities in Kyiv also stepped up threats to seize Fridman and his partner's stake in Ukraine's largest telecoms operator, KyivStar. Months earlier, they had announced plans to sell their stake in Alfa-Bank, a divestment that was part of their efforts to get sanctions lifted, but authorities in Cyprus, where Alfa's parent was registered, hadn't given them permission.

Fridman was still battling the NCA's probe into alleged sanctions violations when he tried to leave the U.K. in May 2023. After he sat down on a flight to Turkey en route to Tel Aviv, a flight attendant walked up to him and told him he needed to get off the plane. Police were waiting at the plane's door and marched him back through immigration, seizing his Russian and Israeli passports. The NCA investigation was ongoing, and the authorities were still trying to prosecute him for sanctions evasion even though they had lifted his bail. But in September, the NCA formally dropped its probe after the billionaire challenged the agency's rights to retain and search the electronic devices it seized during the unlawful raid. Soon after he got his passports back, he boarded a flight to Israel.

U.K. officials got what they wanted—he left—but only after they suffered a humiliating defeat in the courts, including an order to pay Fridman damages. "The sanctions are effectively pushing businesspeople towards Russia, whether they like it or not," Fridman told me. "We don't have any alternatives."

A few weeks later, Hamas launched its surprise attack on Israel, and Fridman fled Tel Aviv for Moscow. Besides Russia, he's now splitting his time between Israel, the UAE, and Turkey, the favored haunts of sanctioned Russian billionaires swerving Western restrictions. But he wasn't exactly welcomed back to Moscow with open arms. In October 2023, the head of the Duma, Russia's lower house of parliament, called for an investigation into Fridman for allegedly supporting the Ukrainian army, an allegation he denied. In December 2023, he attended a high-profile reception for Hanukkah at a well-known Moscow jazz club owned by a saxophonist and prominent supporter of Putin, Igor Butman. Fridman told me the Israeli ambassador to Russia invited him. Pevchikh, Navalny's new leader in exile, was scathing about Fridman's decision to return to Russia. "I would like to ask all those who signed that same ill-fated letter (and there were plenty of people there besides Volkov) to remember an important thing. You have been deceived," she wrote on Twitter. "All these stories about sincere support for Ukraine, hatred of Putin, the desire to help somehow—they were deceiving you."

Ashurkov, the Navalny aide who once worked with Fridman more than a decade ago, told me the billionaire's decision to visit Russia didn't resonate with his campaign to get sanctions lifted. "It doesn't help his case that he's seen in Russia. He knew this would be seen as a kind of spit in the face of efforts to get rid of sanctions," Ashurkov told me. "But I can see why he didn't want to spend more time in Britain where he was under strict sanctions." Ashurkov thinks Western sanctions could have been better at dividing the elite to weaken Putin's regime. "It's a failure of Western sanctions policy that it did not try to get as many Russians on the side of the West as possible," Ashurkov told me. "The sanctions haven't led to any behavior change on behalf of the Russian business and political elite."

Indeed, it looked like Fridman and his partner Aven wouldn't get sanctions lifted unless they publicly condemned Putin's actions, which they refused to do. But in April 2024, they scored a surprise victory when the EU's General Court ruled there wasn't enough evidence to justify the decision to sanction them in March 2022 for ties to Putin or for supporting actions that undermined or threatened the territorial integrity of Ukraine. It looked like they'd gotten off merely for hiring expensive lawyers rather than taking any concrete steps to break with the regime. But they both remained under sanctions having been added to an updated EU list in March 2023, which included different reasons. The new criteria included that Alfa provided insurance to Russia's National Guard and that one of the group's retail subsidiaries was working with a Russian state-controlled company that provides food and other services to the Russian military. Their appeal against the new listing was pending as this book went to press.

Like most of Russia's elite, Fridman lost billions of dollars as sanctions ended his comfortable existence in the West. But without clear conditions for how to get the asset freezes and travel bans lifted, Russia's billionaires (apart from Tinkov) have chosen to stay subservient to Putin's regime in a bid to hold on to their assets in Russia. Khodorkovsky, the exiled opposition leader, told me he supports personal sanctions, but the way they were rolled out had little impact on Putin. "Did this serve to split the elites? No, it didn't work," he told me. "Does Putin care about this? Not very much." One way to make sanctions more effective is to provide relief to individuals who publicly back the Declaration of Russia's Democratic Forces, drawn up in Berlin in April 2023, he said. The declaration, signed by more than thirty thousand people including prominent figures, calls for Russian troops to be removed from all occupied territories, the release of political prisoners, and the elimination of Putin's regime. As Khodorkovsky put it, Fridman and his partners made a choice to not denounce Putin because they saw it as too much of a risk without guarantees from the West. "For me, this is not an argument because during a war everyone is at risk," he told me.

Others similarly saw Fridman's failure to publicly criticize Putin's decision to invade as effectively siding with the Kremlin. A lawyer who has advised some of Russia's leading oligarchs on sanctions says they're unwilling to accept the new reality. "The perception was that it would be a relatively short war and maybe there would be some kind of peace so they could go back to how things were," he told me. "I tell these guys, 'You gotta pick one side or the other because things are never ever going back to normal. If I were you, I would chose NATO because that's the only way you can live in a free society. So divest from Russia, make a public pronouncement, turn over ninety percent of your wealth, and keep a couple hundred million. They're not listening, or if they are, they're not acting."

Picking sides eventually worked for one tycoon. In July 2023, the U.K. finally lifted sanctions on Tinkov, sending a signal to other billionaires that they might get similar treatment if they followed his lead. "I was guilty without being guilty," Tinkov said in an Instagram post after the decision. "Now it is fixed. It would never happen in an authoritarian or dictator's regime."

But for the Russian tycoons who choose to muddle on through, hoping for a change in regime that will alter their circumstances, it could be a long wait. One hypothesis is that Putin's grip on power won't end anytime soon because Russia's elite is stuck in a prisoner's dilemma, a game theory where individuals acting alone pursue courses of action that make them collectively worse off. Most of them would be better off with Putin out of power, but, instead of banding together, each of them is hunkering down trying to make sure their assets aren't seized by the Kremlin. "No one wants to be the first one to actually stand up and metaphorically shoot the first shot," Christo Grozev, the lead investigator at the *Insider*, a Russia-focused media outlet, said at a conference in Aspen in July 2023. "The sanctions work to the extent you cannot find more than a couple of oligarchs who are actually happy with the current situation. But their being unhappy doesn't make a coup."

Londongrad's last major oligarch had left, but Russian money remains embedded in the city. At the time of writing, Fridman's enormous London mansion loomed over the green fields of Hampstead Heath as a reminder of the ongoing economic war.

British authorities eventually allowed him to pay for security at his mansion. But unless the U.K. can prove Fridman violated sanctions and therefore committed a crime, British officials don't have the legal grounds to seize the property, so it's likely to be frozen for years. His mansion is just one of the dozens of oligarch villas, yachts, jets, and bank accounts worth billions of dollars that remain in limbo as Russia continues its barrage of missile and drone attacks across Ukraine.

CHAPTER 13

WILL RUSSIA PAY?

In the early-morning hours of June 6, 2023, explosives detonated at the Nova Kakhovka dam in southeastern Ukraine, sending more than 3 billion gallons of water cascading over the top. The dam was holding back Ukraine's largest reservoir, which supplied homes and farms around the Dnipro, the river that cuts through the country's center. Its collapse allowed water to flood around six hundred square kilometers (232 square miles), causing tens of thousands of people downstream to flee. The torrent left thousands of homes underwater and resulted in more than $4 billion in losses from damage to the region's irrigation systems. It was Ukraine's worst environmental catastrophe since the Chernobyl disaster in 1986, and while both sides traded blame, evidence strongly suggested Russia was responsible. Russian forces had occupied the area for more than a year, and President Zelensky stressed the only way to destroy the dam was through mining it.

The dam's destruction threatened the water supply for 1.5 million people in Ukrainian-controlled territory. Tasked with repairing the damage was the State Agency for the Restoration of Ukraine, a new body established in January 2023 and led by Mustafa Nayyem. Nayyem's agency started building a 145-kilometer-long (90-mile) pipeline to bring clean water to more than six affected cities, all while the country was still at war, and Russian artillery attacks hindered the construction. "It's a huge project, essential to avoiding a crisis with the water supply," Nayyem told me. With some support from the U.S. Agency for International Development (U.S. AID), Nayyem's agency raced to finish the pipeline, completing most of it by April 2024. At a cost of $360 million, the pipeline was just one of hundreds of infrastructure projects Ukraine desperately needs to get going even as Russian missiles continue to pound the country.

Nayyem was at the helm of what should be Europe's biggest reconstruction effort since the Marshall Plan, but without the cash to do it. Rebuilding Ukraine will cost more than $486 billion, according to a World Bank estimate from February 2024. The price tag has only mounted since then. Even by October 2023, the scale of the devastation was mind-boggling: 25,000 kilometers (15,500 miles) of roads, almost 150,000 private homes, and more than 3,500 schools, all destroyed or heavily damaged. Some 154 bridges had been completely destroyed by Russian forces, of which Nayyem's agency had restored 30 with the help of Western governments, but more repairs depend on financing. In the two years after Russia invaded, Ukraine's economy shrank by about a quarter. Ukraine doesn't have enough money to keep the government functioning and pay pensions without foreign aid, let alone rebuild its critical infrastructure. In addition to military assistance, it urgently needs more money for reconstruction than the West is willing to give.

Born in Afghanistan before moving to Kyiv at age nine, Nayyem was once best known as the man who helped spark Ukraine's Maidan revolution. On November 21, 2013, he posted a call on Facebook for his followers to meet at 10:30 p.m. at the monument in Kyiv's Independence Square to protest pro-Russian president Viktor Yanukovych's decision to walk away from an EU association agreement. Hundreds turned out that first night. In the days and weeks that followed, as riot police cracked down on protesters, thousands came, erecting a tent city. Yanukovych eventually fled to Russia, and Putin annexed Crimea, as war kicked off in eastern Ukraine. After the revolution, Nayyem entered politics and became a member of parliament for five years. In 2021, he became deputy minister of infrastructure.

When Russia started bombing the energy grid, bridges, and communications networks across the country, Nayyem found himself running one of the key planks of Ukraine's defense as his agency began trying to help repair and protect critical national infrastructure. He was also running a pilot project to restore five villages in different regions, rebuilding everything from housing to schools. When I spoke to Nayyem, he explained the enormity of the challenges facing Ukraine. The country's ability to withstand Russian attacks depends partly on its ability to fix electricity substations, roads, and bridges destroyed during the war, without waiting until the fighting ends. "It's very difficult to say that it's recovery," Nayyem told me. "It's more about survival." Despite the huge stakes, domestic political infighting led Nayyem to resign in June 2024, leaving Ukraine's reconstruction effort without anyone at the helm. He said crucial funding for rebuilding infrastructure had been stymied and bureaucratic obstacles slowed the agency's work. "I couldn't execute my duties," he told me. Whoever takes over will be faced with the same enormous task: restoring a country devastated by more than two years of Russian attacks.

*   *   *

With Ukraine facing an existential fight and Western nations bickering over aid, there was an increasingly obvious solution: Why not use Russia's roughly $300 billion in central bank reserves that were immobilized in the West in the momentous first days of the war? Why should Western taxpayers pay for Ukraine's reconstruction while a large stash of Russian government funds sat barricaded in Europe, the United States, the U.K., and Japan? For many, seizing Russia's reserves was fully justified under the principle that the "aggressor pays." And the G7 made it clear it won't hand back the central bank cash to Putin or his successor unless Russia agrees to reparations. This proposal has nothing to do with Russian oligarch assets. That's a separate legal track being pursued mostly by the U.S. Justice Department to forfeit the yachts, mansions, and bank accounts of Russian billionaires linked to criminal activity. Not only are the oligarch assets a much-smaller pot of money—around $60 billion globally—but they belong to private individuals who can and are launching court challenges to asset seizures tied to sanctions violations.

The proposal to confiscate, rather than just block, the $300 billion spooked a lot of lawyers, central bankers, and foreign policy experts. After all, international trade and finance depend on respect for both state and private property. Rules for expropriating state assets aren't well established. The United States had seized funds belonging to the central banks of Afghanistan, Iran, and

Venezuela, but Russia's reserves were much larger. Some worried it would set a dangerous legal precedent and give license to the Kremlin to respond by taking over the assets of Western companies caught in Russia. Skeptics worried that seizing the funds would undermine global confidence in the dollar and the euro, leading countries to pare back their holdings of the world's two leading reserve currencies.

In July 2023, the world's top diplomats and national security officials flocked to Aspen, Colorado, for the Aspen Security Forum, an annual summer conference and schmooze-fest. One hot, sunny day during the conference, Larry Summers, the former treasury secretary under Bill Clinton, sat at a picnic table on a stretch of grass, chatting with Jake Sullivan, Biden's national security adviser. The two men talked for almost an hour. Summers was attempting to persuade the White House to use the idle assets from Russia's central bank to fund Ukraine's reconstruction. Summers had become a vocal champion of confiscation. He thought Russia couldn't have it both ways. It couldn't violate the international rules-based order by invading its neighbor and expect the same rules-based order to uphold its property rights. In fact, Summers thought that using Russia's reserves could *deter* other rogue states from similar acts of aggression by showing governments that their globally held assets could be commandeered to repair the damage they do.

As one of the world's most prominent economists, he had the financial clout to try to convince the Biden administration to back the idea. After serving as president of Harvard University, he worked for President Barack Obama as his top economic adviser helping to steer the response to the global financial crisis. "It's crazy to be going to taxpayers for rebuilding Ukraine when this pool of money is available," he told me. "This is one of the rare cases in my experience where the expedient thing is also the right thing. We crossed the Rubicon when we froze the reserves. Nobody thinks these assets are going back. There's a fundamental need for resources to enable Ukraine to function as a viable, economically reconstructed, and successful state."

Summers wasn't alone in trying to influence Sullivan's thinking that day. Just before meeting with Summers, Sullivan had sat down at the same picnic table with Philip Zelikow, a veteran Republican foreign policy adviser and historian who started his career as a trial lawyer, a combination that gave him a unique take on the global implications of using Russian assets to aid

Ukraine. Zelikow and Summers had first started talking about using Russia's reserves in July 2022 in Aspen. They hashed out their ideas with Robert Zoellick, another seasoned Republican, who immediately grasped the legal arguments but also had the markets and foreign policy chops to face down skeptics in diverse fields.

This trio tried to counter naysayers from all angles. Zelikow, with his deep-barreled voice, and Zoellick, with his signature thick mustache, both come from the neoconservative wing of the Republican Party and are ardent advocates of free trade. But with Summers on board, they believed the idea would be able to transcend party politics. For his part, Summers grew more enthusiastic about the idea with the backing of two prominent legal thinkers. "They're not long-haired, radical, lawbreaking, institution-flaunting types," Summers told me. "Their knowledge of international law removed what was my only nagging doubt."

Together, they had some of the world's most powerful people on speed dial. They began writing opinion pieces, both individually and jointly, at leading publications—the *Wall Street Journal*, the *Economist*, and *Foreign Affairs*—to spark a debate and build support for their proposal. "Bank robbers should not expect banks to honor their safe-deposit boxes" was the metaphor Summers, Zelikow, and Zoellick used to explain the concept in a *Foreign Affairs* article they cowrote. When I sat down with Zelikow on the sidelines of the 2023 Aspen Security Forum, he boiled the argument down for me even further. "If you're going to commit all these crimes, I'm going to start taking your stuff," he told me. "I don't respect legal obligations to you because you don't respect legal obligations to anybody else."

As they began shopping the idea around, however, Summers, Zelikow, and Zoellick had to face down fears that utilizing Russian assets would undermine the doctrine of sovereign immunity, which is meant to protect foreign governments from being sued in other countries' courts.

But as Zelikow explained it, transferring Russia's reserves to Ukraine would be a state-on-state act outside any domestic court, meaning sovereign immunity doesn't apply. Under international law, injured states can take "countermeasures" against Russia to compensate the victims of its aggression. Countermeasures don't require a U.N. Security Council resolution. They're designed to induce a law-breaking state to comply with its obligations.

Without Russia's violation of international law by invading Ukraine, it would be illegal to seize its state property, but such a move would set a precedent for using countermeasures.

Zelikow believed that such countermeasures were justified based on Russia's egregious violation of international agreements it had signed. Not only had Putin ignored the U.N. Charter by trying to change borders by force, but he'd also breached the Budapest Memorandum of 1994, when Ukraine agreed to give up its nuclear weapons in exchange for assurances from Russia, the United States, and the U.K. that its territorial integrity would be preserved. But when Russia invaded Ukraine, the U.N. Security Council was paralyzed; Russia, one of its five permanent members, vetoed any resolutions on the war. Instead, the council referred the crisis to the General Assembly for an emergency special session, the first time it had done so in forty years. In early March 2022, the General Assembly voted overwhelmingly in favor of a resolution condemning Russia's invasion, calling it an act of aggression that violated the U.N. Charter. Six months later, the General Assembly adopted a resolution calling on Russia to pay war reparations to Ukraine. The nonbinding vote was supported by ninety-four countries, while seventy-three abstained and fourteen were against it—less than a majority, but it carried political weight. Zelikow believed those resolutions were enough of a legal basis to act.

In fact, a precedent for seizing the reserves already existed. In 1991, the U.N. Security Council set up a compensation commission for Iraq after it invaded Kuwait that forced a percentage of Iraqi oil revenue into an escrow account. Individuals, corporations, governments, and international organizations filed claims with the commission, which paid out more than $52 billion over decades. Russia itself approved the creation of the Iraqi commission.

As permanent members of the Security Council, Russia and China could block any resolution on using Russian assets to compensate Ukraine. But Zoellick thinks it's ridiculous to argue that the world can't use the international legal system unless Russia and China agree. "They would confine international law to ineffectual debating societies," he told me. "I like to forge new policy tools that foes can't use against us. The U.S. doesn't hold its reserves in rubles, so this is a pretty good one." Even without a Security Council vote, the requisition of the assets could be done through other international bodies and agreements.

Zoellick outlined a model similar to the Iraqi commission. Russia's frozen reserves would be deposited into an escrow account that would be used by a multilateral trust fund to pay out claims. Legally, it would be easier to justify using the money to plug holes in Ukraine's budget rather than directly fund military spending; countermeasures are primarily about damages, not financing a war. But the funds could be used to support the government in a range of areas, from health care for injured soldiers to rebuilding the electricity network. Zoellick thinks giving it to the World Bank, where he served as president from 2007 to 2012, would give the move added legitimacy. When we spoke, Ukraine was burning through about $3 billion of foreign funds a month to ensure the central bank in Kyiv didn't print money, triggering hyperinflation. Putin's goal was to destroy Ukraine not only militarily but also economically, leaving it in such a weakened state that it couldn't fight back. "When you have a war of attrition, which this is, you have to focus on the economic sustainability of the parties," Zoellick told me. "You need some money you can use quickly while the conflict is going on."

In the summer of 2022, Zoellick sat down with the Senate Foreign Relations committee staff to make his pitch in the hopes Congress would act to smooth the way. "I was trying to say, 'You know there's three hundred billion dollars here, and you're going to want this money," he recalled telling them. "This is strategically wise, it's appealing policy, it's good politics, and it's ethically correct. How many of those do you get in life?" But Treasury Secretary Janet Yellen said in May 2022 it wouldn't be legal to seize the reserves.

Zoellick believed legislation wasn't even necessary if the United States merely transferred the assets to Ukraine without taking ownership, but congressional action would help smooth the way. It took more than a year for the Democrat-controlled Senate to move on the idea, partly because the Biden administration wasn't responding to requests for feedback on the bill. In mid-June 2023, a bipartisan group of senators introduced legislation—the Rebuilding Economic Prosperity and Opportunity (REPO) for Ukrainians Act—authorizing Biden to move Russian sovereign assets into a fund that the U.S. government would use to rebuild Ukraine. Republican senator James Risch of Idaho, one of the cosponsors of the bill and a longtime Russia hawk, told me Putin would never agree to pay for Ukraine's reconstruction. "To me, this is a no-brainer,"

Risch said. "I hope it happens without their consent. I hope it happens in a way that they're whining and complaining and carrying on. And we say, 'You shouldn't have done this. And anybody else who's thinking about it, this is what's gonna happen to you.'"

But the legislation didn't move for months. Senate staffers thought Sullivan was stalling, while Yellen was opposed. "Sullivan wants to use the frozen Russian sovereign assets as a way to buy peace," one top congressional aide told me in the summer of 2023. "The idea is to use it as a tool in negotiations with Russia."

Many people who favored using the central bank money for Ukraine found this argument foolish. Bill Browder, a London-based hedge fund investor who campaigned for more than a decade for tougher sanctions on Putin's regime after his lawyer died in a Russian prison, was one of them. "It's naive to think we lose a bargaining chip to end the war the moment this money is confiscated," Browder told me. "There's no negotiation that's going to end this war. One thing that could end the war in the wrong way is if the Ukrainians don't have the resources."

As Russian attacks on Ukrainian grain shipments and energy infrastructure escalated over the spring and summer of 2023, the Biden administration shifted in favor of confiscation as long as it was done in coordination with the G7. White House officials, however, denied their thinking changed, telling me they merely needed time to show the proposal adhered to international law. Sullivan, they said, was frustrated by the slow pace of agreeing on the legal argument to support confiscation; the White House only officially backed the REPO bill in November.

Critics worried that confiscating the reserves would undermine the willingness of other central banks to hold U.S. dollars, causing the cost of U.S. government borrowing to jump. The dollar's preeminence as the global reserve currency, some argued, had already been dented as Washington ramped up sanctions over the past two decades. To be sure, the dollar's share of global central bank reserves dropped to about 59 percent from 70 percent in 2000. But most of that shift came from allies such as Switzerland, Canada, and Australia diversifying their currency holdings. Zoellick, for one, thinks anxieties over the prospect of de-dollarization are overblown. "If Russia doesn't get to hold dollars in the future, okay!" he told me. "The Chinese will push for more use of renminbi for trade. Fine. Until the Chinese have a trusted, open, liquid capital account, do you want to put your money there? When people tell me, 'Oh, aren't you worried about the dollar?,' I say, 'Look, if you don't want to hold them, I'll take them.'"

But the United States only held about $5 billion of Russia's central bank assets, which meant Washington's contribution would be relatively small. Getting Europe to back an outright seizure would prove even harder.

*   *   *

From her nineteenth-century yellow stucco-facade headquarters on Neglinnaya Street in central Moscow, Russia's central bank chief, Elvira Nabiullina, began preparing the ground for an economic war years before Putin's mass-scale invasion. Following a wave of sanctions from Washington starting in 2014, Russia began reducing U.S. dollar holdings and buying more euros. When the G7 took the unprecedented step of immobilizing Russia's foreign currency holdings, most of the funds were in euros at various central banks and financial institutions in Europe. Putin and Nabiullina appeared to be betting the United States might freeze Russia's assets in the event of a conflict but that Europe would be too divided to act.

For more than a year after the invasion, it wasn't entirely clear where Russia's assets actually were. Even as this book went to press, there was no definitive report detailing precisely how much is blocked and where. When Brussels required financial institutions to report how much they were holding in frozen assets, a hazy picture began to form. In October 2023, European Commission president Ursula von der Leyen said the EU had frozen 211 billion euros ($223 billion) in Russian reserves. But the exact amounts in other countries were unclear.

By virtue of the esoteric plumbing of international finance, most of that money got stuck in Brussels at an institution that few outside the world of banking had ever heard of: Euroclear, owned by major European financial institutions. Headquartered in a nondescript gray tower in north Brussels, Euroclear is the pipe through which a huge portion of the global trading of bonds, equities, and other securities flow. As the world's oldest and biggest system for settling trades, Euroclear acts as an intermediary between buyers and sellers and a central securities depository that holds bonds for banks. It is a transit point on the highway of international finance, but suddenly there was a traffic jam. Normally Euroclear pays out funds to clients within twelve to forty-eight hours. When G7 countries banned transactions with Russia's central bank, Euroclear suddenly had to block the assets, clogging a normally steady flow of money.

Euroclear was left sitting on about 191 billion euros of Russian central bank assets, much of it in government bonds. That amount quickly grew. As bonds paid out annual interest or matured, the Russian assets generated more and more cash; Euroclear's balance sheet ballooned eightfold from about 25 billion euros at the start of the war to 199 billion by the spring of 2024. Because Euroclear is technically liable to pay the principal back to the Russian central bank, it's required under financial regulations to park it somewhere safe, often with other central banks, which pay interest on the funds. Then, as rates rose in 2022 and 2023 to cool inflation, Euroclear began making billions more from interest rate payments on Russian cash. Euroclear isn't required to pay out those profits to Russia's central bank because its terms didn't include anything about paying interest on balances. In 2023 alone, Euroclear made 4.4 billion euros in interest before tax from investing the cash generated by Russia's immobilized assets.

With so much Russian central bank money in its possession, this boring, apolitical financial institution found itself at the center of a political storm. Pressure mounted in Brussels to figure out how to use the funds for Ukraine. Even though the bulk of the money was in Europe, politicians and central bankers on both sides of the Atlantic believed it was vital for the G7 to agree jointly to use the assets. Some EU leaders initially backed the idea. The EU's foreign policy chief, Josep Borrell, told the *Financial Times* in May 2022 that the idea was "full of logic." He pointed to Biden's vow to use Afghanistan's $7 billion of frozen central bank assets for humanitarian aid and victims of 9/11. "We have the money in our pockets," Borrell said. "This is one of the most important political questions on the table: Who is going to pay for the reconstruction of Ukraine?" Von der Leyen was also an early advocate. In November 2022, she said the bloc would "find legal ways" to use money from Russia to help Ukraine.

Instead Europe dawdled for more than a year. Finding consensus in the twenty-seven EU member states on such a controversial proposal proved elusive. Poland and the Baltic states, long worried about Russia's imperial ambitions, backed the seizure; Germany and France, where some of the assets were held, were wary about the precedent it would set. As Europe sat on the fence, Ukrainian forces were being pushed back on the battlefield. The Kremlin, of course, pounced on talk of confiscation. "We're talking about an international act of thievery, in violation of everything," Kremlin spokesman Dmitry Peskov said.

Divided over how to act, European leaders pursued what looked like the path of least resistance: a proposal to use the profits from investing the cash generated by the immobilized funds, leaving the underlying assets untouched. But from the get-go they encountered opposition from the one figure they needed onside: Christine Lagarde, president of the European Central Bank. In June 2023, the ECB warned Brussels that laying claim to interest from the Russian assets could be seen as "crossing a line" and lead other countries to "turn their back on the euro." But as the war dragged on and EU leaders squabbled over aid to Ukraine, pressure to tap those interest payments soon overwhelmed the ECB's opposition. In the spring of 2024, EU officials had agreed to use Euroclear's windfall profits from managing Russian assets for Ukraine. The plan sidestepped the question of transferring ownership of the principal. In total, Euroclear earned 5 billion euros from Russian immobilized assets before the EU decided to expropriate the interest. Instead of donating those proceeds to Ukraine, Euroclear kept the funds in reserve as a buffer in case of lawsuits from Russia, a decision Zoellick says makes it a war profiteer.

Brussels was twisting itself in knots to devise some legally bulletproof way of tapping the piles of Russian cash parked in Europe. For Browder, the London-based investor who has been lobbying EU officials to use the assets, the windfall tax was the theater of the absurd. "It's convoluted nonsense," he told me. "The moment you start taking any money, then it says you don't care about sovereign immunity, and if you don't care about sovereign immunity, why not take all the money?"

Mario Draghi, the ECB's former president, remained quiet on the issue after resigning as Italy's prime minister in 2022. But people familiar with his thinking told me he favored using all of Russia's reserves, believing that the G7 had already passed the point of no return when it froze the money in the first place.

Meanwhile, there was a growing realization that even if the EU appropriated the windfall profits from Russian assets at Euroclear, the move would raise only about 15 to 20 billion euros over the next four years—a significant sum but tiny compared to Ukraine's military and financial needs. Even as the Biden administration threw its support behind an outright confiscation, France and Germany wouldn't budge, and Lagarde remained opposed. In February 2024, the United States circulated a letter from ten leading international lawyers to G7 countries arguing it would be lawful use frozen Russian state assets to compensate Ukraine given the illegality of Putin's invasion. But French finance minister Bruno Le Maire told a G20 meeting of economy chiefs in Brazil at the end of February that there was no "legal basis" to unlock Russia's central bank reserves. Behind the scenes, U.S. officials were starting to discuss Plan B: how the Russian assets could be leveraged to raise a much larger amount of money for Ukraine up front without confiscation. Multiple ideas were floated that sought to use financial engineering to get around opposition to actually seizing the funds. At the end of March, the United States proposed that G7 allies provide $50 billion to Ukraine through a loan that would be repaid from the future interest payments on Russia's immobilized reserves. In simple terms, it was a bit like a landlord going to a bank to get an upfront loan backed by future rental payments on a property. It was a neat solution pivoting off of Europe's plan to take the windfall gains, one that would effectively dodge taking any decision on Russia's legal ownership of the principal.

At the end of April, the U.S. Congress finally approved a $61 billion foreign aid package for Ukraine that included the REPO Act, giving Biden the clear authority to seize the assets. Former president Dmitry Medvedev promptly warned the Kremlin would retaliate by seizing assets of private U.S. investors in Russia if Washington proceeded with confiscation. The U.S. aid package will help Ukraine through 2024, but Kyiv is facing a massive funding gap for 2025, which the Russian funds could help fill. As this book went to press, U.S. and European officials were trying to iron out the details of the Ukraine loan backed by the interest payments on Russian assets as G7 leaders convened to approve the proposal in Italy in mid-June.

But the United States, the U.K., and Canada all supported outright seizure of the Russian reserves. The U.K.'s foreign secretary, former prime minister David Cameron, was one of the first Western political leaders to publicly support confiscation. At an international conference in Washington in December 2023, he said he'd looked at all the arguments against using the reserves. "So far, I have not seen anything that convinces me this is a bad idea," he said. "Let's take that money, spend it on rebuilding Ukraine, and that's simply like a down payment on the reparations that Russia will one day have to pay." He told a House of Lords committee that he was "pushing hard" for the G7 to back the plan. But the U.K. has only an estimated £26 billion ($33 billion) of Russian sovereign assets, and it's highly unlikely London would go it alone unless the rest of the G7 agrees. No country wanted to stick its neck out and seize the assets unilaterally for fear it would damage the standing and trustworthiness of its currency. Zoellick, for one, thought the United States, U.K., and Canada could act without Europe. While the lion's share of the assets was in euros and only about $5 billion was physically in the U.S., Euroclear was also holding untold billions of Russian cash denominated in U.S. and Canadian dollars or British pounds that it declined to disclose. In theory, Washington, Ottawa, and London could assert their right to use those funds for Ukraine. Zoellick told me the United States could direct Euroclear to transfer dollar assets it holds, asserting jurisdiction much the same way it has used the dollar to enforce sanctions around the world. "It will be hard for Congress to justify economic assistance to Ukraine from American taxpayers when Europeans are fussy about using Russian assets," he told me.

The West may be dithering over what to do with Russian assets, but Ukraine is not. In November 2022, Zelensky launched the Fund for the Liquidation of the Consequences of Russia's Armed Aggression, which held about $1.6 billion, almost half of which came from confiscated Russian assets. Some of that money, in turn, funded Nayyem's agency, which was working to repair the infrastructure destroyed by war. Ukraine was getting some support from the World Bank and U.S. AID, Ukrainian companies were often rebuilding roads and bridges in the expectation of getting paid in the future. Bureaucratic obstacles and political squabbles frequently held up the payments.

In the first half of 2024, Russia was stepping up its bombing campaign, firing missiles at apartment blocks, hospitals, shopping malls, and energy infrastructure across Ukraine, constantly adding to the damage and the spiraling costs of rebuilding the country. Nayyem told me Ukrainians shouldn't have to wait for Russia to agree to pay war reparations. "Thousands of people are losing the chance to come back to their homes. Russia is winning by using the legal procedures of Western countries," he said. "If you say that Russia is guilty and they're killing people, but Russian assets are untouchable, then that just means that you're helping them."

END GAME

In early 2022, when Washington, Brussels, and London devised the most expansive package of penalties ever imposed on a major economy, many Western leaders hoped that the sanctions would quickly kneecap Putin's war machine. That proved overly optimistic. The rollout of additional restrictions was slower than some had hoped. And by nature, sanctions introduce economic distortions that immediately create incentives for evasion. Putin's regime has dodged and weaved through Western economic penalties at considerable expense to the Russian economy—buying a shadow fleet of oil tankers, sourcing Western technology through third countries, and squandering billions propping up the ruble. Forfeiting the property of sanctioned oligarchs has, meanwhile, proven more complicated than anticipated, and an agreement on using Russia's central bank reserves for Ukraine's reconstruction has been elusive. Just like military conflict, economic war doesn't always follow a linear path with a Hollywood ending.

Putin, for his part, expected to declare victory in Ukraine in days. Instead, the war has cost Russia dearly. In the two years following the invasion, Russia had lost an estimated 350,000 troops—dead, injured, or missing soldiers—a staggering toll roughly seven times higher than Soviet losses in ten years of fighting in Afghanistan. Almost seven hundred thousand people left Russia in 2022 alone, many of whom were young, highly skilled tech workers, making for a brain drain of epic proportions. By the middle of 2023, the total number was estimated to be closer to one million. As a result, Russia is facing a labor short-age that's hindering its efforts to staff defense factories and conscript soldiers to send into its "meat grinder" in Ukraine. Russia pledged to double spending on defense to $118 billion in 2024—almost a third of total public expenditure and the highest share of the economy since the collapse of the Soviet Union. Outlays on defense were set to surpass social spending.

In less than two years, the economic war against Russia had reshaped the global economy. Russia rerouted millions of barrels of oil from Europe and the United States to India and China. Its Nord Stream pipelines, stretching more than 750 miles and built at a cost of almost $20 billion, had been shut down, no longer feeding Europe with a steady supply of natural gas. More than a thousand Western companies had exited or curtailed their businesses in Rus-sia, ending three decades of expansion. Export controls blocked Russia from legally importing anything produced with a broad class of U.S. technology, forcing the Kremlin to plot elaborate workarounds. And Russia's oligarchs, who had penetrated everything from European soccer to the global art market and the superyacht industry, had billions of dollars' worth of assets frozen in Europe and the United States, forcing them to retreat to Moscow and Dubai.

The economic war had lasted so long that some of its key players had moved on. In September 2023, KleptoCapture's chief, Adams, finally joined private practice as he had planned, trusting his Justice Department colleagues Michael Khoo and David Lim to continue work on the slew of cases he'd over-seen. Meanwhile, *Amadea* moved from San Diego to a dry dock in Washington state for expensive servicing as as the legal battle over it dragged on. Daleep Singh, who helped craft the Biden administration's sanction policy, left the White House at the end of April 2022 but returned in February 2024 to help craft the next phase of Biden's economic campaign against Putin.

Given the protracted military battle in Ukraine, many have rightly ques-tioned what the economic war has achieved so far. Singh is quick to point out that sanctions were never intended as a stand-alone strategy to end the fighting. Rather, they were designed to be what he calls a "force multiplier," a series of measures that would create a negative feedback loop within the Russian economy and sap the strength of Putin's military-industrial complex. But others argue the sanctions have been a failure. In Moscow, restaurants are busy and the shelves are full. Russia's economy jumped by 3.6 percent in

2023 on the back of bumper defense spending and is expected to grow more than 3 percent in 2024.

It's worth imagining a world where no sanctions were imposed against Russia. What might have happened in Ukraine if Putin was able to tap the country's $300 billion in foreign currency reserves and enjoy unimpeded access to Western technology and petrodollars? Putin would likely have been able to make more territorial gains in Ukraine without any economic restraints in place. Because Russia has classified much of its economic data, it's hard to get a full and accurate picture of the effect of sanctions. But based on a number of measures, the sanctions have been deeply damaging. In 2022 alone, a record $239 billion was pulled out of Russia—equal to 13 percent of the economy—as Russians withdrew money to escape sanctions. Another $27 billion poured out of Russia in the first six months of 2023. The U.S. Treasury estimates that Russia's economy is 5 percent smaller than had been predicted before the full-scale invasion and has experienced slower growth than other energy exporters enjoying high prices for oil and gas. But in many ways, economic growth is not a great way to measure how well Russia is doing. Massive military spending is hiding what's happening in the real economy. Strip out military production, and there's little or no growth. As the Russian economist Sergei Guriev, a professor at Sciences Po living in exile in Paris explained, Putin's defense spending is overheating the economy and crowding out productive sectors. "When you produce tanks, that counts as economic growth, even if those tanks are burned in Ukraine next week," Guriev told me. Likewise, Guriev said generous payments to soldiers or their families was effectively "just printing money," fueling inflation and damaging Russia's long-term prospects.

In some respects, Russia's wealthy elite can weather the sanctions because they have deep pockets to pay inflated prices to get whatever they want. That was on full display in January 2024 at a car showroom on the eastern outskirts of Moscow, where new 2023 models from BMW, Audi, and Toyota were for sale, albeit on average at twice the price as similar models being sold in the United States. Parts could also be sourced from third countries for the right price.

But life for many Russians on lower incomes is getting harder as pressures in the economy mount. However unfair it might seem, sanctions will inevitably affect the wider population, even with exceptions for things such as food and medicine. The ruble's value dropped almost 20 percent in the two years after the war, making everything more expensive. Agriculture production contracted as sanctions hit supply chains. In December 2023, the price of eggs soared 60 percent from a year earlier. Cucumbers were up 47 percent, and oranges were up 72 percent. Long after post-pandemic inflation came down in the West, Russia's overall inflation stood at more than 7 percent in late 2023 through the spring of 2024. The central bank hiked interest rates to 16 percent and introduced capital controls, increasing the economic pain. "Imagine the economy is a car," Russia's central bank chief, Elvira Nabiullina, said. "If we try to drive faster than the design of the car allows and press on the gas with all our might, the engine will overheat early. It's possible we'll drive fast but not for long."

And there are plenty of examples of major Russian industrial projects derailed by sanctions. Take Sukhoi Log, one of the world's largest greenfield gold projects, located in southeastern Siberia. Russian gold producer Polyus had planned to spend $3.3 billion to develop the site using European equipment, but sanctions delayed the project, forcing the company to draw up a new plan. A major project in the Arctic to produce liquefied natural gas has also been delayed because of sanctions on vessels to transport fuel. Long term, isolation from the West will shrink Russia's economy, making it increasingly dependent on China.

It's still too early to say how this economic war will play out. Much will depend on how well Russia plays its cat-and-mouse game to dodge Western restrictions. Likewise, the willingness of the United States and Europe to step up enforcement could put Russia on the back foot. That could be seen at the end of 2023 when Washington threatened to impose sanctions on foreign banks that facilitate payments to Russia's military-industrial complex. The announcement spooked financial institutions from Dubai to Turkey, causing a marked drop in trade with Russia.

But so far, the Kremlin has managed to weather the onslaught of sanctions because of the relatively high global price of oil, the mainstay of the Russian economy. If oil prices fall, the Kremlin's ability to withstand Western penalties could unravel quickly. In a sign that the cost of sustaining the war is mounting, Russia announced plans to introduce a "progressive tax," raising rates on higher earners from 2025. Corporation tax will jump to 25 percent from 20 percent. The hikes are expected to raise another $30 billion.

Putin's ability to sustain the war will hinge on the West's willingness to plug holes in the sanctions against Russia and continue supporting Ukraine. After six months of protracted squabbling over U.S. funding for Ukraine, Congress finally approved a $61 billion aid package for Kyiv in April 2024 and gave President Biden the green light to seize Russian central bank assets held in the United States for use in Ukraine. But the delay in funding had allowed Russian forces to gain momentum on the battlefield and undermined the country's ability to intercept relentless missile attacks. And under pressure from Trump, Congress marked $10 billion of the package as a repayable loan, rather than aid. While the funding boost will help Ukraine defend itself in 2024, the country's future is now inextricably linked to the outcome of the U.S. election. If Biden loses, further Ukraine aid from the United States looks uncertain. Trump himself has claimed that if elected, he would get Putin and Zelensky into a room and end the war within twenty-four hours, raising the prospect of forcing Ukraine to cede territory to agree a ceasefire. For his part, Putin vowed at the end of 2023 to continue fighting until "we achieve our goals," promising to "denazify" Ukraine.

As long as Putin is sitting in the Kremlin, the economic war will continue. In theory, if Trump gets reelected, he could remove many of the sanctions on Russia because so many were imposed under executive orders that could be removed at the stroke of the pen, but he would likely face a storm of opposition from Congress. Short of a revolution in Moscow that installs a liberal pro-Western leader—a highly unlikely prospect in the near term—Russia is likely to remain under heavy sanctions for years to come.

*   *   *

War with a nuclear power such as Russia means it may be impossible for Ukraine to have a decisive military victory. There's always the possibility Putin will do the unthinkable and use tactical nuclear weapons if cornered. In this context, undermining his ability to wage war through economic measures will remain a central tool to counter Putin's territorial ambitions. Still, it's worth considering how things could have unfolded differently. Could the West have done more to avoid such a protracted conflict? Some have suggested that punishing Putin more aggressively in the years following the annexation of Crimea in 2014 might have deterred him from invading in 2022. John Bolton, Trump's former national security adviser, told me he believes "targeted" sanctions is really code for fewer sanctions. "The Russians looked at the Obama sanctions and said, 'This is chicken feed,'" he told me. "If you want sanctions to have an effect, you hit them with the kitchen sink—you hit them with everything all at once." The drip feed of sanctions allowed Russia to adapt and build its economic resilience.

But Putin might have invaded in 2022 anyway, driven by his fantasy that Ukraine had no historical right to exist independently of Russia. Once the invasion got underway, then, could the United States and the EU have done more to shut down the war immediately? Immobilizing Russia's central bank reserves in the days after Putin's forces crossed into Ukraine was a radical step with long-term ramifications. Washington, Brussels, and London rolled out unprecedented sanctions against thousands of individuals and entities in the months that followed.

But, in fact, the West didn't hit Russia with the kitchen sink. Financial sanctions on banks and payment system had less of an impact than some officials originally thought. Western governments adhered to a path of "escalation," motivated by the belief that throwing everything they had at Russia in one go would reduce their ability to respond to events on the ground. In practice, however, this meant that sanctions against the elite were slow and often scattershot, sometimes leaving corrupt officials untouched. For example, the United States waited until September 2023, eighteen months after the invasion, to impose sanctions on several Russian defense contractors and oligarchs with links to organized crime and the military. The EU has still not imposed sanctions on Alexei Miller, the CEO of state-controlled gas giant Gazprom and a key Putin loyalist. And while the U.S. Commerce Department radically expanded export controls to try to deny Russia access to Western technology, U.S.-designed semiconductors and components kept ending up on the battlefield in Ukraine without the companies being held accountable.

But perhaps the biggest mistake: the G7 waited nine months to figure out how to prevent Putin from profiting from sky-high oil prices sparked by the war. And when it did come up with a creative solution—the oil price cap—it failed to enforce it for almost a year, allowing the creation of Russia's shadow fleet of rusty oil tankers to cruise to new markets in Asia.

The single most important thing the West can do to deny Putin resources to fund the war is to lower the price cap on Russian oil and enforce it rigorously. Oil is the key to the health of the Russian economy, and, hence, to its ability to finance defense spending. According to Bloomberg calculations, if Russia's oil export price falls to below $50 a barrel for one to two years, the Kremlin will deplete its National Wealth Fund, which was set up to cushion government finances from swings in energy revenues. That would leave government finances in a precarious position and make it much harder for Putin to continue the war. Reducing it to $30 would be even more effective. But agreeing on the price cap in the first place took protracted negotiations, and lowering it again would require deft political maneuvering—perhaps a greater effort than the West can muster after two years of diplomatic wrangling over sanctions.

*   *   *

Ukraine's future depends in large part on where Russia goes from here. Many of Russia's elites want to turn back the clock to before February 2022, when they had it all—fortunes in Russia, mansions in London and superyachts in Saint-Tropez, and the illusion that Putin's corrupt system could continue without any costs to them or the wider world. I had a lengthy conversation about the future of Russia with one sanctioned Russian businessman who didn't want to be named.

"Putin always told us the West hates us," he said. "Now it's a fact."

It was a sign of the growing anti-Western sentiment among even moderate, Western-facing members of the Russian elite. "The West should be prepared for a long-term fight with Russia," he told me. "Even if Putin leaves in two years, five years, who knows, the next leader will not be pro-Western. The limitless natural resources of Russia and the human resources of China will be a very powerful alliance. Authoritarian regimes learned the lessons of how to run a political monopoly and a market economy."

Indeed, as much as Russia's elite may want to, there's no turning back the clock. As he stokes anti-Western sentiment, Putin is trying to build a new world order challenging Western dominance, positing it as a civilizational conflict. He is betting he can persuade enough countries, from Asia to Africa and the Middle East, to break with the United States and support Moscow, enabling the Russian elite to make enough money outside the West to sustain his regime. In fact, there are already signs that this shift is occurring. Biden's overtures to Saudi Arabia to start producing more oil in 2022 went nowhere. Instead, Saudi crown prince Mohammed bin Salman and the UAE president Sheikh Mohamed bin Zayed al Nahyan welcomed Putin in December 2023 on one of his rare foreign trips. The only other times Putin traveled outside the former Soviet Union since the full-scale invasion was to China and Iran, a reflection of the new world order.

China had turned Russia into a client state. In June 2022, Putin joined forces with Chinese president Xi Jinping at a virtual summit of the leaders of Brazil, Russia, India, China, and South Africa (BRICS) to attack the use of sanctions. "We urge the world to reject the Cold War mentality, bloc confrontation, and oppose unilateral sanctions—and the abuse of sanctions," Xi told the group. Putin accused the West of "using financial mechanisms" as a way to advance the "selfish actions of individual states." It was convenient for Putin to blame the West, rather than his own invasion of a sovereign country, for undermining the post–Cold War peace. A year later, Xi and Putin strengthened their alliance at a March 2023 summit in Moscow, where the Chinese leader declared that their "common interests are multiplying."

With the West facing off against not just Moscow but also Beijing, this new Cold War is unlikely to play out like the old one did, but choices made now will be pored over by historians. "We're facing an inflection point in history," Biden said in televised remarks from the Oval Office, appealing for Congress to approve aid to Ukraine and Israel. "One of those moments where the decisions we make today are going to determine the future for decades to come." Singh thinks it's time to articulate a doctrine of economic statecraft to more effectively counter Russia and China globally. "We're living through the most intense period of great power competition since World War Two," Singh told me, referring to Russia's and China's desire to challenge the United States. "We don't want that conflict to play out through military channels, so it's more likely to play out through the weaponization of economic tools— sanctions, export controls, tariffs, price caps, investment restrictions."

Indeed, sanctions against Russia could provide a playbook for Western countries to follow if Beijing invades Taiwan, but the economic consequences would be far greater given the world's dependency on Chinese manufacturing. Pandemic supply disruptions and rising tensions over Taiwan sparked moves to "derisk" the U.S. economy from Chinese supply chains while cutting Beijing off from cutting-edge technology.

Besides isolating authoritarian regimes such as Russia, Iran, and North Korea, there have been calls for the United States to favor trade and prioritize supply chains with trusted allies. Yellen crystallized this shift in late April 2022 by calling for democratic nations to band together through what she called "friend-shoring" to create principles-based economic alliances—essentially a coalition of neoliberal countries that could deter economic and military threats from authoritarian regimes. "We need to deepen our ties with those partners and to work together to make sure we can supply our needs of critical materials," she said in a speech to the Atlantic Council.

Western powers are also awakening to the need to peel countries away from Russian and Chinese influence using not only the sticks of sanctions but also the carrots of Western finance for infrastructure projects. In the wake of Russia's invasion, the G7 began an effort to counter China and Russia globally in these areas. In June 2022, Biden announced the United States would mobilize $200 billion of investment in global infrastructure projects in the next five years, part of a G7 project to invest $600 billion worldwide as an alternative to China's $1 trillion Belt and Road Initiative. It could be a way to undermine Chinese and Russian economic influence around the world, but progress on real commitments has been incredibly slow.

Western officials seem set on expanding the economic war against Russia. But what U.S. and European policymakers are *not* discussing is perhaps even more important: How to end the war on terms that Ukraine can accept? The U.S. and its allies haven't given Ukraine enough military aid to protect its citizens from missile attacks, let alone defeat Russia. The military and economic response has been in reaction to events on the ground rather than part of a master plan. The West has outlined a promising path for Ukraine's postwar future: a route to membership in the EU and NATO, along with hoped-for reconstruction. But there appears to be no strategy for ending the war, a prerequisite for realizing that vision.

The world needs a stable Russia, which owns more nuclear warheads than any other country. After dozens of interviews with key policymakers on both sides of the pond, I heard very little thinking about a long-term strategy for how to deal with Russia beyond isolation. At the moment, there is a new Iron Curtain keeping Russians out of the West, the flip side to the Cold War, when the Soviets erected barricades to keep their citizens locked up. To put real pressure on Putin, the West needs to accompany its economic war with incentives for Russians who want to oppose the regime.

As Putin throws everything at winning the war, Russia's economy will likely stagnate. It's impossible to predict whether Putin will survive, for how long, or who might succeed him, but a thaw in the economic war, to say nothing of the military battle, is unlikely to come anytime soon.

ACKNOWLEDGMENTS

The idea for this book started on the day Putin launched his full-scale invasion of Ukraine. I knew immediately this was the end of an era, one that began when I first started out as a reporter in Russia in the 1990s. I had considered writing a book about Russia before, but the invasion helped me see a clear narrative arc, from the West's hope of a democratic Russia after the fall of communism to the rise of Putin's authoritarian rule and finally to a new Cold War. Having reported off and on from Ukraine over the years, the senseless destruction of the country and the killing of innocent civilians sparked an obsessive interest in how to limit Putin's ability to wage war.

I could not have written this book without the support and guidance of my editors and colleagues at Bloomberg during my career. I'm grateful to Bloomberg's editor in chief, John Micklethwait, who was not only helpful in sharing contacts but also championed my coverage of Russia and its elite for many years. Deputy editor in chief Reto Gregori has long supported me at Bloomberg and was instrumental in giving me the time away from my day job to report and write this book. And I'm lucky to work for Otis Bilodeau, Robert Blau, and John Voskuhl, who helped me grow as an investigative long-form writer over the years and backed me when I began digging into the unfolding economic war against Russia.

This project grew out of several stories I wrote for *Businessweek*, deftly edited and shaped by Dan Ferrara, Joel Weber, and Susan Berfield. Robert

Friedman, Alex Campbell, Gregory White, Daryna Krasnolutska, David Hellier, Stryker McGuire, Vernon Silver, Alaric Nightingale, Zeke Faux, Tim Gordon, David Voreacos, Aggie Smith, David Gillen, and Matt Campbell provided excellent advice and suggestions. I'm especially grateful to the talented Irina Reznik for generously sharing contacts and recommending excellent reporting lines. I'd also like to thank several other Russian colleagues at Bloomberg who I won't name here to protect them and their families back home; they all helped in ways big and small, both during this project and over the years of reporting stories for Bloomberg. I leaned on Alexander Isakov's economic analysis, which was first rate. Alberto Nardelli, Nick Wadhams, and Dan Flatley's excellent coverage of sanctions was invaluable. Alex Wickham and Jonathan Browning helped me with U.K. reporting. I could not have navigated Cyprus or Dubai without the guidance of Georgios Georgiou and Ben Bartenstein, who were each terrific companions and didn't hesitate to introduce me to their contacts. Makarios Drousiotis in Cyprus was a fantastic resource on the island's golden passport scheme and Russian corruption.

I owe a huge debt of gratitude to my agent, Todd Shuster, who believed in this project early on and offered crucial advice on the contours of the proposal. I am eternally grateful to Colin Harrison at Scribner and Joel Simons at Mudlark for seeing the promise of this book and offering excellent editorial guidance throughout. Colin helped shape the narrative structure and ensured clarity while encouraging me to tease out important themes. Joel helped dream up a fantastic cover for both the U.K. and U.S. editions. My U.K. agent, Toby Mundy, guided me through the pitch process like a pro, while Jack Haug and Emily Polson held my hand throughout. Thanks also to Nan Graham, Stu Smith, Jason Chappell, Paul Samuelson, Mark Galarrita, Zoey Cole, Ash Gilliam Rose, Kyle Kabel, and everyone else at Simon & Schuster.

Rory MacFarquhar taught me a lot about the Russian economy, first as a young reporter in Moscow in the 1990s and later when he explained how sanctions against Russia have evolved since the Obama administration. Thanks to Masha Gordon for sharing her insights on Russian business and to Vasya, who acted as my eyes on the ground in Moscow. I'm grateful to Franz Wild and the International Consortium of Investigative Journalists for arranging access to the group's Cyprus files. Dale Brauner and Will Peischel fact-checked with an attention for detail, while my daughter, Anisa, and Addison Mitchell helped me clean up the endnotes with surprising speed.

There are too many people to thank who helped me as a reporter and writer over the years; I would not have been able to even think about writing a book without you, and you know who you are. I wouldn't be where I am today if Matt Winkler hadn't hired me at Bloomberg twenty-five years ago. Winnie O'Kelley was a terrific editor and boss on all things Russian before she left to join Columbia University. Jackie Simmons has been a fantastic friend and colleague since I joined Bloomberg. And I'm especially grateful to Marc Champion, who took a chance hiring me as a young reporter at the *Moscow Times* years ago, and Geoff Winestock, whose nose for a good Russian business story engendered a love of following the money. Most of all, I'd like to thank all the people who spoke to me for this book, some of whom didn't want to be named, and helped me tell the story of the unfolding new world order.

Writing a book under intense time pressure wasn't easy, especially with the relentless pace of breaking news on sanctions. My greatest debt of gratitude goes to my husband, Cameron, for his enduring support, love, and patience as I disappeared into my home office weekends and evenings. I'd also like to thank my children, Zaki and Anisa, for encouraging me to take breaks along the way and offering endless inspiration to keep going.

NOTES

interviewed more than one hundred people and trolled through thousands of pages of documents for this book. I traveled to Dubai, Cyprus, Brussels, France, and across the United States for research as well as spoke to people in Kyiv by phone or video from my base in London. But I've also drawn from my time reporting from Ukraine before the full-scale invasion and my years of writing about Russia when I interviewed many of the country's billionaires.

Not everyone wanted to speak with me on the record, and I've tried to source where information came from background interviews. While some of my reporting was contemporaneous to events, I also reconstructed a narrative based on interviews conducted months or years later. Some memories were sharp, and others were hazier. When recollections varied, I cross-checked accounts with other sources to reconcile different versions of events.

Even when I have confirmed information myself, I have sought to identify the story that first reported the news. I apologize in advance if I have accidentally missed crediting some media outlet for breaking a news story. While I did not travel to Russia for this book, I conducted some interviews by video and worked with a reporter in Moscow to shed light on how sanctions were playing out on the ground; I also drew from Russian-language news reports to glean how the penalties were affecting businesses across the country. I've both fed into and drawn from the great reporting on sanctions and Russia by my colleagues at Bloomberg, some of whom left Moscow after the invasion and write stories without bylines to protect their families back in Russia. I could not have written this book without them. I would like to acknowledge the fantastic reporting by the *Financial Times*, the *Wall Street Journal*, the *New York Times*, the *Washington Post*, Reuters, the Associated Press, the *Guardian*, and the International Consortium of Investigative Journalists. I'd also like to credit some of the outstanding research from the Kyiv School of Economics, which produced illuminating reports on sanctions and the Russian economy during the two years of war following the full-scale invasion.

PROLOGUE **WE ARE COMING FOR YOUR SUPERYACHT**

3 *On the foredeck*: Sam Fortescue, "*Amadea*: On Board the 106m Lürssen Superyacht Complete with a Dedicated Party Deck," *Boat International*, September 17, 2021, https://www.boatinternational.com/yachts/editorial-features/amadea-106m-lurssen-superyacht; and Olivia Michel, "Amadea: 10 Facts about Lurssen's 106m Superyacht," November 26, 2021, https://www.boatinternational.com/yachts/editorial-features/amadea-superyacht-facts.

3 Amadea *stood out*: This account is based on multiple interviews with sources familiar with *Amadea*'s journey, as well as legal filings. See also Stephanie Baker, "Seizing a Russian Superyacht Is Much More Complicated Than You Think," *Bloomberg Businessweek*, November 7, 2022; and Stephanie Baker, "'Straw Owner' Hides $1 Billion Worth of Yachts, US Says," *Bloomberg News*, May 14, 2022.

6 *almost $60 billion in private Russian assets*: Joint Statement from the REPO Task Force, March 9, 2023, https://home.treasury.gov/news/press-releases/jy1329.

7 *roughly $300 billion*: "Russia Prepares Legal Battle to Stall Seizure of Frozen Reserves," *Bloomberg*, January 12, 2024, https://www.bloomberg.com/news/articles/2024-01-12/russia-prepares-legal-battle-to-stall-seizure-of-frozen-reserves?sref=aJXZGtfw.

7 *more than eighteen thousand designations*: Spencer Vuksic, "Russia Is Now the World's Most Sanctioned Country," Castellum, March 8, 2024. https://www.castellum.ai/insights/russia-is-now-the-worlds-most-sanctioned-country.

7 *Iran was the only*: "Russia Sanctions Dashboard," Castellum, https://www.castellum.ai/russia-sanctions-dashboard.

7 *"Putin put us into"*: Interview with Mikhail Khodorkovsky, April 11, 2024.

8 *In Cold War II*: Niall Ferguson, "How Cold War II Could Turn into World War III," Bloomberg Opinion, October 23, 2022, https://www.bloomberg.com/opinion/articles/2022-10-23/cold-war-2-with-china-and-russia-is-becoming-ww3-niall-ferguson?sref=aJXZGtfw; and "Cold War II: Niall Ferguson on the Emerging Conflict with China," Uncommon Knowledge with Peter Robinson, Hoover Institution, May 1, 2023, https://www.hoover.org/research/cold-war-ii-niall-ferguson-emerging-conflict-china.

10 *doubled defense spending*: "Russia Plans Huge Defense Spending Hike in 2024 as War Drags," Bloomberg, September 22, 2023, https://www.bloomberg.com/news/articles/2023-09-22/russia-plans-huge-defense-spending-hike-in-2024-as-war-drags-on?sref=aJXZGtfw.

11 *lost an estimated $168 billion*: Working Group Paper #18: Energy Sanctions, The International Working Group on Russian Sanctions, February 7, 2024.

11 *lives of tens of thousands*: Helene Cooper, Thomas Gibbons-Neff, Eric Schmitt, and Julian Barnes, "Troop Deaths and Injuries in Ukraine War Near 500,000, U.S. Officials Say," *New York Times*, August 18, 2023, https://www.nytimes.com/2023/08/18/us/politics/ukraine-russia-war-casualties.html. Zelensky gave a lower figure of thirty-one thousand soldiers killed at a press conference on February 25, 2024.

11 *at least $486 billion*: "Updated Ukraine Recovery and Reconstruction Needs," February 15, 2024, https://www.worldbank.org/en/news/press-release/2024/02/15/updated-ukraine-recovery-and-reconstruction-needs-assessment-released.

CHAPTER 1 ATTACKING FORTRESS RUSSIA

13 *Chernobyl nuclear power plant*: "Russian Forces Capture Chernobyl Nuclear Power Plant, Says Ukrainian PM," Radio Free Europe / Radio Liberty, February 24, 2022, https://www.rferl.org/a/ukraine-invasion-russian-forces-chernobyl-/31721240.html.

13 *initial round of U.S. sanctions*: "U.S. Imposes First Tranche of Swift and Severe Costs on Russia," White House Fact Sheet, February 22, 2022, https://www.whitehouse.gov/briefing-room/statements-releases/2022/02/22/fact-sheet-united-states-imposes-first-tranche-of-swift-and-severe-costs-on-russia.

14 *"It's go time"*: Interviews with Daleep Singh, June 26, 2022, and May 10 and January 23, 2023, and Björn Seibert, February 10, 2024. Also see Erin Banco, Garrett M. Graff, Lara Seligman, Nahal Toosi, and Alexander Ward, "Something Was Badly Wrong: When Washington Realized Russia Was Invading Ukraine," *Politico*, February 24, 2023, https://www.politico.com/news/magazine/2023/02/24/russia-ukraine-war-oral-history-00083757.

14 *Putin began testing Washington*: Jim Garamone, "Russia Needs to Answer Questions regarding Military Buildup near Ukraine," Department of Defense News, April 9, 2021, https://www.defense.gov/News/News-Stories/Article/Article/2567812/russia-needs-to-answer-questions-regarding-military-buildup-near-ukraine/.

15 *U.S.-Russia summit*: "Readout of President Joseph R. Biden Jr. Call with President Vladimir Putin of Russia," White House, April 13, 2021, https://www.whitehouse.gov/briefing-room/statements-releases/2021/04/13/readout-of-president-joseph-r-biden-jr-call-with-president-vladimir-putin-of-russia-4-13/.

15 *grievances over Ukraine*: "Telephone Conversation with US President Joe Biden," Kremlin readout, April 13, 2021, http://kremlin.ru/events/president/news/65360.

15 *The penalties were*: "Fact Sheet: Imposing Costs for Harmful Foreign Activities by the Russian Government," White House, April 15, 2021, https://www.whitehouse.gov/briefing-room/statements-releases/2021/04/15/fact-sheet-imposing-costs-for-harmful-foreign-activities-by-the-russian-government/.

15 *the Pentagon canceled*: Natasha Bertrand and Lara Seligman, "U.S. Drops Plans to Send Destroyers into the Black Sea," *Politico*, April 15, 2021, https://www.politico.com/news/2021/04/15/us-navy-ukraine-russia-tensions-481897.

15 *Putin reacted angrily*: "Presidential Address to the Federal Assembly," Kremlin website, April 21, 2021, http://kremlin.ru/events/president/news/65418.

15 *sanctions on Nord Stream 2 AG*: "Nord Stream 2 and European Energy Security," press statement by Anthony Blinken, May 19, 2021, https://www.state.gov/nord-stream-2-and-european-energy-security/.

15 *the president remained opposed*: Interview with former administration officials, April 17, 2023. See also Jennifer Jacobs and Jennifer Epstein, "Biden Says He Waived Nord Stream Sanctions Because It's Finished," Bloomberg, May 25, 2021, https://www .bloomberg.com/news/articles/2021-05-25/biden-says-he-waived-nord-stream -sanctions-because-it-s-finished?sref=aJXZGtfw..

16 *essential for global stability*: "Remarks by President Biden on Russia," White House, April 15, 2021, https://www.whitehouse.gov/briefing-room/speeches-remarks/2021 /04/15/remarks-by-president-biden-on-russia/.

16 *the three-hour summit*: "Remarks by President Biden," White House, June 16, 2021, https://www.whitehouse.gov/briefing-room/speeches-remarks/2021/06/16/remarks -by-president-biden-in-press-conference-4/.

16 *Russian imperial myths*: "On the Historical Unity of Russians and Ukrainians," Vladimir Putin, Kremlin, July 12, 2021, http://en.kremlin.ru/events/president/news/66181.

17 *"false flags"*: Singh interview.

17 *"heavy price"*: *Putin vs. the West, Path to War*, BBC Documentary, January 30, 2023, https://www.bbc.co.uk/iplayer/episode/p0dlzdwr/putin-vs-the-west-series-1-3-a -dangerous-path.

17 *Putin accused the West*: "Extended Meeting of the Board of the Ministry of Foreign Affairs," Kremlin, November 18, 2021, http://kremlin.ru/events/president/news/67123.

17 *"the asymmetric advantages"*: Singh interview.

17 *"It struck me how"*: Seibert interview.

17 *two-hour video call*: "Remarks by President Biden before Marine One Departure," White House, December 8, 2021, https://www.whitehouse.gov/briefing-room/speeches -remarks/2021/12/08/remarks-by-president-biden-before-marine-one-departure-10; and Justin Sink, Ilya Arkhipov, and Henry Meyer, "Biden Told Putin He'd Bolster Ukraine Military If Russia Attacks," December 7, 2021, https://www.bloomberg.com /news/articles/2021-12-07/biden-begins-call-with-putin-seeking-to-avert-ukraine -attack?sref=aJXZGtfw.

17 *"Some allies thought it was a bluff"*: Interview with Eric Green, April 17, 2023.

18 *"We are looking up"*: Luke Harding, "'We Don't Have a *Titanic* Here': Ukraine Plays Down Threat of Russian Invasion," January 28, 2022, https://www.theguardian .com/world/2022/jan/28/ukraine-plays-down-threat-of-russian-invasion-volodymyr -zelenskiy.

18 *wasn't taking a clear stance*: "Remarks by President Biden and Chancellor Scholz," White House, February 7, 2022, https://www.whitehouse.gov/briefing-room/statements -releases/2022/02/07/remarks-by-president-biden-and-chancellor-scholz-of-the -federal-republic-of-germany-at-press-conference/.

18 *"Olaf spoke of"*: Email from Boris Johnson in response to the author's questions, August 8, 2023.

19 *two of Russia's biggest banks*: "US Treasury Imposes Immediate Economic Costs in Response to Actions in the Donetsk and Luhansk Regions," February 22, 2022, https:// home.treasury.gov/news/press-releases/jy0602.

19 *went ahead with sanctions*: "Sanctioning NS2AG, Matthias Warnig, and NS12AG's Corporate Officers," Anthony Blinken, U.S. State Department, February 23, 2022, https:// www.state.gov/sanctioning-ns2ag-matthias-warnig-and-ns2ags-corporate-officers.

19 *Biden had spoken*: "Statement by President Joe Biden on Phone Call with President Volodymyr Zelensky," White House, February 24, 2022, https://www.whitehouse.gov

/briefing-room/statements-releases/2022/02/24/statement-by-president-joe-biden
-on-phone-call-with-president-volodymyr-zelenskyy-of-ukraine/.

19 *"throw everything at them"*: Interview with former senior administration official, April
2023.

20 *wired into the global financial system*: Todd Prince, "'The Nuclear Option': What Is
SWIFT and What Happens If Russia Is Cut Off from It?," RFE/RL, December 9, 2021,
https://www.rferl.org/a/russia-swift-nuclear-option/31601868.html.

20 *block the reserves*: Alex Vasquez, "Venezuela's Guaido Taps $152 Million in Frozen
Funds in the U.S.," Bloomberg, April 22, 2021, https://www.bloomberg.com/news
/articles/2021-04-22/venezuela-s-guaido-taps-152-million-of-frozen-funds-in-the-u
-s?sref=aJXZGtfw; and Patrick Clawson, "Iran's 'Frozen' Assets," Washington Institute, September 1, 2015, https://www.washingtoninstitute.org/policy-analysis/irans
-frozen-assets-exaggeration-both-sides-debate.

21 *The Russian economy depended*: White House Fact Sheet, February 22, 2022.

22 *an anxious call with Zelensky*: Interview with 10 Downing Street source, July 2023.

22 *"SWIFT would really hurt"*: Interview with 10 Downing Street source, May 22, 2023.

23 *a bare-bones sanctions regime*: "The Future Landscape of the UK Sanctions Regime,"
Skadden, Arps, Slate, Meagher & Flom LLP, July 11, 2022, https://www.skadden.com
/insights/publications/2022/07/the-future-landscape-of-the-uk-sanctions-regime.

23 *Johnson privately viewed Scholz*: Interview with 10 Downing Street source, May 22,
2023.

24 *"In the German case"*: Boris Johnson's emailed answers to author's questions, August 8,
2023.

24 *As the G7 leaders debated*: Interview with 10 Downing Street source, May 22, 2023.

24 *"It's always an option"*: "Remarks by President Biden on Russia's Unprovoked and
Unjustified Attack on Ukraine," White House, February 24, 2022, https://www.white
house.gov/briefing-room/speeches-remarks/2022/02/24/remarks-by-president-biden
-on-russias-unprovoked-and-unjustified-attack-on-ukraine/.

24 *Singh had been so central*: Maxi Tani and Alex Thompson, "The Daleep Doctrine,"
Politico, West Wing Playbook, February 24, 2022, https://www.politico.com/newsletters
/west-wing-playbook/2022/02/24/the-daleep-doctrine-00011437.

25 *"Back by popular demand"*: "Press Briefing by Press Secretary Jen Psaki and Deputy National Security Advisor for International Economics and Deputy NEC
Director Daleep Singh," White House, February 24, 2022, https://www.whitehouse
.gov/briefing-room/press-briefings/2022/02/24/press-briefing-by-press-secretary
-jen-psaki-and-deputy-national-security-advisor-for-international-economics
-and-deputy-nec-director-daleep-singh-february-24-2022/.

25 *impose more punishing sanctions*: "'This Might Be the Last Time You See Me Alive,' Zelensky warns EU leaders," *Times of Israel*, February 25, 2022, https://www.timesofisrael
.com/liveblog_entry/this-might-be-the-last-time-you-see-me-alive-zelensky-warns
-eu-leaders/.

26 *block Russia's central bank*: Author interview with senior EU official, February 10, 2024.

27 *"the West is still bickering"*: Interview with 10 Downing Street source, May 22, 2023.

28 *reluctant to support the freeze*: Author interview with sources familiar with the discussion.

28 *discussed conceptually*: Interview with senior U.S. Treasury official, July 20, 2023.

28 *engaged in urban warfare*: "Russia Campaign Assessment," Institute for the Study

of War, February 26, 2022, https://www.understandingwar.org/sites/default/files/20220226%20Russia%20Campaign%20Assessment%20Final_0.pdf.

29 *"They spoke the same language"*: Interview with senior European diplomat, May 26, 2023.

29 *"Italy wants to do this"*: Interview with senior U.S. official, July 20, 2023; and interview with senior European official, November 15, 2023.

29 *broken into their house*: Carol D. Leonnig and Tyler Pager, "Police Investigated Unlawful Entry onto Property of White House National Security Aide," *Washington Post*, March 12, 2022, https://www.washingtonpost.com/politics/2022/03/12/police-investigated-unlawful-entry-onto-property-white-house-national-security-aide/.

29 *removing selected Russian banks*: "Joint Statement on Further Restrictive Economic Measures," White House, February 26, 2022, https://www.whitehouse.gov/briefing-room/statements-releases/2022/02/26/joint-statement-on-further-restrictive-economic-measures/.

30 *"We'll need eyes"*: Singh interview.

30 *the ruble plunged*: Srinivasan Sivabalan and Todd Gillespie, "Ruble Plunges 30% as Markets Briefly Freeze on Sanctions Stress," Bloomberg, February 28, 2022, https://www.bloomberg.com/news/articles/2022-02-28/ruble-plunges-30-as-markets-briefly-freeze-on-sanctions-stress?sref=aJXZGtfw.

30 *"economic and financial war"*: Richard Lough, "France Declares 'Economic War' Against Russia," Reuters, March 1, 2022, https://www.reuters.com/world/france-declares-economic-war-against-russia-2022-03-01/.

30 *"the assumption of sovereign equality"*: Adam Tooze, "Chartbook #89 Russia's Financial Meltdown," *Charbook* (blog), February 28, 2022, https://adamtooze.substack.com/p/chartbook-89-russias-financial-meltdown.

31 *the type of brooch*: "Sledite za broshkami: Signaly Elvira Nabiullina," RBC, February 11, 2022 https://www.rbc.ru/photoreport/11/02/2022/5f92bea39a79475522989725a.

31 *she donned all black*: "Statement by Bank of Russia Governor Elvira Nabiullina," Central Bank of the Russian Federation, February 28, 2022, https://www.cbr.ru/eng/press/event/?id=12730.

31 *"Russia's economic reality"*: "Putin provedet soveshchaniye po ekonomicheskim voprosam," Tass, February 28, 2022, https://tass.ru/politika/13895693.

31 *stabilize the ruble*: This account draws from author interviews with people familiar with central bank officials and "Russia Central Banker Wanted Out over Ukraine, Putin Said No," Bloomberg, March 23, 2022, https://www.bloomberg.com/news/articles/2022-03-23/russia-central-banker-wanted-out-over-ukraine-but-putin-said-no?sref=aJXZGtfw.

32 *"enough to stop an autocrat"*: Singh interview.

33 *fortunes from historical corruption*: "Briefing Paper: Repurposing Frozen Russian Assets for Victims in Ukraine," Redress, June 2022, https://redress.org/publication/briefing-paper-repurposing-frozen-russian-assets-for-victims-in-ukraine/.

33 *Johnson had met Alexander*: Jim Pickard, "Boris Johnson Faces Fresh Questions over 2018 Party at Lebedev Villa," *Financial Times*, June 27, 2023, https://www.ft.com/content/53d32fbc-a1e5-495b-b068-cf7d7a202f78; and Carole Cadwalladr and Mark Townsend, "Revealed: Ex-KGB Agent Met Boris Johnson at Italian Party," *Guardian*, November 17, 2019, https://www.theguardian.com/media/2019/nov/17/boris-johnson-met-alexander-lebedev-without-security-after-nato-summit.

33 *Johnson billed*: Ben Quinn, "PM Says No Official Business Discussed at Lebedev Palazzo 'as Far as I'm Aware,'" *Guardian*, July 26, 2022, https://www.theguardian.com/politics/2022

/jul/26/boris-johnson-says-2018-lebedev-visit-was-in-line-with-security-protocols. Lebedev was not targeted with sanctions in either the U.K., United States, or EU, but Canada and Ukraine have blacklisted him.

33 *freezing his £48 million*: "Government Announces Sanctions against Russian Oligarchs Alisher Usmanov and Igor Shuvalov," U.K. Foreign Office, March 3, 2022, https://www.gov.uk/government/news/government-announces-sanctions-against-russian-oligarchs-alisher-usmanov-and-igor-shuvalov.

34 *"They have now simply"*: Interview with Lavrov to Al Jazeera, Russian Ministry of Foreign Affairs, March 2, 2022, https://mid.ru/ru/foreign_policy/news/1802485/.

34 *"sapping Russian strength"*: "Remarks by President Biden on the United Efforts of the Free World to Support the People of Ukraine," White House, March 26, 2022, https://www.whitehouse.gov/briefing-room/speeches-remarks/2022/03/26/remarks-by-president-biden-on-the-united-efforts-of-the-free-world-to-support-the-people-of-ukraine/.

34 *an attempt to squeeze*: Ambassador James O'Brien, "The Role of Sanctions in U.S. Foreign Policy," at the Institut für die Wissenschaften vom Menschen, Vienna, February 20, 2023, https://www.youtube.com/watch?v=APX4yyHtg20.

CHAPTER 2 HUNTING RUSSIAN KLEPTOCRATS

36 *"We would really love it if"*: Interviews with Andrew Adams, November 16, 2022, and August 16 and September 6, 2023.

36 *"Tonight, I say to the Russian oligarchs"*: "Remarks by President Biden in State of the Union Address," White House, March 1, 2022, https://www.whitehouse.gov/briefing-room/speeches-remarks/2022/03/02/remarks-by-president-biden-in-state-of-the-union-address/.

36 *"different prosecutors"*: Interview with Sharon Cohen Levin, September 8, 2023.

37 *"Sanctions are the new FCPA"*: U.S. Department of Justice, Twitter post, May 26, 2022, https://x.com/TheJusticeDept/status/1529939557449355265?s=20.

37 *Justice Department only started*: "Sanctions Are the New FCPA: The Familiar Evolution of Sanctions Enforcement," Wilson Sonsini Goodrich & Rosati alert, March 30, 2023, https://www.wsgr.com/en/insights/sanctions-are-the-new-fcpa-the-familiar-evolution-of-sanctions-enforcement.html#:~:text=Earlier%20this%20month%2C%20Deputy%20Attorney,Corrupt%20Practices%20Act%20(FCPA).

38 *"carrot-versus-stick conversation"*: Interview with former top U.S. counterintelligence official, July 18, 2023.

39 *"form of civilizational assault"*: "A Conversation with Andrew Adams," Hudson Institute, January 19, 2023, https://youtu.be/tg1KhaJoQJU.

40 *the forfeiture unit*: Levin interview.

40 *seize suspected contraband*: Eric Blumenson and Eva Nilsen, "Policing for Profit: The Drug War's Hidden Economic Agenda," *University of Chicago Law Review* 65 (1998).

40 *civil forfeiture*: Sarah Stillman, "Taken," *New Yorker*, August 5, 2013, https://www.newyorker.com/magazine/2013/08/12/taken.

40 *ropes from Levin*: Robert Lenzer, "The Babe Ruth of Forfeiture Is After Your Ill-Gotten Gains," *Forbes*, August 14, 2012, https://www.forbes.com/sites/robertlenzner/2012/08/14/uncle-sam-forces-crooks-to-forfeit-billions-to-their-victims/.

40 *"parlay the position"*: Adams interview.

41 *a vor*: James O. Finckenauer and Elin Waring, "Challenging the Russian Mafia Mystique," *National Institute of Justice Journal*, April 2001, https://www.ojp.gov/pdffiles1/jr000247b.pdf.

41 *Georgian Mafia group Kutaisi*: Mark Galeotti, "Who Were the Georgian Gangsters Arrested in Europe?," *In Moscow's Shadows* (blog), June 27, 2013, https://inmoscows shadows.wordpress.com/2013/06/27/who-were-the-georgian-gangsters-arrested-in -europe/.

41 *Shulaya was entitled to*: U.S. vs. Razhden Shulaya et al., indictment by the Southern District of New York, June 7, 2017.

42 *the FBI arrested*: Sentencing memorandum from Anthony Cecutti, Shulaya's lawyer, to Judge Forrest, September 9, 2018.

42 *when Shulaya was convicted*: "'Thief-in-Law' Razhden Shulaya Sentenced in Manhattan Federal Court to 45 Years in Prison," Justice Department press release, December 19, 2018, https://www.justice.gov/usao-sdny/pr/thief-law-razhden-shulaya-sentenced -manhattan-federal-court-45-years-prison.

42 *oligarchs close to Putin, who used*: Catherine Belton, *Putin's People* (London: William Collins, 2020), explores at length Putin's use of the *obshchak* model.

43 *take on new meanings*: Mark Galeotti, *The Vory: Russia's Super Mafia* (New Haven, CT: Yale University Press, 2018).

43 *joint U.S.-U.K. project*: Adams declined to discuss specific ongoing cases. This account is based on court documents and my speaking to multiple people familiar with the investigations. For Operation Accordable background, see "National Crime Agency Inspection," Criminal Justice Inspectorates, July 2020, https://assets-hmicfrs.justice inspectorates.gov.uk/uploads/an-inspection-of-the-national-crime-agency-criminal -intelligence-function.pdf.

45 *Hanick came to view Russia as*: "You feel freer in Russia," interview with Jack Hanick, FOMA, August 14, 2013, https://foma.ru/v-rossii-chuvstvuesh-sebya-svobodnee .html.

45 *banks blocked the money*: U.S. v. John Hanick, SDNY, sealed indictment, November 4, 2021, https://www.justice.gov/usao-sdny/press-release/file/1479811/download.

45 *Hanick recalls how*: U.S. v. Konstantin Malofeyev, unsealed April 6, 2022, https://www .justice.gov/opa/pr/russian-oligarch-charged-violating-us-sanctions.

46 *U.K. authorities dragged their feet*: Interviews with people familiar with the investigation, 2023.

47 *Adams's team eventually homed in on*: Adams declined to comment on the specifics of the *Amadea* case. This account of *Amadea*'s seizure by the U.S. government is based on hundreds of pages of legal filings and interviews with people familiar with the vessel as well as lawyers in Fiji and the United States. "'Straw Owner' Hides $1 Billion Worth of Russian Yachts, U.S. Says," Bloomberg, May 14, 2022, https://www .bloomberg.com/news/features/2022-05-14/russian-tycoon-hides-1-billion-worth-of -yachts-us-says?sref=aJXZGtfw; and Stephanie Baker, "Seizing a Russian Superyacht Is Much More Complicated than You Think," *Bloomberg Businessweek*, November 7, 2022, https://www.bloomberg.com/news/features/2022-11-07/russian-oligarch-s-seized -yachts-are-costing-tax-payers-millions.

47 *Gatsby of Putin's Russia*: Catherine Belton, "Suleiman Kerimov, the Secret Oligarch,"

Financial Times, February 10, 2012, https://www.ft.com/content/ad4e8816-52do-11e1 -ae2c-00144feabdco.

47 *reducing the family's shares*: Devon Pendleton, "Sanctioned Russian's Family Sells $6 Billion Stake in Gold Miner," Bloomberg, April 6, 2022, https://www.bloomberg.com/news /articles/2022-04-06/sanctioned-russian-s-family-sells-6-billion-stake-in-gold-miner ?sref=aJXZGtfw.

48 *to set up his own*: The United States sanctioned Khudainatov's company IPC in 2017 for selling oil to North Korea. It delisted the company on March 2, 2020, after the company stopped the trade. Khudainatov has not been resanctioned in the United States, but the EU added him to its list in June 2022 for "benefiting from the government" and being "associated with listed persons."

48 *around $11 billion*: "Rosneft Will Pay the Ex-President $11 Billion for Assets in Taimyr," *Moscow Times*, February 12, 2021, https://www.moscowtimes.ru/2021/02/12/rosneft -zaplatit-eks-prezidentu-11-mlrd-za-aktivi-na-taimire-a102793; and "Rosneft ne poskupilas na Taimyr," Kommersant, February 12, 2021, https://www.kommersant.ru/doc /4691394.

49 *Russia's Federal Guard Service*: "The Secret of Scheherazade," *Navalny* (blog), March 21, 2022, https://navalny.com/p/6620/.

49 *of a third superyacht*: Baker, "Seizing a Superyacht."

50 *Supreme Court rejected*: Fiji director of public prosecutions, June 7, 2022.

50 *"pay for upkeep"*: Christopher Woody, "The 'Craziest Thing' about Seizing Russian Superyachts," *Business Insider*, June 16, 2022, https://www.businessinsider .com/craziest-thing-about-russian-yacht-seizure-upkeep-cost-jake-sullivan-2022 -6?r=US&IR=T.

50 *again appealed the seizure*: Eduard Khudainatov and Millemarin Investments Ltd. vs U.S.A., "Memorandum in Support of Motion for Return of Property Pursuant to Federal Rule of Criminal Procedure 41(g)," October 23, 2023, 28; and *USA v. Amadea*, Forfeiture Complaint, SDNY, October 23, 2023, 11.

51 *his daughter's charter*: Author interview with Adam Ford, Khudainatov's lawyer, January 18, 2024.

51 *"Ensure the carpet"*: G1 Guest preferences, disclosed in *USA v. Amadea* court filings.

51 *Khudainatov sold* Amadea: *USA v. Amadea*, Forfeiture Complaint.

51 *"boat has been sold"*: *USA v. Amadea*, Forfeiture Complaint.

52 *Washington had targeted Kochman*: "U.S. Treasury Severs More Networks Providing Support for Putin and Russia's Elites," U.S. Treasury, June 2, 2022, https://home .treasury.gov/news/press-releases/jy0802.

52 *Kochman was renowned*: Author interview with source, April 25, 2022.

CHAPTER 3 **DEMOCRACY DERAILED**

Inevitably, my attempt to recount fifteen years of Russian economic history in one chapter meant leaving out some key twists and turns. This potted history is designed to help readers understand the backstory to the current sanctions campaign.

57 *One in two workers*: Kaspar Richter, "Wage Arrears and Economic Voting in Russia," *American Political Science Review* 100, no. 1 (February 2006), https://www.cambridge

.org/core/journals/american-political-science-review/article/abs/wage-arrears-and
-economic-voting-in-russia/4CE1332755A04C08179B4C8234DDDED5.

58　*Yeltsin harnessed the frustrations*: Celestine Bohlen, "Yeltsin Galvanizes Russians'
Will and Taps into Their Frustration," *New York Times*, August 22, 1991, https://www
.nytimes.com/1991/08/22/world/after-the-coup-yeltsin-galvanizes-russians-will-and
-taps-into-their-frustration.html?searchResultPosition=3.

59　*Yeltsin sided with the radicals*: Chrystia Freeland, *Sale of the Century* (Boston: Little,
Brown, 2000), 33.

59　*communist-dominated legislature*: Anders Aslund, "Russia: The Arduous Transition to
a Market Economy," in *The Great Rebirth: Lessons from the Victory of Capitalism over
Communism*, ed. Anders Aslund and Simeon Djankov (Washington, DC: Peterson
Institute for International Economics, 2014).

59　*a much-more complicated patient*: Jeffrey Sachs, "What I Did in Russia," https://www
.jeffsachs.org.

60　*"less shock and more therapy"*: Strobe Talbott, *The Russia Hand: A Memoir of Presidential
Diplomacy* (New York: Random House, 2002), 106.

60　*the West never stumped up*: Sachs, "What I Did."

61　*hundreds of billions of dollars*: Stephanie Baker, "Russia: Deal on Paris Club Entry Seen
as Political Victory," RFE/RL, June 9, 1997, https://www.rferl.org/a/1085238.html.

61　*With the country effectively broke*: James Boughton, "Russia: From Rebirth to Crisis
to Recovery," in *Tearing Down Walls: The International Monetary Fund, 1990–1999*
(Washington, DC: IMF, 2012).

62　*about a financial scheme being hatched*: Ibid.; and author interview with Martin Gilman,
the IMF's senior representative in Moscow in the 1990s.

62　*Russia's vast natural resources*: Stephanie Baker, "From Russia with Cash," Bloomberg Markets, May 2010, https://stephaniebakerwriter.com/stories-archive/mikhail-prokhorov
-from-russia-with-cash,

62　*an audacious program*: Daniel Treisman, "'Loans for Shares' Revisited," *Post-Soviet
Affairs* 26, no. 3 (July–September 2010).

63　*buying London's Chelsea Football Club*: Boris Berezovsky, claiming he owned a 50
percent stake in Sibneft, sued Abramovich in London but lost the case in 2012.
Abramovich argued Berezovsky was never a beneficial owner of trusts that owned the
assets but that he had acted as his *krysha* or "protection." *Berezovsky v Abramovich*,
"Executive Summary of the Full Judgment," October 1, 2012, https://www.judiciary
.uk/wp-content/uploads/JCO/Documents/Judgments/berezovsky-abramovich
-summary.pdf.

63　*Russia's original sin*: See Freeland, *Sale of the Century*.

63　*"Yeltsin drunk is better than"*: Talbott, *Russia Hand*, 185.

64　*promise to attend*: Phil Reeves, "Yeltsin Tries to Outshine the Red Star of Davos,"
Independent, February 7, 1996, https://www.independent.co.uk/news/world/yeltsin-tries
-to-outshine-red-star-of-davos-1317726.html.

64　*swilling champagne*: William Drozdiak, "Russian Communist Grabs Attention at
Forum," *Washington Post*, February 4, 1996, https://www.washingtonpost.com/archive
/politics/1996/02/05/russian-communist-grabs-attention-at-forum/fc3d06f7-92b2-4b3d
-9fdf-4ac47bf2e52d/.

64　semibankirschina: William Safire, "One Language; Crony Capitalism," *New York*

Times, February 1, 1998, https://www.nytimes.com/1998/02/01/magazine/on-language-crony-capitalism.html.

64 *redheaded economic reformer*: Freeland, *Sale of the Century*, 187. See also her widely cited *Financial Times* story from October 29, 1996, which first revealed the group; and David Hoffman, *The Oligarchs* (New York: Public Affairs, 2002), 329.

64 *"deal with social problems"*: Memorandum of telephone conversation with Yeltsin, Clinton Presidential Library, February 21, 1996.

64 *another $10 billion*: Boughton, *Tearing Down Walls*.

65 *another heart attack*: Boris Yeltsin, *Midnight Diaries* (New York: Public Affairs, 2000), 35–36.

66 *industrial output plunged*: Sergey Smirnov, "Economic Fluctuations in Russia," *Russian Journal of Economics*, May 31, 2015, https://rujec.org/article/27945/.

66 *"He's brought the country"*: Stephanie Baker-Said, "Paid Off Then Laid Off," *Moscow Times*, April 21, 1998.

67 *oligarchs made fortunes*: Stephanie Baker-Said, "Uneximbank to Lose State Customs Funds," *Moscow Times*, August 8, 1997; and Stephanie Baker-Said, "Chubais Pledges Federal Treasury by 1998," *Moscow Times*, August 26, 1997.

67 *the IMF released $4.8 billion*: Boughton, *Tearing Down Walls*.

67 *Camdessus was at his*: Ibid.; and Freeland, *Sale of the Century*, 301.

67 *most officials were gone*: Boughton, *Tearing Down Walls*.

68 *"forty-watt bulb"*: Talbott, *Russia Hand*, 286.

68 *"toxic nuclear waste"*: Ben Aris, "Russia's Bondageddon," BNE IntelliNews, April 26, 2018, https://www.intellinews.com/russia-s-bondageddon-140704/.

68 *When protesters descended*: Masha Gessen, *The Man without a Face: The Unlikely Rise of Vladimir Putin* (New York: Riverhead Books, 2012), 68–69.

69 *foreign economic activity*: Gessen explores Putin's early years in St. Petersburg. See also "Putin's Stamp and the $2 Million Heist," RFE/RL, May 26, 2022, https://www.rferl.org/a/putin-bribe-scandal/31867449.html.

69 *working in the Kremlin*: Yeltsin, *Midnight Diaries*, 326.

69 *the appointment of Putin*: Ibid.

69 *Berezovsky claimed*: Gessen, *Man without a Face*, 18–22.

69 *helping Putin select*: Dominic Midgley and Chris Hutchins, *Abramovich: The Billionaire from Nowhere* (Neville Ness House, 2004), 89.

69 *old KGB types*: Author interview with Alexander Goldfarb, July 30, 2018. See also Goldfarb's book *Death of a Dissident: The Poisoning of Alexander Litvinenko* (London: Simon & Schuster UK, 2008), 182.

70 *"you have built this state yourself"*: Sabrina Tavernise, "Putin, Exerting His Authority, Meets with Russia's Tycoons," *New York Times*, July 29, 2000, https://www.nytimes.com/2000/07/29/world/putin-exerting-his-authority-meets-with-russia-s-tycoons.html.

70 *Putin excluded anyone who*: Amelia Gentleman, "Tycoon Resigns from Duma," *Guardian*, July 18, 2000, https://www.theguardian.com/world/2000/jul/18/russia.

70 *Kursk submarine sank*: Gessen, *Man without a Face*, 172.

70 *fled Russia a few months later*: Ibid.

70 *"see his heart and soul"*: "President Bush and President Putin Talk to Crawford Students," George W. Bush White House Archives, November 15, 2001, https://georgewbush-whitehouse.archives.gov/news/releases/2001/11/20011115-4.html.

70 *The Russian leader talked up*: Peter Baker, "'I'm Thrilled He's Here,'" *Washington Post*, November 15, 2001, https://www.washingtonpost.com/archive/politics/2001/11/15 /im-thrilled-hes-here-bush-says-as-putin-visits-his-texas-ranch/d9928257-b7e4-428c -9d44-865a1ce6e5f5/.

71 *he wanted to retire*: Stephanie Baker-Said, "Russia's Oil Czar Looks West," Bloomberg Markets, July 2002. Khodorkovsky sued me for libel over this story, but he dropped the claim in the spring of 2003, just months before he was arrested.

71 *in talks with ExxonMobil*: Andrew Jack and Carola Hoyos, "Exxon May Offer $25 Billion for 40% of Yukos," *Financial Times*, October 2, 2003.

71 *"eaten more dirt than I need"*: John Browne, *Beyond Business* (London: Orion Publishing, 2011), 145.

71 *Rosneft gradually took over*: Catherine Belton, "Rosneft Seals Takeover of Yukos," *Financial Times*, May 10, 2007, https://www.ft.com/content/9e293f12-fed3-11db-aff2 -000b5df10621.

73 *"you'll be swallowing dust"*: "You'll Be Tired of Swallowing Dust," Kommersant, June 20, 2002, https://www.kommersant.ru/doc/328322.

73 *first state visit to Britain of a Russian leader*: "UK State Banquet Honors Putin," CNN, June 24, 2003, https://edition.cnn.com/2003/WORLD/europe/06/24/britain.putin/.

73 *After a signing ceremony*: George Wright, "UK and Russia Strike 'Historic Energy Deal," *Guardian*, June 26, 2003, https://www.theguardian.com/uk/2003/jun/26/russia .politics.

73 *barred from reentering*: Stephanie Baker-Said, "Browder, Branded a Danger to Russia, Posts 2,549 Percent Return," Bloomberg Markets, May 22, 2006, https://www .bloomberg.com/news/articles/2006-05-22/browder-branded-a-danger-to-russia -posts-2-549-percent-return?sref=aJXZGtfw.

74 *"I really don't feel safe"*: Author interview with Boris Berezovsky, March 9, 2007, London. See also Stephanie Baker-Said, "Spy Murder Shakes Russian Émigrés Flooding Britain with Cash," Bloomberg Markets, March 29, 2007.

74 *they were Putin's men*: Catherine Belton, *Putin's People: How the KGB Took Back Russia and Then Took on the West* (Glasgow, Scotland: William Collins, 2020), is the definitive account of the tycoons who got rich off Putin's presidency.

75 *from state-controlled Gazprom*: "Rotenberg prodal krupneshevo podryadchika Gazproma," *Vedomosti*, November 7, 2019, https://www.vedomosti.ru/business/articles /2019/11/07/815728-krupneishii-podryadchik-gazproma.

75 *his consigliere and played an important role*: Author interview with source, November 6, 2023. See also Betsy McKay, Thomas Grove, and Rob Barry, "The Russian Billionaire Selling Putin's War to the Public," *Wall Street Journal*, December 2, 2022, https://www .wsj.com/articles/russian-billionaire-selling-putins-war-ukraine-11669994410.

75 *Rupert Murdoch of Russia*: Stephen Grey, Brian Grow, and Roman Anin, "Comrade Capitalism," Reuters, November 18, 2014, https://www.reuters.com/investigates /special-report/comrade-capitalism-rocket-men/.

75 *the Kremlin's financial dependency*: "Rossiya vernulas' v Parizhskiy klub dolgi SSSR," *Rossiyskaya Gazeta*, August 22, 2006, https://rg.ru/2006/08/21/dolg-procenti.html.

76 *imperial ambitions*: Claire Bigg, "Was Soviet Collapse Last Century's Worst Geopolitical Catastrophe?," RFE/RL, April 29, 2005, https://www.rferl.org/a/1058688 .html. Putin spoke about NATO including Russia in 2001. See Baker, "'I'm Thrilled He's Here.'"

76 *"against whom is this expansion intended?"*: "Speech at the Munich Conference," February 10, 2007, http://en.kremlin.ru/events/president/transcripts/24034.

76 *ring alarm bells about Putin*: Yegor Gaidar, *Collapse of an Empire: Lessons for Modern Russia* (Washington, DC: Brookings Institution Press, 2007).

76 *membership in the future*: Bucharest Summit Declaration, April 3, 2008, https://www.nato.int/cps/en/natolive/official_texts_8443.htm.

76 *direct threat against Russia*: "Putin Warns NATO over Expansion," *Guardian*, April 4, 2008, https://www.theguardian.com/world/2008/apr/04/nato.russia.

76 *the transfer was illegitimate*: "Text of Putin's Speech at NATO Summit," Unian, April 2, 2008, https://www.unian.info/world/111033-text-of-putin-s-speech-at-nato-summit-bucharest-april-2-2008.html.

76 *"Robin to Putin's Batman"*: "Medvedev's Address and Tandem Politics," cable from U.S. ambassador to Russia John Beyrle, Wikileaks, November 19, 2008, https://wikileaks.org/plusd/cables/08MOSCOW3343_a.html.

76 *finding common ground*: Michael McFaul, *From Cold War to Hot Peace: An American Ambassador in Putin's Russia* (Boston: Mariner Books, 2018).

76 *"like a ward boss"*: Barack Obama, *A Promised Land* (New York: Penguin Random House, 2020), 466.

77 *53 percent of seats*: Elections to the State Duma, OSCE Observation Mission Final Report, January 12, 2012, https://www.osce.org/files/f/documents/f/5/86959.pdf.

77 *The demonstrations continued*: Robert Person and Michael McFaul, "What Putin Fears Most," *Journal of Democracy*, April 2022, https://www.journalofdemocracy.org/articles/what-putin-fears-most.

78 *40 percent of Russia's oil*: Anna Shiryaevskaya, "Rosneft Completes $55 Billion TNK-BP Russian Oil Acquisition," Bloomberg, March 21, 2013, https://www.bloomberg.com/news/articles/2013-03-21/rosneft-completes-55-billion-acquisition-of-oil-producer-tnk-bp?sref=aJXZGtfw.

78 *suggesting he had been strangled*: Jeremy Hodges, "Berezovsky Cause of Death Can't Be Determined, Coroner Says," Bloomberg, March 28, 2014, https://www.bloomberg.com/news/articles/2014-03-27/berezovsky-cause-of-death-can-t-be-determined-coroner-says?sref=aJXZGtfw.

CHAPTER 4 **PUTIN'S CALCULUS**

79 *the help of Paul Manafort*: Stephanie Baker, "Paul Manafort's Lucrative Ukraine Years Are Central to the Russia Probe." May 22, 2017, https://www.bloomberg.com/news/features/2017-05-22/paul-manafort-s-lucrative-ukraine-years-are-central-to-the-russia-probe?sref=aJXZGtfw.

79 *"suicidal" for Ukraine*: "Trading Insults," *Economist*, August 24, 2013, https://www.economist.com/europe/2013/08/24/trading-insults.

80 *(one hundred lives)*: "Remembrance Day of the Heavenly Hundred Heroes," We Are Ukraine, February 20, 2023, https://www.weareukraine.info/remembrance-day-of-the-heavenly-hundred-heroes/.

80 *voiced their concerns*: Author interview with Dan Fried, July 18, 2023.

80 *stormed the local parliament*: "Crimean Parliament Seized by Unknown Pro-Russian Gunmen," *Guardian*, February 27, 2014, https://www.theguardian.com/world/2014/feb/27/crimean-parliament-seized-by-unknown-pro-russian-gunmen.

82   *reshaped financial warfare*: Juan Zarate, *Treasury's War: The Unleashing of a New Era of Financial Warfare* (New York: Public Affairs, 2013), 7.

83   *vote was widely condemned*: John Bellinger III, "Why the Crimean Referendum Is Illegitimate," Council on Foreign Relations, March 16, 2014, https://www.cfr.org/interview/why-crimean-referendum-illegitimate.

83   *Obama administration's response*: "Ukraine-Related Sanctions," Obama White House, March 17, 2014, https://obamawhitehouse.archives.gov/the-press-office/2014/03/17/fact-sheet-ukraine-related-sanctions.

83   *"I didn't think it was right"*: Interview with Rory MacFarquhar, May 6, 2023.

83   *"drive us into some corner"*: "Obrashcheniye Presidenta Rossiskoi Federatsii," March 18, 2014, http://kremlin.ru/events/president/news/20603.

84   *targeted Bank Rossiya*: "Russian Leadership's Inner Circle," U.S. Treasury, March 20, 2014, https://home.treasury.gov/news/press-releases/jl23331. Timchenko famously sued the *Economist* magazine over similar allegations.

84   *Timchenko's Labrador retriever*: Interview with Tass, August 3, 2014, https://tass.com/top-officials/743432.

84   *sold his stake*: "Rossiskiy milliarder Timchenko prodayet svoyu dolyu v Gunvor Tornkvistu," Tass, March 21, 2014, https://tass.com/economy/724708?utm_source=google.com&utm_medium=organic&utm_campaign=google.com&utm_referrer=google.com.

84   *"ashamed for my friends"*: "Pryamaya liniya s Vladimirom Putinym," Kremlin, April 17, 2014, http://kremlin.ru/events/president/news/20796.

84   *$18 million worth of art*: "The Art Industry and U.S. Policies That Undermine Sanctions," Staff Report of the U.S. Senate Permanent Subcommittee on Investigations, Committee on Homeland Security and Governmental Affairs, 116, https://www.hsgac.senate.gov/wp-content/uploads/imo/media/doc/2020-07-29%20PSI%20Staff%20Report%20-%20The%20Art%20Industry%20and%20U.S.%20Policies%20that%20Undermine%20Sanctions.pdf.

85   *"Russia is a regional power"*: "Press Conference with President Obama," March 25, 2014, https://obamawhitehouse.archives.gov/the-press-office/2014/03/25/press-conference-president-obama-and-prime-minister-rutte-netherlands.

85   *the president's claims of American exceptionalism*: Putin interview with the German newspaper *Bild*, January 12, 2016, http://www.en.kremlin.ru/events/president/transcripts/statements/51155.

85   *confrontation could be contained*: John Bolton, *The Room Where It Happened: A White House Memoir* (New York: Simon & Schuster, 2020), 131.

85   *"sign of weakness"*: Interview with John Bolton, December 12, 2023.

85   *"people's republic"*: "Ukraine Crisis: Protesters Declare Donetsk 'Republic,'" BBC, April 7, 2014, https://www.bbc.co.uk/news/world-europe-26919928.

85   *mercenaries led by Yevgeny Prigozhin*: Evidence Submission by the Dossier Center to the U.K. Parliament, May 2022, https://committees.parliament.uk/writtenevidence/108385/html/.

85   *stepped up its sanctions*: "Additional Treasury Sanctions on Russian Government Officials and Entities," U.S. Treasury, April 28, 2014, https://home.treasury.gov/news/press-releases/jl2369.

86   *"less blowback to the U.S."*: Interview with Brad Setser, July 14, 2023.

86   *"damage an economy"*: Singh interview, January 23, 2023.

86   *"can we cause one?"*: Setser interview.

87 *"an obvious choice"*: Singh testimony, https://www.congress.gov/116/meeting/house
/109498/witnesses/HHRG-116-BA10-Wstate-SinghD-20190515.pdf.

87 *pinprick sanctions*: "Sanctions on Entities within the Financial Services and Energy Sectors," U.S. Treasury, July 16, 2014, https://home.treasury.gov/news/press-releases/jl2572.

87 *downed plane*: "Readout of President's Call with President Putin of Russia," July 17, 2014,
https://obamawhitehouse.archives.gov/the-press-office/2014/07/17/readout-president
-s-call-president-putin-russia.

87 *Malaysian Airlines Flight*: "Body Parts, Debris Scattered at Malaysia Airlines Wreckage
Site," ABC News, July 18, 2014, https://abcnews.go.com/International/body-parts
-debris-scattered-malaysia-airlines-wreckage-site/story?id=24623388.

87 *the EU barred*: "EU Restrictive Measures," Council of the European Union, Background
Note, July 29, 2014, https://www.consilium.europa.eu/media/22023/144159.pdf.

88 *United States also cut off*: "Additional Treasury Sanctions on Russian Financial Institutions," July 29, 2014, U.S. Treasury, https://home.treasury.gov/news/press-releases
/jl2590; and "U.S. Commerce Department Expands Export Restrictions on Russia," BIS
press release, July 29, 2014, https://www.bis.doc.gov/index.php/all-articles/107-about
-bis/newsroom/press-releases/press-release-2014/710-u-s-commerce-department
-expands-export-restrictions-on-russia.

88 *agricultural products*: "Russia Announces Ban on Many U.S. Agricultural Products,"
U.S. Department of Agriculture, August 7, 2014, https://fas.usda.gov/data/russia
-announces-ban-many-us-agricultural-products; and Whitney McFerron, "Russia Seen
as Main Loser from Food Import Ban with EU," Bloomberg, August 7, 2014, https://
www.bloombe agricultural products rg.com/news/articles/2014-08-07/russia-seen
-as-main-loser-from-food-import-ban-with-eu?sref=aJXZGtfw.

88 *tightened the noose further*: "Expanded Treasury Sanctions," U.S. Treasury, September
12, 2014, https://home.treasury.gov/news/press-releases/jl2629.

88 *forced Exxon out*: Ilya Arkhipov, Stephen Bierman, and Ryan Chilcote, "Rosneft Says
Exxon Arctic Well Strikes Oil," Bloomberg, September 27, 2014, https://www.bloomberg
.com/news/articles/2014-09-27/rosneft-says-exxon-arctic-well-strikes-oil?sref=aJXZGtfw.

89 *ordered the bulldozing*: Andrew Kramer, "Russia Destroys Piles of Banned Western
Food," *New York Times*, August 6, 2015, https://www.nytimes.com/2015/08/07/world
/europe/russia-destroys-piles-of-banned-western-food.html.

89 *before it officially launched*: Anna Eremina, "Rosneft provela pervuyu operatsiyu v
Ruskoi SWIFT," March 22, 2018, https://www.vedomosti.ru/finance/articles/2018
/03/22/754655-rosneft-provela-pervuyu-operatsiyu-swift.

90 *its ambassador to Ukraine had signed*: "Kompleks mer po vypolneniyu Minskikh soglash-
enii," Minsk II agreement, February 15, 2015, https://www.osce.org/files/f/documents
/5/b/140221.pdf.

90 *his side of Minsk II*: Steven Pifer, "Minsk II at Two Years," Brookings, February 15, 2017,
https://www.brookings.edu/articles/minsk-ii-at-two-years/.

90 *consider recognizing Crimea*: "Trump Tries to Clarify After Mistakenly Saying Russia Has
No Forces in Ukraine," ABC News, August 1, 2016, https://abcnews.go.com/Politics/
donald-trump-attempts-clarify-comments-russian-forces-ukraine/story?id=41045975.

91 *"two guys injured"*: Author interview with Oleg Deripaska, Moscow, January 2011;
and Stephanie Baker, "Metals Mogul," Bloomberg Markets, April 2011, https://www
.bloomberg.com/news/articles/2011-02-21/deripaska-rebounding-from-near-disaster
-stares-down-potanin-as-metals-soar?sref=aJXZGtfw.

91 *"very politically connected"*: Deripaska interview.

91 *FBI sought him out for questioning*: Author interview with source, July 2023. See also David Ignatius, "The GOP's Spin on the Russia Probe Doesn't Add Up," *Washington Post*, September 25, 2018, https://www.washingtonpost.com/opinions/a-gop-spin-on-the-russia-probe-reads-like-a-noir-thriller--but-doesnt-add-up/2018/09/25/1b940c92-c0ca-11e8-be77-516336a26305_story.html.

91 *tycoon was suing him*: Stephanie Baker, David Voreacos, and Volodymyr Verbianyi, "Manafort's Offer to Russian Oligarch Was Tied to Disputed Deal," Bloomberg, September 27, 2017, https://www.bloomberg.com/politics/articles/2017-09-27/manafort-s-offer-to-russian-is-said-to-be-tied-to-disputed-deal?sref=aJXZGtfw.

91 *sanctions on Prigozhin's companies*: "Treasury Designates Individuals and Entities Involved in the Ongoing Conflict in Ukraine," U.S. Treasury, June 20, 2017, https://home.treasury.gov/news/press-releases/sm0114.

91 *propping up dictators*: Simon Marks and Stephanie Baker, "What Wagner's Mutiny Means for Its Sprawling Business Empire," Bloomberg, June 27, 2023, https://www.bloomberg.com/graphics/2023-wagner-presence-in-central-african-republic/?sref=aJXZGtfw.

92 *continued to cruise*: Stephanie Baker, "Seizing a Russian Superyacht Is Much More Complicated Than You Think," Bloomberg, November 7, 2022, https://www.bloomberg.com/news/features/2022-11-07/russian-oligarch-s-seized-yachts-are-costing-tax-payers-millions?sref=aJXZGtfw.

93 *"indices of corruption"*: Countering America's Adversaries Through Sanctions Act, August 2, 2017, https://congress.gov/115/plaws/publ44/PLAW-115publ44.pdf§§.

93 *long and random*: "Report to Congress Pursuant to Section 241 of the CAATSA Act," January 29, 2018, https://assets.bwbx.io/documents/users/iqjWHBFdfxIU/rJRW6x rdtLJE/v0.

93 Forbes *list of the richest Russians*: "DOJ Doesn't Deny Treasury's Russian 'Oligarch' List Was Copied from *Forbes*," *National Law Journal*, April 23, 2019, https://www.law.com/nationallawjournal/2019/04/23/doj-doesnt-deny-treasurys-russian-oligarch-list-was-copied-from-forbes/?slreturn=20231005050544.

93 *Putin joked that*: Henry Meyer and Stepan Kravchenko, "U.S. Names Oligarchs, Kremlin Elite but Avoids New Sanctions," Bloomberg, January 30, 2018, https://www.bloomberg.com/politics/articles/2018-01-30/u-s-releases-sweeping-list-of-russian-billionaires-officials?sref=aJXZGtfw.

94 *"don't trust the president"*: Kevin Breuninger, "People Don't Trust the President on Russia," CNBC, January 30, 2018, https://www.cnbc.com/2018/01/30/senators-grill-treasury-secretary-mnuchin-on-sanctions.html.

94 *"investigated for money laundering"*: "Treasury Designates Russian Oligarchs, Officials, and Entities in Response to Worldwide Malign Activity," April 6, 2018, https://home.treasury.gov/news/press-releases/sm0338.

94 *"groundless, ridiculous, and absurd"*: Yuliya Fedorinova and Thomas Wilson, "U.S. Sanctions Turn Putin Tycoons into International Pariahs," Bloomberg, April 6, 2018, https://www.bloomberg.com/politics/articles/2018-04-06/tycoon-goes-from-flights-with-putin-to-top-u-s-sanctions-target?sref=aJXZGtfw.

94 *hide Putin's money laundering*: *Oleg Deripaska v Janet Yellen*, "Memorandum Opinion," U.S. District Court for the District of Columbia, June 13, 2021.

95 *price of aluminum*: "Deripaska's Rusal Roiled by Sanctions as Aluminum Prices Jump,"

Bloomberg, April 9, 2018, https://www.bloomberg.com/news/articles/2018-04-09/deripaska-s-rusal-sees-defaults-looming-after-u-s-sanctions?sref=aJXZGtfw.

95 *global supply chain into chaos*: Thomas Biesheuvel and Jack Farchy, "Russia Sanctions Throw Global Aluminum Industry into Chaos," Bloomberg, April 17, 2018, https://www.bloomberg.com/news/articles/2018-04-17/russia-sanctions-throw-global-aluminum-supply-chain-into-chaos?sref=aJXZGtfw.

95 *"expect Treasury to"*: Author interview with John Smith, May 17, 2023.

95 *"not a good idea"*: Author interview with former Treasury official, June 6, 2023.

96 *"rescue the minority shareholders"*: Barker interview, Bloomberg TV, January 28, 2019.

96 *"Our objective was"*: "Mnuchin interview with Bloomberg TV's Stephanie Flanders," April 30, 2018.

96 *"a minority shareholder"*: Barker interview.

96 *Over dinner at Deripaska's apartment*: Interview with person familiar with the talks, November 17, 2023.

97 *reducing his control*: Ibid.

97 *"Rusal impacts"*: Letter from Ambassador Peter Wittig, Fara filing, May 30, 2018, https://efile.fara.gov/docs/6170-Informational-Materials-20180530-5.pdf.

97 *"'We've just pounded him'"*: Bolton interview.

97 *limiting the export of*: State Department Sanctions Notice, August 24, 2018.

98 *Barker persuaded Deripaska*: Interview with person familiar with the discussions, November 17, 2023.

98 *reduced his stake in*: Ibid. See also Polina Trifonova, "Kak budet ustroyeno upravleniye v EN+ posle utraty Deripaskoy kontrolya nad kompaniyey," Vedomosti, January 28, 2019, https://www.vedomosti.ru/business/articles/2019/01/28/792643-kak.

98 *Deripaska also pledged*: Treasury letter to Senator Ron Wyden, April 26. 2019.

98 *"removed control"*: Barker interview.

98 *He asked the court to*: Oleg Deripaska v Steve Mnuchin and Andrea Gacki and the U.S. Treasury's OFAC, March 15, 2019, https://assets.bwbx.io/documents/users/iqjWHBFdfxIU/rxcgfJK3dbfg/vo.

99 *petition was denied*: Sabrina Willmer, "Supreme Court Denies Russian Oligarch Deripaska's Plea to Lift Sanctions," Bloomberg News, October 3, 2022, https://www.bloomberg.com/news/articles/2022-10-03/russian-oligarch-deripaska-rejected-by-top-us-court-on-sanctions?sref=aJXZGtfw.

99 *"alternative reserve currencies"*: Natasha Doff and Anya Andrianova, "Russia Buys Quarter of World Yuan Reserves in Shift from Dollar," Bloomberg, January 9, 2019, https://www.bloomberg.com/news/articles/2019-01-09/russia-boosted-yuan-euro-holdings-as-it-dumped-dollars-in-2018?sref=aJXZGtfw.

99 *"all too weak"*: Johnson emailed answers to author's questions, August 8, 2023.

100 *"the price of international political conflict"*: Bolton interview.

CHAPTER 5 **OLIGARCHS IN AMERICA**

101 *owned not by him*: Jake Rudnitsky, Yuliya Federinova, and Chris Strohn, "FBI Raids Russian Billionaire Oleg Deripaska's Washington Mansion," Bloomberg, October 19, 2021, https://www.bloomberg.com/news/articles/2021-10-19/fbi-raids-russian-tycoon-deripaska-s-washington-home-nbc-says?sref=aJXZGtfw.

101   *"Did they find a load of"*: Deripaska Telegram post, October 20, 2021, https://t.me /olegderipaska/323.

102   *People who know him*: Author interview with source, October 7, 2023.

102   *he bought three homes*: U.S. v. Graham Bonham-Carter, SDNY indictment, unsealed October 11, 2022, https://www.justice.gov/usao-sdny/pr/uk-businessman-arrested-sanctions -evasion-benefitting-russian-oligarch-oleg-deripaska.

103   *planning to plow $100 million*: Interview with source familiar with the plan, October 7, 2023, and with Freddie Piro. December 20, 2007.

103   *over $3 million*: Piro interview, Deed of Trust.

104   *transfer the proceeds*: U.S.A. v Oleg Vladimirovich Deripaska, Olga Shriki, Natalia Mikhaylovna Bardakova, Ekaterina Olegovna Voronina, SDNY indictment, September 28, 2022, https:// www.justice.gov/d9/press-releases/attachments/2022/09/29/22cr518_s1_indictment _0.pdf.

104   *(It wasn't the first time)*: Michael Weiss, "Sergei Lavrov and Oleg Deripaska Traveled with a Sex Worker to Japan in 2018," April 20, 2022, https://newlinesmag.com/reportage /sergei-lavrov-and-oleg-deripaska-traveled-with-a-sex-worker-to-japan-in-2018/; and "Deripaska and Escort Joined Lavrov and Mistress on Official Trip to Japan," Insider, April 20, 2022, https://theins.ru/en/corruption/250507.

105   *After she gave birth*: U.S.A. v Deripaska.

106   *"sort of a cowboy"*: Interview with U.S. intelligence source, July 24, 2023.

106   *she emailed the FBI*: Greg Woodfield, "Former Mistress of Top Ex–FBI Agent Charles McGonigal Calls Him a Traitor," *Daily Mail*, December 20, 2023, https://www.dailymail .co.uk/news/article-12880905/Mistress-FBI-agent-Charles-McGonigal-traitor-Russian -oligarch-Oleg-Deripaska.html.

106   *Fokin's daughter get an internship*: U.S. v. Charles McGonigal, "Government's Sentencing Submission," December 7, 2023.

107   *was asking for as much as $3 million*: Ibid.

107   *to ensure secrecy*: Interview with source, July 18. 2023.

107   *McGonigal betrayed his*: https://www.justice.gov/usao-dc/pr/retired-fbi-executive -charged-concealing-225000-cash-received-outside-source.

107   *"most disappointing thing"*: Interview with source, July 2023.

107   *"I never intended to hurt"*: Bob Van Voris, "Ex-FBI Agent Pleads Guilty to Work for Russian Billionaire," Bloomberg, August 15, 2023, https://www.bloomberg.com/news /articles/2023-08-15/ex-fbi-agent-pleads-guilty-to-working-for-russian-billionaire?s ref=aJXZGtfw.

107   *he was sentenced*: "Former Special Agent in Charge of New York FBI Counterintelligence Division Sentenced to 50 Months," Justice Department, December 14, 2023, https:// www.justice.gov/opa/pr/former-special-agent-charge-new-york-fbi-counterintelligence -division-sentenced-50-months.

108   *"Peace is very important!"*: Deripaska Telegram post, March 3, 2022, https://t.me/oleg deripaska/376.

108   *Appearing to panic*: U.S.A. v Deripaska.

109   *$2 million bond*: Bail Disposition for Olga Shriki, September 29, 2022.

110   *When squatters broke into*: Simon Childs, "Take a Look Inside the Russian Oligarch's Mansion Occupied by Squatters," *Vice*, March 15, 2022, https://www.vice.com/en /article/wxdkn5/oleg-deripaska-house.

110   *Soon after Washington*: U.S.A. v Graham Bonham-Carter indictment, September 21, 2022,

https://www.justice.gov/usao-sdny/pr/uk-businessman-arrested-sanctions-evasion-benefitting-russian-oligarch-oleg-deripaska.

111 *more than $12 million*: Ibid.

111 *London's response*: Author interview with sources in London and Washington, July/August 2023.

112 *"life in a democracy"*: Andrew Adams, talk, Hudson Institute, Washington, DC, January 19, 2023.

113 *for $110 million*: Author interview with source, August 30, 2023; and Stephanie Baker, Yuliya Fedorinova, and Irina Reznik, "Putin's 'American' Oligarch Privately Boasted of Trump Ties, Then He Lost Billions," Bloomberg, December 7, 2018, https://www.bloomberg.com/news/features/2018-12-07/viktor-vekselberg-met-michael-cohen-then-he-lost-billions?sref=aJXZGtfw.

113 *fulfilling his duty*: Elena Berzanskaya and Nikolai Uskov, "Ya vsegda schital, chto khorosho ponimayu zapadnyy mir," *Forbes*, February 1, 2021, https://www.forbes.ru/milliardery/419713-viktor-vekselberg-forbes-ya-vsegda-schital-chto-horosho-ponimayu-zapadnyy-mir.

113 *a tech incubator*: Baker, Fedorinova, and Reznik, "Putin's 'American' Oligarch."

113 *When then California governor*: Alexander Sazonov, "Sanctioned Russian Tycoon Transforms Palace into a Fabergé Mecca," Bloomberg, August 30, 2019, https://www.bloomberg.com/news/articles/2019-08-30/sanctioned-russian-tycoon-transforms-palace-into-a-faberge-mecca.

113 *"for the Russian government to access"*: Lucia Ziobro, "FBI's Boston Office Warns Businesses of Venture Capital Scams," *Boston Business Journal*, April 4, 2014, https://www.bizjournals.com/boston/blog/startups/2014/04/fbis-boston-office-warns-businesses-of-venture.html?page=all.

114 *Vekselberg was stopped*: Baker, Fedorinova, and Reznik, "Putin's 'American' Oligarch."

114 *The U.S. Treasury never permitted him*: Berzanskaya and Uskov, "Ya vsegda schital."

114 *a childhood friend*: Author interview with source, August 30, 2023.

114 *The billionaire leased*: Sazonov, "Sanctioned Russian Tycoon."

115 *home in Southampton*: Author interview with source, August 30, 2023.

115 *through a company*: This account is drawn from sources familiar with the situation and *U.S.A. v Vladimir Voronchenko* indictment, SDNY, February 7, 2023.

115 *to cover taxes*: U.S. v. Robert Wise, Superseding Information, SDNY, April 25, 2023.

115 *Instead, he fled*: Through an associate Voronchenko declined to comment for this book.

115 *carting away boxes*: "Feds Search Park Ave. High-Rise, Southampton Estate in Russian Oligarch Probe," NBC New York, September 1, 2022, https://www.nbcnewyork.com/investigations/feds-search-park-ave-high-rise-southampton-estate-in-russian-oligarch-probe/3847764/.

115 *"promote the violation"*: Chris Dolmetsch, "Lawyer Laundered Russian Oligarch's Money by Paying Bills for His NY Homes," Bloomberg, April 25, 2023, https://www.bloomberg.com/news/articles/2023-04-25/lawyer-laundered-oligarch-money-by-paying-bills-for-his-ny-homes?sref=aJXZGtfw.

116 *"worst mistake I ever made"*: Wise didn't respond to multiple requests for comment for this book. Chris Dolmetsch, "Lawyer for Sanctioned Russian Oligarch Avoids Jail for Money Laundering," Bloomberg, December 4, 2023, https://www.bloomberg.com/news/articles/2023-12-04/sanctioned-oligarch-s-ny-lawyer-avoids-jail-for-money-laundering.

116 *traced* Tango *to a shell company*: U.S. District Court for DC, Case 22-sz-5, Application for a Warrant to Seize Property Subject to Forfeiture, in the Matter of the Seizure of the Motor Yacht *Tango*, with IMO 1010703.

117 *made 800,000 euros*: Sam Jones, "Briton Arrested in Spain for Allegedly Helping Russian Oligarch Evade Sanctions," *Guardian*, January 25, 2023, https://www .theguardian.com/world/2023/jan/25/briton-arrested-spain-allegedly-helping-russian -oligarch-evade-sanctions.

117 *Spanish police arrested Masters*: Masters declined to comment for this book.

117 *But the High Court*: Andrew Ede, "Briton Based in Mallorca Will Not Be Extradited to the U.S. over Russian Yacht," *Majorca Daily Bulletin*, July 20, 2023, https://www.majorca dailybulletin.com/news/local/2023/07/20/115231/mallorca-based-briton-will-not -extradited-the-us.html.

118 *"We simply cannot"*: Stephanie Baker and Joe Mathieu, "Russian Oligarchs Are Running out of Safe Places to Hide Their Yachts and Jets," Bloomberg, November 16, 2022, https://www.bloomberg.com/news/articles/2022-11-16/us-hunter-of-hidden -russian-wealth-says-global-net-is-tightening?sref=aJXZGtfw.

118 *froze 21 billion euros*: General Secretariat of the Council, Ad Hoc Working Party on Frozen Assets, March 21, 2023.

119 *"get inside Putin's head"*: Adams stepped down from the Justice Department to join Steptoe & Johnson, a Manhattan law firm, in September.

120 *In World War II*: "Deadline Set for Schemes Compensating Victims of WWII Property Confiscation," U.K. Department for Business, Energy & Industrial Strategy, September 23, 2022, https://www.gov.uk/government/news/deadline-set-for-schemes-compensating -victims-of-wwii-propertyconfiscation#:~:text=Under%20the%20Trading%20with%20 the,and%20countries%20occupied%20by%20them.

CHAPTER 6 MICROCHIP MONTE

123 *An Israeli citizen*: According to Brayman's now-deleted Facebook profile.

124 *Prosecutors alleged the supplies included*: This account is based on court documents disclosed in the *U.S. v. Grinin et al.* case, including the superseding indictment, Eastern District of New York, December 5, 2022, https://www.justice.gov/usao-edny/press -release/file/1557531/download.

124 *media reports were quick*: Dugan Arnett, Hanna Krueger, and Brendan McCarthy, "Like a Plot from 'The Americans,'" *Boston Globe*, December 13, 2022.

124 *hypersonic Kinzhal missiles*: "Stop Missile Terror," Ukrainian government report on Western components in Russian missiles, June 2023.

125 *450 foreign-made components*: James Byrne, Gary Somerville, Joe Byrne, Dr. Jack Watling, Nick Reynolds, and Jane Baker, "Silicon Lifeline: Western Electronics at the Heart of Russia's War Machine," RUSI, https://www.rusi.org/explore-our-research/publications /special-resources/silicon-lifeline-western-electronics-heart-russias-war-machine, 12, 22.

125 *Largest single Western suppliers*: "Stop Missile Terror."

125 *Both companies stopped*: Sheridan Prasso, "Chips from Texas Instruments and Other U.S. Makers Flow into Russia, Despite Ban," Bloomberg, December 21, 2023, https://www .bloomberg.com/news/articles/2023-12-21/chips-from-texas-instruments-txn-analog

-devices-adi-flow-into-russia?srnd=undefined&sref=aJXZGtfw; and "Challenges of Export Controls Enforcement," Kyiv School of Economics, January 2024.

125 *RUSI found a Kalibr cruise*: Byrne et al., "Silicon Lifeline," 14.

125 *no earlier than March 2023*: "NACP Adds to the Database of Foreign Components in Weapons," National Agency on Corruption Prevention, January 19, 2024, https://nazk .gov.ua/en/news/nacp-adds-to-the-database-of-foreign-components-in-weapons -parts-of-the-missile-that-have-hit-the-center-of-chernihiv-in-the-summer-of-2023/.

126 *organization called the Coordinating*: Free Russia Foundation, "Effectiveness of U.S. Sanctions Targeting Russian Companies and Individuals," 7, https://www.4freerussia .org/effectiveness-of-u-s-sanctions-targeting-russian-companies-and-individuals/.

126 *half a decade behind the United States*: Chris Miller, *Chip War: The Fight for the World's Most Critical Technology* (New York: Scribner, 2022), 42–43, 141–42.

127 *Washington imposed a blanket ban*: Emily Kilcrease, "The New Russia Export Controls," Center for a New American Security, March 7, 2022, https://www.cnas.org /press/press-note/noteworthy-the-new-russia-export-controls.

127 *stranding around four hundred jets*: Siddharth Vikram Philip, "Lessor Avolon Writes Off $304 Million on Planes Tied to Russia," Bloomberg, May 3, 2022, https://www.bloomberg.com /news/articles/2022-05-03/lessor-avolon-writes-off-304-million-on-planes-tied-to-russia?s ref=aJXZGtfw; and http://static.government.ru/media/acts/files/1202206270017.pdf.

127 *Russia's civil aviation*: Maria Ehrlich, "Flying Blind," *Novaya Gazeta Europe*, September 21, 2023, https://novayagazeta.eu/articles/2023/09/21/flying-blind-en; and "Russia's Civil Aviation in Slow Collapse," BNE IntelliNews, November 27 2023, https://www .intellinews.com/russia-s-civil-aviation-in-slow-collapse-302901/.

128 *the tech battle*: Interview with senior federal law enforcement source, January 19, 2024.

128 *FBI "wanted" notice*: FBI Wanted Notice for Boris Yakovlevich Livshits, https://www .fbi.gov/wanted/counterintelligence/boris-yakovlevich-livshits/@@download.pdf.

130 *By then, the website of Sertal*: According to a Web archive of Sertal.ru: https://web.archive. org/web/20220218142230/http://sertal.ru/catalog/elektronnaya-komponentnaya-baza/.

130 *the U.K.'s continued failure to prevent*: Photon Pro LLP, U.K. Companies House filing, https://find-and-update.company-information.service.gov.uk/company/OC425116 /filing-history; and "Treasury Targets Sanctions Evasion Networks," U.S. Treasury, March 31, 2022, https://home.treasury.gov/news/press-releases/jy0692.

131 *federal agents descended*: October search of Brayman's home cited in letter of Artie McConnell, assistant U.S. Attorney for the Eastern District, to Judge Gonzalez regarding bail, December 13, 2022.

131 *communicating frequently with Livshits*: Letter from Artie McConnell, assistant U.S. Attorney for Eastern District, to Judge Ramon Reyes, July 14, 2023.

135 *Uss operated from Italy*: "Bosnia and Herzegovina National Arrested for Aiding in the Escape of Russian Defendant," U.S. Justice Department press release, December 5, 2023, https://www.justice.gov/opa/pr/bosnia-and-herzegovina-national-arrested-aiding -escape-russian-defendant.

135 *"criminal enablers of oligarchs"*: "Five Russian Nationals and Two Oil Traders Charged in Global Sanctions Evasion and Money Laundering Scheme," U.S. Justice Department, October 19, 2022, https://www.justice.gov/usao-edny/pr/five-russian-nationals-and -two-oil-traders-charged-global-sanctions-evasion-and-money.

136 *The Italian Justice Ministry*: "Clear Up Anomalies in Uss Case, Says Meloni," ANSA,

April 15, 2023, https://www.ansa.it/english/news/world/2023/04/15/clear-up-anomalies
-in-uss-case-says-meloni_5b95fffa-b021-49f9-b2dd-8f80fd34f79d.html.

136 *pretending to deliver groceries*: "Bosnia and Herzegovina National Arrested."

136 *The Serbian gang arrived*: Ibid.

137 *"I'm in Russia!"*: "Syn gubernatora Ussa soobshchil, chto nakhoditsya v Rossii," RIA
Novosti, April 4, 2023, https://ria.ru/20230404/uss-1862910566.html.

137 *"not just the head of our state"*: "Uss poblagodaril tekh, kto pomog yevo synu vernutsya
vs Rossiyu," RIA Novosti, April 9, 2023, https://ria.ru/20230409/uss-1864075950
.html.

137 *U.S. prosecutors were "apoplectic"*: Interview with senior U.S. law enforcement official,
September 6, 2023.

137 *investigation of the judges*: Chiara Albanese, "Italy Freezes Assets of Russian Who Dodged
U.S. Sanctions Charges," Bloomberg. April 21, 2023, https://www.bloomberg.com
/news/articles/2023-04-21/italy-freezes-assets-of-russian-who-dodged-us-sanctions
-charges?sref=aJXZGtfw.

138 *surged at the end of 2021*: Kyiv School of Economics / Yermak-McFaul International
Working Group on Russian Sanctions, "Russia's Military Capacity and the Role of
Imported Components," June, 19, 2023, 14.

138 *accounted for 87 percent*: Ibid., 17.

138 *"no limits" partnership*: Kremlin readout, February 4, 2022, https://kremlin.ru/supple
ment/5770.

138 *Putin stood for thirty-five minutes*: "Putin schitayet, chto sanktsionnaya likhoradka
Zapada neset ugrozu vsemu miru," Tass, September 7, 2022, https://tass.ru/ekonomika
/15676095.

138 *"We have not lost"*: "We Have Not Lost and Will Not Lose Anything," Meduza, September 7, 2022, https://meduza.io/en/news/2022/09/07/we-have-not-lost-and-will
-not-lose-anything-putin-on-the-consequences-of-the-war-in-ukraine.

138 *lost more than 2,900*: For a running count of Russian tanks lost, see "Document-
ing Russian Equipment Losses during the Russian Invasion of Ukraine," *Oryx*
(blog), https://www.oryxspioenkop.com/2022/02/attack-on-europe-documenting
-equipment.html. Paul Schwartz, "A War of Attrition," Center for Strategic & International Studies (CSIS), July 2023, 6.

138 *export controls and sanctions*: Schwartz, "War of Attrition," 7.

138 *more than 1,500*: "Russian Ground Forces receive 1,500 new upgraded tanks," Tass,
December 19, 2023, https://tass.com/defense/1723815.

139 *roughly 1,200*: Interview with Michael Gjerstad, analyst at the International Institute
for Strategic Studies. See also "Equipment Losses in Russia's War," *Military Balance*
(blog), International Institute for Strategic Studies, February 12, 2024, https://www
.iiss.org/online-analysis/military-balance/2024/02/equipment-losses-in-russias-war
-on-ukraine-mount/.

139 *fired 7,400 missiles*: "During the Invasion Russia Launched 7,400 Missiles," Radio
Svoboda, December 21, 2023, https://www.radiosvoboda.org/a/news-ihnat-rosia
-rakety-drony/32741855.html.

139 *unleashed another 1,000*: "Since the Beginning of the Year, Russia Has Launched a
Thousand Missiles," UNN, April 12, 2024, https://unn.ua/en/news/since-the-beginning
-of-the-year-russia-has-launched-a-thousand-missiles-and-almost-2800-shaheds
-at-ukraine-kislytsya.

139 *more than 1,400 missiles*: "VS RF Poluchil v 2023 Godu Boleye 1.5 tys Tankov i 22 tys Bespilotnikov," Tass, December 29, 2023, https://tass.ru/armiya-i-opk/19650835.

139 *Russia's production volumes*: "Budanov's Stockpile of Russian Missiles," Slovo i Dilo, September 13, 2023,https://www.slovoidilo.ua/2023/09/13/novyna/bezpeka/budanova -oczinyly-zapasy-rosijskyx-raket-pislya-publikacziyi-nyt.

139 *such as the Kh-101*: Schwartz, "War of Attrition," p. 17; and Conflict Armaments Research, December 2023, https://storymaps.arcgis.com/collections/29eb0c 63b0444572ab0a8740c9c3b3a8?item=4.

139 *head of Russia's Tactical Missile*: Oleg Falichev, "Na krutykh povarotakh sudby," *Nezavi-simaya Gazeta*, January 20, 2023, https://nvo.ng.ru/realty/2023-01-20/8_1221_obnosov .html.

139 *doubled the production*: "Missile Producer CEO Informs Shoigu about Doubling Pro-duction," TASS, September 27, 2023, https://tass.com/defense/1681237.

139 *hampering Russia's military production*: Western officials' briefing, November 16, 2023.

139 *set back twenty to thirty years*: Western officials' briefing.

139 *Kremlin turned to Pyongyang*: "US Says Russia Using North Korea Ballistic Missiles," BBC, January 5, 2024, https://www.bbc.co.uk/news/world-us-canada-67888793.

140 *Iran began sending combat drones*: Reid Standish, "Chinese Drones Flow to Training Centers Linked to Russian War in Ukraine," RFE/RL, October 3, 2023, https://www .rferl.org/a/russia-ukraine-chinese-drones-training-centers/32621432.html; and Aamer Madhani, Colleen Long, and Zeke Miller, "Russia Aims to Obtain More Attack Drones from Iran," Associated Press, May 15, 2023, https://apnews.com/article/russia-iran -military-cooperation-d982dd3faf78fbb17dfc8b9c1cb9dae7. For the axis of ill will, see Niall Ferguson, https://www.hoover.org/research/understanding-new-world-disorder -stephen-kotkin.

140 *developing domestic drones*: "Putin: obyem otrasli bespilotnykh letatelnykh apparatov v RF mozhet dostigat 1 trln rubley," Tass, April 27, 2023, https://tass.ru/ekonomika/17632747.

140 *Iranian Shahed-136 kamikaze drones*: The *Wall Street Journal* was the first to report on the plans: Dion Nissenbaum and Warren Strobel, "Moscow, Tehran Advance Plans for Iranian-Designed Drone Facility," *Wall Street Journal*, February 5, 2023, https:// www.wsj.com/world/moscow-tehran-advance-plans-for-iranian-designed-drone -facility-in-russia-11675609087. The Albatross company announced plans to build drones in Alabuga, Tatarstan, in a press release on January 23, 2023, https://alb.aero /about/news/kompaniya-albatros-otkryla-proizvodstvo-bespilotnykh-vozdushnykh -sudov-v-oez-alabuga-/.

140 *leaked by the Prana network*: "It became known how much Shahed-136 costs for Rus-sia," Militarnyi, Feb. 6, 2024, https://mil.in.ua/uk/news/stalo-vidomo-skilky-koshtuye -shahed-136-dlya-rosiyi/

140 *apparent delays*: Vladimir Solovyov posted images of the factory on Telegram on March 5, 2024, https://t.me/SolovievLive/244102/; and Thomas Newdick, "Our First Look at Russia's Shahed-136 Attack Drone Factory," War Zone, March 5, 2024, https://www .twz.com/news-features/our-first-look-inside-russias-shahed-136-attack-drone-factory.

140 *Western electronic inputs*: "Electronics in the Shahed-136 Kamikaze Drone," Institute for Science and International Security, November 14, 2023.

140 *to $2.45 billion in 2022*: Free Russia Foundation, "Effectiveness of U.S. Sanctions Targeting Companies and Individuals," 4.

140 *exports to Russia surged*: Natalia Konarzeska, "Turkey Will Not Give Up on Its Lucrative

Trade with Russia," Turkey Analyst, June 26, 2023, https://www.turkeyanalyst.org
/publications/turkey-analyst-articles/item/709-turkey-will-not-give-up-on-its-lucrative
-trade-with-russia.html.

140 *island state of the Maldives*: Katherine Creel and Shoji Yano, "Small Island Nation with
Big Role Shipping Chips to Russia," Nikkei Asia, July 21, 2023.

140 *Russia often struggled to source*: Kyiv School of Economics, June 2023, 7.

141 *"a new strategic asset"*: "Remarks by National Security Advisor Jake Sullivan at the
Special Competitive Studies Project Global Emerging Technologies Summit," White
House, September 16, 2022, https://www.whitehouse.gov/briefing-room/speeches
-remarks/2022/09/16/remarks-by-national-security-advisor-jake-sullivan-at-the-special
-competitive-studies-project-global-emerging-technologies-summit/.

141 *"there's a specific catalyzing event"*: Interview with Kevin Wolf, December 10, 2023.

142 *BIS rules would ban*: Ibid.

142 *1 trillion chips*: "Global Semiconductor Sales Increase 23.5% in Year-on-Year in November," Semiconductor Industry Association, January 3, 2024.

143 *"export controls has been unprecedented"*: Interview with Mattew Axelrod, January 26, 2023.

143 *they found Western semiconductors*: Jeanne Whalen, "Sanctions Forcing Russia to
Use Appliance Parts in Military Gear," *Washington Post*, May 11, 2022, https://www
.washingtonpost.com/technology/2022/05/11/russia-sanctions-effect-military/.

143 *more than 600 percent*: Alberto Nardelli, Bryce Baschuk, and Marc Champion,
"Putin Stirs European Worry on Home Appliance Imports Stripped for Arms,"
Bloomberg, October 29, 2022, https://www.bloomberg.com/news/articles/2022-10
-29/putin-stirs-european-worry-on-home-appliance-imports-stripped-for-arms?lead
Source=uverify%20wall&sref=aJXZGtfw.

144 *fraud and money laundering*: "Russian International Money Launderer Arrested for
Illicitly Procuring Large Quantities of U.S. Manufactured Dual-Use, Military Grade
Microelectronics," U.S. Justice Department, September 8, 2023, https://www.justice
.gov/usao-sdny/pr/russian-international-money-launderer-arrested-illicitly-procuring
-large-quantities-us.

145 *the semiconductor industry*: "The Semiconductor Decade," McKinsey, April 1, 2022, https://
www.mckinsey.com/industries/semiconductors/our-insights/the-semiconductor
-decade-a-trillion-dollar-industry.

145 *"We're in the midst of a shift"*: Axelrod interview.

CHAPTER 7 CORPORATE HOSTAGES

147 *a poll found*: "Americans Overwhelmingly Want Companies to Take Actions against
Russia," Morning Consult, February 28, 2022, https://pro.morningconsult.com
/instant-intel/russia-ukraine-invasion-companies-take-action.

148 *"Are you insane?"*: Author interview with Oleg Paroev, November 10, 2023.

148 *On March 7, 2022, Jeffrey Sonnenfeld*: "Yale's Sonnenfeld Makes the Case for Companies
Ceasing Operations in Russia," interview on CNBC, March 7, 2022, https://www.cnbc
.com/video/2022/03/07/yales-sonnenfeld-makes-the-case-for-companies-ceasing
-operations-in-russia.html; and Jeffrey Sonnenfeld, "The Great Business Retreat of
2022 Matters in Russia Today," *Fortune*, March 7, 2022, https://fortune.com/2022/03
/07/great-business-retreat-matters-russia-sanctions-1986-south-africa-putin-ukraine
-world-politics-jeffrey-sonnenfeld/.

149 *in his memoir*: George Cohon, *To Russia with Fries* (Toronto: McClelland & Stewart, 1999), 17–18.

149 *Cohon finally clinched*: Ibid., 191.

149 *new processing center*: Ibid., 176.

149 *27,000 applications*: Ibid., 193.

150 *"Big Mac is* perestroika": Ibid., 195.

150 *gala party*: Ibid., 223.

150 *had 235 restaurants*: Andrew E. Kramer, "Russia's Evolution, Seen through Golden Arches," *New York Times*, February 1, 2010, https://www.nytimes.com/2010/02/02/business/global/02mcdonalds.html.

150 *its ingredients locally*: Carol Matlack, "Could McDonald's Be the Latest Victim of Russian Retaliation?," *Bloomberg Businessweek*, August 20, 2014, https://www.bloomberg.com/news/articles/2014-08-20/russian-sanctions-bite-europe-mcdonalds-in-russia-suffer-too?sref=aJXZGtfw.

150 *increase investment by*: "McDonald's Will Increase Investments in Russia in 2019," Interfax, February 6, 2019, https://www.interfax.ru/business/649409.

150 *"We had total ownership"*: Interview with Craig Cohon, November 14, 2023.

151 *2 billion liters*: "Coca-Cola to Cease Production and Sales in Russia," Interfax, June 17, 2022, https://interfax.com/newsroom/top-stories/80370/.

151 *Long lines formed*: Kamil Galeev, Twitter post, March 9, 2022, https://x.com/kamilkazani/status/1501688135960379395?s=20.

151 *stuffed his refrigerator*: "'The Hoarder Pounder': Russian McDonald's Fan Stocks Up as Restaurants Close," *Newsweek*, March 10, 2022, https://www.newsweek.com/russia-mcdonalds-fan-stocks-restaurants-close-hoarder-pounder-1686631.

151 *$50 million a month*: Kevin Ozan, transcript of his talk at the UBS Global Consumer and Retail Conference, March 9, 2022.

151 *McDonald's employees had personal accounts*: Paroev interview. See also Geoff Colvin, "Inside McDonald's Months-Long Decision to Sell All 853 Stores in Russia," *Fortune*, July 27, 2022, https://fortune.com/2022/07/27/mcdonalds-closing-all-stores-russia-revenue-employees/.

152 *"by a U.S. person"*: "Prohibiting New Investment in and Certain Services to the Russian Federation," White House, April 6, 2022, https://www.whitehouse.gov/briefing-room/presidential-actions/2022/04/06/prohibiting-new-investment-in-and-certain-services-to-the-russian-federation-in-response-to-continued-russian-federation-aggression/.

152 *"'de-Arching' a major market"*: Email from CEO Chris Kempczinski to McDonald's employees, May 16, 2022, https://corporate.mcdonalds.com/corpmcd/our-stories/article/chris-russia-update.html.

152 *flew to Dubai*: Paroev interview. See also Colvin, "Inside McDonald's."

153 *"entrust" him with*: Alexander Govor interview, RBK, March 5, 2023, https://www.youtube.com/watch?v=bbyaT9qKX_c.

153 *retain all sixty-two thousand*: "Novy vladelets seti McDonald's v RF zayvil o 'simvolicheskoy plate' za neye," Interfax, June 12, 2022, https://www.interfax.ru/russia/845991.

153 *the giant* M: "'Golden Arches' Come Down near Moscow," Reuters, May 23, 2022, https://www.reuters.com/business/retail-consumer/golden-arches-come-down-near-moscow-mcdonalds-russia-rebrand-begins-2022-05-23/.

153 *"had to be destroyed"*: Paroev interview.

153 *with sandpaper even deployed*: "Izbavlyayutsya ot logo c pomoshchyu nazhdachki," MSK1,

June 8, 2022, https://msk1.ru/text/food/2022/06/08/71396534/; "Tasty Name but No Big Mac," Reuters, June 13, 2022, https://www.reuters.com/world/europe/mcdonalds -russia-reopens-under-new-ownership-renamed-vkusno-tochka-2022-06-12/.

153 *McGovor as "immodest"*: "Alexander Govor: Tochku stavit rano," Tass, September 4, 2023, https://tass.ru/business-officials/18586343.

153 *running out of french fries*: Paroev interview.

154 *refused to work with Vkusno*: Ibid.

154 *was growing faster than anticipated*: Olga Popova, "Russia's McDonald's Heir Growing Quickly," Reuters, June 6, 2023, https://www.reuters.com/business/retail-consumer /russias-mcdonalds-heir-growing-quickly-long-haul-2023-06-05/.

155 *more than two thousand*: "65th Digest on the Impact of Foreign Companies' Exit from the RF Economy," Kyiv School of Economics, June 3, 2024, https://kse.ua/about-the -school/news/65th-issue-of-the-regular-digest-on-impact-of-foreign-companies-exit -on-rf-economy/.

155 *Levi's decided to leave*: Levi's emailed statement, April 10, 2024, "Levi's nashel pok- upatelya v rossiskikh magazinov," RBC, July 21 2022, https://www.rbc.ru/business/21 /07/2022/62d9299d9a7947d3cf25971f.

156 *renamed it Pizza H*: "Pizza Hut v Peterburge smenila nazvaniye na 'Pitstsa H,'" July 12, 2022, https://www.fontanka.ru/2022/07/12/71482304.

156 *for $6 million*: "Partner Timati raskryl stoimost pokupki Starbucks v Rossii," RBC, June 13, 2023, https://www.rbc.ru/business/13/06/2023/64880b899a794714ba3eaca5.

156 *(1 million dislikes)*: "Pro-Government Rap Video Smashes Russian YouTube Record with 1M Dislikes," *Moscow Times*, September 9, 2019, https://www.themoscowtimes.com /2019/09/09/pro-government-rap-video-smashes-russian-youtube-record-with-1m -dislikes-a67206.

156 *saw buying Starbucks*: "Anton Pinskiy: Biznesmen Pobedil Vo Mne Khodozhnika," Tass, June 13, 2023, https://tass.ru/business-officials/17955161.

157 *Loro Piana, part of LVMH, remained open*: Author interview with shop staff. See also Gustaf Kilander, "Petition Launched for Maker of Vladimir Putin's $13,000 Jacket to Denounce Him," *Independent*, March 21, 2022, https://www.independent.co.uk/news /world/vladimir-putin-jacket-loro-piana-b2040450.html§§.

157 *stores in Moscow were selling*: I hired a Russian reporter to scout out what was available in Moscow through parallel imports in January 2024. Kraft Heinz said in a statement on March 8, 2022, that it would suspend new investment and exports to Russia. Mars made a similar statement on March 10, 2022.

158 *"are already hostages"*: Andrii Onopriienko interview, October 13, 2023.

158 *take "temporary control"*: Russian Presidential Decree no. 302, April 25, 2023, http:// publication.pravo.gov.ru/Document/View/0001202304250033.

159 *$3 billion before*: Carlsberg 2021 annual report.

159 *sell it to Arnest*: Author interview with source familiar with the sale, November 2, 2023.

159 *Taimuraz Bolloyev*: Anastasia Kovoleva and Margarita Sobol, "Upravlyat aktivami Baltiki budet vladets BTK Grupp Taymuraz Bolloyev," Vedomosti, July 18, 2023, https://www .vedomosti.ru/business/articles/2023/07/18/985915-upravlyat-aktivami-baltiki-budet -bolloev.

159 *didn't consult or inform*: Carlsberg CEO Cees T. Hart speaking to analysts on August 16, 2023.

159 *"stolen our business"*: Michael Race, "Carlsberg Cuts Ties with 'Stolen' Russian Business," BBC, October 31, 2023, https://www.bbc.co.uk/news/articles/cgxkx9g2kn40.

160 *Siluanov, shot down, saying*: Anastasia Koveleva, "Natsionalizatsiya Baltika ne planiruyetsya," Vedomosti, December 18, 2023, https://www.vedomosti.ru/business/articles/2023/12/18/1011538-natsionalizatsiya-baltiki-ne-planiruetsya.

160 *Baltika could continue*: "Court Permits Baltika to Use Carlsberg Beer Brands," Interfax, December 18, 2023, https://interfax.com/newsroom/top-stories/97748/.

160 *French yogurt maker Danone*: Danone press release, March 22, 2024. Courtney Weaver and Adrienne Klasa, "Danone Plans to Sell Russian Operations to Chechnya-Linked Businessman," *Financial Times*, February 21, 2024, https://www.ft.com/content/6c1c5fe0-5a98-4d67-acfb-caf482e109cf.

160 *game of Russian roulette*: Sarah Anne Aarup, "Russian Roulette for Western Companies That Stayed," *Politico*, August 8, 2023, https://www.politico.eu/article/western-companies-stayed-russia-war-face-consequences/.

161 *such as airbags and antilock brake*: "AvtoVaz Starts Making Cars with Airbags Again," BNE IntelliNews, August 24, 2022, https://www.intellinews.com/avtovaz-starts-making-cars-with-airbags-again-but-car-sales-remain-depressed-254427/.

161 *car sales plunged*: "Russia—Automotive Sales Volume," MarkLines, January 12, 2023, https://www.marklines.com/en/statistics/flash_sales/automotive-sales-in-russia-by-month-2022#:~:text=In%20all%20of%202022%2C%20687%2C370,down%2067.2%25%20to%2054%2C811%20units.

161 *agreed to sell*: Renault press release, May 16, 2022, https://media.renaultgroup.com/renault-group-signs-agreements-to-sell-renault-russia-and-its-controlling-interest-in-avtovaz/; and "Renault perdeast 68% doli v AvtoVaze v plzu NAMI, zavod v Moskve," Interfax, April 26, 2022, https://www.interfax.ru/business/838101.

161 *"historic event"*: "Sobyanin nazval zapisk novoi model 'Moskvich' istorichekim cobitiem," November 23, 2022, https://ria.ru/20221123/moskvich-1833597551.html.

162 *reassembling a Chinese car*: Denis Ilyushenkov, "Avtovazod Moskvich nachal sborku avtomobil po kitaiskomu obrazu," Vedomosti, November 23, 2022, https://www.vedomosti.ru/business/articles/2022/11/23/951792-avtozavod-kitaiskih.

162 *began assembling JAC*: "Sollers budet vypuskat kitayskiye mashiny JAC pod sobstvennoy markoy," Vedomosti, September 8, 2022, https://www.vedomosti.ru/auto/articles/2022/09/08/939797-sollers-budet-vipuskat-kitaiskie-mashini.

162 *Volkswagen sold its operations*: "Avilon Closes Acquisition of VW's Russian Assets," Interfax, May 23, 2023, https://interfax.com/newsroom/top-stories/90744/.

162 *assemble kits from Chery*: "Byvshiy zavod Volkswagen mozhet nachat vypusk avtomobiley Chery," Autotstat, August 23, 2023, https://www.autostat.ru/news/55442/.

162 *about 80 percent*: "Russia's Key Economic Sectors Shrug Off Sanctions," Bloomberg, November 15, 2023, https://www.bloomberg.com/news/articles/2023-11-15/russia-s-war-economy-sees-key-sectors-shrugging-off-sanctions?sref=aJXZGtfw.

163 *"avoid the politics"*: Bernard Looney interview with Bloomberg TV, February 8, 2022, https://www.bloomberg.com/news/articles/2022-02-08/bp-ceo-mounts-robust-defense-of-his-company-s-russian-connection?sref=aJXZGtfw.

163 *"wanted them to be aligned"*: Author interview with Kwasi Kwarteng, May 23, 2023.

163 *"values-based decision"*: Interview with senior BP executive, June 22, 2023.

164 *BP went hunting*: Dinesh Nair, Ruth Daivid, Debjit Chakraborty, and Fiona MacDonald, "BP Approaches State-Owned Energy Majors in Bid to Offload Russia Assets,"

Bloomberg, March 20, 2022, https://www.bloomberg.com/news/articles/2022-03-30/bp-said-to-approach-state-owned-energy-majors-on-russia-assets?sref=aJXZGtfw.

164 *dividends from Rosneft*: Rosneft reported it would pay a 2022 dividend of 38.36 rubles per share and 30.77 in 2023. BP owns 2,093,140,119 shares, according to Bloomberg data.

164 *"the right thing"*: Interview with senior BP executive, June 22, 2023.

164 *initially promised to not deploy new technology*: SLB company statement, July 14, 2023, https://www.slb.com/resource-library/updates/2023/update-on-slbs-russia-operations.

164 *wrote off $4.2 billion*: Shell frequently asked questions, July 3, 2023.

165 *talking to China's key state-run energy companies*: "China Energy Giants in Talks for Shell's Russian Gas Stake," Bloomberg, April 21, 2022, https://www.bloomberg.com/news/articles/2022-04-21/china-state-energy-giants-in-talks-for-shell-s-russian-gas-stake?sref=aJXZGtfw.

165 *In June 2022, he signed a decree*: Decree no. 416 of the Russian president, June 30, 2022, http://publication.pravo.gov.ru/Document/View/0001202206300033?index=1&rangeSize=1.

165 *struggling to replace Western oil and gas extraction technology*: Seb Kennedy and Zach Simon, "Russia's Stunted LNG Coup," *Energyflux* (blog), December 20, 2023, https://www.energyflux.news/p/russia-coup-arctic-lng-2-sanctions-natural-gas.

166 *17 percent of Russia's*: Andrii Onopriienko, Oleksii Hrybanovskyi, and Nataliia Shapoval, "How the Income of Foreign Businesses in Russia Has Changed in 2022 and Why So Many Companies Still Do Not Leave," Kyiv School of Economics, May 2023, 6.

166 *half of them remained*: "60th Issue of the Regular Digest on Impact of Foreign Companies' Exit on RF Economy," Kyiv School of Economics, January 8, 2024, https://kse.ua/about-the-school/news/60th-issue-of-the-regular-digest-on-impact-of-foreign-companies-exit-on-rf-economy/.

166 *$20 billion in total*: Onopriienko interview.

166 *Nestlé continued to*: "International Sponsors of War: 80 Years after World War II, Nestlé Again Feeds the Aggressor," National Agency on Corruption Prevention, November 2, 2023, https://nazk.gov.ua/en/news/international-sponsors-of-war-80-years-after-world-war-ii-nestle-again-feeds-the-aggressor/; letter from B4Ukraine to Jon Moeller, CEO, Procter & Gamble, February 14, 2023, https://leave-russia.org/procter-gamble.

166 *five hundred franchised restaurants*: "Fast Food That Really Kills," National Agency on Corruption Prevention, January 10, 2024, https://nazk.gov.ua/uk/novyny/fastfud-yakyy-diysno-vbyvae-nazk-vneslo-subway-do-pereliku-mizhnarodnyh-sponsoriv-viyny/.

166 *fall into the hands*: Alan Jope interview with ITV, January 18, 2023, https://www.itv.com/news/2023-01-17/boss-of-unilever-defends-decision-to-retain-business-in-russia.

166 *would rather keep*: Oliver Barnes, "Tobacco Group Philip Morris Admits It May Never Sell Its Russian Business," *Financial Times*, February 22, 2023, https://www.ft.com/content/656714b0-2e93-467b-92d6-a2d834bc0e2b.

166 *narrowing the exit doors*: B4Ukraine, "The Business of Leaving," 21.

CHAPTER 8 HOW TO SELL A SOCCER CLUB

169 *"This is classic Putin"*: Author interviews with sources, February 8, 2022, and July 12, 2023.

169   *the troop buildup*: Author interview with source, January 23, 2023.

170   *broker a peace deal*: "Roman Abramovich in Belarus Assisting Talks at Kyiv's Request," *Jerusalem Post*, February 28, 2022, https://www.jpost.com/international /article-698891; and author interview with Alexander Rodnyansky Jr., April 12, 2022. Versions of Abramovich's role were later reported by Max Seddon, Arash Massoudi, Laura Hughes, and Chris Cook, "Poison, Planes and Putin: Abramovich's Race to Save a Fortune and Stop the War," *Financial Times*, April 1, 2022, https://www.ft.com /content/d80a42c1-bd1f-48e1-8dcf-f01ebdb304fb; and Max Colchester, Jared Malsin, and Thomas Grove, "Roman Abramovich's Abrupt Transformation from Shunned Oligarch to Wartime Envoy," *Wall Street Journal*, April 1, 2022, https://www.wsj.com /articles/roman-abramovich-putin-ukraine-war-envoy-11648823720. See also: Stephanie Baker, Daryna Krasnolutska, and Nick Wadhams, "Abramovich at Risk of U.S. Sanctions as Peace Talks Sputter Out," Bloomberg, April 22, 2022.

170   *The Ukrainians wanted a "full-fledged intermediary"*: Irina Shikhman interview with Alexander Rodnyansky Sr., "A pogovorit?," YouTube, January 19, 2023, https://www .youtube.com/watch?v=FCOYVWTC19k 26 minutes–32 minutes.

171   *he splashed money*: Fordstam 2021 accounts, 37.

172   *Berezovsky claimed he had an unwritten agreement*: Executive Summary of the Full Judgment of Gloster H in *Berezovsky v Abramovich*, October 1, 2012.

172   *Abramovich denied*: Ibid.

172   *150 Russian diplomats*: "EU Imposes Sanctions against Salisbury Suspects," U.K. Foreign Office press release, January 21, 2019, https://www.gov.uk/government/news /eu-imposes-sanctions-against-salisbury-suspects.

173   *the roman empire*: Stephanie Baker, David Hellier, and Irina Reznik, "Has Anyone Seen Roman Abramovich?," *Bloomberg Businessweek*, September 25, 2018, https://www .bloomberg.com/news/features/2018-09-25/has-anyone-seen-roman-abramovich-the -last-days-of-londongrad?sref=aJXZGtfw.

173   *£1 billion plan on hold*: Ibid.

173   *"I warned them"*: "Pryamaya liniya c Vladimirom Putinim," June 7, 2018, http://kremlin .ru/events/president/news/57692.

174   *valuing the club at £3 billion*: Author interview with source, July 12, 2023.

174   *the European Super League*: Ibid.

174   *threatening the health of domestic competitions*: Mark Kleinman, "Top English Clubs in Bombshell Talks to Join European Premier League," Sky News, October 20, 2020, https:// news.sky.com/story/top-english-clubs-in-bombshell-talks-to-join-european-premier -league-12109175.

175   *His application breezed through*: See Willem Marx, "The Oligarch's Passport," *Vanity Fair*, June 2023, https://archive.vanityfair.com/article/2023/6/the-oligarchs-passport.

175   *"He finally managed to find a country"*: Alexei Navalny, Twitter post, December 23, 2021, 8:02 a.m., https://x.com/navalny/status/1473926817300033537?s=20.

175   *beneficiaries of two trusts*: U.S. v a Boeing 787-8 Dreamliner Aircraft Tailnumber P4-BDL and a Gulfstream G650 Aircraft Tailnumber LX-Ray, affidavit in support of seizure warrant, SDNY, June 6, 2022.

175   *$4 billion in assets*: Harry Davies, "Leak Reveals Roman Abramovich's Billion-Dollar Trusts Transferred before Russia Sanctions," *Guardian*, January 6, 2023, https://www .theguardian.com/world/2023/jan/06/roman-abramovich-trusts-transfer-leak-russia -sanctions.

175   *according to a lawsuit filed by*: Securities and Exchange Commission v Concord Management LLC and Michael Matlin, Southern District of New York, September 19, 2023.

176   *"We were hoping"*: Author interview with source, July 12, 2023.

176   *Norma Investments Ltd.*: David Davidovich responses to emailed questions, May 10, 2022. See also Max Colchester and Margot Patrick, "Abramovich Investment Vehicle Shifted Control Shortly After Russia Invaded Ukraine," *Wall Street Journal*, March 15, 2022, https://www.wsj.com/articles/abramovich-investment-vehicle-shifted-control -shortly-after-russia-invaded-ukraine-11647380381?mod=article_inline.

176   *"The danger is that"*: "Sanctions," debate, March 1, 2022, *Hansard Parliament* 709, https://hansard.parliament.uk/commons/2022-03-01/debates/6EF274E3-57A6-46ED -BFE2-348AEB926501/Sanctions.

176   *"all victims of the war"*: Statement from Roman Abramovich, Chelsea FC, March 2, 2022, https://www.chelseafc.com/en/news/article/statement-from-roman-abramovich.

176   *symptoms consistent with poisoning*: Author interview with source, November 6, 2023. See also "Abramovich Suffered Suspected Poisoning during Ukraine Talks," Bloomberg News, March 28, 2022, https://www.bloomberg.com/news/articles/2022-03 -28/abramovich-suffered-suspected-poisoning-during-ukraine-talks?sref=aJXZGtfw.

177   *he was collateral damage*: Author interview with source, November 6, 2023.

177   *Zelensky asked Western nations*: Stephanie Baker, Daryna Krasnolutska, and Nick Wadhams, "Abramovich at Risk of U.S. Sanctions as Peace Talks Sputter Out," Bloomberg, April 22, 2022, https://www.bloomberg.com/news/articles/2022-04-22/abramovich-at -risk-of-u-s-sanctions-as-peace-talks-sputter-out?sref=aJXZGtfw.

178   *optimistic about a possible breakthrough*: Author interview with source, April 8, 2022.

178   *Kyiv negotiators proposed*: Sergiy Sydorenko, "No Peace, No Guarantees," European Pravda, March 30, 2022, https://www.eurointegration.com.ua/eng/articles /2022/03/30/7136915/; author interview with source close to the talks, November 6, 2023; Olena Roschyna, "Arahamiya Stated That the Russians Lured Ukraine with 'Peace for Neutrality,'" *Ukrainska Pravda*, November 24, 2023, https://www.pravda .com.ua/news/2023/11/24/7430282/.

178   *change the country's constitution*: Ibid.

179   *If Russia remained*: Author interview with Podolyak, May 27, 2024.

179   *froze $7 billion in assets*: Interview with source in Jersey, January 2024; and Jonathan Browning, "Roman Abramovich Has $7 billion of Assets Frozen in Tax Haven Jersey," Bloomberg, April 13, 2022, https://www.bloomberg.com/news/articles/2022-04-13 /roman-abramovich-has-7-billion-of-assets-frozen-in-jersey?sref=aJXZGtfw.

179   *One of his biggest holdings*: "UK Sanctions Major Manufacturer of Russian Steel," Foreign Office press release, May 5, 2022, https://www.gov.uk/government/news /russia-uk-sanctions-major-manufacturer-of-russian-steel.

179   *to seize the two planes*: Boeing, Gulfstream affidavit, June 6, 2022.

180   *Every time Chelsea*: Author interview, July 12, 2023; and "Chelsea: What You Need to Know," Office of Financial Sanctions Implementation, https://ofsi.blog.gov.uk/2022 /03/10/chelsea-football-club-what-you-need-to-know/.

180   *the U.K. imposed sanctions*: "UK Hits Key Russian Oligarchs with Sanctions," Foreign Office, April 14, 2022, https://www.gov.uk/government/news/uk-hits-key-russian -oligarchs-with-sanctions-worth-up-to-10bn.

181   *scandal led them to be ruled out*: Interviews with sources familiar with the sale. Also see Jon Greenberg, "Tom Ricketts Responds to Latest, Most Offensive Batch of Joe Ricketts

Emails," *Athletic*, February 5, 2019; "Chelsea Fans Protest against Ricketts' Bid for Club," *Sky Sports*, April 2, 2022, https://www.skysports.com/football/news/11668/12580215 /chelsea-fans-plan-protest-against-ricketts-bid-for-club-before-brentford-clash.

181   *the stringent terms*: Statement from the board of directors of Chelsea Football Club, May 30, 2022, https://www.chelseafc.com/en/news/article/statement-from-board-of -directors-of-chelsea-football-club-limit.

181   *considering diverting*: Steven Swinford, "Plans to Divert Cash from Sale of Chelsea for Grassroots Football," *Times*, May 2, 2022, https://www.thetimes.co.uk/article /plan-to-divert-cash-from-sale-of-chelsea-for-grassroots-football-032h62zjt.

181   *the rumors stopped*: Author interview with sources, July 2023, February 2024.

181   *most expensive deal*: It was overtaken as the most expensive deal in sporting history in July 2023 with the $6.05 billion takeover of the Washington Commanders football team in the United States.

181   *"not terribly well managed"*: "Behdad Eghbali Takes on Chelsea Exit Plan," Football.London, December 24, 2022, https://www.football.london/chelsea-fc/news/behdad-eghbali-chelsea -25823329.

181   *paying a 10 million euro fine*: "Chelsea Fined £8.6 million for FFP Breach," *Sky Sports*, July 29, 2023, https://www.skysports.com/football/news/11095/12929532/chelsea -fined-8-6m-for-ffp-breach-as-juventus-banned-from-europe-for-23-24-in-separate -financial-case; and Martyn Ziegler and Matt Lawton, "Chelsea Investigated over Willian and Samuel Eto'o Transfers," *Times*, October 30, 2023, https://www.thetimes .co.uk/article/chelsea-investigated-over-willian-and-samuel-etoo-transfers-premier -league-23fndzmdl.

182   *for exclusively humanitarian purposes*: "Unilateral Declaration regarding the Sale of Chel- sea Football Club," Department for Culture, Media & Sport, May 30, 2022, https://www .gov.uk/government/publications/unilateral-declaration-regarding-the-sale-of-chelsea -football-club/unilateral-declaration-regarding-the-sale-of-chelsea-football-club.

182   *U.K. officials denied*: Briefings by Western officials, July 7, 2023, and September 29, 2023. See also Paul MacInnes, "Roman Abramovich Representatives Believe the UK Government Changed Terms over Frozen £2.5 Billion," *Guardian*, October 17, 2023, https://www.theguardian.com/football/2023/oct/17/roman-abramovich-representa tives-uk-government-frozen-chelsea-sale-funds.

183   *"largest purely humanitarian foundation"*: Author interview with Mike Penrose, Novem- ber 9, 2022.

183   *British officials wanted*: Briefing with Western sources, June 19, 2023.

183   *would refuse to approve*: Alberto Nardelli, Stephanie Baker, and Alex Wickham, "Ukraine Aid from Chelsea Sale Delayed as Approval Process Drags," April 7, 2023, https://www .bloomberg.com/news/articles/2023-04-07/ukraine-aid-from-chelsea-sale-delayed -as-approval-process-drags.

183   *"suffered a lot of casualties"*: Author interview with source, November 6, 2023.

184   *Some 15 million Ukrainians*: Figures from the United Nations Refugee Agency, February 2024, https://www.unrefugees.org/emergencies/ukraine.

184   *215 Ukrainian fighters*: Stephanie Baker and Ben Bartenstein, "Billionaire Abramovich Met Saudi Prince for Russia-Ukraine Prisoner Exchange," *Bloomberg*, September 23, 2022, https://www.bloomberg.com/news/articles/2022-09-23/why-roman-abramovich -met-mbs-in-saudi-arabia-last-month?sref=aJXZGtfw.

184   *he was part of negotiations*: Interview with people familiar with Abramovich's

negotiations, February, 26, 2024, and April 10, 2024. See also Henry Meyer, Jennifer Jacobs, and Michael Nienaber, "Deal to Swap Navalny Was in the Works When He Died, Official Says," Bloomberg, February 26, 2024, https://www.bloomberg.com /news/articles/2024-02-26/navalny-was-set-for-release-in-swap-before-he-died-aide -says?sref=aJXZGtfw.

185 *"The person talking"*: "Putin Says He Agreed to Navalny Swap before Activist's Death," Bloomberg, March 18, 2024, https://www.bloomberg.com/news/videos/2024-03-17 /putin-agreed-to-navalny-swap-before-activist-s-death-video?sref=aJXZGtfw.

185 *By the summer of 2023*: Author interview with source, December 9, 2023.

185 *"his power is much stronger"*: Author interview with source, November 6, 2023.

CHAPTER 9 **CYPRUS: THE TROJAN HORSE**

189 *Greek pop star entertained*: Fresh Events, "It was an immense honor," Facebook post, September 14, 2018, https://www.facebook.com/fresh.events.cy/posts/it-was -an-immense-honor-to-be-part-of-this-wedding-to-dream-and-bring-to-life-th /10160712744715517/.

189 *ribbon-cutting ceremony*: Oenou Yi, "Sunday wouldn't have been such a wonderful day," Facebook post, June 4, 2019, https://www.facebook.com/oenouyi.ktimavassiliades /posts/pfbid02K6cbKLq8z7Py889dmxT81yJqvWzBuj1uLePH1yowG92c624wDaYojN C82u2XBR8nl.

190 *His law firm*: "The Kremlin Playbook in Europe," Center for the Study of Democracy, October 15, 2020, https://csd.bg/publications/publication/the-kremlin-playbook-in-europe/.

190 *Russians used Cyprus*: I am grateful to the journalist Makarios Drousiotis for sharing an English draft of his book on corruption in Cyprus, where he calls the island's citizenship-by-investment scheme a Trojan horse for Chinese investors. I believe the same holds true for Russians in Cyprus. Others have previously described Cyprus as a Trojan horse for Russia. Makarios Drousiotis, *Putin's Island: How Cyprus became a Russian Client State in the Heart of the European Union* (Alfadi Publications, 2024).

190 *Sutton Place estate*: "UK Sanctions Abramovich and Usmanov's Financial Fixers," U.K. Foreign Office, April 12, 2023, https://www.gov.uk/government/news/uk-sanctions -abramovich-and-usmanovs-financial-fixers-in-crackdown-on-oligarch-enablers.

190 *Washington also sanctioned Vassiliades*: "Further Curbing Russia's Efforts to Evade Sanctions," U.S. State Department, April 12, 2023, https://www.state.gov/further -curbing-russias-efforts-to-evade-sanctions-and-perpetuate-its-war-against-ukraine-2/.

191 *hide $960 million*: "UK sanctions Abramovich and Usmanov's."

192 *Vassiliades told*: "'No Assistance' . . . Vassiliades Denies Involvement with Russian Oligarchs," *Cyprus Times*, April 13, 2023, https://cyprustimes.com/koinonia/oudemia -syndromi-arneitai-ebloki-me-rosous-oligarches-to-dikigoriko-vasileiadi/.

192 *In July 2023*: "They Fired at the Lawyer's House," *Cyprus Times*, July 28, 2023, https://cyprustimes.com/astynomiko-reportaz/gazosan-tin-oikia-tou-dikigorou-me -peran-ton-5-pyrovolismon-martyries-gia-motosikleta-pics/.

192 *1 billion euros stolen*: "Pokhishchennoye na Kipr otmyli v Sank-Peterburge," November 10, 2023, Kommersant. https://www.kommersant.ru/doc/6267992.

192 *suited to hiding*: Steve Coll, "Serbian Money Trail Leads to Cyprus," *Washington Post*, June 6, 1992, https://www.washingtonpost.com/archive/politics/1992/06/07/serbian -money-trail-leads-to-cyprus/3f92c601-bbf3-4236-9394-1f54d687c4c7/.

193 *largest foreign investor*: Yalman Onaran, "Cyprus Euro Controls May Last Years as Sarris Vows Weeks," Bloomberg News, March 27, 2013, https://www.bloomberg.com /news/articles/2013-03-27/cyprus-capital-controls-first-in-eu-could-last-years?sref=a JXZGtfw.

193 *Browder was one of the first*: Bill Browder, *Freezing Order: A True Story of Money Laundering, Murder and Surviving Putin's Wrath* (New York: Simon & Schuster, 2022), and *Red Notice: A True Story of High Finance, Murder and One Man's Fight for Justice* (New York: Simon & Schuster, 2015).

193 *a 2.5 billion euro loan*: Natalie Weeks and Scott Rose, "Cyprus, Russia Sign 2.5 Billion Euro Loan Deal in Moscow," Bloomberg, December 23, 2011, https://www.bloomberg .com/news/articles/2011-12-23/cyprus-russia-sign-2-5-billion-euro-loan-deal-in-moscow -1-?sref=aJXZGtfw.

193 *a third of the total deposits*: Yalman Onaran, "EU Closer to Bank Union Fails to Help Cyprus in Crisis," Bloomberg, March 21, 2013, https://www.bloomberg.com/news /articles/2013-03-21/eu-closer-to-bank-union-fails-to-help-cyprus-in-crisis?sref=aJX ZGtfw.

193 *forced to write off*: IMF Cyprus Country Report no. 13/293, September 2013, https:// www.imf.org/external/pubs/ft/scr/2013/cr13293.pdf.

194 *a client of the Cypriot president's old law firm*: Drousiotis, *Putin's Island*.

194 *acted as a proxy*: Bank of Cyprus announcement, August 28, 2014, https://www.mar ketscreener.com/quote/stock/BANK-OF-CYPRUS-PUBLIC-COM-6494482/news/Bank -of-Cyprus-Public-Announcement-according-to-Cyprus-Law-L-190-I-2007-18963232; and "Kremlin Playbook," 91.

195 *launder money and evade the restrictions*: Alice Kantor, "Europe's Golden Visas Are Booming, despite Calls to Get Rid of Them," Bloomberg, August 15, 2023, https:// www.bloomberg.com/news/articles/2023-08-15/europe-s-golden-visas-are-booming -despite-calls-to-get-rid-of-them?sref=aJXZGtfw.

195 *Some described RCB*: Luke Harding, "Segei Roldugin, the Cellist Who Holds the Key to Tracing Putin's Hidden Fortune," *Guardian*, April 3, 2016, https://www.theguardian .com/news/2016/apr/03/sergei-roldugin-the-cellist-who-holds-the-key-to-tracing -putins-hidden-fortune.

195 *a close friend of Putin's*: "The Kremlin Connections behind Cyprus's RCB Bank," Organized Crime and Corruption Reporting Project, April 2, 2022, https://www.occrp.org /en/investigations/the-kremlin-connections-behind-cypruss-rcb-bank.

195 *signs they'd been falsified*: Drousiotis, *Putin's Island*, p 257.

196 *more than sixty citizenship applications*: Interview with Myronas Nicolatos, former head of the Cyprus Supreme Court, June 2023.

196 *Between 2007 and 2020*: "Cyprus to Revoke Passports of Four Sanctioned Russians," Reuters, April 7, 2022, https://www.reuters.com/world/europe/cyprus-revoke-passports -four-sanctioned-russians-sources-2022-04-07/.

197 *Deripaska's application*: Unredacted excerpt obtained by the author from the report issued by the government-appointed inquiry chaired by Myron Nicolatos.

197 *Cyprus granted him*: Ibid.

197 *U.S. officials raised concerns*: Ibid.

197 *They also covertly recorded*: "How I Exposed the Politicians Willing to Sell Passports in Cyprus," Al Jazeera, October 13, 2020, https://www.aljazeera.com/features/2020 /10/13/hi-my-name-is-angie-im-an-undercover-reporter.

197   *Russians the biggest applicants from 2017 to 2019*: "Cyprus Sold Passports to Criminals and Fugitives," Al Jazeera, August 23, 2020, https://www.aljazeera.com/news/2020 /8/23/exclusive-cyprus-sold-passports-to-criminals-and-fugitives.

197   *continued to process*: "'Golden Passport' Schemes," European Commission, April 6, 2022, https://ec.europa.eu/commission/presscorner/detail/en/ip_22_2068.

198   *Over the previous decade*: Author interview with U.S. official.

198   *Finally, in April 2022*: "Four More Russian Billionaires Blacklisted by EU to Lose Cypriot Citizenship," RFE/RL, April 21, 2022, https://www.rferl.org/a/cyprus-russian-billionaires -passports/31814484.html.

198   *hadn't been officially informed*: Author interview with former Cyprus official, July 12, 2023.

198   *it surrendered its banking license*: RCB statement, October 24, 2022, https://rcbcy.com /en/news/announcement-surrendering-banking-license.

199   *additional 1.2 billion euros*: "Cyprus Finance Ministry: More than 1.2 Billion Euros in Russian Assets Frozen," Associated Press, May 16, 2023, https://apnews.com/article /cyprus-russia-sanctions-frozen-assets-eb3871790c000ea9dd91a1e034842e2c.

199   *British officials traveled*: https://x.com/UKinCyprus/status/1661328302059954 177?s=20.

199   *The central bank governor said*: Dean Starkman, "How Cyprus Rose to Become the Beating Heart of the Putin Regime's Shadow Financial System," ICIJ, November 14, 2023, https://www.theguardian.com/world/2023/apr/22/cyprus-russia-sanctions -us-uk.

199   *10,000 accounts belonging to about four thousand*: Interview with Marios Skandalis, chief compliance officer of the Bank of Cyprus, June 2023.

199   *Among the leaked documents*: I am grateful to the ICIJ for sharing their Cyprus files with me. Neil Weinberg, "Cyprus Ignores Russian Atrocities, Western Sanctions to Shield Vast Wealth of Putin Allies," ICIJ, November 14, 2023, https://www.icij.org /investigations/cyprus-confidential/cyprus-russia-eu-secrecy-tax-haven/.

200   *PwC and Mordashov*: Simon Goodley, "PwC Cyprus Moved £1 Bn for Russian Tycoon on Day He Was Put under Sanctions," November 14, 2023, *Guardian*, https://www .theguardian.com/business/2023/nov/14/pwc-cyprus-russian-tycoons-ukraine-invasion -sanctions.

200   *"No one is above"*: "ICIJ Report Will Be Investigated," Cyprus Business News, November 15 2023, https://www.cbn.com.cy/article/2023/11/15/743078/president-icij -report-will-be-investigated/.

200   *the United States sent twenty-four FBI agents*: Nikolaos Prakas, "US Agencies to Deploy Team to Island amid 'Cyprus Confidential' Revelations," December 1, 2023, *Cyprus Mail*, https://cyprus-mail.com/2023/12/01/us-agencies-to-deploy-team-to-island -amid-cyprus-confidential-revelations/.

200   *"zero tolerance" policy on Russian sanctions*: Andria Kades, "Government Focuses on Sanctions Compliance," *Cyprus Mail*, November 8, 2023, https://cyprus-mail.com /2023/11/08/zero-tolerance-for-sanctions-evasion-says-government-spokesman/.

201   *"Not only in Dubai"*: Names withheld for legal reasons.

201   *She'd recently won her appeal*: Stephanie Bodoni, "Wagner Group Founder's Mother Wins Challenge to EU Sanctions," Bloomberg, March 8, 2023, https://www.bloomberg .com/news/articles/2023-03-08/wagner-group-founder-s-mother-wins-challenge-to -eu-sanctions?sref=aJXZGtfw.

CHAPTER 10 **A GLITTERING MOSCOW-ON-THE-GULF**

204 *"ties to organized crime"*: "Treasury Designates Russian Oligarchs, Officials and Entities in Response to Worldwide Malign Activity," U.S. Treasury, April 6, 2018, https://home .treasury.gov/news/press-releases/sm0338.

204 *voted to officially recognize the occupied Ukrainian regions*: EU sanctions regulations, February 23, 2022, https://eur-lex.europa.eu/legal-content/EN/TXT/HTML/?uri=O J%3AL%3A2022%3A042I%3AFULL.

205 *seizure warrant for*: "U.S: Obtains Warrant for Seizure of Airplane of Sanctioned Russian Oligarch Andrei Skoch," U.S. Justice Department, August 8, 2022, https:// www.justice.gov/opa/pr/united-states-obtains-warrant-seizure-airplane-sanctioned -russian-oligarch-andrei-skoch-worth.

205 *Rental Solutions & Services*: Stewart Murray, CEO of Rental Solutions & Services, declined to comment for this book.

206 *caught Russian intelligence officers bragging*: Nomaan Merchant, Ellen Knickmeyer, and Jon Gambrell, "Leaked US Intel: Russian Operatives Claim New Ties with UAE," Associated Press, April 12, 2023, https://apnews.com/article/intelligence-leak-russia -uae-pentagon-9941a3bb88b48d4dbb5218649ea67325.

207 *guest of honor*: "Meeting with President of UAE Mohammed Al Nahyan," June 16, 2023, Kremlin readout, http://kremlin.ru/events/president/news/71444.

207 *already met with Putin*: "Meeting with President of the UAE," Kremlin readout, October 11, 2022, http://kremlin.ru/events/president/news/69574.

207 *meet with MBZ*: "Russia-UAE Talks," Kremlin, December 6, 2023, http://kremlin.ru /events/president/news/72918.

207 *million Russians visited*: "Turpotok mezhdu Rossiyey I OAE prevysil 1 mln chelovek v 2022," Tass, March 15, 2023, https://tass.ru/ekonomika/17276719.

207 *"absurd and nonsensical"*: Hugo Miller, "Russia Inc.'s Swiss Trading Hub Wrestles with 'Dark Side,'" Bloomberg, March 11, 2022, https://www.bloomberg.com/news/articles /2022-03-11/russia-inc-s-swiss-trading-hub-wrestles-with-its-dark-side?sref=aJXZGtfw.

207 *he kept his yacht anchored off*: Interview with sources familiar with the situation, June 2023.

207 *setting up shop in the UAE*: "Russian Yachts and Money Are Going Where US Influence Has Waned," Bloomberg, June 1, 2022, https://www.bloomberg.com/news/features /2022-06-01/billionaire-russians-yachts-and-money-flow-where-us-influence-has -waned?sref=aJXZGtfw.

208 *Dubai's biggest international real estate buyers*: Abeer Abu Omar, "Russian Buyers Help to Propel Dubai Property Sales to Record," Bloomberg, January 16, 2023, https:// www.bloomberg.com/news/articles/2023-01-16/russian-buyers-help-to-propel-dubai-s -property-sales-to-record?sref=aJXZGtfw.

208 *UAE to its "gray list"*: "Jurisdictions under Increased Monitoring," FATF, March 2022, https://www.fatf-gafi.org/content/fatf-gafi/en/publications/High-risk-and-other -monitored-jurisdictions/Increased-monitoring-march-2022.html.

209 *In July 2022*: UAE Ministry of Economy Circular no. 05/2022, June 26, 2022, https:// www.moec.gov.ae/documents/20121/387526/Circular+No.+5-2022+MOE_REAR+final +clean.pdf/2770819d-999a-d2eb-66e5-2b84141eda48?t=1656231114928.

209 *off-plan purchases*: "FY 2022 Residential Market Report," Betterhomes. January 17, 2023, https://www.bhomes.com/en/blog/market-reports/fy-2022-residential-market -report-betterhomes.

209 *transferred $30 million*: Author interviews, June 15, 2023.

209 *a license to Sam Bankman-Fried's*: Virtual Assets Regulatory Authority, Enforcement Notice, November 22, 2022, https://www.vara.ae/en/regulations/regulatory-notices /ftx-exchange-fze-vara-revocation-of-approval-and-suspension-of-mvp-licence/#:~:text =FTX%20Exchange%20FZE%20%5BFTX%20MENA,Licence%20stands%20 suspended%20in%20consequence.

209 *Binance users were converting*: Angus Berwick and Patricia Kowsmann, "Binance, the Biggest Player in Crypto, Is Facing Legal Risks over Russia," *Wall Street Journal*, August 22, 2023, https://www.wsj.com/finance/binance-cryptocurrency-russia-sanc tions-ddb948c3?mod=article_inline.

210 *sold its Russia business*: Suvashree Ghosh and Emily Nicolle, "Binance Exits Russia with Sale to Just-Launched Exchange," Bloomberg, September 27, 2023, https://www .bloomberg.com/news/articles/2023-09-27/binance-exits-russia-with-sale-of-unit-to -just-started-exchange?sref=aJXZGtfw.

210 *United States charged Binance*: USA v. Binance Holdings Ltd., U.S. District Court for the Western District of Washington at Seattle, November 14, 2023.

210 *pitch for new wealth*: Sarmad Khan, "Abu Dhabi's Move to Cut Business Set-Up Fees Set to Boost FDI and Non-Oil Economy," National, July 26, 2021, https://www.the nationalnews.com/business/economy/2021/07/26/abu-dhabis-move-to-cut-business -set-up-fees-set-to-boost-fdi-and-non-oil-economy/.

210 *nowhere to be found*: Abu Dhabi Global Market registry of Blackbridge Holdings Ltd. and ArrowSwift Holdings Ltd., https://newreg.adgm.com/s/public-registrar?entity id=0011v00003DpAMYAA3, https://newreg.adgm.com/s/public-registrar?entityid =0011v00003DpAMYAA3.

211 *"Wealth sits easily"*: Author interview with Abu Dhabi official, June 14, 2023.

211 *transferred his stakes*: "Abu Dhabi Lures Russian Steel Tycoon's Holdings Away from Cyprus," Bloomberg, June 30, 2023, https://www.bloomberg.com/news/articles/2023-06 -30/abu-dhabi-lures-russian-steel-tycoon-s-holdings-away-from-cyprus?sref=aJXZGtfw.

211 *to warn officials*: "Wally Adeyemo's Visit to the UAE," U.S. Treasury readout, June 22, 2022, https://home.treasury.gov/news/press-releases/jy0828.

211 *wouldn't hesitate to target non-U.S. citizens*: "Remarks by Deputy Secretary of the Treasury Wally Adeyemo at the UAE Banks Federation Roundtable," U.S. Treasury, June 22, 2022, https://home.treasury.gov/news/press-releases/jy0827.

211 *couldn't plead ignorance*: Author interview with Dubai banking executive, June 13, 2023.

212 *"there isn't leakage"*: Author interview with UAE banking executive, June 16, 2023.

212 *"'We are the U.S.'"*: Author interview, June 13, 2023.

212 *Russia's largest trading partner*: "Tovarooborot mezhdu RF I OAE v 2022 godu vyros do $9 mlrd," Tass, February 20, 2023, https://tass.ru/ekonomika/17094049.

212 *seven hundred Russian companies*: Tatiana Voronova and Ilya Usov, "Sber zakrivayet podrazdelenie v UAE," Frank Media, December 15, 2022, "https://frankmedia.ru /105518.

212 *an attempt to serve the Russian community*: "Statement regarding MTS Bank Branch in Abu Dhabi," Central Bank of the UAE, February 24, 2023, https://www.centralbank .ae/media/jgigng3q/cbuae-statement-regarding-mts-bank-branch-en.pdf.

212 *about 80 percent of Russia's*: Author interview, June 14, 2023.

212 *"permissive of dark money"*: "Remarks by U.S. Department of the Treasury's Under Secretary for Terrorism and Financial Intelligence Brian Nelson in Turkiye," U.S.

Treasury readout, February 3, 2023, https://home.treasury.gov/news/press-releases/jy1248.

213 *"warn" officials about*: Daphne Psaledakis and Humeyra Pamuk, "Top U.S. Treasury Official to Warn UAE, Turkey over Sanctions Evasion," Reuters, January 28, 2023, https://www.reuters.com/world/top-us-treasury-official-warn-mideast-countries-over-sanctions-evasion-2023-01-28/.

213 *prepared to impose sanctions*: Author interview, July 20, 2023.

213 *sanctions on MTS*: "Targeting Key Sectors, Evasion Efforts," U.S. Treasury, February 24, 2023, https://home.treasury.gov/news/press-releases/jy1296.

213 *central bank relented*: "CBUAE Revokes the License of MTS Bank Branch in Abu Dhabi," Central Bank of the UAE, March 31, 2023, https://www.centralbank.ae/media/vfohtjei/cbuae-revokes-the-licence-of-mts-bank-branch-in-abu-dhabi-en.pdf.

213 *helping wealthy Russians*: "With over 300 Sanctions, U.S. Targets Russia's Circumvention and Evasion," U.S. Treasury, May 19, 2023, https://home.treasury.gov/news/press-releases/jy1494.

213 *"citizenship by investment"*: "New Investment Option for Vanuatu's CBI Program," Huriya Privae, LinkedIn post, March 31, 2023, https://www.linkedin.com/pulse/new-investment-option-vanuatus-cbi-programme-huriya-john-d-/?trackingId=t3gZXw%2FCOzjNxYUKW0OY%2BA%3D%3D.

214 *In designating Hanafin*: Office of Foreign Assets Control sanctions designation, https://sanctionssearch.ofac.treas.gov/Details.aspx?id=43085; "OFAC Sanctions Dubai-Based Financial Services Firm and CEO for Role in Russian Sanctions Evasion," Chainalysis, May 19, 2023, https://www.chainalysis.com/blog/ofac-sanctions-russia-john-hanafin-huriya/; and Etherscan, https://etherscan.io/address/0x38735f03b30fbc022ddd06abed01foca823c6a94.

214 *appeared with Cherie Blair*: "International Women's Day: A Mentorship Success Story," Luxury Network, March 7, 2023, https://www.theluxurynetwork.ae/international-womens-day-a-mentorship-success-story-by-katerina-pawlowska-hanafin-coo-and-co-founder-of-huriya-private/; and Amy Sharpe, "Cherie Blair's Charity Linked to Firm Sanctions for 'Supporting Russia,'" *Mirror*, May 27, 2023, https://www.mirror.co.uk/news/politics/cherie-blairs-charity-linked-firm-30093729. The U.S. Treasury spells her name "Katarzyna." "With Wide-Ranging New Sanctions, Treasury Targets Russian Military-Linked Elites," U.S. Treasury, September 14, 2023, https://home.treasury.gov/news/press-releases/jy1731.

214 *his "money laundering globally"*: "Treasury Hardens Sanctions with 130 New Russian Evasion and Military-Industrial Targets," U.S. Treasury, November 2, 2023, https://home.treasury.gov/news/press-releases/jy1871.

215 *gold for U.S. dollars*: "Treasury Sanctions Illicit Gold Companies Funding Wagner Forces," U.S. Treasury, June 27, 2023, https://home.treasury.gov/news/press-releases/jy1581.

215 *blocks on gold traders*: "UK Cracks Down on Gold and Oil Networks Propping Up Russia's War Economy," U.K. Foreign Office, November 8, 2023, https://www.gov.uk/government/news/uk-cracks-down-on-gold-and-oil-networks-propping-up-russias-war-economy.

215 *biggest Russian gold traders*: Eddie Spence, "Russian Gold Is in Hands of Obscure Firms," Bloomberg, May 2, 2023, https://www.bloomberg.com/news/articles/2023-05-02/russian-gold-is-in-hands-of-obscure-firms-as-jpmorgan-hsbc-exit?sref=aJXZGtfw.

CHAPTER 11 **CAPPING PUTIN'S WAR PREMIUM**

217   *"a gas station masquerading"*: Burgess Everett, "McCain: Russia Is a 'Gas Station,'" *Politico*, March 26, 2014, https://www.politico.com/story/2014/03/john-mccain-russia -gas-station-105061.

218   *"We were trying to"*: Interview with Daleep Singh, January 23, 2023.

218   *"not cause a global recession"*: Interview with former White House official, March 15, 2023.

219   *comprised 45 percent*: "Energy Fact Sheet: Why Does Russian Oil and Gas Matter?," International Energy Agency, March 21, 2022, https://www.iea.org/articles/energy -fact-sheet-why-does-russian-oil-and-gas-matter.

219   *snowballed from there*: Brian Platt, "Trudeau Says Canada to Ban Russian Crude Oil Imports," Bloomberg, February 28, 2022, https://www.bloomberg.com/news/articles /2022-02-28/trudeau-says-canada-to-ban-russian-crude-oil-imports?sref=aJXZGtfw.

219   *"or we'll legislate"*: Singh interview.

219   *"giving money to a terrorist"*: Roman Petrenko, "'Let the War Feed Them,'" *Ukrainska Pravda*, March 7, 2022, https://www.pravda.com.ua/eng/news/2022/03/7/7329072/.

219   *"Doesn't Russian oil smell"*: Dmytro Kuleba, Twitter post, March 5, 2022, 12:02 p.m., https://twitter.com/DmytroKuleba/status/1500090023877746692?s=20.

219   *Only 8 percent*: "U.S. Energy Information Administration—EIA—Independent Statistics and Analysis," https://www.eia.gov/todayinenergy/detail.php?id=51738.

219   *Gasoline prices in the United States*: David Baker, "Drivers Facing Record Gas Prices Say They'd Pay More to Stop War," Bloomberg, March 7, 2022, https://www.bloomberg .com/news/articles/2022-03-07/drivers-facing-record-gas-prices-say-they-d-pay-more -to-stop-war?sref=aJXZGtfw.

220   *Italy's prime minister, Mario Draghi*: Chiara Albanese and Alberto Brambilla, "Italy Signs Gas Deals in Angola, Congo to Cut Russia Ties," Bloomberg, April 20, 2022, https:// www.bloomberg.com/news/articles/2022-04-20/italy-snaps-up-angolan-gas-after -deals-for-north-african-supply?sref=aJXZGtfw.

220   *By April, Putin was earning*: "Putin May Collect $321 Billion Windfall If Oil, Gas Keep Flowing," Bloomberg, April 1, 2022, https://www.bloomberg.com/news/articles/2022 -04-01/putin-may-collect-321-billion-windfall-if-oil-gas-keep-flowing?sref=aJXZGtfw.

221   *cap on natural gas*: Daniele Lepido, "Italy to Discuss Price-Cap Mechanism for Energy From Russia," Bloomberg, March 5, 2022, https://www.bloomberg.com/news/articles /2022-03-05/italy-to-discuss-price-cap-mechanism-for-energy-from-russia?sref=aJXZGtfw.

221   *would trigger a recession*: Patrick Donahue, "Germany Signals Opposition to Cutting Off Essential Russian Energy," Bloomberg, March 7, 2022, https://www.bloomberg.com /news/articles/2022-03-07/germany-signals-opposition-to-cutting-essential-russian -energy?sref=aJXZGtfw.

221   *"everybody wanted more sanctions"*: Interview with Björn Seibert, February 10, 2024.

222   *"the ultimate irony"*: Interview with Catherine Wolfram, May 11, 2023.

222   *a tax or tariff on Russian oil*: Ricardo Hausmann, "The Case for a Punitive Tax on Russian Oil," Project Syndicate, February 26, 2022, https://www.project-syndicate. org/commentary/case-for-punitive-tax-on-russian-oil-by-ricardo-hausmann-2022-02. Treasury officials discussed this influential piece by Hausmann, professor at Harvard's John F. Kennedy School of Government.

223   *outlining the pros and cons*: Craig Kennedy, a Russian-energy expert at Harvard

University's Davis Center, wrote about a smart embargo option that influenced Treasury's thinking. "Russian Oil's Achilles' Heel," *Navigating Russia* (blog), April 8, 2022, https://navigatingrussia.substack.com/p/russian-oils-achilles-heel?utm_source=profile.

223 *"There was skepticism"*: Author interview with Ben Harris, July 14, 2023.

224 *"I'm a free market person"*: Author interview with Kwasi Kwarteng, May 23, 2023.

224 *"Janet Yellen's baby"*: Interview with Elizabeth Rosenberg, September 28, 2023.

224 *"the real solution"*: Interview with Oleg Ustenko, August 2, 2023.

225 *Orbán stubbornly refused*: Interview with EU diplomats, Brussels, September 5, 2023.

225 *she tweeted diplomatically*: Ursula von der Leyen (@vonderleyen), "This evening's discussion with PM Viktor Orbán was helpful," Twitter post, May 9, 2022, 7:05 p.m., https://x.com/vonderleyen/status/1523725927834075136?s=20.

226 *"wouldn't get a deal"*: Harris interview.

226 *Draghi was willing*: Author interview with source, November 15, 2023.

226 *"one of the most complicated"*: Interview with Jonathan Black, July 12, 2023.

227 *"This is going to fail"*: Adam Posen (@AdamPosen), "This is going to fail," Twitter post, June 26, 2022, 11:14 p.m., https://twitter.com/AdamPosen/status/1541183138348445696?s=20.

227 *"We figured out we didn't need"*: Harris interview.

227 *"we had the leverage"*: Ibid.

227 *"Russia will not supply"*: "Novak: Rossiya ne budet postavlyat neft pri vedeni potolka tsen nizhe zatrat na dobychu," Tass, July 20, 2022, https://tass.ru/ekonomika/15268109.

228 *"impingement on his sovereignty"*: Harris interview.

228 *Russia's cost of oil production*: Georg Zachmann, Ben McWilliams, and David Kleimann, "How a European Union Tariff on Russian Oil Can Be Designed," *Bruegel* (blog), April 29, 2022, https://www.bruegel.org/blog-post/how-european-union-tariff-russian-oil-can-be-designed.

228 *Gazprom suspended supplies*: "Europe's Energy Crisis Deepens After Russia Keeps Pipeline Shut," Bloomberg, September 3, 2022, https://www.bloomberg.com/news/articles/2022-09-02/gazprom-says-nord-stream-to-remain-shut-after-technical-issue?sref=aJXZGtfw.

229 *"freeze the wolf's tail!"*: Oleksii Pavlysh, "Putin Tries to Scare Europe with Cold Winter," *Ukrainska Pravda*, September 7, 2022, https://www.pravda.com.ua/eng/news/2022/09/7/7366446/.

229 *"We will not be blackmailed"*: "Our Country Is Capable of New Beginnings at a Rapid Speed," Bundesregierung, December 17, 2022, https://www.bundesregierung.de/breg-en/issues/scholz-wilhelmshaven-2154424.

230 *"I had to repeat"*: Harris interview.

230 *"a shortage of tomatoes"*: Putin press conference, Kremlin transcript, December 22, 2022.

230 *diplomatic charm offensive*: Interview with EU diplomat, September 5, 2023.

230 *he branded the move "stupid"*: Vladimir Soldatkin and Guy Faulconbridge, "Putin Says Russia Could Cut Oil Production over 'Stupid' Price Cap," Reuters, December 9, 2022, https://www.reuters.com/business/energy/putin-russia-will-not-lose-out-oil-price-cap-2022-12-09/.

231 *Siluanov, was more gloomy*: "Wider Budget Deficit in 2022 Caused Partly by Bringing Some Additional Spending Forward," Interfax, December 27, 2022, https://interfax.com/newsroom/top-stories/86515/.

231   *The Kremlin was forced to raid*: "Russia's National Wealth Fund Falls," Interfax, February 5, 2024, https://interfax.com/newsroom/top-stories/99103/.

231   *Russia's oil export revenue*: "Oil Market Report—July 2023," International Energy Agency, https://www.iea.org/reports/oil-market-report-july-2023.

231   *Russia's budget deficit was bigger*: "Russia Budget Deficit Hits $45 Billion, Exceeding Full-Year Goal," Bloomberg, May 11, 2023, https://www.bloomberg.com/news/articles /2023-05-11/russia-budget-gap-hits-45-billion-exceeding-full-year-goal?sref=aJXZGtfw.

231   *"nothing short of a theft"*: "Foreign Minister Sergei Lavrov's Statement," Russian Ministry of Foreign Affairs, March 2, 2023, https://www.mid.ru/en/press_service/minister _speeches/1856607/.

231   *"It's been a remarkable"*: "The Russian Oil Price Cap Is 'Actually Working,'" CNBC, May 15, 2023, https://www.youtube.com/watch?v=XknXOP9JAdc.

232   *billions of Indian rupees*: Gleb Sotnikov, "Lavrov: Indiya poobeshchala pomoch s investirovaniyem milliardov rupiy kompaniy iz RF," *Rossiyskaya Gazeta*, September 10, 2023.

232   *"Their costs are up"*: Roundtable with Wally Adeyemo, October 27, 2023.

233   *price of Russia's Urals crude*: Alaric Nightingale and Lucia Kassai, "Russia's Flagship Crude Oil Surpasses G7 Price Cap for First Time," Bloomberg, July 12, 2023, https:// www.bloomberg.com/news/articles/2023-07-12/russia-s-flagship-crude-surpasses-g -7-price-cap-for-first-time?sref=aJXZGtfw.

233   *almost $82 a barrel*: Ben Hilgenstock, Elina Ribakova, and Nataliia Shapoval, "Bold Measures Are Needed as Russia's Oil Is Slipping Beyond G7 Reach," Kyiv School of Economics, November 16, 2023.

233   *"migrating into the Russian fleet"*: Interview with Liz Rosenberg, September 28, 2023.

233   *"reliant on a piece of paper"*: Alex Longley, "Rising Oil Prices Complicate Russian Price Cap Checks for Insurers," Bloomberg, April 27, 2023, https://www.bloomberg.com /news/articles/2023-04-27/-we-rely-on-a-piece-of-paper-insurers-uncomfortable-with -russian-oil-price-cap?sref=aJXZGtfw.

233   *About a third of*: Hilgenstock, Ribakova, and Shapoval, "Bold Measures Are Needed."

234   *"It was pinging from the"*: Interview with Samir Madani, July 10, 2023.

234   *He soon tracked*: "Cold Case: Thirteen (out of Sixteen) Mysterious Foreign Supertankers in Iran Finally Positively Identified," TankerTrackers.com, August 8, 2020. https:// tankertrackers.com/articles/cold-case-thirteen-out-of-sixteen-mysterious-foreign -supertankers-in-iran-now-positively-identified.

235   *The next day*, Pollux *reappeared*: TankerTrackers.com note to clients, February 1 and 7, 2023.

235   *In one classic case*: "Russia's Shadow Fleet," Bloomberg Originals, December 6, 2023, https://www.youtube.com/watch?v=Azm4yKKIlqE.

236   *A Marshall Islands front*: "Dark Fleet: Out of Mind, but Not out of Sight," Lloyd's List, March 31, 2023, https://www.lloydslist.com/LL1144570/Dark-fleet-Out-of-mind-but -not-out-of-sight.

236   *Russia's ghost tankers*: Jakob Kjogx Bohr, "For Almost a Year, Russia's Shadow Fleet Has Had Free Access to Denmark," Danwatch, November 15, 2023, https://danwatch .dk/i-knap-et-aar-har-ruslands-skyggeflaade-haft-fri-adgang-til-danmark/.

236   *didn't have recognized insurance*: Michelle Wiese Bockmann, "Dark Fleet Tanker Loses Engine Power Transiting Danish Waters," Lloyd's List, May 17, 2023, https://lloydslist .com/LL1145107/Dark-fleet-tanker-loses-engine-power-transiting-Danish-waters.

236 *But international maritime rules*: Kristina Siig, "Why Denmark Can't 'Block' Dark Tank-
     ers," *EJIL:Talk!* (blog of the *European Journal of International Law*), December 14,
     2023, https://www.ejiltalk.org/why-denmark-cant-block-dark-tankers/. See also
     Craig Kennedy, "Measuring the Shadows," *Navigating Russia* (blog), August 23,
     2023.

236 *It fired off*: Timothy Gardner, "US Probes 30 Ship Managers for Suspected Russia
     Oil Sanctions Violations," *Reuters*, November 13, 2023, https://www.reuters.com
     /business/energy/us-sends-notices-30-ship-managers-over-suspected-russia-oil
     -violations-2023-11-13/.

237 *half of Moscow's shadow vessels*: "'Shadow' Tankers Not Enough to Transport the
     Majority of Russia's Oil," Center for Research on Energy and Clean Air (CREA),
     September 26, 2023, https://energyandcleanair.org/wp/wp-content/uploads/2023/09
     /CREA_Press-release_Russias-shadow-tankers.pdf.

237 *The number of Greek-owned*: Julian Lee, "Greek Shipowners Are Stampeding out of
     the Russian Oil Trade," Bloomberg, February 5, 2024, https://www.bloomberg.com
     /news/articles/2024-02-05/greek-shipowners-are-stampeding-out-of-the-russian-oil
     -trade?sref=aJXZGtfw.

237 *"an alternative ecosystem"*: Wally Adeyemo, Council on Foreign Relations, February 23,
     2024.

237 *Russia was selling*: Russian Sanctions Digest by KSE Institute, May 2024.

238 *is shrinking the ability*: International Energy Agency Oil Market Report, January 18,
     2024.

238 *"It's completely illogical"*: Ustenko interview.

CHAPTER 12 **FREEZING LONDONGRAD**

242 *Graeme Biggar, said the unit*: "Wealthy Russian Businessman Arrested on Suspi-
     cion of Multiple Offences," National Crime Agency, December 1, 2022, https://
     www.nationalcrimeagency.gov.uk/news/wealthy-russian-businessman-arrested-on
     -suspicion-of-multiple-offences.

243 *a story I'd written*: Stephanie Baker and Matthew Monks, "Russians Drop Texas Oil Bid,
     Averting Trump Security Review," Bloomberg, June 26, 2017, https://www.bloomberg
     .com/news/articles/2017-06-26/russia-s-alfa-moguls-drop-texas-oil-deal-amid-security
     -concerns?sref=aJXZGtfw.

245 *a "brazen history of collusive"*: Gregory L. White, "At Russia's Alfa, Hardball Still Reigns,"
     Wall Street Journal, June 2, 2009, https://www.wsj.com/articles/SB124389901406474381.

246 *"When you get used"*: "Fridman: How I Became an Oligarch," Open Democracy,
     November14, 2010, https://www.opendemocracy.net/en/odr/fridman-how-i-became
     -oligarch/.

246 *Fridman sometimes skipped*: "Not All Russian Oligarchs Pay Homage to Putin," Warsaw
     Institute, March 21, 2019, https://warsawinstitute.org/not-russian-oligarchs-pay-homage
     -putin/.

246 *with Putin one-on-one*: Mueller Report, March 2019, 1:146, https://www.justsecurity.org
     /63708/word-searchable-version-of-mueller-report/.

246 *"Putin just gave"*: Interview with Petr Aven, March 26, 2024.

246 *brawled for years with BP*: Torrey Clark and Stephanie Baker-Said, "BP Says TNK-BP
     Billionaires Seek to Wrest Control," Bloomberg Markets, June 11, 2008, https://

www.bloomberg.com/news/articles/2008-07-24/bp-losing-23-of-output-looms-in
-russia-venture-fight?sref=aJXZGtfw.

247   *"We're always in touch"*: "Q&A: Russia's Mikhail Fridman," *Wall Street Journal*, June 29,
2012, https://www.wsj.com/articles/SB10001424052702303649504577495852883865194.

247   *"We sincerely believed"*: Stephanie Baker, "Broke Russian Oligarch Says Sanctioned
Billionaires Have No Sway over Putin," *Bloomberg Businessweek*, March 17, 2022, https://
www.bloomberg.com/news/features/2022-03-17/broke-russian-oligarch-fridman
-says-sanctioned-billionaires-can-t-sway-putin?sref=aJXZGtfw.

247   *doing Putin's bidding*: European Union Regulations, February 28, 2022, https://eur-lex
.europa.eu/legal-content/EN/TXT/PDF/?uri=CELEX:32022R0336.

248   *a degree of randomness*: Email correspondence from the Foreign Office, March 2022,
obtained by the author.

248   *"Our approach should"*: Emails obtained by the author.

249   *gave the billionaire an allowance*: NCA pre-interview disclosure, December 20, 2022,
in case against Nerijus Kuskys, Athlone House estate manager.

249   *£1 million in frozen funds*: Upmanyu Trivedi, "Sanctioned Tycoon Denied Extra Cash by
UK Court," Bloomberg, October 26, 2023, https://www.bloomberg.com/news/articles
/2023-10-26/sanctioned-billionaire-mikael-fridman-denied-extra-cash-for-uk-mansion
?sref=aJXZGtfw.

249   *to donate £10 million*: U.K. Treasury email, July 5, 2022.

249   *thirty NCA officers descended*: Stephanie Baker and Jonathan Browning, "Russian Billionaire Investigated by UK for Sanctions Violations," Bloomberg, May 25, 2022,
https://www.bloomberg.com/news/articles/2022-05-25/russian-billionaire-investigated
-by-uk-for-sanctions-violations?sref=aJXZGtfw.

249   *investigating around £3.7 million*: Jonathan Browning, "Billionaire without UK
Bank Account Fights Sanctions Probe," Bloomberg, September 27, 2022, https://
www.bloomberg.com/news/articles/2022-09-27/billionaire-without-a-bank
-account-fights-uk-sanctions-probe?sref=aJXZGtfw.

249   *his art collection*: As detailed in Andrew Jack, "Petr Aven: The Russian Oligarch with
an Eye for Art, Not Yachts," *Financial Times*, July 12, 2017, https://www.ft.com/content
/f328a740-6233-11e7-8814-0ac7eb84e5f1.

249   *froze about £1.5 million*: Katharine Gemmell and Jonathan Browning, "Russian Billionaire
Haggles with UK over Expenses at Mansion," Bloomberg, July 19, 2022, https://www
.bloomberg.com/news/articles/2022-07-19/russian-billionaire-haggles-with-uk-over
-expenses-at-mansion?sref=aJXZGtfw.

250   *"By mistake!"*: "Squeezed by Sanctions, Some Oligarchs Are Heading Home to Putin's
Russia," Bloomberg, October 31, 2023, https://www.bloomberg.com/news/articles
/2023-10-31/russian-oligarch-expats-driven-home-by-anti-putin-sanctions-abroad?s
ref=aJXZGtfw.

250   *regret that he'd spent less time*: *The Man Who Was Too Free*, film directed by Vera
Krichevskaya, 2016, https://www.asnconvention.com/the-man-who-was-too-free.

250   *"Fridman said that"*: Interview with Vladimir Ashurkov, March 2022.

251   *six thousand state officials*: Update to the ACF 6,000 List, Anti-Corruption Foundation,
October 21, 2022, https://acf.international/news/obnovlenie-spiskov-fbk-new.

251   *a short list of two hundred Russians*: "The ACF Has Compiled the List of Top 200 War
Enablers for the UK," August 29, 2022, https://acf.international/news/fbk-podgotovil
-top-200.

252 *Putin should be made czar*: Oleg Tinkov (@olegtinkov), Instagram post, March 26, 2017, https://www.instagram.com/p/BSGsNj8jJH7/?utm_source=ig_web_copy _link&igsh=MzRlODBiNWFlZA==; and Tinkov interview with Yuri Dud, May 11, 2022, YouTube, https://www.youtube.com/watch?v=wDkztLMNK9k.

253 *sold his 35 percent stake*: Anton Troianovski and Ivan Nechepurenko, "Russian Tycoon Criticized Putin's War. Retribution Was Swift," *New York Times*, May 1, 2022, https:// www.nytimes.com/2022/05/01/world/europe/oligarch-putin-oleg-tinkov.html.

253 *"I have lost nine billion dollars"*: Author WhatsApp exchange with Tinkov, May 16, 2023.

253 *"presented with a clear option"*: Author interview with Leonid Volkov, September 2, 2022.

253 *"target businesspeople acting"*: Letter from Volkov to Josep Borrell, October 14, 2022, as cited in "Kremlin Critics Seek Sanctions Relief for Anti-War Tycoons," Bloomberg, March 1, 2023, https://www.bloomberg.com/news/articles/2023-03-01/kremlin-critics -seek-sanctions-relief-for-anti-war-tycoons?sref=aJXZGtfw.

254 *"live in a seized mansion"*: "Presidential Address to Federal Assembly," Kremlin, February 21, 2023, http://en.kremlin.ru/events/president/news/70565.

254 *On March 1, 2023*: "Kremlin Critics."

255 *Volkov wrote on his*: Leonid Volkov, Telegram post, March 9, 2023, 10:40 a.m., https://t .me/leonid_volkov/3811.

255 *reiterate his message*: Leonid Volkov, "Alexei Navalny's Chief of Staff Says Personal Sanctions Need Rethinking," *Economist*, March 14, 2023, https://www.economist.com /by-invitation/2023/03/14/alexei-navalnys-chief-of-staff-says-personal-sanctions-need -rethinking.

255 *Navalny replaced him*: @Navalny, "Maria Pevchikh @pevchikh, the founder and permanent head," Twitter post, March 22, 2023, 3:32 p.m., https://x.com/navalny/status /1638564226322055170?s=20.

256 *Alfa Group's insurance companies*: Mikhail Fridman, Proekt, July 2023, https://war-proekt .media/spisok-oligarkhov/provider/mihail-fridman/; Georgy Shabaev, "The Owner of Kyivstar and Morshinska Cooperates with the Russian Guard and Putin's Security," Radio Svoboda, May 1, 2023, https://www.radiosvoboda.org/a/skhemy-fridman -alfastrakhovanye-roshvardiya/32382279.html; and "Russian Tycoons to Unload Alfa-Bank Stake to Escape Sanctions," Bloomberg, March 10, 2023, https://www.bloomberg .com/news/articles/2023-03-10/russian-tycoons-in-deal-to-unload-alfa-bank-stake -amid-sanctions?sref=aJXZGtfw.

256 *nationalized Alfa Group's bank*: Olesia Safronova, "Ukraine Says It Completes Nationalization of Tycoons' Sense Bank," Bloomberg, July 22, 2023, https://www.bloomberg. com/news/articles/2023-07-22/ukraine-says-it-completes-nationalization-of -tycoons-sense-bank?sref=aJXZGtfw.

256 *United States finally imposed sanctions on Fridman*: "Treasury Imposes Sanctions on Russian Elites and a Russian Business Association," U.S. Treasury, August 11, 2023, https://home.treasury.gov/news/press-releases/jy1690.

257 *NCA formally dropped its probe*: Jonathan Browning, "UK Drops Probe into Sanctioned Russian Billionaire Mikhail Fridman," Bloomberg, September 15, 2023, https://www .bloomberg.com/news/articles/2023-09-15/uk-drops-probe-into-sanctioned-russian -billionaire-mikhail-fridman?sref=aJXZGtfw.

257 *called for an investigation*: "Gosduma prosit proverit Fridmana," Business Online, October 12, 2023, https://m.business-gazeta.ru/news/610238.

257 *"All these stories"*: Maria Pevchikh @pevchikh_, "Khochetsya proprosit vsekh,"

Twitter post, December 7, 2023, 10:17 p.m., https://x.com/pevchikh/status/17328 87199773855919?s=20.

258 *EU's General Court ruled*: "The General Court Annuls the Inclusion of Petr Aven and Mikhail Fridman on the Lists of Persons Subject to Restrictive Measures Between February 2022 and March 2023," https://curia.europa.eu/jcms/upload/docs/application /pdf/2024-04/cp240061en.pdf.

258 *Khodorkovsky, the exiled*: Interview, April 11, 2024.

259 *"I tell these guys"*: Author interview, May 30, 2022.

259 *"The sanctions work to"*: Christo Grozev, Aspen Security Forum, July 19, 2023.

CHAPTER 13 **WILL RUSSIA PAY?**

261 *more than $4 billion*: Ukraine International Monetary Fund, Country Report No. 23/247, July 2023.

261 *Russia was responsible*: Kateryna Chursina and Olesia Safronova, "Ukraine Dam Blast Blamed on Russia Tips War into New Phase," Bloomberg, June 6, 2023, https://www .bloomberg.com/news/articles/2023-06-06/destruction-of-dam-in-ukraine-threatens -flooding-in-battle-zone.

261 *"It's a huge project"*: Author interview with Mustafa Nayyem, July 10, 2023.

261 *Rebuilding Ukraine will*: "Updated Ukraine Recovery and Reconstruction Needs," February 15, 2024, https://www.worldbank.org/en/news/press-release/2024/02/15 /updated-ukraine-recovery-and-reconstruction-needs-assessment-released.

262 *the scale of the devastation*: "The Total Amount of Damage Caused to the Infrastructure of Ukraine," Kyiv School of Economics, October 3, 2023, https://kse.ua/about-the -school/news/the-total-amount-of-damage-caused-to-the-infrastructure-of-ukraine -due-to-the-war-reaches-151-2-billion-estimate-as-of-september-1-2023/.

262 *he posted a call*: Mustafa Nayyem, Facebook post, November 21, 2013, https://www .facebook.com/Mustafanayyem/posts/pfbid02tYMKJjUUjwFGUPqqqwoU79777Ga5x hZxLW98X5N2RjnegGcEvUMGTmVm8NoY1P7Gl.

263 *the "aggressor pays"*: "Responsibility of States for Internationally Wrongful Acts," United Nations, 2001, https://legal.un.org/ilc/texts/instruments/english/draft_articles /9_6_2001.pdf.

263 *$60 billion globally*: Joint Statement from the REPO Task Force, March 9, 2023, https:// home.treasury.gov/news/press-releases/jy1329.

264 *"This is one of the rare cases"*: Author interview with Larry Summers, December 19, 2023.

265 *"Bank robbers should not"*: Lawrence H. Summers, Philip Zelikow, and Robert Zoellick, "The Other Counteroffensive to Save Ukraine," *Foreign Affairs*, June 15, 2023, https:// www.foreignaffairs.com/ukraine/other-counteroffensive-save-ukraine.

265 *"I don't respect legal"*: Author interview with Philip Zelikow, July 21, 2023.

266 *breached the Budapest Memorandum*: Budapest Memorandum, December 5, 1994, https:// policymemos.hks.harvard.edu/files/policymemos/files/2-23-22_ukraine-the_budapest _memo.pdf?m=1645824948.

266 *General Assembly voted*: "General Assembly Overwhelmingly Adopts Resolution Demanding Russian Federation Immediately End Illegal Use of Force in Ukraine," United Nations, March 2, 2022, https://press.un.org/en/2022/ga12407.doc.htm.

266 *calling on Russia to pay*: "General Assembly Adopts Resolution on Russian Reparations

for Ukraine," United Nations, November 14, 2022, https://news.un.org/en/story/2022/11/1130587; and https://press.un.org/en/2022/sc14801.doc.htm.

266 *filed claims with the commission*: "Security Council Unanimously Adopts Resolution Confirming UN Compensation Commission Has Fulfilled Its Iraq-Kuwait Mandate," February 22, 2022, https://press.un.org/en/2022/sc14801.doc.htm.

267 *"When you have a war"*: Author interview with Robert Zoellick, July 22, 2023.

267 *a bipartisan group of senators*: Rebuilding Economic Prosperity and Opportunity (REPO) for Ukrainians Act, June 15, 2023, https://foreignaffairs.house.gov/press-release/mccaul-risch-kaptur-whitehouse-reintroduce-legislation-to-repurpose-sovereign-russian-assets-for-ukraine/; and https://www.foreign.senate.gov/imo/media/doc/06-14-23_repo_act.pdf.

268 *"I hope it happens without"*: Author interview with James Risch, July 23, 2023.

268 *Yellen was opposed*: David Lawder, "Yellen Says Legal Obstacles Remain on Seizure of Russian Assets to Aid Ukraine," Reuters, February 27, 2023, https://www.reuters.com/world/yellen-says-legal-obstacles-remain-seizure-russian-assets-aid-ukraine-2023-02-27.

268 *"There's no negotiation"*: Author interview with Bill Browder, April 28, 2023.

268 *White House only officially backed*: National Security Council email, November 17, 2023.

268 *dropped to about*: "Currency Composition of Official Foreign Exchange Reserves," International Monetary Fund, December 22, 2023, https://data.imf.org/?sk=e6a5f467-c14b-4aa8-9f6d-5a09ec4e62a4.

269 *For more than a year*: Interview with official from the EU working group on Russian assets, May 9, 2023.

269 *had frozen 211 billion euros*: "Opening Remarks by President von der Leyen," European Commission, October 27, 2023, https://ec.europa.eu/commission/presscorner/detail/en/statement_23_5373. At the time this book went to press there was still no definitive breakdown of where the assets were.

270 *Euroclear's balance sheet*: "Euroclear Achieves Strong First Quarter Results," April 30, 2024, https://www.euroclear.com/newsandinsights/en/press/2024/mr-11-strong-first-quarter-results.html.

270 *"Who is going to pay"*: Sam Fleming, "EU Should Seize Russian Reserves to Rebuild Ukraine, Top Diplomat Says," *Financial Times*, May 9, 2022, https://www.ft.com/content/82b0444f-889a-4f3d-8dbc-1d04162807f3.

270 *"find legal ways" to use money from Russia*: "Statement by President von der Leyen on Russian Accountability and the Use of Russian Frozen Assets," European Commission, November 30, 2022, https://ec.europa.eu/commission/presscorner/detail/en/statement_22_7307.

271 *"We're talking about"*: "Peskov zayvil, chto Rossiya ne teryayet nadezhdu na razmorozku valyutnykh rezervov," Tass, October 31, 2022.

271 *"crossing a line"*: ECB internal note, June 2023.

271 *use Euroclear's windfall*: Alberto Nardelli, "EU Drafts Law to Send Russian Central Bank Profits to Ukraine," Bloomberg, March 18, 2024, https://www.bloomberg.com/news/articles/2024-03-18/eu-drafts-law-to-send-russian-central-bank-profits-to-ukraine?sref=aJXZGtfw.

271 *passed the point*: Author interview with source, November 15, 2023.

272 *Le Maire told*: Alessandra Migliaccio, "Le Maire: We don't Have Legal Basis to Seize Russian Assets," Bloomberg, February 28, 2024.

273 *"So far, I have not"*: "Fireside Chat with David Cameron," Aspen Institute, December 7, 2023, https://www.youtube.com/watch?v=QT4uOWQsMaI&t=3s.

273 *"pushing hard"*: David Cameron hearing with the U.K. House of Lords, European Affairs Committee, December 14, 2023, https://parliamentlive.tv/event/index/81eaf5d0-80ab-40e4-8334-991ccecbc9e7.

273 *£26 billion of Russian sovereign assets*: "Repurposing Russian Assets to Rebuild Ukraine," *Hansard* 735 (June 27, 2023), https://hansard.parliament.uk/commons/2023-06-27/debates/1557FA76-F69E-4E14-B459-10BD7BBB0917/RepurposingRussianAssetsTo RebuildUkraine.

273 *Zoellick, for one, thought*: Robert Zoellick, "REPO Act Lets Biden Boost Ukraine," *Wall Street Journal*, April 25, 2024, https://www.wsj.com/articles/repo-lets-biden-boost-ukraine-russia-war-frozen-russian-reserves-6253cd4e.

273 *In November 2022*: "Almost US$1.6 billion Accumulated to Deal with Aftermath of Russia's Aggression," *Economichna Pravda*, May 15, 2023, https://www.pravda.com.ua/eng/news/2023/05/15/7402295/.

EPILOGUE **END GAME**

275 *350,000 troops*: Estimate from James Heappey, minister for the armed forces, U.K. Defence Ministry, January 29, 2024, https://www.parallelparliament.co.uk/question/11255/russia-ukraine.

275 *seven hundred thousand people left*: Rachel Lyngaas, "Sanctions and Russia's War: Limiting Putin's Capabilities," U.S. Treasury, December 14, 2023, https://home.treasury.gov/news/featured-stories/sanctions-and-russias-war-limiting-putins-capabilities.

276 *closer to one million*: "Russians Have Emigrated in Huge Numbers Since the War in Ukraine," *The Economist*, August 23, 2023, https://www.economist.com/graphic-detail/2023/08/23/russians-have-emigrated-in-huge-numbers-since-the-war-in-ukraine.

276 *pledged to double spending*: "Putin utverdil rost raskhodov na armiyu," *Moscow Times*, November 27, 2023, https://www.moscowtimes.ru/2023/11/27/putin-utverdil-rost-rashodov-naarmiyu-dorekorda-sovremen-sssr-a114367.

277 *record $239 billion*: Center for Macroeconomic Analysis and Forecasting, Russian Central Bank, July 24, 2023, http://www.forecast.ru/_ARCHIVE/Mon_13/2023/TT2023_8.pdf.

277 *5 percent smaller*: Lyngaas, "Sanctions and Russia's War."

278 *Agriculture production contracted*: Anna Frants, "Russian Consumer Feel Themselves in a Spot as High Inflation Persists," Associated Press, November 24, 2023, https://apnews.com/article/russia-economy-inflation-food-shopping-515a5dfec7ea4f71ad b1aa5dc5674bfc.

278 *"economy is a car"*: "Russia Signals Tight Policy to Stay After Hiking Rate to 16%," Bloomberg, December 15, 2023, https://www.bloomberg.com/news/articles/2023-12-15/bank-of-russia-hikes-key-rate-to-16-in-fight-to-curb-inflation?sref=aJXZGtfw.

278 *Polyus had planned*: "Chinese Engineers Are Keeping Russia's Metal Furnaces Firing," Bloomberg, January 28, 2024, https://www.bloomberg.com/news/articles/2024-01-28/china-s-engineers-are-keeping-russia-s-metal-furnaces-firing?sref=aJXZGtfw.

278 *a "progressive tax"*: Putin interview with Dmitry Kiselev, Kremlin, March 13, 2024, http://kremlin.ru/events/president/transcripts/73648.

279 *end the war*: Trump interview on *Meet the Press*, NBC, September 15, 2023, https://

www.nbcnews.com/politics/donald-trump/trump-pleased-putins-praise-ukraine
-russia-meet-the-press-rcna105298.

279 *could remove many*: While the 2018 CAATSA sanctions on Russia require Congress
to approve any removals, the 2014 and 2022 rounds of sanctions were issued under
executive orders authorized by the International Emergency Economic Powers Act,
which gives the president sweeping powers.

280 *sanctions on several Russian defense*: The U.S. Treasury sanctioned Iskandar Makhmudov
and Andrei Bokarev, saying both had links to organized crime. "With Wide-Ranging
New Sanctions, Treasury Targets Russian Military-Linked Elites and Industrial Base,"
U.S. Treasury, September 14, 2023, https://home.treasury.gov/news/press-releases
/jy1731.

281 *below $50 a barrel*: Alex Isakov, "Oil Shock Would Mean Just 2 Years of Cash Stash,"
Bloomberg Economics, January 11, 2024.

282 *"Cold War mentality"*: "Xi Jinping: BRICS Countries Need to Act with a Sense of
Responsibility," Xinhua, June 23, 2022, https://english.news.cn/20220623/7e62a3329
7644e77a52aa0c6e5413bdc/c.html.

282 *their "common interests"*: Xi statement, Insight EU Monitoring, March 21,2023, https://
ieu-monitoring.com/editorial/chinese-russian-summit-statements-of-presidents
-vladimir-putin-and-xi-jinping/403365.

282 *"determine the future"*: "Remarks by President Biden," White House, October 20, 2023,
https://www.whitehouse.gov/briefing-room/speeches-remarks/2023/10/20/remarks-by
-president-biden-on-the-unites-states-response-to-hamass-terrorist-attacks-against
-israel-and-russias-ongoing-brutal-war-against-ukraine/.

282 *"weaponization of economic tools"*: Author interview with Daleep Singh, January 23,
2023.

283 *called "friend-shoring"*: "US Treasury Secretary Janet Yellen on the Next Steps for
Russia Sanctions and 'Friend-Shoring' Supply Chains," April 13, 2022, https://www
.atlanticcouncil.org/news/transcripts/transcript-us-treasury-secretary-janet-yellen
-on-the-next-steps-for-russia-sanctions-and-friend-shoring-supply-chains/.

283 *$600 billion worldwide*: "Factsheet on the G7 Partnership for Global Infrastructure
and Investment," Ministry of Foreign Affairs of Japan, G7 Summit, Hiroshima, May
2023, https://www.mofa.go.jp/files/100506918.pdf; and "President Biden and G7
Leaders Formally Launch the Partnership for Global Infrastructure and Investment," White House, June 26, 2022, https://www.whitehouse.gov/briefing-room
/statements-releases/2022/06/26/fact-sheet-president-biden-and-g7-leaders-formally
-launch-the-partnership-for-global-infrastructure-and-investment/#:~:text=To
day%2C%20President%20Biden%20will%20announce,2027%20in%20global%20
infrastructure%20investments.

283 *progress on real commitments*: "Remarks by World Bank Group President Davis Malpass
at G7 Hiroshima Summit," May 20, 2023, https://www.worldbank.org/en/news/speech
/2023/05/20/david-malpass-g7-hiroshima-summit-side-event-partnership-global-in
frastructure-and-investment.

PHOTO INSERT CREDITS

1   Peter Klaunzer/Bloomberg
2   Photo courtesy of the White House
3   Julia Kochetova/Bloomberg
4   Chris Kleponis/Bloomberg
5   U.S. Department of Justice
6   Julien Hubert
7   Simon Dawson/Bloomberg
8   Tomohiro Ohsumi/Bloomberg
9   Julien Hubert
10   U.S. Department of Justice
11   National Agency on Corruption Prevention
12   U.S. Department of Justice
13   FBI
14   Liesa Johannssen-Koppitz/Bloomberg
15   Laurent Laughlin/Bloomberg
16   Marc Atkins/Getty Images
17   Angel Navarrete/Bloomberg
18   Hollie Adams/Bloomberg
19   *New Lines Magazine/The Insider*
20   Sopa Images/Alamy
21   State Agency for Restoration of Ukraine
22   Qilai Shen/Bloomberg

INDEX

Pagliuca, Steve, 180–81
palladium, 106
Palm, 204
Paloma Precious, 216
Panama Papers, 195
Paper Trail Media, 182
Paroev, Oleg, 148, 151, 153, 154
Pearl Harbor bombing, 81
Penrose, Mike, 182–83
Pentagon, 15, 206
Pepsi, 149, 150, 151, 157
perestroika, 149, 150
Peskov, Dmitry, 46, 177, 271
Peterson Institute for International
 Economics, 227
Pevchikh, Maria, 184, 255, 257
Philip Morris, 166
Photon Pro LLP, 130
Pinskiy, Anton, 156
Piro, Freddie, 103
Pizza Hut, 155–56
PJSC Polyus, 47
Podolyak, Mykhailo, 177, 179
poisonings, 43, 74, 172–73, 176, 251
Poland, 59, 156, 221, 230, 270–71
Pollux (tanker), 235
Polyus, 278
Portugal, 175
Posen, Adam, 227
Potanin, Vladimir, x–xi, 62, 64, 65, 106–7,
 158, 253
Prana network, 140
Prevezon Holdings Ltd., 193
PricewaterhouseCoopers (PwC), 197, 199–200
Prigozhin, Yevgeny, 85, 91–92, 159, 201, 215
prisoner's dilemma, 259
Procter & Gamble, 166
Proekt Media, 256
Promised Land, A (Obama), 76
Promsvyazbank, 19, 192
Psaki, Jen, 25
Putin, Vladimir, 8, 58, 68–78, 99, 189, 193, 194,
 195, 196, 203, 267, 277, 279
 Abramovich and, 69, 169, 170–71, 173, 177,
  184–85
 amassing of troops on Ukraine border,
  14–17

anticipation of quick victory in Ukraine,
 275
anti-Western rhetoric of, 83, 281–82, 284
Aven and, 246
Biden's negotiation attempts and, 14–16, 17
bin Zayed Al Nahan's talks with, 207
central bank asset freeze and, 30–31
centralization of power by, 72
corporate exodus from Russia and, 158–60,
 165, 166
Deripaska and, 94
European Union–Ukraine agreement, 79
expansion of state's grip on oil, 72–73,
 77–78
food import bans of, 88, 150
Fridman and, 243, 244, 245, 246, 247,
 258–59
indifference to economic decline, 89, 90
Johnson on, 23
Kerimov and, 47
Khodorkovsky on, 7
kleptocrats and, 35, 37, 38, 41, 42–43
Malofeyev and, 44
military modernization and, 126, 140
natural gas weaponized by, 228–29
nuclear weapons threat, 21
Obama's call with, 87
Obama's criticism of, 85
oil price cap and, 227, 228, 229, 230–31, 232
oil revenues and, 9–10, 72, 217, 218–19, 220
oligarchs and, 70–75, 158–60, 170–71, 185,
 244–45, 254
"On the Historical Unity of Russians and
 Ukrainians," 16
orders bulldozing of food and cheese, 89
personal sanctions on, 26
presidential elections won by, 69, 77
as prime minister, 68–69, 76–77
Tinkov and, 252, 253
Trump's summit with, 97
Ukraine invasion ordered by, 3, 13
United Arab Emirates visited by, 282
Uss and, 136, 137
violations of international agreements
 by, 266
West's initial support of, 70
Xi's meeting with, 138